GOVERNANCE
South Asian Perspectives

GOVERNANCE

South Asian Perspectives

edited by

Hasnat Abdul Hye

MANOHAR
2002

First published 2000
Second impression 2001
First paperback edition 2002

Hardbound: ISBN 81-7304-399-X
Paperback: ISBN 81-7304-458-9

Published by
Ajay Kumar Jain for
Manohar Publishers & Distributors
4753/23 Ansari Road, Daryaganj
New Delhi 110002

Printed at
Print Perfect
Delhi 110064

Dedicated to
fellow FSLP Scholar Kofi Annan
Secretary General, UN
for his commitment to Good Governance

Contents

ADMINISTRATION

LOCAL GOVERNMENT

GOVERNANCE AND ECONOMY

Preface

The papers in this anthology were presented in an international seminar jointly organised by the Local Government Division of the Ministry of LGRD and Co-operatives, Government of Bangladesh and the UNDP in August 1998. Though there had been other seminars/meetings on the subject this was the first international event held in Bangladesh bringing together scholars, practitioners and policy makers from countries of South Asia and the international development agencies. In terms of scope, the subjects included in the seminar programme were the most comprehensive. For the first time almost all the subjects and issues that come under "governance" were covered for analysis and discussion. The international dimension, the South Asian perspectives and the exhaustive nature of the agenda were manifestly the main justification for yet another seminar. Participation in the different sessions was broad-based representing cross-section of the Bangladesh society and facilitated spontaneous and valuable exchange of views. For limitation of space the resume of discussion does not appear in this anthology.

In including wide ranging but related themes and issues in the agenda the seminar highlighted the broad universe of discourse and the integrated framework for reform measures in respect of governance. Attention was focused on both the "Trees" and the "Forest", pointing out the relation between the two and the outcome of the relationship for the "ecology" of governance.

The main conclusion in the papers presented and the consensus that emerged in the discussions were that the quality of governance in South Asia was much less than desired and it could be improved. Since 'governance' has come to be seen as the handmaiden of the executive branch of the state, much of the criticism for failure was laid at its door. The reasons for this failure as identified ranged from 'systemic' to 'historical' and the reform measures recommended called for a thorough overhaul of the system, particularly the executive branch. Restructuring and reformulating the executive branch were felt necessary both for its own efficiency and to allow the other participants in governance, actual and potential (e.g., legislature, judiciary, local government, civil society), to fully flourish and make their rightful contributions.

An interesting aspect in the on-going discussion on 'governance' is that it is the international development agencies (World Bank, UNDP, etc.) which have been most vocal about the need for reform to bring about qualitative improvement. But it is these very agencies, among others, which are responsible to a great extent, for the "quantity" (size) of the government that prevails to-day in most developing countries. So, neither for the expansion nor for the recommendations to reform the 'government', the initiative rested and lie with the countries concerned. The most important consensus arising out of the seminar is that the agenda for reform should be nationally designed and owned. Imposed from above and outside, the reform programme will lack commitment and cannot be sustained for long. If for nothing else, for this simple conclusion the seminar should be considered as an important milestone in the passage to good governance. The papers presented in the seminar and included in this book, are food for thought as well as sources for actions to *those* who have undertaken the difficult journey towards the desired destination of "good governance". It is imperative to talk in the plural, because 'governance' is and should be a collective endeavour and not the preserve of a few closeted in the inner sanctum of power. Individually, we are at the receiving end of governance, but collectively we both deliver and receive. This is the thought underlying most of the papers and this is the message of the seminar.

The book was planned to be jointly edited by myself and Prof. Zarin Rahman Khan. After making some initial input Prof. Khan was not available for the editorial work and the responsibility devolved on me. Nevertheless, I would like to acknowledge the contribution made by Pro. Khan as well as for her participation in the seminar as a rapporteur. The help and technical assistance received from UPL are very much appreciated, particularly the advice of Mr. Mohiuddin Ahmed.

December, 1999 *Hasnat Abdul Hye*

CONTRIBUTORS

Abul Maal A. Muhith: Former Minister of Planning and Finance.

Atiur Rahman: Senior Research Fellow, Bangladesh Institute of Development Studies (BIDS).

B.K. Jahangir: Pro-Vice Chancellor, National University, Gazipur.

Barrister M. Amir-Ul Islam: Vice President, Bangladesh Bar Council.

Dilara Chowdhury: Professor, Department of Government and Politics, Jahangir Nagar University, Savar, Dhaka.

Dinesh Mehta: Regional Advisor, South Asia, Urban Management Programme for Asia and Pacific, UNDP/UNCHS.

G.D. Cyril Gunapala: Additional Secretary to the President, Sri Lanka.

G.M. Ramesh Kumar: Special Officer, Planning, CIRDAP.

G. Shabbir Cheema: Director, Management Development and Governance Division, United Nations Development Programme, New York, U.S.A.

Hasnat Abdul Hye: Secretary, Local Government Division of the Ministry of LGRD & Co-operatives, Govt. of Bangladesh.

Imtiaz Ahmed: Associate Professor, Department of International Relations, University of Dhaka.

Jeffrey E. Key: Professor, Sweet Briar College, Virginia, U.S.A.

Justice Ranganath Misra: Former Chief Justice of India.

K.C. Sivaramakrishnan: Visiting Professor, Centre for Policy Research, New Delhi, India.

Justice K.M. Subhan: Former Judge, Appellate Division, Supreme Court of Bangladesh.

Krishna P. Khanal: Professor of Political Science, Tribhuvan University, Katmandu, Nepal.

M. Kabir Hassan: Associate Professor of Financial Economics, Department of Economics and Finance, University of New Orleans, U.S.A.

Meghna Guhathakurta: Associate Professor, Department of International Relations, University of Dhaka.

Mizanur Rahman Shelley: Chairman, Centre for Development Research, Bangladesh (CDRB) and Editor, Asian Affairs.

Mizanur Rahman: Associate Professor of Law, Dhaka University.

Mohammed Abu Eusuf: Junior Consultant, Bangladesh Institute of Development Studies (BIDS).

Nazrul Islam: Professor, Department of Geography and Environment, University of Dhaka and Chairman, Centre for Urban Studies, Dhaka.

Norma Mansor: Associate Professor, Faculty of Economics and Administration, University of Malaya, Kuala Lumpur.

Peter Lyon: Academic Secretary, Institute of Commonwealth and Australian Studies, University of London.

Rehman Sobhan: Chairman, Centre for Policy Dialogue, Dhaka.

Robert LaPorte, Jr.: Professor of Public Administration and Political Science, Department of Political Science, The Pennsylvania State University, U.S.A.

Salma Khan: Chairperson, UN Committee on the Elimination of Discrimination Against Women (CEDAW).

Syed Naimul Wadood: Lecturer, Department of Business Administration, The University of Comilla (UNIC).

Syedur Rahman: Coordinator, Hubert H. Humphrey Fellowship Programme, The Pennsylvania State University, U.S.A.

Tasneem Ahmed Siddique: Chairman, SAIBAN, Action Research for Shelter, A Non-Governmental Organization, Karachi, Pakistan.

Yousuf Abdullah Harun: President, FBCCI, Bangladesh.

Zaidi Sattar: Consultant, The World Bank, Dhaka.

Designations of authors refer to those held by them at the time of writing the papers.

GOOD GOVERNANCE: A SOCIAL CONTRACT FOR THE NEW MILLENNIUM

Hasnat Abdul Hye

Introduction

In the recent past, issues of governance have received increasingly serious attention from researchers, policy makers and the international development community. "Governance" now not only occupies central stage in the development discourse but is also considered as the crucial element to be incorporated in the development strategy. Apart from the universal acceptance of its importance, differences, however, prevail in respect of theoretical formulations, policy prescriptions and conceptualization of the subject itself. Governance as a theoretical construct, separate from the theory of state, is not only in an inchoate stage, but its formulation also differs among researchers depending on their ideological convictions. Policy analysis based empirically on the historical experiences of governance gives prominence to "government failures" to deliver leading to propositions for downsizing or rightsizing, while policy prescriptions for good governance take an evolutionary view of the matter questioning relevance of public sector management of certain activities in a changed context. In conceptualization, divergent views either represent governance as a narrowly defined phenomenon in the form of activities of only the executive branch of the State i.e. the government or as one where the State comprising the Legislature, the Executive and the Judiciary are the parts that constitute a whole without the positive synergistic relation with the private sector and civil society. The third and the recent interpretation of "governance" introduces the private sector and the civil society including the local government system as participants in and promoter of good governance, through changes in their subsidiary roles and direct involvement in areas hitherto kept exclusively in the public domain.

A Conceptual Framework

Since conceptualization is the basis of theoretical formulation and influences policy making in a significant way, it is important to define "governance" and to identify the institutions and the loci of power that exercise "governance" as legitimate authorities. From the point of view of any structured discussion, it is necessary to have a framework to set the various sub-themes within the broader spectrum of discourse. Without trying to be pedantic, and to state in a simple and straightforward manner, it is proposed to interpret "governance" as the undertaking of activities, management of resources, organization of men and women by groups of people, communities, local government bodies, business organizations and the branches of the state (Legislature, Judiciary and Government) through social, political, administrative and economic arrangements that meet the daily needs of people and ensure sustainable development. According to this view, institutionalization of rule of law — including coercive measures required to enforce laws and rules for protection of lives and property — and development activities of the government for promotion of common welfare are the foundation as well as the superstructure of governance while spontaneous autonomous activities of people acting out of their free will reinforce both when they are allowed to flourish. Neither the executive government nor the civil society, singly and separately, can ensure this. Though the conventional constituents of "State", namely, Parliament, Judiciary and Executive Government, may encompass this diverse area of governance at some particular point of time, changes often take place subsequently that make a combination of these constituents of the State and other actors, collaborative partners in governance with clear-cut and sometimes overlapping jurisdictions. To accommodate the broadly defined "governance" proposed here, one has to go beyond the conventional definition and composition of "State" and look at both its formal and informal constituents or organs. Schematically this is shown below through comparison in Figures I and II:

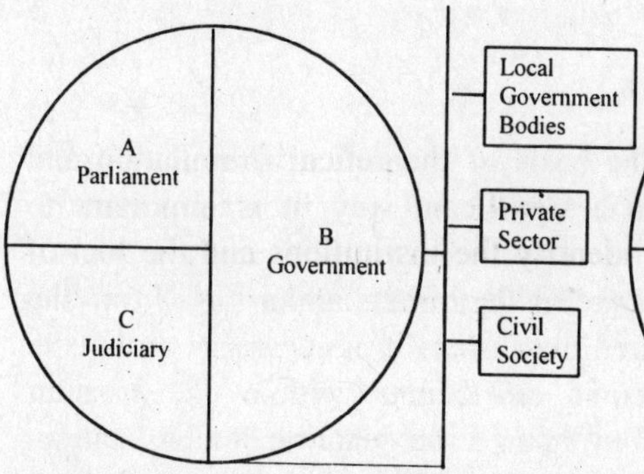

Fig. I: Conventional State

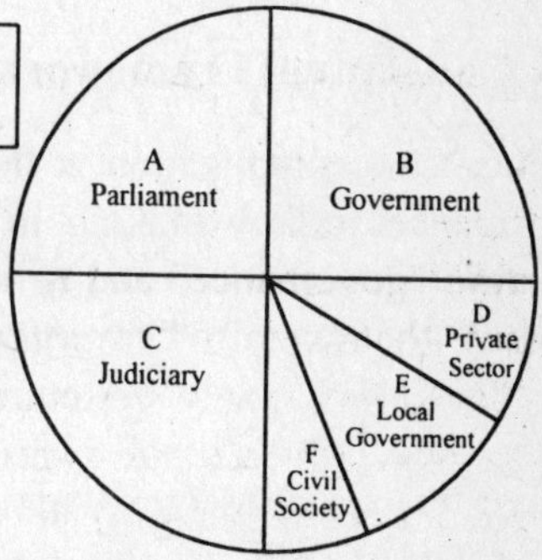

Fig. II: State Redefined

State Redefined

It is argued that modern nation states in their early stage, and for many years subsequently, remained responsible for "Governance" only or mainly through formal organs as represented by A, B and C in Figure I. Private sector of business and industries and the community based organizations (civil society) either exist in their fledgling conditions or are non-existent at this stage, while local government bodies are used as mere adjuncts of the government branch lacking autonomous existence. Though all three organs of "State" exercise powers and discharge functions of governance, it is the executive branch — the "government" — which plays the dominant role because of its sponsoring of legislation, enforcement of laws and undertaking of multifarious activities, both regulatory and developmental. Where local government bodies, private sector and the community based organizations exist, they are controlled and regulated by the government. Though the treatment meted out to them by government may be discussed in Parliament, and they may have access to courts for protection of legal rights, the dominance of government makes them almost subordinate to its executive power. In this scheme of things, even in a democratic polity, the informal branches become the object of the act of "governance" i.e. they are governed rather than seen governing in their own areas as autonomous actors. In most of the developing countries that became independent from colonial rule, this was the common pattern of governance because lack of freedom did not allow the informal organs of state to develop while the formal organs were created to serve the needs of the alien rulers. After independence of these countries, the three formal constituents of "State" monopolized or nearly monopolized "governance" because the informal organs viz. the private sector or the community based organizations were weak or non-existent.[1] Local government bodies lacking autonomy did not fare better. As this arrangement enjoyed legitimacy, and there was tacit acceptance from the people, the system of governance that came to be established can be said to be the outcome of the prevailing configuration of institutions with corresponding allocation of powers and jurisdictions. In other words, the particular type of governance that emerged was the "political contract" agreed to by the people at the time and was articulated in the constitution of their countries. The state came into existence through the legal action of the people in making a constitution. The legal action of the people was the contract that bound them in a body politic. But the theory of a "political contract" with "State" as one of the party and the "People" as the other presumes, as a prior development, the theory of a "contract of society" in which the members of society have many unwritten contracts supporting the State. Lock, Russeau and Hobbes laid emphasis on this concept of social contract based on their assumption that a "contract of government" could not exist without a "social contract" (Barker, 1978). It is obvious that social contract is more of an ideology than a legal document like constitution which is a legal contract. No society anywhere was ever constituted on the basis of a formal and legally binding contract. But the ideology of a society as a set of shared beliefs, goals and practices constituted the unwritten social contract and determined the contract of government bringing into existence the legal entity of State through a constitution. Following this line of reasoning, it can be argued that post-colonial societies inheriting the colonial legacy did not have a social contract or at least not a full-fledged one and their constitutions, as the document legitimizing States, did not always inhere an ideology in the form of a social contract. Thus governance in post-colonial societies was mainly a product of "political contract" reflecting the incomplete social formations of the colonial period.

A New Social Contract

But society and social formations are not immutable. Society changes autonomously and more significantly by dint of the very experiences of "governance". With varying time span, alongside the formal organs of State, community based organizations emerge, gain in strength and show their capacity to participate, even to independently undertake some of the activities that were in the public domain before. Private sector of manufacturing and business centering around the market and within the regulatory framework of the government steadily expands and gains comparative advantages in doing many of the activities that were hitherto in the public sector. Where the "State" through its formal organs — Parliament, Judiciary and Executive (government) encourages the private sector and the civil society, the development of the "informal" organs of the state becomes rapid and significant. This gives rise to a new configuration of institutions or "organs" in terms of their social acceptance, autonomy and resources which calls for a new pattern of governance. This change can take place dramatically through private sector-led activities, and initiatives of civil society or through active patronage of government, in an evolutionary manner through incremental steps, the informal organs "stepping in" in certain areas and the formal organ of the state, particularly the government, correspondingly withdrawing. A new pattern of governance thus emerges either because of deliberate policies pursued by the state in an evolutionary way or spectacularly through an increasingly confident private sector and an expanding civil society. The stage is then set for a new "social contract" on which the "political contract" of the state can be based.

Political Commitment

In the midst of this slow but inexorable transition to a new system of governance, donor pressures for policy changes and institutional reforms sometimes act as catalyst coming with the incentive of additional resources to implement the structural adjustment package. But the most effective and enduring intervention is by that of elected politicians who legislate laws, make rules and oversee the performance of the government. They have or can have the holistic view of governance being at the highest policy making level and can exercise the objectivity to recognize changes in the configuration of institutions. Even when some credit can be claimed by bureaucracy within the "government" for bringing about the new configuration of institutions (emergence of private sector, promotion of civil society etc.), because of their direct involvement redefinition (re-engineering?) of "governance" suffers in various ways — delays, tokenism, confusion and misgivings. Inertia and predilection for status quo contribute to this in no small measure. It is, therefore, only through political commitment that the evolutionary incremental changes can be accelerated to gather sufficient momentum and the new configuration of institutions becomes sustainable. When this task is accomplished "governance" assumes the characteristic of Figure II where both the formal and informal organs of state become partners, sharing power and exercising "governance" in their own rights in clearly demarcated areas. Each organ exercises governance in its own jurisdiction under legally recognized rules and procedures. "Governance" in this scheme ceases to be confined to governing others and instead tend to include both 'other-directed' governing organs (as in the case of government) and 'inner-directed'[2] self-governing bodies with the jurisdiction and the authority of the former undergoing necessary transformation.

Political democracy through freedom of association, free expression, rule of law and participation in governance has a better chance of ushering in new configuration of "institutions" in society paving the way for new and broad-based patterns of governance as envisaged in Figure II. The formal organs of state in a democratic polity viz. Legislature, Judiciary and the Executive have contributed to this change in varying degrees in different countries at different times depending on the exercise of their historic roles and the strength and confidence of the civil society representing the informal organs.

Good Governance

The above is a simplistic explanation and a tentative attempt at conceptualization of "governance" from the institutional point of view. Governance, of course, is not only about the "organs" or actors. More importantly, it is about the quality of governance which expresses itself through such attributes as accountability, transparency, efficiency, empowerment, participation, sustainability, equity and justice. But just as the dancer cannot be separated from the dance,[3] the organs or actors executing governance in their respective spheres cannot be relegated to the background. Since the attributes of good governance are the outcome of the institutional behaviour of the organs, analysis of the qualitative aspects of good governance has to cover the functioning of all the organs and in different contexts: independently, in their mutual relation and as a collective. Having conceptualized the parameters of governance, its desirable attributes can be seen in proper perspective, with both form and content placed in an inter-linked network where each of the organs postulates its own attributes of good governance. Seen from this point of view, good governance is not something to be desired by the "government" delegating some of its powers and functions to the informal organs but as formal outcome of a new configuration of institutions resulting in a new social contract (as an ideology) and redefining the pluralistic State in the constitution.

The conceptualization proposed above, based on historical experiences and inductive method, sets the backdrop to the main theme by highlighting the changing nature of the configuration of institutions in a society calling for new pattern of governance and pave the way to deal with the qualitative aspects of governance. It frees the subject of "governance" from extraneous pressures of donor conditionalities and polemics of ideologues. Empirical analysis based on this conceptualization should be able to make out a case for change in the conventional pattern of governance in a deliberate and planned manner. Just as in evolving new configuration of institutions the formal organs of the state have positive roles, in institutionalizing new pattern of governance also they can and make necessary contribution.

It should be the objective of any discourse on "governance" to delineate the manner in which the formal organs can play out their historic role in promoting good governance through improvement in their day to day activities and through promotion of civil society including private sector. As integral part of this, the ways and means of integrating the "informal" organs of governance viz. private sector, civil society etc. into the mainstream of governance should be explored. But before outlining the future, the past and the present need to be looked at, even if briefly, to find out how and why social, political and economic developments have been what they are. In shaping the parameters of a social contract for the new millennium explanation of the cause and effect relationship is the starting point of intellectual efforts and the beginning of the new discourse on governance.

Before concluding this section, a point has to be clarified. When "good governance" is discussed the implication is that there is failure of governance or mis-governance. It does not require robust imagination to recognize that excepting under tyrannical regimes or exploitative colonial rulers, no government (i.e. no state) deliberately follows a policy of bad governance. Particularly in democratic polity with regular elections and accountability to the people, a political party can sacrifice good governance only at its own peril. So the case of "good governance" does not rest on experiences with "bad governance" deliberately pursued by a government or broadly speaking by a state (except in the cases mentioned above) but on promoting it more vigorously because "good governance" remains the continuing ideal under almost all circumstances. The acts of omission and commission that compromise or undermine it like corruption, violation of human rights etc., are aberrations that may characterize any government anywhere, be it in a developed or a developing country and should be seen as failures that circumscribe good governance and not as the product of bad governance. The subtle difference between the two being that in the former, the aberrations take place in spite of the general norm, while in the latter case, they are the intended consequences of bad governance and as such are not aberrations. The two situations with apparently subtle differences have implications for policy reforms that are wide-ranging and diverse. Keeping these nuances of "good governance" in mind the "universe of discourse" as delineated earlier can now be traversed looking for experiences of the recent past and the present and exploring the road map for the future.

The analytical exercise within the proposed conceptual framework can now be organized thematically keeping the emerging scope of discourse in respect of "governance" in view. Its ideological underpinning is provided by the need to have a new "social contract" as we enter the third millennium. Under the general theme of "good governance" the discourse can be envisaged to cover the subjects that are considered relevant to it and may include: (1) Governance and Legislature, (2) Governance and Judiciary, (3) Governance and Administration, (4) Governance and Local Government System (in rural areas), (5) Governance and Local Government System (in urban areas), (6) Governance and Economy, (7) Governance and Civil Society, (8) Governance and the International Development Community.

Sub-Themes of Governance

1. Legislature

Legislature is a general term which subsumes various other specific names like parliament, congress, national assembly and country-specific names (Diet in Japan, Cortes in Spain, Jatiya Sangshad in Bangladesh, etc.). There can be legislature both under dictatorial regimes and in representative democracies. The relationship between legislature and executive defines the nature of government and the scope of "governance" to a great extent. In Parliamentary democracy sovereignty of the people rests in and is upheld through legislature. It is this role as the custodian of the people's sovereignty which makes legislature the most important organ of state.

The principal task of legislature is, of course, law-making. In legislation the supreme act is adoption of the constitution which lays down the fundamental rights of people, state principles and powers and functions of the principal branches of the State viz. Legislature, Judiciary and Government. The very first act of a legislature (in its role as constituent assembly) enshrines the fundamental principles of governance and embodies the institutions entrusted with them. Both in constitution-making and enactment of various laws subsequently, legislature can ensure good governance if the wishes of the people, their hopes and aspirations are truly reflected in the constitution and in the laws enacted thereafter. Lord Bryce in his seminal work, "Modern Democracies", recognized that legislatures constituted an indispensable part of the machinery of government in democracies, but felt that because of party caucuses and growth of pressure groups the "dignity and moral influence of representative legislatures have been declining" (Bryce, 1921). His words date back to 1921 and much water has flown under the bridge since then witnessing many changes in the working of legislatures. But the question about populist character of laws passed and their rationale from the point of view of the greatest welfare of the largest number of people remains valid even to-day. Another aspect of legislation refers to the life span of laws enacted. A law meant for the commonweal of the people should be based on general consensus so that they remain as perpetual law irrespective of changes in government. Legislature in its role of law-making can contribute to good governance by ensuring this through multi-party, unanimous approval.

People elect their representatives to legislature not only for making laws to govern the country based on their desires, but also to oversee their enforcement and administration. It is this function which gives legislature a meaningful role in governance almost exercising executive powers and as such is the key to promoting good governance. "But if the legislative power in a free state has no right to stay the executive, it has a right and ought to have the means of examining in what manner its laws have been executed" (Montesquieu, 1848). Legislative supervision and control over the activities of the executive branch of the state i.e. the government is required not only for ensuring enforcement of laws but also to check and control excesses committed or transgressions made by the public servants. This power is exercised by legislature through general discussions in the sessions and in various parliamentary committees. The more vigorous, active and regular are these forums for overseeing and controlling the executive branch, the greater is the promotion of the cause of good governance.

Besides the traditional focus in studies of legislatures on the relationship of government and the formulation of public policy, recent works have looked at legislature in a broader context, particularly in relation to the citizens and the political system generally. According to one of these new perceptions, legislature is one of the agencies that mobilize consent of the people and from them acceptance of its policies. This is so because the electoral commitments made during election commit not only the government i.e. the party in power but also the voters. They constitute a set of expectations about the future course of government policy and these expectations lay the foundation of consent and acceptance for relevant government programmes in the future.

But the government i.e. the party in power have to take many decisions in the form of laws and public policy in addition to the commitments made before election. How to legitimize these decisions or mobilize consent in their favour are issues that take legislature into a more difficult terrain. Legislature, through the representatives, particularly the treasury bench members, can mobilize consent between, as well as, at elections. Through mass media and public meetings this mobilization of opinion can be attempted, as is done sometimes. New laws can be discussed in detail and on a multi-party basis as much within the legislature as in public. This gives the people not only better information about the legislative process but enables them to participate also.

The focus of any discussion on "Governance and Legislature" should be on the process of law-making (participatory, mobilization of opinion), the background and rationale behind most of the laws (group interests or general welfare), enforcement of accountability of the government to the legislature (parliamentary committees, etc.), its use as a forum for multi-party discussion on governance and on its role in promoting good governance through these processes. Past and present practices and experiences over the same may be used as bases for recommended changes in futures.

2. Judiciary

Judiciary with the system of laws and the institutions involved in making legal decisions is the basis of a stable and just society. By upholding the rule of law judiciary protects the rights of individuals to live, work and enjoy without fear or favour. When Hobbes described life in the State of Nature as "poor, solitary, nasty, brutish and short", he had in mind the absence of laws and any authority to enforce rule of law. Laws are the life blood of a civilized society while judiciary is its throbbing heart keeping it alive and well.

Rule of law begins with the laws framed to protect the lives of citizens, their right to property, for enforcement of contracts and enjoyment of fundamental rights. The existence of this body of laws and its comprehensiveness are essential pre-conditions as well as crucial determinants of good governance. With the passage of time the need for new laws or for amendment of existing laws may arise. Legislature is the forum for law making; and though legislation is initiated mostly by administrative ministries, they are not the only source. Law Reforms Commission continuously reviewing the working of the legal regime can effect these changes and, therefore, can be an integral part of the law making procedure. Popular movement advocating social change (as in the case of domestic violence against women or against dowry system) or stricter enforcement of law (as in rape cases) may also act as catalyst for legislation as an instrument of social change. National and international declarations in favour of a multi-dimensional and holistic concept of human rights adding social, economic and cultural rights to the traditional civil, political and legal rights can broaden the scope and pace of legislation that enhances the dignity and freedom of people.

Judiciary in the restricted sense of courts of trial and for appeals gives decisions based on laws in cases brought to their notice. Decisions of courts are essentially interpretation of laws and as such become laws themselves. It is not uncommon to have judgmental laws emanating from court decisions that not only capture the letter but also the spirit behind laws. Judicial review of new laws involving interpretation of the constitution also falls in this category though in a different context using different authority. Judiciary in the former role of making judgmental laws, and as interpreters of constitution in the latter case ceases to have a passive role. The more dynamic and active is the role of courts in these respects, the greater is the refinement of the rule of law which is an important attribute of good governance.

In the matter of judicial review the highest court in a country can apply certain principles developed by courts of foreign jurisdiction and thereby make them part of constitutional law even when they are not mentioned in the constitution. Then, there are the cases of precedents and practices that occur in the day to day management of affairs of state under the constitution. These precedents and practices can be declared by the highest court as constitutional conventions which then become rules of political practice even when they are not enforceable in courts. Conventions may sometimes develop into constitutional law from non-legal rule and can be enforced in court. Thus the highest court through its use of various instruments other than law proper can expand the function and strengthen the effectiveness of judiciary. In ensuring good governance through judiciary these are important considerations. Thus conceived, judiciary is not a passive body interpreting laws mechanically.

The interpretation of constitutional provision does not, however, make judiciary at the highest level superior to the other organs of state e.g. legislature, government (Islam, 1996). But by ensuring compliance with constitutional provisions by them, particularly by the executive branch (the government), judiciary promotes good governance in a significant way. This is an important check on the abuse or misuse of power by the administrative branch and as such is an important attribute of good governance through judiciary. The highest court also exercises this subtle check on legislature in the matter of making of new laws. Though the role of the court in deciding constitutional questions involved in law making can be an activist one, it has been pointed out that frequent and wanton engagement of judges in "ideological-legislative" and "operational-executive" activities may violate the doctrine of separation of powers affecting the performance of judiciary's proper role as an independent and neutral body.

The promotion of good governance through Judiciary depends on its independence to a great extent. The manner of appointment, promotion and the method of remunerating the judges at all levels are important considerations in this respect. Related to this issue is the principle of separation of judiciary from the executive.

An adequate and comprehensive body of laws that evolves with time in response to social changes is the foundation of judiciary. Independence and creativity of the mind of judges reinforce this foundation. But these alone do not ensure rule of law. Legal process involving pre-trial investigation and the trial procedure can be such that court cases linger making litigation so expensive (both in terms of time and money) as to be practically out of reach of the poor. Moreover, there may be requirements of evidence that are stacked against the victim (as in rape cases) making dispensation of quick and adequate justice very difficult, if not altogether impossible.

Judiciary depends on the administrative branch not only for investigation but equally importantly for carrying out the court orders and decisions. Ends of good governance require that perception of justice and rule of law is shared equally and with the same urgency by the Judiciary and the Administrative branches. Discordance here can be an obstacle frustrating whatever efforts might be taken at the preceding stages. A detailed analytical discussion on the subject should look at the various issues mentioned above and others that are deemed relevant and important. The focus need to be on promoting the integration of judiciary in its broadest sense (laws, legal procedure and courts) into the overall framework of good governance.

3. Governance and Administration

This sub-theme is somewhat tautological and does not immediately convey the intended meaning. Governance by the executive branch i.e. the government is carried out through public administration. Being the means by which it governs no binary or subject-object relation is contemplated between governance and public administration. Governance and public administration are synonymous here, though the latter can also be seen as an institution while the former is the activity undertaken through it. Public administration has often been used broadly to include development administration as well, a broadening of the definition necessitated by the prevailing extent of "governance" by the government.

As is well known, in the beginning government's traditional role included only maintenance of law and order, revenue collection and a modicum of public services — all of which were treated as basic public goods. The justification for raising public resources was the provision of these basic services. In Europe and North America even these minimal functions contributed positively to the development and growth of markets playing catalytic role. At the end of the nineteenth century the government's role in promoting social welfare through income redistribution was first seen in Bismarck's Germany. But Government remained small until the Russian Revolution in 1917 and the Great Depression in the USA in the Thirties. The paradigm of government's role that took shape after the Second World War in the developed countries was based on several cardinal principles which included (a) provision of welfare benefits to the poor and unemployed; (b) a strong public sector for production and distribution of goods and services; (c) economic growth with stability i.e. full employment with price stability (World Bank, 1997). This expansion of role led the size of governments in the industrially developed countries to double between 1960 and 1995.

In the newly independent developing countries the expansion of the public sector took place not only all at once but was also all pervasive for the simple reason that at the time of their independence, there was a very small private sector, a moribund local government and no civil society worth its name.

Apart from sheer force of necessity, public sector rapidly expanded as a result of the conviction among leaders and bureaucrats about public sector-led growth strategy which was seen as not only capable of accelerating the pace of development but also of ensuring equity and justice. Government control of the economy, at least of the "commanding heights", and use of central planning as the mechanism to allocate resources to priority sectors became common credo in all these countries even when they professed faith in democratic polity. New Deal in America to overcome the Great Depression, the coming of welfare state in Great Britain after the Second World War and in the Scandinavian countries soon afterwards, the popularity of Keynesian demand management to kick-start the economy in recession and the rapid industrialization of Soviet Union through central planning were all grist to the mill of public sector-led growth strategy. Nationalism that found its political expression in an independent sovereign state, embraced economic self-reliance as the natural corollary. Public sector thus became involved in a multitude of activities — from traditional maintenance of law and order, to infrastructure development, management of public utilities and operation of manufacturing enterprises.

The expansion of public sector activities required proliferation of public administration in the form of offices, bureaucrats, technicians and numerous functionaries. The industrially developed countries of the west and the development agencies where they wielded influence were fully supportive of this state dominated economic development as long as the countries remained on the right side of the ideological divide or at least sat astride the divide. Technical assistance was provided liberally both by the UN and the bilateral agencies to enhance capacity of public administration so that it could take on their burgeoning responsibilities. Even central planning was considered useful and economists from developed countries were placed in the Planning Commissions of developing countries as part of technical assistance. The emergence of Big Government did not take place overnight and in its creation both the government of the developing countries and their external development partners played important roles.

Though the burden of criticism is on the failure of government in delivering goods and services effectively, there is also a theoretical undertone of neo-liberalism and of neo-classical economics behind it. Looking at the current discourse on governance it appears that two major strands stand out prominently. According to the first, government with its public sector has failed and so it should move over and allow others (private sector, civil society) to take its place. The second view contends that though government has failed it is not as a result of its inherent weakness, nor because it was inevitable, but mostly due to wrong or inadequate use of its resources.

In other words, governance has not been properly carried out, fully using all the potentials of governmental institutions. A third view may be added based on the argument that there has not been a total failure of government, but it has become ineffective and inefficient in many areas with relative neglect of priority areas (gender development, poverty alleviation, environmental protection, etc.) because of over-stretching and being overwhelmed with too many responsibilities. On the other hand, government directly or indirectly has enabled the private sector and the civil society to gradually emerge and expand their areas of activity even while it started faltering. Because of these two parallel developments government can now withdraw into its core areas of responsibilities and competence producing pure public goods.

On the basis of the third view of government and governance (in the broadest sense of doing the traditional activities and as provider of public goods) discussion can take place on the direction of its future involvement and the manner of achieving it. Public Administration, as the instrument of government for carrying out the "core" activitie can then become leaner and fitter and through them gentler and kinder. The important thing to ensure is the proper balance along the public-private-local government-civil society spectrum determined not only by considerations of comparative advantage but equally importantly by the criteria of equity and justice. In this new milieu ethos of work will change with competitiveness and transparency becoming the order of the day for sheer survival of the public sector. This transformation together with the withdrawal of licensing and permit giving and the exercise of discretionary powers will reduce the incidence of corruption. Multilateral and bilateral aid/loan giving agencies being not required to channel their resources exclusively through public sector will not be encouraging corruption either by some of their staff or the public sector employees of the recipient countries. A frontal attack on corruption can begin when the symbiotic relation between the public sector and the aid/loan giving agencies is terminated or significantly minimised.

The main problem with the above scenario is that it assumes a final stage in the development of government's role. But the reality is that as the socio-economic context changes, so does the role of the government. Just as it is too myopic to think about "end of history", it is short-sighted to think about a final and fixed role of the government, ignoring dialectics of change. Keeping this in mind the present task is to identify the functions of various actors in the society particularly government, local government institutions, private sector and civil society, to delineate the relationship among them to obtain the maximum of synergy and to enhance the capacity of all these institutions so that the new configuration of institutions gains in momentum scaling ever newer heights in a dynamic setting.

Irrespective of the stage of development in governance through public administration and its scope, the attributes of good governance will, however, remain the same: accountability, transparency empowerment, participation, justice and equity. These are the eternal verities of governance through public administration that do not mutate, though their context may change.

4. Local Government System (Village, Union, Thana, District)

Local Government is part of overall governance. In countries where it is recognized in the constitution it is at par with the other formal organs of State. Like the central government authority local government institutions at various levels perform almost the same functions (agriculture, health, education, road development) within their jurisdictions. The scale and scope of these activities are, however, limited. But being nearer to the community the development activities and services provided by local government institutions can have immediate impact on their lives. The central government, on the other hand, relieved of myriads of small scale activities and services can concentrate on major works. When this division of work between the national government and the local government institutions is determined, distinct and clear-cut principles can ensure productivity and efficiency for both. More often than not, they are also likely to be cost-effective.

Local government institutions being nearer to people can involve them in various ways: (a) planning and implementation of projects; (b) supervision of educational institutions, hospitals and other government financed units; (c) mobilization of support for new initiatives like campaign against dowry, child labour etc.; (d) enforcement of laws regarding gender discrimination, violence against women, environmental protection; (e) mobilization of resources in the form of taxes, fees, tolls etc. Popular participation also assumes importance because of its potentials for holding the local government institution accountable to the community. On the other hand, local government institutions as the representative organization of the people can enforce accountability of the central/national government authorities. The more aware, vigilant and active the community becomes through their participation in local government bodies, the greater is the pressure on both local government institutions and the government authorities to become transparent and responsive.

The potentials of local government institutions can be realized more effectively where there is decentralization and devolution of powers. Accountability, transparency, participation, empowerment, equity and all the other attributes of good governance can be in full play and become a part of the daily work of both the government and local government bodies when decentralization and devolution take place.

Decentralization and devolution ensure that the needs of the disadvantaged groups in the community are addressed adequately and environmental issues receive due attention because of their proximity to the decision-making authority. Transparency and accountability in decentralized units encourage people to take more interest in local affairs and to pay their dues timely. Without decentralization and devolution local government bodies remain paper organizations without any effective role. It will be no exaggeration to say that it is in a decentralized local government system that most of the attributes of good governance have a chance to survive and prosper. Strengthening of local government institutions can, therefore, be seen as a positive trend towards good governance.

Analytical discussion is expected to analyze the role of local government bodies at grass roots level from the point of view of promoting good governance using the criteria of accountability, transparency, efficiency and equity.

5. Local Government — City Corporations and Municipalities

Urbanization is taking place rapidly and on a massive scale all over the world. This is particularly pronounced in Asia and Latin America. It is estimated that by 2020 Asia will become predominantly urban with an urban population of 2.4 billion or 55 per cent of the total population. Of the 27 megacities (with population exceeding 10 million) 17 are projected to be located in Asia while the number of smaller towns will multiply. The challenge of sustainable development in the next millennium will be faced with greater intensity in these urban settings.

Increasing urbanization is a normal process of development as seen from the experiences of developed countries. Rather than trying to stem the tide of urbanization, the goal should be to make this growth as much planned as possible so that it is sustainable, efficient and equitable. This planning process should be based on the premise that urban centres are not only places where a large number of people live in a concentrated manner making demands on roads, transportation, parks, electricity, gas, water supply, sanitation, health, educational facilities and housing but they are also centres of intensive economic activities, both in the formal and informal sector. Urban centres of all types hold great potentials not only of improving the standard of life of their inhabitants but also of the rural population through backward and forward linkages and as such are useful mechanisms for promoting human development. Whether these potentials will be realized fully, reasonably well or inadequately will depend on the management of urban life and activities. The record so far in many developing countries indicates that human development has lagged behind the phenomenal explosion of urban population resulting in growing incidence of crime, violence, poverty, exploitation of women and child labour and environmental degradation because urban management authorities have failed to maintain a reasonable level of activities and provide services to all irrespective of class, sex or age. Life in many big cities has become chaotic, risky, unhealthy and even dehumanizing because of mismanagement. This is disconcerting as major cities everywhere have the benefit of concentration of wealth and talented people including public leaders. The failure in governing cities is, therefore, symptomatic of the overall failure in governance.

Urban management has various forms in different countries. The most common is the functioning of an elected body (city corporation for big cities, municipality for small towns) which is responsible for provision of the civic amenities, public utilities and development and maintenance of infrastructures. The urban management authorities carry out their mandated activities in situations where supply is outstripped by growing demand, exacerbating not only the problem of quantity or volume of services provided but also their quality. Though paucity of resources is often cited as the greatest constraint, absence of advance planning, new initiatives and lack of innovativeness have been pointed out as other contributory factors for the prevailing unsatisfactory state of affairs. On the other hand, accountability, transparency and participation have not been found to characterize the management style and practice of urban authorities in many countries.

The prevailing trend of centralization of most of the activities has become untenable in the context of growing urban population and their burgeoning demands. Inefficiency and corruption are endemic in such management culture, though there are honourable exceptions. Being centralized and distant from the citizens, it is also difficult to establish accountability. On the other hand, centralization of activities by urban authorities have ignored the important role of coordination in situations where some of the basic services and infrastructure facilities remain within the jurisdiction of other agencies. Spontaneous and regular coordination with other authorities will continue to be a major task in any type of urban management structure and as such is an important attribute of good governance by urban management authorities. Administrative and financial autonomy from the national government is another important criterion of good urban governance which is not often ensured for lack of financial self-sufficiency. Redefinition and clarification of the role of the central government agencies emphasizing facilitation and coordination rather than direct operation or control and regulation through guidelines are important for sustainability of city governance.

Good governance in the management of big cities require partnership with private sector and the civil society organizations. While partnership with private sector can help the urban authorities to deliver services efficiently, that with civil organizations can enforce accountability and transparency through participation. Civil society organizations can also mobilize the support of the community for collection of revenue and maintenance of facilities created by urban authorities. Though for smaller urban areas the need and scope of partnership with private sector may not be great, the involvement of local community through participation in decision-making and implementation on supervision of activities undertaken by municipalities can be very helpful. Urban governance being limited to specific and small areas stand to benefit more from public participation and as such is an important criterion of judging their performance.

6. Governance and Economy

Governance and economy are inseparable. Throughout the ages governance has relied on economy for its sustenance and has influenced its nature and development. At one level this relationship has been reflected in fiscal and monetary policies, foreign trade and foreign investment and their operational instruments like taxation, interest rate, money supply, exchange rate, capital control, etc. At the other end, governance has directly impinged on economy through its role as allocater of resources and direct investment in various sectors. Though operationally inter-linked and almost inseparable, for the convenience of analysis these two aspects of governance in relation to economy may be treated separately. The first part—the policy aspects should deal with "Governance and Economy" while the second part should cover the broader framework of "Governance and Public Administration".

Executive branch of the State i.e. Government raises revenue through various taxes, fees, rates, etc. and uses these in the form of public expenditure. People through their representatives in legislature have a say on the incomes and expenditures of government when budgets are presented for approval. The extent and effectiveness of this budgetary control of people through their representatives need to be analyzed just as the social, economic and political rationale of public finance and expenditure call for close scrutiny. The current fiscal crisis facing many countries in the form of growing public debt cannot be treated independent of public expenditure, while the discrete subjects of taxation and revenue collection deserve critical analysis in their own right. Excise and customs duties and the overall tariff regime need to be looked at from the point of view of not only revenue collection but also because of their impact on competitiveness of domestic industries both under overly protective regimes and under reform programmes of rapid liberalization that withdraw protection overnight. Critical imbalance created in the balance of payment situation through liberalization of trade in the face of non-tariff barriers like alleged human rights abuse, environmental and other qualitative criteria applied by industrially developed countries need to be highlighted to complete the picture. The absence of medium term fiscal planning, forecast of revenue earnings, trend in public expenditure and debt servicing make the projected resource mobilization in official documents like Five Year Plans operationally insignificant. The declining influence of long-term analysis and forecast in Five Year Plans also aggravates the distribution of income because conscious efforts to structure taxes and formulate fiscal incentives to reduce income inequality do not always receive due emphasis in the annual budgetary exercise.

Monetary and credit policies are important instruments for governance of economy. Their effectiveness depend on realistic data and critical analysis of trends in money supply and price indices on a regular basis. More importantly, monetary and credit policy as well as exchange rate policies need to be taken by authorities like the Central Bank independent of the political imperatives of almost daily nature. Interest rates determined by administrative fiat not only lead to less than desirable allocation of resources adversely affecting efficiency but is also inequitable as the benefit of subsidized credit is enjoyed by those having access to formal credit. Direct payment of subsidy targetting specified sectors and groups may overcome this to some extent but its duration and administration need to be determined according to a systematic plan framework and not on ad-hoc basis. The experience with both administered interest rates for credit and subsidy may be an important part of the analysis under this sub-theme of governance.

Banks and financial institutions operate within the monetary and credit policies of government and are important institutions for the outcome of governance in this sphere. Just as too rigid control in their decision-making (in interest determination, sanction of loan to clients, etc.) can thwart this initiative and affect their viability, inadequate and irregular supervision of their activities or absence of guidelines can spell financial chaos as has been the case in quite a few countries in recent years. Strict enforcement of capital-adequacy ratio, bad loan provisioning and check against speculative investment have now become part of the folk-lore of neo-liberal economics.

Policy formulations regarding foreign exchange, exchange rate and capital flow have assumed critical importance in the governance of the economy following the turmoil in the financial markets of Mexico and South-East Asian countries requiring bail-out efforts by multilateral and bilateral authorities. As globalization of the economy proceeds and the national markets are integrated more closely backed up by the revolution in information technology, exchange rate, current account deficit, debt servicing liabilities of both the public and private sector will come to determine the stability of the economy with a far greater intensity. Paradoxically, it will seem that with greater liberalization national governments' capacity to govern economy has been eroded and they are helplessly being buffeted by external forces unleashed through the very forces of liberalization. Is it a case of a lack of regular analysis of trends and realistic forecast of development in the financial and capital markets as some allege? Or is it a case of too much, too soon, at least for the developing countries as others hasten to point out? No one would, of course, argue for a return to the status quo ante when exchange rates remained inflexibly fixed and there was tight control on movement of capital across borders. But the manner and the time-frame of deregulation and decontrol in this area perhaps deserve closer scrutiny, particularly after the recent upheavals in the financial markets in Asia.

The above issues under the macro economic policies for governance of economy affect both public and private sectors including the direct foreign investors (DFI and portfolio investment). Along with the macro economic policies, the policies at micro level like price fixing for some products both in public and private sectors, rent, fee, rates etc. charged for utilities and various services by government agencies are important policy matters affecting economy. The ramifications of both macro and micro economic policies for private sector require to be highlighted to find out whether these help or hinder its operation and expansion. The goal of these policies should be not only the creation of a level playing field but strengthening the enabling role of government so as to allow greater participation by private sector in economy both as producer and consumer.

The above discussion of macro-economic and micro economic issues bring us to the various liberalization and structural adjustment reforms undertaken in many developing countries including Bangladesh, under conditionalities of loan and aid. Based on recent experiences particularly in Africa, it is being contended that failure of economic reforms has been largely because of the failure of governance. On the other hand, failure is attributed by others to the very nature of the wide ranging reforms that ignore the realities of particular situations. It is pointed out that stabilization measures recommended to address a short term crisis often succeed because they are limited and there can be support for these (devaluation, partial convertibility, reduction of fiscal deficit, raising interest etc.). But far-reaching long term macro-economic measures designed to bring about structural adjustment involving reduction of public expenditure, drastic reduction of tariffs, full convertibility etc. expose domestic private sector to the outside world all of a sudden and as such require well thought out planning and phased implementation. Shock therapy through drastic reforms may produce desired results in a few cases but its beneficial effects being fortuitous in nature can never be the general rule, and as such is not a sound policy.

Though the attack on central planning and the role of the interventionist state is based mostly on ideological considerations of the neo-liberals, very few developing countries are caught in the time-warp of old convictions. They are prepared to change the pattern of economic governance not because they have failed, but having borne the responsibility of economy-wide governance, they feel overwhelmed and overextended. Fortunately, institutions like the private sector have emerged over the years to which the erstwhile Interventionist State can transfer many of the activities that are not in the nature of pure public goods. The policy reforms for expansion of the domestic private sector and attraction of foreign investors have become somewhat complex because of the unforeseen consequences of liberalization and structural adjustment reforms measures. Thus even while government is in the mood to reduce its scope of governance in economy, its agenda for policy making and regulatory framework has become crowded and urgent, though from a different perspective.

7. Civil Society

"Wherever therefore any number of men are so united into one society as to quit everyone his executive power of the law of nature and to resign it to the public, there and there only is a political or civil society. And this is done wherever any number of men, in the state of nature, enter into society to make one people, one body politic under one supreme government: or else where anyone joins himself to and incorporates with any government already made" (Lock, J. 1632-1704).

The above is an apt description of civil society given by Lock where he contrasted it with the state of nature or law of nature. It is obvious that what he had in mind was the modern day concept of State or Government. But this is not how "civil society" is being used by people now a days. On the one hand, it is being contrasted with non-civilian, that is military society. At the other extreme, it is defined to include all institutions other than the formal organs of State, particularly Government. Neither of these two descriptions are realistic and operationally significant. The definition of civil society should include private sector, voluntary organizations (NGOs), social welfare organizations, professional bodies, trade unions, community based organizations, special interest groups, research organizations, "advocacy group" and, last but not the least, media in private sector. By this definition civil society excludes legislature, judiciary, government, local government institutions and private sector trading and manufacturing units.

Civil Society as defined above covers multifarious activities, from provision of limited public goods (micro-credit, primary health care, etc.) to advocacy for social reforms (gender equality, education for all, human rights for disadvantaged group etc.). The following description of various types of institutions within civil society and their usual functions/activities is meant to be illustrative:

Civil Society Profile

Sl.No.	Type	Activities
1.	Media (Press, Radio, TV)	Public opinion forming, information dissemination, entertainment, etc.
2.	Trade Unions	Collective bargaining, awareness creation among members about their rights and public policies relating to them.
3.	Professional Bodies	Maintaining high standard of the profession, protecting the rights of the members, promotion of interests etc.
4.	Private Voluntary Organization	Advocacy of social change in particular areas, provision of limited public goods to their clientele (credit, primary health, adult literacy, etc.) manufacture and distribution of consumer goods to members of the public (milk processing, fisheries, textiles, etc.) protection of the rights of disadvantaged groups (e.g. minorities, tribal people, destitute women, street children, etc.).
5.	Sports and Cultural Bodies	Promotion of sports and culture through the activities of their members.
6.	Social Welfare Organizations	Promotion of social welfare of members or limited clientele in particular areas through voluntary services of various types.

From the above it is evident that members of civil society are active in diverse and wide ranging areas. It is significant that in almost all countries their number is increasing as is the type and scope of activities. To the extent civil society expands, government can withdraw into core areas of competence and where lumpy investment is required (major public infrastructure projects).

Not only as substitute of government in selected areas but also for articulating demand of their members for services provided by government agencies, civil society can assume a crucial role. On the other hand, in cases where some of the institutions in civil society provide limited public goods (primary health care, primary education etc.) and consumer goods they set a standard of quality and price fixing against which performance of public sector agencies and private companies can be compared. Because of these actual and potential roles expansion of civil society is an effective mechanism for promotion of good governance. In recent years the role of civil society has been seen as contributing to the accumulation of "social capital" which is the community's capacity to participate in and benefit from development activities. Related to the concept of social capital is the useful idea that it functions through and with government and markets, not in place of them. Thus the apparent competitive or substitutive relation between civil society on the one hand, and government and private sector on the other, dissolves into an interdependent network with synergistic development potentials. Good governance thus can be promoted not only through autonomous emergence of civil society as a dynamic sector of development and change but also on the basis of active promotion by government through public policies and healthy competition with the private sector.

Civil society as contemplated here does not always cover the potential clientele comprehensively and therefore, may give rise to discrimination or lead to unbalanced development. The strategy of governance has, therefore, to be designed both by promoting "social capital" accumulated through civil society and serving the areas and communities that have not become part of the existing civil society in a kind of holding operation by the government.

Civil society as participant in the business of good governance has to demonstrate many of the same attributes applicable to government and private sector. Among these attributes, accountability (to the clientele/community), transparency (to the greater public and the clientele), participation, empowerment, efficiency (least-cost operation) fairness of price and fees charged (e.g. interest rate for micro credit) may be mentioned. Some of the contentious issues here are the high cost of operation per unit and earning of profit by otherwise non-profit organizations enjoying tax breaks and other exemptions, participation in open political activities (as during election) by agencies funded largely by foreign donors. Whether the large number of wholly foreign funded NGOs functioning in developing countries can be regarded as part of civil society or not also need to be examined. The confidence and faith on the vibrant and dynamic civil society can be strengthened through satisfactory resolution of these questions. The onus of doing this rests on the civil society itself.

It is important to analyze the context in which civil society has emerged, review its present role and then focus on the measures required to promote this role within the paradigm of good governance.

8. Governance and the International Development Community

"Governance" in the developing countries of Asia and Africa has been greatly influenced by the development assistance received by them from bilateral and multilateral aid/loan giving agencies. This has been particularly strong in the economic sphere with resultant impact on public administration. While "political governance" remained the preserve of domestic politicians and their parties, "economic governance" bore the stamp of external development agencies even when the prevailing dogma embraced different shades of socialism ranging from welfare statism to nearly complete "command economy". Foreign aid and loan were provided generously to bridge both the savings-investment and foreign exchange gaps. In adopting the theory of "big-push" investment strategy the developing countries found willing and helpful development partners who were anxious to see them take-off into "self-sustained growth" on way to the mass consumption society. End justified the means and it did not matter that public sector was becoming all pervading using central planning as the mechanism and a vast army of bureaucrats.

The genesis of big government can be traced to this joint collaboration between the recipient and the external aid giving agencies. In the fifties and sixties public sector took charge not only of the "commanding heights" of the economy but was almost a 'lone ranger' in the valleys and depressions, there being no other sector (private, civil society) or only faint stirrings of others. As has already been pointed out, those were the heydays of public and development administration that flourished on the public sector-led growth strategy. Bureaucrats undertook every conceivable tasks ranging from motivation for family planning to adoption of high yielding varieties of seeds. Technical assistance was provided generously by the international development community to give training to their increasing number and public administration institutes were set up with foreign aid.

Foreign assistance through various development agencies (bilateral, multilateral, UN) at the early stages primarily focused on the activities (investment) and the delivery system and was not concerned much about macro-economic or micro-economic policy matters. Policy reform was almost beyond the pale of external aid and its influence on "economic governance" was more pronounced on quantity (number of projects, physical targets, number of new technologies introduced, number of technical experts working etc.). Improvement of planning procedure, implementation methods, evaluation of development projects were some of the few operational areas where technical assistance sought to strengthen capacity. Not to speak of promoting private sector or civil society vigorously, even the issue of improving "economic governance" based on criteria like accountability and transparency did not receive much attention.

The development efforts initiated through public sector with foreign assistance had many success stories. Growth rate rose slowly but steadily, social and physical infrastructures developed significantly and the quality of life showed reasonable improvement. But there were cases of failures or of limited results also. The majority of people did not benefit from development efforts, poverty both widened and deepened, environmental degradation took place, inefficiencies and corruption thrived and inflation got out of control aggravating the cost of living of the poor. Disillusionment with these and other negative consequences of planned development was soon joined by aid fatigue. One by one, the bilateral and multilateral aid giving agencies started re-appraising their aid strategy. Soon, beginning in the early eighties the pendulum swung towards policy reforms and structural adjustment programmes. Reducing budgetary deficit, public debt, change in exchange rate policy to address current account deficit, privatization of public sector enterprises, encouraging private sector and civil society, emphasis on poverty alleviation and gender development became standard prescription for promotion of sustainable development. The collapse of the former Soviet Union and the East European communist countries gave a fillip to this trend away from a dominant public sector and placed democratic participation high in the agenda.

The above reform measures are now underway as part of the new development assistance strategy of the international development community. Government's role is not being rolled back; it is being adapted to its capability and adjusted with the emergent private sector and the civil society. Good governance is being seen as the process of acquiring excellence by government in the areas where it's role is indispensable and at the same time is one of enabling private sector and civil society to grow. The latter two are receiving assistance from the development community, directly and indirectly, as part of the new strategy. As in the past, the international development community is exerting powerful influence in determining the course of governance and it is more direct and less subtle now. In accepting and implementing these policy reforms developing countries must use their own judgement and decide on the scope and timing of the programmes because governance that is home grown has greater chance of being sustainable. For countries that still depend on foreign assistance significantly the subject is of more than academic interest. It is vital for sustainable human development in a world that is becoming closely integrated rapidly.

Conclusion

Changes over time and experiences gained have set the backdrop for a new social contract that can meet the prevailing needs of society and challenges of the new millennium. This not only calls for broadening the concept and practice of 'governance' but also requires defining the role of different partners, severally and collectively, and delineation of their scope of collaboration.

Notes

1. Similar unbalanced development characterized societies where feudal and semi-feudal institutions coexisted with desultory modernization of political institutions that oscillated between autocracy and some semblance of representative democracy.
2. The expressions "inner-directed" and "other-directed" appeared first in "Lonely Crowd" written by David Riesman, Nathan Glazer and Renel Denny (Doubleday, 1954). I have used these in a different context taking their literal meanings.
3. The expressions is borrowed from W.B. Yeats' work.

References

Bryce, Lord, *Modern Democracies*. 1921.

Hart, H.L., *The Concept of Law*. Clarendon Press, U.K., 1961.

Islam, Mahmudul, *Constitutional Law of Bangladesh*, BILIA, 1995.

Lock, J., *An Essay Concerning the True Original Extent and End of Civil Government*, 1632-1704.

Lock, J., Hume, D., Russeau, J.J., *Social Contract* with an introduction by Ernest Baker, Oxford University Press, 1978.

Montesquieu, *The Spirit of the Laws*. 1848.

World Bank, *The State in a Changing World*. World Development Report, Washington D.C., 1997.

CONSENSUS, PROBLEMATICS AND REFORM AGENDA

B.K. Jahangir

Introduction

Bangladesh is not a surplus state, and its capacities are minimal over social and economic policy. Within this arena, the state is experimenting with democracy, in the wake of globalization. The state is constructed to create global and/or regional markets and the ideology of globalization is democratization. Since Bangladesh is not a surplus state and its capacities are minimal, the political construction of democratization has created problems. This has occurred in spite of market economy and global and/or regional trends and the pressures produced by the needs of street politics. If state is power, then, power is to be constituted around internal and external linkages. Both involve building power alliances: (a) inter-state coalitions at the regional and international level and (b) state-business alliances in the internal market. The whole issue of state capacity means adaptability of the state in this new role, and Bangladesh is groping to find a way out to be independent from other elements of the coalition and the alliances. Compulsion is growing in Bangladesh economy to become regionalized, and this regionalization of the economy has generated the propulsion for inter-state coalitions involving South Asian states and sub-regional states.

States, including Bangladesh, are engaged in facilitating regionalization/internationalization to increase the state capacity for coordination between market economies and the governments. This compulsion for regionalization is political in the sense that the government deliberately is opening up capital markets to facilitate regionalization/internationalization of corporate activity in trade, investment and production. Government, in the light of East Asian experience, is trying to enlarge the state capacity for industrial and trade transformation. State adaptability for market economy is increasing, and a sense for collaboration between government and business is growing. The agenda of inter-state coalitions and state-business alliances, perhaps in the future, will produce a different kind of state where power of the state will be reconstituted within coalitions and alliances to enhance national economic co-ordination. This is an indication that state is in the process of a change in which territorial limit is not the be-all and end-all of everything of relationship, rather the state is responsive to change, and out of the responses, a different kind of state is gradually taking shape giving a new meaning to inter-state and government-business relationship.

This process of democratization has generated internal challenges which radicalizes the notions of power and sovereignty. In place of undivided sovereignty comprising the relationships between territory, community and region, it is evolving — stretching relationships in time and space — beyond the fixed political borders of nation-state. These stressed relationships link nation with nation, state with state, and are multi-dimensional: economic, political, cultural, environmental and regional. These links and stressed relationships produce a sense of sharing in all fields mentioned above including sovereignty. The contemporary forms of regionalization have changed the shape of nation, state and national economies. The proliferation of powerful international and/or regional actors in national politics and accommodation of national politics enmeshed within regionalization and/or internationalization has transformed the efficacy of the tools of national governance. State means a given space in a region and Bangladesh is deepening a sense of regionalization within its state boundary along with other states. This phenomenon is new and Bangladesh national markets in capital, products and labour are more sensitive to the movements and crises of other markets.

Changing Role of Nation State

These changes are radical and deeply influences the theory of sovereignty emerging out of liberal democracy. Location of a political community is not strictly confined within the boundaries of a single nation state. Locus of political power is not necessarily based in the national government. Therefore, sovereignty is located in various overlapping and spatially variable sovereign institutions. This changing scenario has legitimized multiple citizenships and citizens are now members of multitude of political communities. In place of a single government, there are multitudes of governments; in place of a single citizenship, there are multitude citizenships; in place of an undivided sovereignty, there are overlapping sovereign institutions. All these point to a shared concept of governance combining a nation state and a region. As governing power, the role of nation-state is changing. Since state is embedded in an inter-state system, the case for democratization investigates the connection between political community and democracy.

The way democracy is functioning in Bangladesh raises certain issues regarding individuals and institutions. Democratic experiment here is pluralistic in theory and attempts to achieve consensus and homogeneity. This premise is false because people are not a unified and homogeneous entity. In the project for democracy, therefore, an accommodation is needed for resolution of conflicts and antagonisms in the institutions, to guarantee respect for human rights and to avoid descending into tyranny. Does democracy express the authentic longings of the people? Democracy incorporates the popular content as well as its distortion: the relations of domination and exploitation. People or the majority of people live within the relations of domination and exploitation and the authentic popular content of democracy is expressed in terms of freedom. Extreme ideology distorts the popular longing for community and social solidarity against competition and exploitation. In the case of Bangladesh the right wing political parties distort this longing to legitimize the continuation of the relations of domination and exploitation. In such a scenario, democratization means either active engagement in civil society or passive consumerism. Both sorts are gaining ground here. Simultaneity is the norm. In the society, divisive antagonisms, such as class struggle, is dominant, and post-ideological pragmatic universe of rational administration and negotiated consensus are the talking points of the stationed World Bank chief and the donor agencies which the intellectuals play with aestheticism, hedonism and pluralistic ways of life. All these point to the contradiction of the liberal democratic project. Another dimension to the democratization project has also emerged: opposition between the logic of dissent and the logic of antagonism. This opposition generates tension between the logic of dissent and the logic of antagonism, between the liberal-democratic universe of negotiation and the fundamentalist universe of good and evil. This tension between the two — class struggle divisiveness and the negotiated consensus, the logic of dissent and the logic of antagonism — is irreducible. The emergence of unsettling-destabilizing forces out of the two, is difficult to be integrated into a social whole. The site of the tension, therefore, is the state: post-nation state versus the nation-state. The elements of post-nation-state in Bangladesh are globalization trends of the economy which are advocated simultaneously by the transnational corporations and by the national government. Economic integration within region and global world is the agenda and the nation-state extends its capacity beyond historically framed national sovereignty. Nation-state and the global market are not antinomies, rather they supplement each other changing: (a) state's previous role to protect economic sovereignty and (b) expanding state's capacity to negotiate sovereignty into the new international environment.

Issues at Democratization

Democratization process has raised certain issues in Bangladesh: (a) Is the state neutral permitting different ways of life? and (b) Does the state promote specific causes like secularism or personal autonomy? Rawls (1972), one of the most important advocates of neutrality thesis, defines neutrality as non-interference and pluralism as toleration of different ways of life. This formulation begs the question. Acceptance of Rawls' formulation means increasing tolerance for violence in the name of dissent and indifference for minority rights in the name of the majority. The recognition of multiple identities presumes multiple communities and these are construction, sharing: (a) a space of a single, shared rationality and (b) place whose unity depends on a division, a polemical community for imposing discourse of equality. The problem is: how to transform the governing ideas of community into an organizing concept of social experience.

Democratization project, as theorized and practiced in Bangladesh, reveals the tension between the superior future (west) and the inferior past (east) and conceals power relationship between the two. Democratization processes are seen, in Bangladesh, as expression of a double movement; stretching the western notion of democracy and deepening the western values. Bangladesh is part of the structures and organizations of modern societies and within the orbit of instantaneous communication and global capitalism which stimulate economic and social process and interlock the local and global. Democratization project has key implications for the national state and sovereignty. There are two ways of erosion. One is: globalism — economic, political, legal and military. Which has its own way of pressure for changing the nature of sovereignty. The other way of erosion is growth of local and regional nationalism. This growth is a pointer to destabilization of previously constituted national sovereignty. Bangladesh has become a site of this kind: of disruption and erosion.

Can it be said that the democratization project is West's outward expansion — a kind of disguise to keep going its dominant continuities? It has been suggested that two elements are prominent in democratization process. Globalization/democratization problematic has two elements: (a) it is centred in the west and talks English (English as international language, as Anglo-Indian, as Anglo-Bangla, as Anglo-Japanese or as Anglo-Germany) and (b) its form of homogenization is essentially an American conception of the world. This analysis takes us straight to the heart of the problem: the impact of the neo-liberal thought on the peripheral societies. Neo-liberalism is the frame of the present day development theory which is a combination of private property, market relations and possessive individualism. Along with these, participatory development and good governance are now in official agenda of development.

Good Governance in Democratization

Good governance is in the heart of democratization process. In Bangladesh, good governance stands for the strengthening of judiciary system (separation of judiciary from the executive), election monitoring, administrative decentralization, ethnic relation CHT (Chittagong Hill Tract), protection of minorities and conflict resolution (with opposition political parties). OECD produced a report on development outlining the key features of the donor countries. In the words of the report, this creates new scope for mutual understanding and synergy among policy makers in donor governments as they tackle developments as part of achieving a 'global agenda'.

Mastering development as part of a 'global agenda' is the slogan of the World Bank, OECD, IMF and other donor agencies and international organizations. Prescriptions are: a role for civil society, for good governance, Western-style democracy, decentralization and participation. The neo-liberal thesis has made, on the one hand, imperialism visible because it has the greatest capacity to subvert national sovereignty of a poor country like Bangladesh and on the other, positively celebrates the moral record of the West — a sort of return of imperialism, because of the failure of nationalism, emergence of more conservative intellectual climate and the collapse of the Soviet Union. Bangladesh is part of this system. An angst is underlying the democratization process and Bangladesh is experiencing the hegemony of the World Bank and the IMF, the chaos of the privatization and liberalization and the sad demise of the autonomy of the state.

Democratization does not mean merely the politics of universal suffrage. The question is: Do people govern actually? Since government is a form of decision-making body, it cannot function or govern against the people or without it. In Bangladesh, two insurrections of 1990 and 1996 prove this point eloquently. The common people entered into the history of Bangladesh to exercise their rights and all kinds of regime, democratic or non-democratic, derived this authority from them. This way people intervened in public affairs passively, or actively. A public sense of the regime's legitimacy is people's acceptance of the government where obedience is linked. When, as in 1990, or in 1996, this obedience was withdrawn from the Jatiya Party (JP) and the Bangladesh Nationalist Party (BNP) government, these regimes abdicated, though they had certain support of civil functionaries, armed services and security forces. Citizens' support legitimizes regimes, authority and withdrawal of citizens' support produces political, economic, social and cultural insecurities and tensions in the governing process: contemporary Bangladesh is a testimony to this.

Conflicting Values

This process of linking decision-makers and people is another name of Western neo-liberal thinking. For Bangladesh this represents emancipation from the colonial past, permitting the advent of a liberal society. A society needs pluralism for creating the modern values. This is a longing, a sort of romanticism born in Mill's England and imposed in colonial Bengal, proclaiming the free creation of values. From Bankim to Rabindranath to Lalan, from Fazlul Huq to Abul Hashim to Sheikh Mujib all spoke out for a pluralistic society. When its ideals were transferred to politics under General Zia's military hegemony and reinterpreted by General Ershad, it eventually instigated the furies of a Muslim Bangladesh, of communalism and fundamentalism. Pluralism, which democratization wants to establish, speaks for human values and is inherently multiple and conflictual. A model society based on one single goal leads to despotism. In Bangladesh, we have experienced a model society-oriented despotism in the times of Zia and Ershad and also experienced the problems of establishing multiple and conflictual human values. The point is: are we aware of pluralism? Is there any attempt to construct tolerance of different individual choices of life? Pluralism is a vision between societies (Pakistani military society *vis-à-vis* Mujib's Sonar Bangla) and the growth of Bengali nationalism is an attempt to explore contrasting cultures and a testimony to multiplicity of such cultures. These two elements of nationalism are the proving ground of pluralism. Pluralistic cultures may be incompatible, but their variety cannot be unlimited, for the nature of men, however various and subject to change, must possess some generic nature if it is to be called human at all.

The crux of the problem is: did we inherit a liberal civilization? Our political experience is obsessed by the great despotic visions of the right and left political leaders of the past passionately attached to the theories that were not their own, (Fazlul Huq to Abul Hashim), but borrowed from the West and Islam and imperfectly understood and rushed to blind passion. (On the one hand Fazlul Huq's Krishak Praja Party and Abul Hashim's initial phase of Bengal Muslim League and Moulana Akram Khan's Congress phase to Muslim League phase, and on the other, Shariatullah, Titumir and Dudu Mia's reading of Islam), dragging their followers after them. The distance between their fascination with ideas and their effects on political practice is vast and contradictory. The monist practice and pluralist visions have led to perversions of politics and weakened the basis of a liberal civilization. The dichotomy between the right and the left and the yearning for the absolutes produced a vision which is inconsistent with pluralism. It does not mean co-existence of the devil and God, rather it generates values of conflicting nature and involves agonizing choices and possibility of moral uncertainty. These agonizing choices were made during the colonial time and the military regimes for the individual's right to self direction, as opposed to direction by a theocratic military state or military state or military-led political party. Colonialism and cultures are conjoined through relations of ruling: the ruling apparatus is that familiar complex of management, government, administration, professions, and intelligentsia, as well as the textually mediated discourses that coordinate and interpenetrate it. It's special capacity is the organization of particular places, persons, and events into generalized and abstracted modes vested in categorical systems, rules, laws and conceptual practices. The former thereby become subject to an abstracted and universalized system of ruling mediated by texts. Through this process of abstraction the colonial and the post-colonial state legislate differences in order to legitimize authority and marginalize the agonizing burden of pluralism. We have lived through the ideals of democratization process and involved in inner conflicts, in support of perceiving reality in its multiplicity but believing in unitary whole. For us democratization process means suffering through the truth, the stripping off of political and moral despotism. This leads to a critique, with far reaching implications, of the assumption at the base of everyday social and political conduct.

State and Civil Society

Bangladesh is positioned between globalization and regionalism. The stress of globalization and the strain of regionalism stamped their marks on the policies of the state. Bangladesh at the level of decision-making is trying desperately to accommodate new institutions including the diversity of intergovernmental, transnational and NGOs and regional organizations (for example, South Asian Association for Regional Co-operation and Organization of Islamic Conference), new issues like the environment, gender, democracy, migration and new approaches at the levels of both analysis and praxis, from neo-liberalism to post-modernism.

Is it possible to build up pluralism within the Bangladesh civil society: a pluralist world of co-operating and mutually dependent interests? In order to construct a structure of interdependence a certain amount of interventionism, for instance, in the form of transfer of resources from rich to poor through a strengthened local governance system, is needed. The crucial actor, is still, the state, with limited sovereignty and possibly restricted by a system of shared norms based on systems of management in various realms (trade, finance, energy) where civil society comply with established norms without hegemonic pressures.

The state has become a site of rehabilitated state, strengthened non-state actors and anti-democratic tendencies. Throughout eighties and nineties there was a global pressure for a shrunken state, an outcome of economic and political liberalization. This ideological decline, it seems, has stopped and the state is set for rehabilitation. Bangladesh has learnt slowly the lessons of both Newly Industrialized Countries (NICS) and Structural Adjustment Programmes and the lessons point to a necessary role for a new state in terms of economic direction, infrastructural development and welfare provision. A new consciousness is growing out of popular movement, civil society, activists, and NGOs regarding the unacceptable human and financial costs of un/under employment, infrastructural decay and rising levels of crime and insecurity, especially to women and vulnerable groups. This consciousness necessitates the imperative of a 'strong' state rather than a shrunken state challenging the global ideological pressure of neo-liberalization. Some of the consequences of Structural Adjustment Programmes and continuing structural changes may have lead to a policy of rejuvenation of state in Bangladesh in the late nineties. Its rejuvenation is closely related to state performance in the areas of accountability and transparency. Again, Bangladesh has accommodated to global pressure of democracy and activity of influential non-state actors as the criterion for sate management. The inclusion of International NGO and NGO's together with the media, constituted a civil society within the state which exists, increasingly at global as well as national levels. The territoriality of the state and the de-territoriality of the civil society are part of contemporary democratization rocess and Bangladesh is learning to cope with the formal multi-party arrangement and elections and informal popular movements.

In Bangladesh, the site of the state is increasingly becoming an arena of ideology of democracy and the submerged threat or authoritarianism of corporatist tendencies. Whereas ideology of democracy includes civil society and constitutional politics, authoritarian or corporatist tendencies point to arbitrary or military rule and anarchy. The dichotomy between democratization and corporatism constitutes the possibilities of distortion of the nature of state: the weakened state or the resurgent state may come to rely on coercion if resources shrink. Therefore, the apparent trend towards official democratization, needs closer interrogation. Economic liberalization releases competitiveness and genres of globalization and regionalism present divergent and contradictory assumptions and definitions regarding directions for Bangladesh as a whole and for classes and civic groups within Bangladesh particularly.

Parallel Pressures of Liberalization

Indeed, a fundamental tension is brewing between the parallel pressures generating out of economic liberalization and political liberalization. Economic liberalization may necessitate political centralization and coercion whereas political liberalization may necessitate widest participation in the decision-making process. Since the room to manoeuvre is slender, repressive/imposed discipline for economic management may be an essential corollary of Structural Adjustment Programmatic Reforms costing democratization process. Since the regime will be endangered, the lure of various types of corporatism and coercion may lead towards political concentration demising the democratization process.

Despite globalization process, considerable fissiparous tendencies are apparent in Bangladesh, for instance, construction of Export Processing Zones (EPZ) for economic and political reasons, autonomy of ethnic communities and formation of divisions for the establishment of mini political rights fragmenting the unitary state.

Two trends are visible. One is the continuing globalization of the world economy in terms of communication, distribution, production and technology. And the other is minuscule level of representative structures in terms of both economic efficiency and political representation.

In the global area the scenario is also changed. The West is divided and lacks a will to impose conditionalities for sustained structural adjustment. The South seems slipping out of hands of the West and the conditionalities constructed by the West regarding political and environmental and devolution of power are now the preserve of the local and global NGOs. They have assumed the responsibility on behalf of the West to put pressure on the state.

Here, Bangladesh, could seize the chance to recapture the global agenda for sustainable development and human security to escape from interventionist conditionalities and redefine its own development direction. This could be possible in Bangladesh where civil society has proved its mettle and has experienced two insurrections against two dictatorial regimes. The internalization of experience matured the civil society to constitute an alternative source of policy innovation and programme implementation. An area of co-operation is feasible exploring regional and global developmental conditions outside the domain of inter-state organizations through inter-civil society.

Bangladesh, in response to such trends, is reacting to continuing regionalization following the end of Bretton Woods and cold war scenario. Inter-state relationship within the region is no longer the exclusive preserve of ministerial arrangements. It encompasses organized elements in political economy, civil society: business, media and women, for continuing consultation and cooperation. This has reinforced informal regionalisms alongside formal regionalism.

This inter-twining of formal features with informal regionalism has produced a new development contact within South Asia. Bangladesh has something to contribute to such a mutual dialogue regarding growing interdependence involving communication and redistribution of resources. After two lost decades Bangladesh could possibly return to more realistic, humane, long term development policies stressing on interdependence within the region. This is a step towards rejuvenation stopping marginalization of Bangladesh in political and policy debates and to turn a disadvantageous position into an advantageous situation.

State and Development Strategy

Bangladesh state is redefining development, exploring issues like democracy, environment, gender, informal sector and privatization. The state has started to discard worn out notions of one person regime. Formal multi-party elections and governance has redefined civil society and the civil society has enlarged its capacity to accommodate indigenous discourses, experiences and pressures. A parallel force has also emerged from the market and constituted something of a departure. Will these factors transform the political economics and political cultures of the state in a significant way?

The above question is addressed to the state. The crisis in Bangladesh development generated critiques on both the role of the state and the development strategy. Structural adjustment packages prepared by the international financial institutions prescribed a reduced role for the state in economic development. Hence the stress on the reduction of the public sector, enlargement of the privatization of the productive activities and liberalization of foreign investment policy. The limitation of structural adjustment packages followed by the BNP government is increasingly becoming obvious and a new realization is growing in social policies and investment in human resources on the part of the state.

The lost decades made us wise and now we recognize that the economic and the social are inseparable and that state and market should interact. Development necessitates a role for the state and the role should be to overcome deficiencies in two areas: equity and international/regional competitiveness. This is a compulsion for difference and the state should be different in order to promote equity within the country and to promote competitiveness outside the country. Apart from equity and competitiveness, the state has a certain role to build national consensus. These are central issues for a people wishing to become different. The question is whether the Bangladesh state has the capability to combine these objectives. Is it possible for a weak state to play a central role in building national consensus in a society which is heterogeneous and polarized on almost all issues of national life? In other words, how to resolve the tension between what should be the new role of a state and a state as it is.

Consensus Building

Consensus is the demand of the day. Since the emergence of Bangladesh, the state experimented with political regime and military dictatorship to ease various areas of contestations/contradictions in national life and to further economic development. But the result was counter-productive. The initial years of one-party domination and the post-1975 military hegemony made clear that freedom, participation and toleration need to be built into the political system. Dissent became a national movement and dismissed the Party-State bloc as well as the Military-State bloc and the state versus civil society conflict evolved into a struggle for civic powers. The idea of consensus emerged out of the commitment to a negotiated solution within the framework of the existing constitution. We have witnessed the degradation of democracy into tyranny and authoritarianism and this degradation has taught us that democracy needs to be authentic. Perhaps the pre-condition of authenticity is consensus and consensus shuns violence. This idea is derived from pluralist democratic theory. The integration of state and society is needed to construct consensus and to ensure social and political stability. Without construction of consensus, manifold problems of Bangladesh cannot be addressed and here lies the strength of the argument for a pluralist society. This kind of society is not conflict and contradiction-free, rather this kind of arrangement stresses on reconciling interests in the increasingly heterogeneous society.

Perhaps there is self-defeat limitation in pluralist democratic theory. Self-defeat or limitation arises out of the process of dialogue or opening up of communication with the oppositions, counterparts and marginalized sectors. Is it possible or how far is it possible to start dialogue with the BNP, the main political opposition? Or to open up channel of communication with the marginalized sectors? The BNP perhaps is not enthusiastic to enter into a minimal value consensus programme and is more interested to harness agitation-resistance programme against the government, which points to the limitation of the pluralist democratic theory. The integration of state-society divide is needed to guarantee social and political stability, but the divide poses a threat against the construction of consensus value. The scenario is: the main opposition party wants to stay out of the consensus terrain. Then, how to reach the marginalized sectors or the poor? If the state could open up communication channel with the marginalized sectors or the poor through the NGO's through the ruling party, then perhaps it would be possible to hear the voices of the poor. Opening up new channels of communication could lead to more conflicts between different sectors or precipitate sectional interest and arrest growth rates. In such a scenario of limited and fragile democratization process, consensus construction begs manifold problems too complex to manipulate for the state management. In the case of Bangladesh the state is weak and its listening capacity is limited and management skill is poor. In such a terrain, the strengthening of pluralist democratic theory and the construction of consensus value could lead to more challenge for the governance problematic. In spite of problems of manifold nature, the promotional role of the state for construction of national consensus is a new developmental paradigm.

Reformist Agenda

It is obvious that reformist agenda is inevitable, but there are constraints of adjustment measures and the social costs need to be addressed within the overall constraints in order to minimize or to contain the pain of adjustment. In what way the Bangladesh state is going to increase social support while decreasing overall expenditure? It is a dilemma of serious magnitude and an answer is expected to address this problem. Two alternatives are before the policy makers. First: the re-allocation of existing social expenditure to increase efficiency and equity. It could be done by shifting funds/resources from secondary to primary schooling, from curative to preventive health care, from urban to rural sectors. Second: supplementary programmes designed to reach the poor and those affected by adjustment. It could be done by public works programmes, infrastructure development, nutrition interventions, credit and other support for micro level development. The first is a way to correct budget distortions and to increase welfare expenditures shifting from well-off groups to needy ones within a given budget constraint. The second is to limit interventions to particular groups and to administer practical measures within the theoretical model and the real world of Bangladesh. Policies have two types of natures: (a) universal policies become regressive when they ignore certain characteristics of the recipients, for instance inefficiency and (b) selective policies become regressive when they are part of a strategy of dismantling policies.

Another aspect should not be belittled: internal political opposition to adjustment measures. Left political parties and poor and middle class groups organized in trade-unions have articulated their opposition to adjustment programmes. In order to diffuse opposition, adjustment programmes need to be delinked from the ruling party and operate in a transparently non-partisan manner. Perhaps here lies the compulsion of the national consensus scenario. Appointments are to be made on a neutral basis and efforts are to be made to involve groups from across the political spectrum.

Reference

Rawls, J., *A Theory of Justice*, Oxford University Press, 1972.

LEGISLATURE AND GOVERNANCE IN BANGLADESH

Dilara Chowdhury

Introduction

Bangladesh opted for a parliamentary democracy following independence in 1971 in which establishment of a sovereign legislature was sought. The main thrust was to ensure the sovereignty of the people exercised through a democratically elected representative body called the legislature. Though the concept of nineteenth century sovereign legislature, which was to govern the polity, has undergone a profound transformation giving rise to the dominance of the executive in the context of the complexities of modern state, its role and significance in making the government behave has not diminished in any way. And it was hoped that the legislature in Bangladesh would function in such a way that effective governance would be ensured.

But even after twenty-seven years of independence, various structural changes of the legislative organ, and with the re-establishment of a sovereign parliament since 1991, the effectiveness of the legislature in promoting good governance has remained somewhat elusive. In this paper attempts would be made to briefly outline a conceptual framework dealing with legislature's role in developed societies and its evolution in Bangladesh since independence. Finally, there would be a discussion on how far the legislature in Bangladesh has been able to effectively ensure good governance.

Conceptual Framework

The evolution of modern legislature and its role in democratic governance date back to the gradual working of parliamentary democracy in England. Though its origin lies not 'in the legislation, not even in the supply of finance' but in the king's need for 'some process, however rough and ready, by which he could obtain the consent, or at least the acquiescence, of the influential sections of the people to his acts of governance, (Butt, 1968) it became increasingly identified with the law-making functions (Locke & Monstesque). This aspect of the legislature was further strengthened when during the eighteenth century the Americans, in their fight to safeguard their interests against the royal governors, emphasized the policy-making functions of the legislature. Basically the legislature remained identified with the law-making function, as the general idea was that the representatives should make the rules under which they would live. As such the battle cry during the last half of nineteenth-century was to reinforce the supremacy of the parliament and limit the powers of the executive. The legislature was, thus, viewed as the most important organ of the government.

Historically, however, the powers and supremacy of the legislature began its ascendancy after the glorious revolution of 1688 in England. But thanks to the changing role of the state, the executive's ascendancy has become more visible since the late nineteenth century. Sir Ramsay Muir, in his brilliant study of the British Parliament, has very candidly pointed out the ineffectiveness of the legislature in performing its designated role (Muir, 1930). Although Sir Ramsay over-emphasized the decline of the British Parliament, there is no denying that the British Parliament or the Mother Parliament's role has changed in view of the emergence of an assertive, structured and well-disciplined party-system in Great Britain and the consequent dominance of the executive. Sir Ivor Jennings has pointed out that the 'transcendent and absolute' power of Parliament has now shifted to the hands of the Government and ultimate control on the executive is with the electorate or public opinion (Jennings, 1969). Similar trends were visible in West European countries where the emergence of well-disciplined parties gave rise to strong executives.

The latter issue has posed a serious lop-sided executive-legislature relations since post-World War II period to date. The increasing responsibilities of the State of the twentieth century call for greater initiative and dynamism from the executive, which almost compels it to interfere in the legislative sphere. The line between the two spheres, as a result, became blurred, especially in the parliamentary framework. This phenomenon has been termed by Lord Bryce as the 'decline of legislatures' (Bryce, 1921).

In spite of such development, 'once the idea of direct popular government was rejected as impractical, representative assemblies were the only known device by which executives could be restrained (liberalism) and restrained on the basis of the peoples' will (Blondel, 1979). The legislature has, thus, emerged as the symbol of liberalism and democracy though its functions and roles have undergone profound changes. As such, though there has been the recent trend towards a 'decline of parliament' and the rise of cabinet dictatorship, no one can deny or challenge the importance of the legislature, not only in the parliamentary system, but even in a presidential system as it exists in the US.

Today, Dicey's concept of a legislature through which the people govern themselves, is somewhat tarnished, but in its new role, it provides twin purposes of securing popular representation and government accountability. Through popular representation, it provides, on the one hand, conflicting interests with a platform for negotiation and compromise, and on the other, it provides a forum where government's accountability is secured and its actions are evaluated. The legislature, in a modern state, though does not engage itself so much with the initiation of legislation, its role in law-making is crucial, and "its capacity to control the potential excesses of executive initiative and power has been considered a basic task of legislatures in modern theories of representative government" (Rossiter, 1961). Its "decisional" role, according to Marvin Weinbaum, "to initiate legislation, to modify, delay or defeat bills, to influence administration through parliamentary questions, interpellations, and investigations, and to alter departmental budgets, authorizations, and personnel", is, thus, vital in performing its crucial task i.e., ensuring good governance (Weinbaum).

It is to be noted that the weakness or the strength of the legislatures depend on their capacity or oversight activities to do their designated tasks. And these criteria vary from legislature to legislature. In the developed societies these capacities or the oversight activities are highly structured and continuous. British Parliament which is executive-centered and gives an impression of subordinating the legislature in effect, is continuously under scrutiny by the legislature so that policy-formulation are mass oriented and there is no abuse of power by the government. These have been possible due to strong party-system, traditions, conventions as well as providing greater opportunities to the Opposition and the back-benchers. Parliamentary techniques during plenary sessions are also highly successful. Similar legislative strength is also discernible from the activities of Indian parliament.

The US Congress is another example of strong legislative control over executive actions. It possesses the most 'telling constraint,' i.e., the power to saying 'no' to executive without being intimidated into dissolution. Through its well-structured committee system the United States Congress has been acting as a vigilant 'watch-dog' in scrutinizing executive's activities and playing decisive role in the policy-making process. Very few legislatures enjoy such prestige, power, and strength to deal with the potential abuse of power of the executive.

Legislature in a modern state, thus, may have given up its direct role in governance but in its new role it has certainly not abandoned its task of making the government behave and ensuring good governance. Besides influencing the law-making functions it uses various techniques and modus operandi such as adjournment motions, question and answer sessions, investigation by committees etc. to do the designated task.

Evolution of Bangladesh's Legislature

The Constituent Assembly of Bangladesh was formed in March 1972, through a Presidential Ordinance known as 'Bangladesh Constituent Assembly Order.' The Constituent Assembly consisted of members of the National Assembly and the Provincial Assembly who were elected between December 1970 and 1st March 1971.

This sovereign body was entrusted with the task of framing the Constitution of the Peoples' Republic of Bangladesh, but it was not to operate as a legislature. From the outset, the sovereignty of the Constituent Assembly was set on a wrong footing. The sovereignty of Constituent Assembly of Bangladesh had been circumscribed by another Presidential Order, namely the Constituent Assembly Members (Cessation of Membership) Order, which stipulated that if a member of the Constituent Assembly either resigned or was expelled from the party which nominated him to the election, his seat would be declared vacant. Since the Awami League had captured most of the National Assembly and Provincial Assembly seats in the elections of 1970 and 1971, the Constituent Assembly automatically became subservient to the ruling party.

A constitutional draft committee was formed during the first session of the Constituent Assembly and it proceeded with the framing of a sovereign parliament. Constitutional provisions were incorporated in order to make the parliament a truly sovereign body so that it could perform its designated task. All legislative authority of the Republic was entrusted to Parliament, which is officially known as the Jatiya Sangsad. Method of choosing representatives through direct elections on the basis of universal adult franchise was provided to preserve the intrinsic aspect of a sovereign parliament.

In order to enhance the prestige, status and sovereignty of Parliament a number of other provisions were included. According to J. Blondel, there are four indicators which determine the high status of a legislature; i.e., (i) Parliamentary immunity (the right to make statements in the House), (ii) Parliamentary inviolability (the right not to be detained except in certain circumstances), (iii) Procedural independence (the right to freely draft the Rules of the Chamber), (iv) Freedom of meeting (the right to meet whenever members so decide. It was given the 'highest status' symbols. The House was given the power to frame its own rules and procedure.

The constitution makers of Bangladesh also incorporated devices and mechanisms through which the Jatiya Sangsad would be able to fulfil its assigned task. Incorporation of provision to set up a committee system in parliament was done. Keeping the committee system in mind and inspired by the golden vision of establishing an effective parliament, Articles 76(1) and (2) were incorporated. These articles stipulated that during the first meeting of each session of the legislature, parliament would appoint standing committees of which the most prominent ones would be: (1) A Public Accounts Committee (PAC); (2) A Committee of Privileges; (3) Other such standing committees as Rules of Procedure of Parliament required in order to examine, (i) draft bills and other legislative proposals; (ii) review enforcement of laws; (iii) handle those matters referred to by parliament; (iv) investigate or inquire into the activities or administration of the ministries and furnish information. To ensure further accountability of the executive, Article 77 provided for an Ombudsman. For further effective scrutinizing the public accounts of the Republic, Article 127 of the 1972 Bangladesh Constitution stipulated that the office of a Comptroller and Auditor General would audit all expenditures of the government and relay the reports of public accounts to the President to be laid before parliament. The terms and conditions of his office were set to ensure the independence and impartiality of such an office. For the efficient working of the House a parliamentary secretariat was provided by Article 79.

The Constituent Assembly Members (Cessation of Membership) Order was incorporated, as a constitutional provision, in order to deal with the circumstances under which a member must vacate his seat. The most novel one was Article 70, which stipulated that if a member resigned or voted against the party which nominated him to the election, his seat would be declared vacant. He would, however, not be debarred from contesting the subsequent election. There is no doubt that this Article circumscribed the independence and free spirit of the individual MPs. Such a relationship between the party and parliament in Bangladesh had serious repercussions on the working of parliament itself.

It is amply evident, despite Article 70, that the framers of the Constitution of 1972 took all necessary measures to establish the supremacy of the Jatiya Sangsad so that it could keep the executive on its toes for the effective governance of the country. But unfortunately the history of Bangladesh's legislative development has not been encouraging despite the strong (as mentioned earlier), constitutional provisions to make it a sovereign body. The point here is to make a distinction between theory and practice.

In the context of the above discussion let us now analyse the role played by the legislature under various regimes in ensuring governance in the country.

'Vulnerable' Legislature

With the general election held on 7 March 1973, the life of a sovereign parliament seemed to have begun in Bangladesh. Constitutional provisions ensured the independence and sovereignty of the legislature in clear terms but the existence of an 'executive-centered elite' and absence of strong party system indeed raised serious questions about its capacity in either policy-making process or oversight activities. Two other factors also aroused suspicions and apprehensions about the smooth functioning of the Jatiya Sangsad: (1) Article 70, as pointed out earlier, circumscribed the independence and free spirit of the MPs. It was incorporated in the context of lack of existing party discipline in the country, which previously had created acute political instability in the then East Pakistan. It was a dilemma, which did not have an easy solution. In England the party whip forbids voting against one's own party but the leader of the party remains constantly in touch with the back-benchers in order to feel public opinion and prevent dissension/ rebelliousness within the party. But in case of Bangladesh, the MPs did not have any such prerogatives. They had to toe the executive-centered party line; (2) the results of March election failed to produce an established Opposition which required a membership of at least twenty whereas the Opposition captured only six seats out of 300 parliamentary seats.

The absence of an established Opposition created a serious draw-back, as the role of the Opposition is very crucial in a parliamentary system. Without a responsible opposition in parliament, its functions are seriously hampered. According to Professor Morris-Jones, "In the absence of a proper Opposition, with adequate strength and enjoying recognition, there can be, it is said, no healthy parlia-mentary government, for the government will be uncontrolled and unresponsive" (Morris-Jones, 1957). K.C. Wheare, an authority on legislature, also comments that the chief burden of making the government behave is on the Opposition. He further continues that it is the job of the members of the Opposition to examine and to criticize what the government has done and proposes to do through questions to ministers, through motions of censure and no-confidence and through debates that accompany the passing of financial legislation (Wheare, 1965).

Unfortunately, in the 1973 Jatiya Sangsad, there was no such phenomenon. The success of Congress dominated one-party parliamentary system in India is often cited, as an example, but it has to be noted that the Indian success story is mainly a creation of the leadership quality of Jawaharlal Nehru, the democratic structure of the internal organization of the Congress Party and criticism/suggestions put forward by the parliamentary committees. The Nehru government, in spite of having an absolute majority, treated and behaved with the Opposition with the respect that a parliamentary opposition deserves (Morris-Jones, 1957).

No such attitude on the part of the ruling party was discernible in the first parliament of Bangladesh. During 1973-75 the six members of the Opposition tried to take upon themselves the responsibilities of an Opposition. But this opposition was feeble, frustrated and unable to offer an alternate government. The fact of the matter is that it was not a constitutionally recognized Opposition and as such the government did not treat them accordingly. Moreover, curtailment of freedom of the MPs allowed the government a free hand in dealing with the Opposition. It was evidenced by the parliamentary activities of the First Sangsad.

Various parliamentary devices like Question Hour, the Short-notice Questions and Supplementary Questions through which grievances are ventilated and individual rights are protected could neither generate much interest nor any debate on public policies as it happens in most developed democracies where the 'back-benchers' take a delight in heckling a Minister (Jennings, 1969). During the Question Hour, debates are not supposed to run along party lines but most Treasury Bench MPs were apprehensive and extra-careful not to step out of line making the whole procedure more a charade than real.

The familiar parliamentary procedure of the adjournment motion, used to call attention to problems of government, was not allowed although there were daily reports in the newspapers about the deteriorating law and order situation. By late 1973 and early 1974, the situation had deteriorated to such an extent that the government had to deploy the army to handle it. In all there were seven adjournment motions but none was accepted. Motions relating to the army's power and alleged use of excessive and repressive measures were not tabled in the House. It should, however, be pointed out that in modern parliaments, adjournment motions are rarely allowed, but this does not mean that its significance in calling attention of the government to its failures can be completely dismissed, for it does allow the House to be aware of the situation and arouses public reactions to its consequences. Unfortunately, the first Jatiya Sangsad decided to turn a blind eye and tried to brush aside the issue of the government's arbitrary actions and infringement on civil liberties in the name of maintaining law and order situation. Four notices for half-an-hour were similarly ignored. It, thus, became obvious that the House, because of the 'brute majority' of the ruling party and its high-handed attitude, could neither criticize, scrutinize, check the government's arbitrary actions, nor stop the government from infringing on individual liberties and civil rights. To quote K.C. Wheare, "the House was unable to make the government behave." On the contrary, by September 1973 the powers of Parliament were curtailed through the Constitution (Second Amendment) Bill, 1973.

Even with regard to the policy making activities the first parliament demonstrated the classical weakness of a 'marginal' legislature with little or no policy-making power. Although it is an accepted knowledge that modern day legislatures do not initiate the laws which previously were its sole prerogatives, as mentioned earlier, with the rise of the strong executive, it has effectively passed on to latter's arena. But "it is the overall effect on the making of law which is crucial, and in that regard the power which legislative assemblies have to influence the direction and contours of public policy-making is decisive. So fundamental is this process that it is difficult to imagine legislatures performing any other functions effectively" (Sissonileo R. and M. Snowiss). But this crucial function in modern legislatures, especially in a parliamentary system is complex unless the parliament possesses what Blondel has termed as "constraint" but not the kind which "placed on the legislature that prevent it from influencing the policy-making process, but rather the 'constraints' that the legislature is capable of placing on the policy-related activities of the executive" (Blondel, 1979). The government finds it difficult to have a smooth sailing if there are strong legislative constraints. But without the existence of substantive constraints there cannot be a salient policy making role in the legislature. One of the most 'telling constraint' is the veto power but in the context of weaker constraint i.e., when it does not have viable power to reject government proposals, it can extract modifications or compromise in policy proposals which can be done through private consultation with legislators or through open legislative debate. In such cases government may feel compelled to make amendments. There are instances where government's proposals are bound to be approved but the legislature can influence policy formulation through private discussion between the government and its supporters. The government would consider amendments to mollify the dissidents even though party discipline can be used. It may not also introduce a proposal due to anticipated opposition and wait until the climate is more congenial.

But the activities of the First Parliament demonstrated such lack of legislative constraints on the executive that its role in policy making process was almost minimal. It was kept not only out of the policy formulation process but its oversight activities in the process were also marginalized.

As a result most of the Acts passed were placed before the parliament in the form of Presidential Ordinances. Out of 110 Acts passed as many as 91 were Presidential Ordinances. Accordingly, various controversial Ordinances were put before Parliament in the form of bills. Acts like the Special Powers Act, 1974; the Special Powers (Amendment) Bill, 1974, the Emergency Powers Bill, 1975, and the controversial Constitution (Fourth amendment) Bill, 1975, were all passed without either eliciting public opinion or being sent to the Select Committees or having private discussion with the legislators. The Parliament's ineffective powers in scrutinizing these bills are evidenced by the short lengths of debates on them, the deliberation time was sketchy with only a handful MPs taking part in the deliberation.

Ineffective scrutiny of bills by the first parliament was also due to the weak committee system. Unlike the reactive legislatures, there were no effective committees. The opposition was not strong enough to insist on having a powerful committee system. There were only seven Standing Committees, including a Public Accounts Committee, and only a few Select Committees on non-important bills. The government took up all the time in parliamentary business. Unlike in India, no specific period was set aside for private members' business as such. During the first parliament there were neither any private members' bills nor any private members' resolutions before the House. This clearly demonstrated the dominating position of the executive over parliament.

Similarly, it also failed miserably in exercising financial control over the executive. It is a common knowledge that one of the effective weapons available to the legislature to control and make the executive behave properly, is its power over financial matters. Judged by this criterion the first Parliament could not discharge this vital role effectively for the reasons mentioned above. The passing of the budget and its subsequent scrutiny remained in the executive's domain.

The legislature's post-auditing procedure of the government's financial accounts was flawed as well and more cosmetic than genuine. Though an office of a Comptroller and Auditor-General (C & A-G) was established through the Comptroller and Auditor-General Order, 1972, but unlike the C & A-G of Great Britain who is directly responsible to the House of Commons and works independently in close co-operation with the Public Accounts Committee, the C & A-G of Bangladesh was responsible to the President. Article 61(1) stipulated that the C & A-G would perform such functions and exercise such powers, and prepare such reports, in relation to the expenditures and accounts of the government of Bangladesh as may be determined by the President. The C & A-G would keep the reports in such form with the approval of the President; finally, he would submit the reports relating to the accounts of the People's Republic of Bangladesh to the President who would lay it before the parliament. Similarly, the Public Accounts Committee, which was formed on April 7, 1973, to oversee, remained ineffective due to executive's control over it. It was evidenced by to the fact that the chairmanship of the committee went to a Treasury Bench member and not an opposition member which is the usual practice. Both in Great Britain and India, the ministers are excluded from the chairmanship of either the Public Accounts Committee (PAC) or the Estimates Committee. By convention, a top ranking Opposition MP chairs the PAC, in these countries. In England between 1959 and 1963, Harold Wilson chaired the PAC. The effectiveness of legislature's financial control over the executive is, thus, easily discernible. Throughout the first Jatiya Sangsad the PAC met only thrice, to consult the C & A-G and discussed modus operandi, etc. but no audit reports were submitted in the House.

From the above discussion of the functioning of the first Jatiya Sangsad, it becomes crystal clear that the Sangsad could not fulfil the glorious vision of its role i.e., to ensure effective governance of the executive as envisaged in the 1972 Constitution of Bangladesh. Sheikh Mujib with his long-standing commitments to a parliamentary system had no doubt dreamed of institutionalizing parliament. During the first session of the Constituent Assembly he had reminded the Speaker of his role as a Speaker in a parliamentary democracy, and how fundamental was a neutral stance and objectivity in the evolution of parliamentary convention (Proceeding, 1972). The statement probably demonstrated his good intentions. But events turned out quite the opposite. In the absence of an established constitutional Opposition, effective political parties, the pre-eminence of the executive was ensured instead of legislative one. The passage of the Constitution (Fourth Amendment) Bill, 1975, was a monumental example of the impotence of the first Parliament of Bangladesh.

"Lame and Tame" Legislature

In assessing the strength of the legislature it has been pointed out that legislative-executive relationship could be extremely lopsided if the former is deprived of its right of censure whereas the latter is endowed with the power of dissolution. The precarious effectiveness of the Second Parliament in scrutinizing the government can, thus, easily be understood by the fact that it did not have any right of censure whereas the executive retained the power of dissolution.

President Ziaur Rahman introduced a curious mixture of parliamentary and presidential system in which constitutional provisions were amended in order to bring about a changed legislative-executive relations. The power of the executive was strengthened at the cost of legislature. There were no provisions that the cabinet would be 'responsible to the parliament' and it held office at the pleasure of the President. The power of the dissolution lay entirely with the president. This power has not been given entirely to the executive either in a genuine presidential system like that of the United States or in France under the Fifth Republic with which Zia's system was often compared. The collective responsibility of the French Cabinet to Parliament and the financial authority exercised by the latter make it more effective, as well as more powerful, than the legislature under Zia.

Most important constitutional provision that Zia brought with regard to the role of the legislature related to parliament's power over budget and financial matters. Under a new Article 92(A), the chief mechanism to scrutinize the executive was curtailed detrimental to the development of a healthy legislative politics. Without the financial control the legislature loses the main source of influence in restraining and controlling the executive. Article 145(A) curtailed the legislature's power relating to international treaties. This was a gross violation of the faith in constitutionalism and democracy. Even with regard to legislative procedure, initiation of bills as well as their deliberations was neither in line with the parliamentary form of government nor a presidential one.

The committees set up by the Zia parliament resembled neither in structure nor in action with the ones found in a genuine presidential system. In a genuine presidential system, as in the US, members of the legislature belonging to the president's party may chair the departmental committees but these committees are zealous about investigating actions of the executive. Not only are the bills referred to the appropriate committees, but also most committees 'question the executive and investigate departments.' In the US, the House of

Representatives and Senate committees not only question the relevant secretaries and senior civil servants, but they also call outside witnesses. Obviously, the committees do more thorough and detailed investigation of the executive than an individual MP can do. The legislature, thus, had so many restrictions and limits on its powers that its effectiveness in checking, scrutinizing and controlling the executive was undoubtedly beyond any question.

Zia, thus, established a legislature, which was endowed with the activities and trapping's that gave it the aura of an effective parliament. But actually, parliamentary activities and departmental committees and debates were designed to 'train' parliamentarians while the chief executive maintained a tight control over it. Zia himself stated in his inaugural speech that it takes long to learn parliamentary conventions and traditions. Each MP needs to have knowledge about the structure and administration of the government before he can really fulfil his designated role. He hoped that through the experience gathered in the second Parliament, the Honourable MPs would be able to establish conventions and traditions, which would help, and promote democracy. He also lectured the MPs about their expected role as MPs of a 'Sovereign Parliament'. Zia's Parliament was, however, not a 'sovereign parliament' but a 'lame and tame' one, tailored to fulfil the needs of an all-powerful executive. It had very little control over the executive's actions. And it could not also be expected.

Apogee of 'Rubber Stamps' Parliaments

Former President Ershad's two parliaments of 1986 and 1988 were the apogee of 'rubber stamps' parliaments. Though he did not make any changes in the composition of the legislature but its role and prestige were severely damaged because of widespread electoral rigging by the ruling party. No legislature can function and discharge its role unless it is elected fairly and without which its representational character is difficult to maintain. Even the Opposition in such Parliament is manipulated by the executive whereas the members belonging to both Treasury Bench and so-called Opposition can be easily intimidated as their 'victories' in the election were mainly due to ruling party's courtesy. Legislature under President Ershad without any representational character uniquely fitted into the above mentioned paradigm.

But there was no dearth of the parody of parliamentary activities. It was reflected in the pattern of politics in Bangladesh. A hand-picked Opposition was there and the parliamentary activities were nothing but caricature of the actual ones. Rules were suspended when controversial bills were introduced and they were passed with shortest possible deliberations. As many as 21 Ordinances were placed during the first session of the Third parliament. Executive's unfettered actions and legislative impotency created widespread discontent in the country. The frustrated Opposition took politics to the streets. Countrywide agitation, repeated strikes and demonstrations forced President Ershad to dissolve his 1986 parliament in December 1987. But the Fourth legislature established following an unprecedented rigged election, which, as boycotted by all major political parties, was even worse than the previous one. It, however, went through the charade of having real legislative activities and took up voluminous plenary activities. It also set up an impressive committee system.

As mentioned, from the parliamentary activities it appeared that it was performing its designated task. But deeper analysis reveals that the parliamentary activities were performed by a legislature which was constitutionally 'lame and tame'. The legislators' existence as MPs depended on the goodwill of the President and their performance was nothing but a charade. Parliamentary activities like adjournment motions, question hour, even the question of adjournment motions, in the context of the chief executive's non-dependence on parliament for his tenure, became meaningless. Ershad's legislature in effect was merely a parody of a true democratic one.

Legislature under the Revised Parliamentary System

Bangladesh reverted back to parliamentary form of government after a mass movement and once again sovereign parliament was established. For the first time in Bangladesh's legislative history the Fifth Parliament constituted under Twelfth Amendment Bill 1992 demonstrated its ability in conflict management. The issue of Presidential system *vis-à-vis* parliamentary system was resolved through usual legislative procedures. And hopes were raised that in the context of a nascent two-party system, emergence of strong parliamentary Opposition, the legislature would effectively begin supervising the executive and curtail its potential excess of powers.

It is now evident that though the Fifth and Seventh legislatures have been kept out of policy-formulation, which require caucus consultation, activities in the committees and plenary areas, the Fifth Parliament demonstrated certain amount of skills in influencing the policy-making process. During the existence of this legislature, bills were regularly sent to the Select Committees and later accepted in the floor, through regular procedure, with the stipulated committee recommendations. Unfortunately, this practice is not being followed by the present one. The note of dissent on bills at the committee stage is being ignored by the Seventh Parliament, which is not a healthy development.

Also detrimental to legislative development is the tendency of the executive to by-pass the parliament by placing the Ordinances in the form of bills. The Fifth Parliament, in this regard has done more so than any other. But both have been by-passing the legislature by bulldozing bills of national interests such as Upazilla Abolition Bill, Special Security Force, 1992 and Chittagong Hill Tracts bills. Like the First parliament neither the Fifth nor the Seventh Parliaments have allowed the introduction of Private Member's bills. It is a truism that the Private Members bills have little or no chance of being enacted but the MPs usually get a chance to express his opinion in "either criticizing the Government's programmes or publicizing new proposals" (Hyson). They are used for tactical purposes to influence the details of Government bills, or to press Cabinet for action. All these undoubtedly undermine the legislative oversight capacities to a great extent.

With regard to committee system although the Fifth Parliament formed ministerial committees as early as during the Third Session and an impressive committee system was setup, its oversight activities had been marginal and it needed a thorough over-hauling (Hasanuzzaman, 1994-95). It was commendable to have sent important bills to the appropriate Select Committees, but its Standing Committees, especially the PAC and the departmental committees, were not efficient enough to keep a check on the executive. The PAC was chaired by a Treasury Bench MP and the concerned ministers including the non-MP ministers headed the departmental committees. The fact that the non-MP ministers had been denied voting rights was not sufficient to make these committees do their designated task. Most departmental committees were busy with micro-level administrative management rather than with initiating policy, which were needed for debates and for scrutinizing departmental mismanagement. An office of Ombudsman also was needed.

Unfortunately the development of committee system, instead of making further progress, has had difficulties during the present legislature. There were differences between the Opposition and the ruling party over the composition of membership and chairmanships of the ministerial committees. After prolonged period an agreement has been reached in which the membership in the committees has been proportionally distributed but the chairmanships are still held by Treasury Bench MPs saving one to Jatiya Party. The executive control in the oversight of these committees can easily be discernible.

One of the main reasons for non-effectiveness of the committee system is the total lack of professional support. The legislators are no match to the knowledge and expertize of the bureaucracy. In order to conduct thorough departmental investigations the committee members must be provided background information, reports etc. without which the task is insurmountable. In the US—huge administration with professional expertize provide needed services to the lawmakers. It is interesting to note that as late as in 1947 there were 400 professionals in this category but today the number is 4000. Besides, the research division of Library of Congress is engaged in preparing report etc. for the Congressmen (Hasanuzzaman, A.M., 1996).

The legislature must have the power to demand information from the executive because without such knowledge and power to mould the law, effective control over bureaucracy and effective governance cannot be established. And as long the oversight activities of the legislature remain at the mercy of the executive no interest group or lobby can be expected to associate themselves with those assemblies (Smith and Musolf).

It is imperative that the committee system must be made powerful and efficient without which modern day legislature would always be dominated by the executive. This is a serious weakness in Bangladesh's legislature. Among other weaknesses another factor is the lack of responsibility of the ministers to the legislature. The ministers feel more responsible to executive since their very existence is dependent on it. Moreover, the legislators themselves require so many favours from the administration that they are reluctant to use sanctions even if they have any against the executive. Popular distrust and sentiment about the legislators, especially their alleged reputation of being corrupt also undermine its efficiency.

Most important of all, its stature and power could also not be enhanced due to the failure of the political parties. They have not yet been able to set the parameters within which the House must operate. And their marginal presence in the legislature has contributed vastly to its weak oversight activities. The executive must give more importance and time to the Opposition as well as the back-benchers. Opposition's recent allegations that as many as two thousand and five hundred adjournment motions are still pending is a horrendous example of how the legislature's capacity to scrutinize executive is being undermined by the present parliament.

Conclusion

Parliamentary democracy has been established in Bangladesh in 1991 with a sovereign parliament. There is no doubt about its institutional continuity. In spite of a few constitutional provisions, which curtail some of the legislature's powers and influences, people in general are hopeful about its success and effectiveness due to the presence of a powerful Opposition in the House. But in order to have the House perform its main function, its committee system, especially the Departmental Committee system needs to be strengthened. To establish full parliamentary control over public expenditures its PAC needs to be reorganized with 'an executive arm' similar to the General Accounting Office attached to the US Congress. The C & A-G office, keeping in line with the British system, should be made independent of the executive branch and responsible to the legislature. Besides these developments, the factor which would make the legislature effective is democratization within the political parties. Unless the leaders are susceptible to public opinion, the legislature's main task, i.e., to check the arbitrary actions of the executive, will remain as elusive as ever.

References

Blondel, J., *Comparative Legislatures* (New Jersey: P. Hall, Inc., 1979).

Bryce, Lord James, *Modern Democracies* (London: Macmillan Co. Ltd., 1921), pp.367-77.

Butt, Ronald, *The Power of Parliament* (London), 1968, p.31.

Hasanuzzaman, Al Masud, "Parliamentary Committee System in Bangladesh", in *Regional Studies*, Vol.XIII, No.1, Winter 1994-95, pp.31-39.

Hasanuzzaman, Al Masud, "The Congressional Committee System in the United States", in Md. Imdadul Hoque and M. Nazrul Islam (eds.), *Markin Juktorastro, Samaj O Sanskriti*, No. 5, Bangladesh Association for American Studies and USIS, Dhaka, December 1996, p.61.

Hyson, S.R.V., "The Role of the Back-Benchers — An Analysis of Private Members' Bills in the Canadian House of Commons", *Parliamentary Affairs*, 28, Summer, pp.262-72, cited in Mezey, Michael L., op. cit., p.88.

J. Blondel in Michael L. Mezey, *Comparative Legislatures* (Durham: Duke University Press, 1979), p.25.

Jatiya Sangsad Debates, Vol. 1, No. 1, April 2, 1979, pp.32-33.

Jennings, Sir Ivor, *Parliament* (London: Cambridge University Press, 1969).

Jennings, Sir Ivor, *Parliament* (London: Cambridge University Press, 1969), p.117.

Locke, John, *Second Treaties on Civil Government*, Chapter XI, and Monstesque, *Spirit of Laws*, Book XI, Chapter 8.

Morris-Jones, W.H., *Parliament in India* (London: Longmans Green & Co., 1957), pp.43-71.

Morris-Jones, W.H., op. cit., p.326.

Muir, Ramsay, *How Britain is Governed* (New York: Richard R. Smith Inc., 1930).

Proceedings of the Constituent Assembly, 1972, p.28.

Rossiter, C. (ed.), *The Federalist Papers* (New York: American Library, 1961), cited in Joel Smith and Llyod D. Musolf (eds.), *Legislatures in Development Dynamics of Change in New and Old States* (Durham: Duke University Press).

Smith, Joel, and Musolf, Lloyd D. (eds.), p.52.

Snowiss, Richard Sissonileo M., "Legislative Viability and Political Development". Joel Smith and Llyod D. Musolf (eds.), p.50.

Weinbaum, M.G., "Toward a Classification of Legislative Systems: Its Application and Implications for Developing Nations", prepared for delivery at the Sambaugh Conferences on Legislatures in Developing Countries.

Wheare, K.C., *Legislatures* (London: Oxford University Press, 1965), p.115.

Wheare, K.C., op. cit., p.19.

GOVERNANCE AND PARLIAMENTS

Peter Lyon

> Governance is the sum of the many ways individuals and institutions, public and private, manage their common affairs. It is a continuing process through which conflicting or diverse interests may be accommodated and co-operative action may be taken. It includes formal institutions and regimes empowered to enforce compliance, as well as informal arrangements that people and institutions either have agreed to or perceive to be in their interest. (OUP, 1955)

In relation to forms of governance, parliaments are located in that enormous area between putative world government and various forms of local government. Lexicographically and historically, governance and parliaments have rich pasts and potentially very variable futures. Their relationships can be highly complementary or deemed inherently competitive, as the vicissitudes of Bangladesh's political history since 1971 amply reveal.

Unwritten History of Parliaments and Governance

Parliamentary government is a broad meandering river fed by many streams. A full history of its vicissitudes would need many volumes. Such a survey would surely need to assess, *inter alia* the significance of such different personalities and thinkers-cum-polemicists as John Locke, Edmund Burke, John Stuart Mill or Enoch Powell and Michael Foot.

Twentieth-Century Vicissitudes

The record of performance of parliamentary government in the 20th century, and contemporary assessments of their workings, have been highly variable, even at times volatile. Three main phases can be identified which correspond roughly to the dissolution of some empires, the consequent emergence of successor states (often ostensibly bent on establishing their own parliamentary, democratic system) and efforts to restructure international order.

1914-1939/45

1919 and the peace of Versailles seemed to many contemporaries to mark the triumph of democracy, the adoption of British or American models of government by the newly independent states of eastern Europe and the institutionalization of a new democratic international order whose principal expression and embodiment was the League of Nations. Optimism was not to last long, however, in the face of Fascist, National Socialist and Bolshevik challenges.

Certainly, if one were compiling an anthology of abuse against parliamentary government and its pretensions, the scatology showered by the likes of Lenin and Trotsky, or by Mussolini, would feature prominently in any denunciatory litany.

Within the British Empire/Commonwealth, however, in these inter-war years, there were some interesting evolutions towards more indigenous parliamentarianism, towards what was later to be called autochtony, within the still semi-enclosed British world.

Canada first cracked the facade of imperial unity and lessened the primacy of the Westminster parliament in matters pertaining to Canadian legislation. Constitutional conventions were adapted for new, more formal duties. Drained of their erstwhile elusive fluidity and particularity, they became defined and embedded in formal resolutions of successive imperial conferences, from the 1920s onwards, to identify the structure of the evolving Commonwealth. Thus Canadian, South African and Irish nationalists pressed home their claim, and their persistently repeated — and at times intemperate — demands for an explicit renunciation of the surviving elements of inequality of status were conceded. After the Imperial Conferences of 1926, 1929 and 1930, these Premiers could cite agreed declarations to the effect that the Dominions were in no way subordinate to the United Kingdom in any aspect of their domestic or external affairs; that it would be improper for the UK parliament to alter their laws except at their request and with their consent; that the UK government had no commanding voice in the appointment of a Governor-General to a Dominion or in the discharge of his duties; that reservation of Dominion Bills was to be an empty formality and that disallowance of Dominion Acts (with one class of exception — regarding fundamental constitutional revision) was a dead letter; and that the assent of their parliaments was required for any change in the law touching the succession to the throne or the royal style and titles.

On the great issue of whether the Westminster parliament could again, as in 1914, commit the whole British Empire-Commonwealth to war, it was a Canadian voice which pointed the way forward, sometimes to the exasperation of British politicians and officials. Mackenzie King's catchword phrase was 'Parliament (meaning the Canadian House of Commons) will decide', and that was what happened in 1936 when Canada declared war against Hitlerite Germany one week after the Westminster parliament. By a narrow majority, the South African parliament went to war. Eire, already in effect a sleeping member of the 'British' Commonwealth, stayed neutral during 1939-45.

1945-1969/91

Throughout the long years of the Cold War, *circa* 1945 to 1989/91, spokesmen for 'the West' (roughly the NATO/OECD clubs) tended to assume that their opposition to communism automatically proved their devotion to democracy, despite the dubieties of such an assumption in many specific cases. Furthermore, a pervasive American Jeffersonian-Wilsonianism tended to assume that decolonization naturally begat democracy, even though the immediate record of rapid decolonization in the 1960s and 1970s produced many post-colonial regimes where parliament was a frail and floundering institution or was soon shunted aside.

It would be wrong, however, to assume axiomatically that 'the third world' of the 1960s, '70s and '80s was entirely inimical to parliamentary democracy. Generally, this was still the most popular form of government, even if practice often fell far short of profession. This 'third world' was in fact so large, so diverse, so heterogeneous that the record of what exactly happened in detail within its governmental systems is hard to summarize briefly, but *dirigisme*, state socialism and central planning were often prominent in both profession and practice. Army rule or single-party dictatorship was not uncommon. Thus genuine parliamentary systems were relatively rare.

Of course, not all Americans endorsed a Jeffersonian-Wilsonian optimism. None of the three major continental nations — France, Germany and Italy — consistently maintained a parliamentary system through the first six decades of this century. Thus, American political scientist, Leon Epstein, asserted that the evidence was 'not yet conclusive as to the adaptability of parliamentary government outside its limited western homelands'.

1989/91-Till Today

Since the end of the Cold War, an unprecedented amount of praise has been lavished on the ideals of parliamentary government and many countries (especially in eastern Europe) seem, or at least claim, to have adopted parliamentary government. A historical perspective should caution against undue optimism, remembering, for instance, what happened in eastern Europe after 1919.

Even so, the English-speaking world, and the Commonwealth component of it most notably, has played a significant part in commending and promoting parliamentary government in recent years, through election monitoring and assistance, encouraging liberalization, decentralization and devolution and non-governmental organizations, whilst also favouring pluralism, civil society and governments which are both transparent and accountable.

One central aspect of current debate concerns the role, significance and durability of 'the State', and this is a matter of some complexity and wide ramifications. It is worth recalling in a discussion of parliamentarianism as well as national parliaments, that there is currently lively discussion and signs of heightened salience in the Euro-parliament, in such associations as the IPU and the CPA, as well as about matters of global governance.

Inevitably, such preoccupations and preferences have met with mixed results and some pessimistic analyses have been forthcoming lately to doubt and challenge the claim that a high-tide towards democratization is now dominant.

Some Cassandra-like contemporary analysts pronounce pessimistically about the prospects for parliamentary government and warn about the growth of 'illiberal democracy', ascribing increasing violence and creeping or escalating anarchy to the shortcomings and actions of weak new democratic regimes rather than to the insurgencies or coups to which they fall prey.

Two writers, Robert Kaplan and Fareed Zakaria, may be cited as exemplifying such views. Kaplan has written that today, and especially in West Africa, newly installed democracies excite ethnic and nationalist passions, frequently leading to social banditry, turmoil and quasi-anarchy, perhaps eventually to rampant anarchy.

Zakaria, the current editor of the prestigious American quarterly *Foreign Affairs*, in an article which has attracted much interest and comment, insists that democracy cannot be manufactured swiftly, that it requires centuries-long maturing of societies and institutions in a framework of 'constitutional liberalism' — which is a highly debatable, contemporary American reformulation of a familiar Whiggish, Burkean view.

In marked contrast, the current president of Freedom House in New York, Adrian Karatnycky, has argued recently that pessimism about the general prospects for liberal democracy is unjustified and not supported by the recent record.

Each year Freedom House issues an end of the year survey of the state of political rights and civil liberties around the world. In 1995 there were 117 democratically elected governments, of which 76 were free. The survey for 1997 concluded that, whilst the number of democracies remained static at 117, the roster of 'free' countries increased to 81. Similar claims could be, and have been, made of trend lines in the Commonwealth.

What accounts for these trends? A full account would need to consider the gestation and patchy implementation of the Helsinki accords from the mid-1970s onwards, the end of the Cold War, post-colonial trends in many countries and in the Commonwealth to the Harare declaration of 1991 and its subsequent refinements in the Millbrook declaration of 1995. But, in general, we can say that successive 'free and fair' competitive elections encourage stronger — and perhaps more responsible — political parties and tend to stimulate genuine debate over policy alternatives and force leaders to face the verdict of the electorate. Pluralism and liberalism tend to be enhanced. Constant negotiation and compromise are more likely if leaders know that their policies are subject to regular public review and electoral judgement. Transparency, accountability, and legitimacy, are related terms here.

IPU and CPA

The two principal plenary associations for parliament and parliamentarians in the contemporary world are the Inter-Parliamentary Union (IPU) and the Commonwealth Parliamentary Association (CPA).

IPU

First set up in 1889, the Inter-Parliamentary Union (IPU) is the world organization of the parliaments of sovereign states. The IPU is the principal focus for world-wide parliamentary dialogue and works for peace and co-operation among peoples and for the establishment, maintenance and efficient functioning of representative democracy. With its headquarters in Geneva, the IPU today has over a hundred national parliaments as its members and three international parliamentary assemblies as Associate members.

As a major reference point globally, the IPU relates to the United Nations (and its network of related international organizations), whose objectives it generally endorses whilst working in close conjunction with it. IPU also co-operates with the regional inter-parliamentary organizations, as well as with international, inter-governmental and non-governmental organizations motivated by the same ideals.

CPA

Founded in 1911 as the Empire Parliamentary Association, with six founder-members (Australia, Canada, Newfoundland, New Zealand, South Africa and the United Kingdom) and evolving with the Commonwealth, the Commonwealth Parliamentary Association (CPA) adopted its present name in 1948, changed its rules to enable all member-branches to participate in the management of the Association, and established a separate Secretariat to manage is affairs.

Today, the CPA has branches in 139 national, state, provincial and territorial parliaments, with a total membership of over 14,000 parliamentarians. The recent and continuing resurgence of parliamentary democracy is evident in the growth of the CPA. Since 1990, more than 20 new parliaments and legislatures have been admitted to or resumed membership of the CPA.

CPA provides the sole means of regular consultation among members of Commonwealth parliaments. It seeks to foster co-operation and understanding among them and to promote the study of and respect for parliament.

CPA Activities

Eight Noteworthy Features:

1. Commonwealth Parliamentary Conferences for Small Countries

The CPA has since 1981 held conferences of its members from small countries — from more than 30 jurisdictions with populations of up to a demographic ceiling of 400,000. Members discuss political problems and the operation of small, democratic systems in some of the world's smallest jurisdictions.

2. Commonwealth Women Parliamentarians

The CWP was founded by women delegates at the 1989 plenary conference so that at future conferences there could be more discussion of ways to increase female representation in parliament and ensure that gender issues are raised in the CPA. A Steering Committee of 25 members has been set up. The CPA Secretariat maintains a biographical data base of women members.

3. Post-Election Seminars

Since the 1991 Harare Commonwealth Declaration in which Heads of Government recognized the CPA role in promoting democracy, the association has undertaken an intensive programme of 16 seminars (between 1991 and mid-1998) in Commonwealth countries. Focussing mainly on countries with new parliamentary systems or an unusually high intake of new members at elections, seminars have been held in: Zambia (twice); the Bahamas, Ghana (twice); Kenya, Lesotho, Seychelles, Malawi, Botswana, Zimbabwe, Barbados, Tanzania, Uganda, KwaZulu-Natal and Bangladesh.

4. Election Observation

The CPA co-operates with the Commonwealth Secretary-General in forming Election Observation Groups. A register of current and former members is maintained so experienced politicians can be nominated to serve on Commonwealth missions.

5. Publications

The Parliamentarian, published quarterly by the CPA Secretariat, contains articles, analyses and bibliographical information on parliamentary, political and constitutional developments written by senior Speakers, Ministers, Members or parliamentary officials involved in the issues. Factual reports are also published on major proceedings in several sovereign Commonwealth Parliaments and on legislative initiatives in a selection of Houses.

Newsletters: two newsletters are issued approximately every two months, one on CPA developments and the other on parliamentary and political news.

Specialist Publications: the CPA publishes other material on parliamentary subjects, such as: summaries of certain conferences and seminars, a report on the Barriers to Women's Participation in

Parliament, a Commonwealth parliamentary map, a Parliamentary Directory, a survey of parliamentary salaries and allowances, a Members' guide to procedural issues etc.

6. Parliamentary Information and Reference Centre

This Centre, at the CPA Secretariat, maintains, in co-operation with parliamentary officials, an extensive collection of material on Commonwealth Parliaments. It provides an information service for Members and Branches, produces monographs and book lists for those working or studying in the parliamentary field, and generates comparative material for publication.

7. Parliamentary Training

An expert group of senior parliamentary officials, representing all Commonwealth regions, met twice in 1996 to formulate a model training manual for parliamentary staff. This manual is now available to all Parliaments to help them formalize or improve their staff training, based on the variety of programmes in place in Commonwealth Parliaments and Legislatures.

In late 1997, the CPA held a training seminar in Calcutta for Secretaries of the Parliaments and Legislatures of the Asian Region.

A new programme, launched in 1997, facilitates the attachment of senior Members and officials from one Parliament to another so that they can assess at first hand different practices and procedures which may be adapted to strengthen their own institution.

8. Beyond the Commonwealth

The Association seeks to extend the influence of Commonwealth Parliamentarians into the wider international community and to expose Commonwealth Members to views elsewhere. Joint conferences have been held with a British Foreign and Commonwealth Office agency, Wilton Park, to bring Commonwealth Members together with a group of mainly European civil servants and diplomats to assess global issues. The 1994 conference examined electoral practices, while relations between Parliament and people were discussed in 1995, followed by democracy and development in 1996 and conflict prevention and resolution in 1997. These meetings have led to the publication of definitive texts on their subjects, as well as a pocket manual for election observers.

The IPU and the CPA are international associations which are suasive rather than mandatory. They provide advice and expertise and offer deliberative and comparative opportunities for the participants in their proceedings. They have no coercive power but some persuasive influence. Currently, they are both advocating fashionably ascendant political ideas and help to make and maintain an international consensus of opinion about parliamentary government, its practices and possibilities. They thus aid parliamentary governance quietly, incrementally and for the most part unobtrusively without much publicity or knowledge of their proceedings apart from those who directly participate or are specifically informed. Is this a matter for regret or congratulation?

Euro-Parliament

Ever since the Rome Treaty, establishing the European Economic Community (EEC), was signed in March 1957, the European movement has had some institutional expression for the much older idea of a European parliament. Until recently, however, it was more accurate to speak of a proto- or para-Europarliament. Only ten years ago, a well informed British Europhile summed up the weaknesses of the European parliament in succinct terms which are worth quoting at some length:

> Those who originally pressed for the European Parliament to be given a direct mandate by the electorate of the Community did so in the belief that by the time it came to pass the Common Market would have reached something close to economic and political union. There would then, they assumed, be a need to subject a powerful European executive to democratic control by European voters rather then indirect scrutiny by national Parliaments through appointed members. Ironically, the directly elected European Parliament came into being without there being anything remotely like a Community government in the making. The elected assembly was left as a purely consultative assembly without a clear executive interlocutor.

Ten years later the European parliament has acquired more powers, though informed public awareness of this within member-countries seems very slight.

Today, the Eur-oparliament has a right to be consulted on a wide range of legislative proposals, and forms one arm of the Community's Budgetary Authority. Since the Single European Act of 1987 it has an increased role in legislation, through the 'concertation' procedure, under which it can reject certain Council drafts in a second reading procedure. With the ratification of the Maastrict Treaty, it gained the right of 'co-decision' on legislation with the Council of Ministers on a restricted range of domestic matters.

What might make the Euro-parliament more popular or at least more acceptable to its electorate? A prime test is, of course, elections. Turn-outs lately have been low (57% all told last time round, with 40% of registered British, Irish, Portuguese and Dutch voters bothering to cast their ballots). Electoral campaigns still tend to be narrowly national rather than embracing Euro-wide issues.

Formally speaking, the Euro-parliament seems to be gathering weight and authority. The Amsterdam treaty of June 1997 once again strengthened the parliament's powers. It may now reject nominees for the Commission's presidency. In terms of vetting legislation, the Euro-parliament has become near-equal to the Council of Ministers, which represents national governments. Vast arrays of lobbyists swarm the corridors in Strasbourg nowadays, even though most of the EU's 370 million people remain stoically, even bleakly, indifferent to their parliament.

Some Euro-enthusiasts fear that national parliaments, pleading the cause of 'subsidiarity' — the doctrine of taking decisions at the lowest possible level — will grab back powers ceded to the EU. Others think that national parliaments should have scrutiny over EU decisions. Some observers insist that national parliaments should more rigorously monitor their own governments' actions in the Council.

Good Global Governance?

The end of the Cold War has also encouraged fresh consideration of world governance, notably through the work of the Commission on

Global Governance initiated by Willy Brandt and Co-chaired by Ingvar Carlsson (Sweden) and Shridath Ramphal (Guyana). What is striking about their wide ranging main report, Our Global Neighbourhood, published in 1995, is its avoidance of advocating any one formula or recipe for World Government and its stress on the multi-dimensionality of the challenges and needs for good governance globally.

Five points in particular are emphasized:

- that good governance needs to adapt to change and to multiple values,
- that security concerns must be dealt with realistically,
- that economic interdependence needs to be managed,
- the United Nations be reformed, and
- the rule of law needs strengthening worldwide.

Conclusion

There are more parliaments extant today than ever before in human history. It follows inevitably that they display tremendous variety and sometimes great contrasts between their avowals and performances. Evidence can be found of a few apparently healthy examples, and many (of which Bangladesh currently is one) which are not. The apparent indeterminacy of our immediate future make it impossible to foresee exactly which ones will prosper and which will fail.

A constitutional pluralistic regime for Bangladesh surely is preferable to autocracy and/or army rule which more than once have proved to be cul-de-sacs — political (and in other respects also) blind alleys. Constitutional pluralism, unhappily however, has not yet sunk deep roots in Dhaka and throughout the country of Bangladesh, even though it does constitute a shield, perhaps only a frail shield against the threat and renewed eruption of civil strife and violence. The silken thread of legitimacy needs to be preserved. This is not easy. The political classes of Bangladesh (which certainly includes NGOs as well as those formally involved in parliamentary politics) have onerous consequential roles to play.

It is usual for people, parliaments and nations to peruse several goals simultaneously e.g., peace, prosperity, or development, and genuinely to regard each of these as intrinsically worthwhile and desirable. It would be naive however, as the late Isaiah Berlin often warned, to believe that each of these values is naturally complementary or consonant with one another. The pursuit of one may have to be purchased at some cost of another. Parliamentary government cannot necessarily guarantee economic development or a national consensus. It needs to be valued for its intrinsic rather than its instrumental value and this intrinsic worth is pre-eminently political.

References

Commission on Global Goverance, "Our Global Neighbourhood", Oxford University Press, 1995, p.2.

Palmer, I., *Europe without America?* Oxford University Press, 1988, pp.144.

PARLIAMENT AND GOVERNANCE IN NEPAL

Krishna P. Khanal

Introduction

In today's parliamentary system, most of the works related to governance is carried out by the executive branch of the government headed by a prime minister, who is accountable to the parliament. The parliament is supposed to exercise control over the government through legislative business, for which the government has to rely on parliamentary approval. Besides, ministers including the prime minister, are answerable to the parliament for their actions. Therefore, the parliament has significant role to improve the quality of governance.

Political System

Nepal witnessed a democratic transition following a mass upsurge in 1990. The Monarchy, which was previously the fountain-head of all the state powers and actions, conceded to be the constitutional head, and sovereignty of the state was transferred to the people. The constitution, drafted by a Commission consisting of constitutional experts and politicians, was promulgated by the King on the recommendation of the Council of Ministers. It has incorporated fundamental democratic values, principles and institutions. Political pluralism, civil and political rights, popularly elected parliament, representative government, independent judiciary, free press, etc. have become the basic ingredients of the political system. The parliament, today, constitutes the fundamentals of governance in Nepal.

The 1990 constitution limited the absolute power of the King, relegating his role to that of a non-active constitutional monarch. The King is required to act on the advice and the consent of the Council of Ministers. Monarchy is regarded as the symbol of national unity and its duty is "to preserve and protect" the Constitution. The government is carried on in his name but the executive powers of the state is exercised by the Council of Ministers. Article 35 of the Constitution states, "Except as otherwise expressly provided has to be exercised exclusively by His Majesty or at his discretion or on the recommendation of any institution or official, the powers of His Majesty under this Constitution shall be exercised upon the recommendation and advice, and with the consent of the Council of Ministers. Such recommendation, advice and consent shall be submitted through the Prime Minister."

The Constitution provides for a parliamentary system of government wherein the cabinet is collectively responsible to the parliament. The prime minister is appointed by the King from amongst the members of *Pratinidhi Sabha*, who is a leader of the parliamentary party enjoying majority in the House. In case of hung parliament, i.e., no political party having majority in the *Pratinidhi Sabha*, a coalition government of two or more political parties may be formed. If the political parties fail to make such a coalition, the leader of the largest party in the parliament is called upon to form a minority government. In both cases, the prime minister requires to prove within thirty days that he enjoys the support of the majority in the house through a vote of confidence. If the minority government fails to get the majority support, the *Pratinidhi Sabha* is dissolved and new elections are to be held.

The Constitution also provides for a cabinet system of government of which the prime minister is the leader. The ministers are appointed on her/his recommendation and continue in office at her/his confidence. The Parliament has the power to censor the government through various means. Ministers are accountable to the house both collectively and individually. The government requires to get the policies, programmes and budget approved through the parliament. Likewise, the lower house of the parliament can also remove the government from office by passing a vote of no-confidence.

Besides, the parliament consists of various standing and select committees which are instruments to improve the quality of legislation as well as to ensure accountable government.

Composition of the Parliament

The Nepali parliament consists of His Majesty the King and two houses: *Pratinidhi Sabha* (House of Representatives) and *Rastriya Sabha* (National Assembly). The lower house, i.e. *Pratinidhi Sabha* has 205 seats directly elected by the people based on adult franchise. For this purpose, each of the seventy-five administrative districts have been converted into electoral districts which send a minimum of one or more representatives depending on the ratios of population compared to that of national population. The electoral constituencies in a district are determined and delimited by a separate commission appointed for this purpose on the basis of the last census preceding the parliamentary elections. *Rastriya Sabha*, i.e. the upper house, consists of sixty members of whom ten are to be nominated by the King; thirty-five including three women members to be elected by the House of Representatives based on the proportional strength of political parties in the House; fifteen members, three each from five development regions of the country are elected on the basis of single transferable vote by electoral colleges for each region consisting of the elected representatives at the local level. The House of Representatives has a tenure of five years provided it is not dissolved earlier. The National Assembly is a permanent House with a tenure of six years for its members, of whom one-third retires every two years.

Problems of Stability

Compared to the presidential system, the parliamentary system is relatively unstable by its very nature. It is created by the parliament and has to constantly rely on the confidence of the parliament. Particularly, when there exists multiplicity of political parties with sizeable strength in the parliament, it is prone to be unstable. Besides, the government in this system is the product of the majority in the parliament and the moment it is in short of majority it is certain to fall down. In a situation when no political party commands an absolute majority in the house of the parliament, stability becomes an acute problem.

After the restorations of parliamentary democracy, Nepal has been facing this problem. Even when the Nepali Congress (NC) enjoyed an absolute majority in the parliament following 1991 elections, its government could not complete the tenure due to intra-party conflicts. Failure to manage the relationship between the government and the party executives by the NC ultimately led to the fall of NC Government in 1994. A group of Members of Parliament belonging to the ruling NC, who were opposed to Prime Minister G.P. Koirala, abstained from voting in the House of Representatives in a crucial motion related to government policies. Prime Minister Koirala resigned and recommended for the dissolution of the House and called for fresh elections.

The issue of stability became more acute in the second Parliament following the mid-term polls held in November, 1994. This time, the House of the Representatives lacked a majority of either party. This had direct bearing upon making and breaking of the government. No single party was in a position to form the government on its own strength. The equation of the government, therefore, depended on the unity and understanding between and among three major parties namely the NC, the United Markist-Lenninist (UML) and the Rastriya Projatantra Party (RPP). Besides, minor parties like Nepal Sadvabana Party (NSP), Nepal Workers and Peasants Party (NWPP) or even individual MPs had become decisive factors to determine the fate of government. This brought chronic instability in the government.

From November 1994 onwards, the parliament in Nepal produced five prime ministers heading different types of governments. Minority government of CPN-UML was in office for about nine months, followed by the NC-led coalition which lasted for about eighteen months, only to be replaced by another coalition led by the RPP having only 19 seats in the lower house of the parliament with the support of the UML. This government could continue hardly for six months in office to be succeeded by another coalition headed by another leader of the RPP again, with the support of the NC.

However, this coalition also could not survive. And now, due to a split in the UML, there is a minority government headed by the NC, by virtue of being the largest party in parliament.* Nevertheless, this government, too, is shaky and struggling for survival. During this period, there had been two attempts to dissolve the House of Representatives and seek fresh mandates. On both occasions the judiciary prevented the dissolution. As a result, the authority of the prime minister to dissolve the house, which is considered as a 'long stick' to control the house, has been jeopardized.

In the exercise of survival game, the second parliament has encountered many unhealthy practices. The UML government introduced the practice of the constituency development fund to be used by the MP in his/her constituency. Allowances and other financial benefits were increased. Besides, they were given financial support to keep their personal secretariat and an unlimited amount for medical treatment. They were also allowed to import a vehicle with duty exemption. Furthermore, the special fund under the Home Ministry was made available to those who were politically influential and accessible under the pretext of medical treatment. The number of ministers were also increased beyond proportion to ensure the support of MPs to the incumbent government. As a result, the MPs lost considerably their prestige and status among the general people, and a great damage was inflicted upon the credibility of parliamentary democracy and accountability of the government.

Both the treasury and the opposition often tried to reach understanding and compromise on several issues but failed to create an environment of national consensus and conciliation. Accountability of the government to the parliament was limited to mere formalities rather than evolving the norms. The parties in the parliament faced serious problems to differentiate the parliamentary role and the general functions of the party. Most of them encountered problems between the party executives and the behaviour of the MPs. It became acute when the party was in power. Even in opposition, the party's control over MPs was frequently challenged and there were incidences of violating the party whips. In the second parliament,

* The article was written in July, 1998.

these issues and problems became further acute and conspicuous. Defiance and defection were almost open, and both the Speaker and Chairman of the House of Representatives and the National Assembly respectively could not respect the anti-defection provision of the Constitution. The MPs belonging to the NSP and the NWPP had entered into individual alliance with the NC and the UML abandoning the party on whose ticket they had won the seat. The RPP remained split on the floor of the house over the issue of shifting coalition partners in the government. It eventually split in January 1998 over the question of the government headed by its own President. Likewise, the CPN-UML which had emerged as the largest party in the present parliament has also split. Party position in parliament is shown a Table 1 at the end.

Deterioration in the behaviour of political parties and concomitant effect on the members of the parliament has spoilt political culture. There has been flow of illegitimate money 'up and down the political network'. As a consequence, no political leader, today, no matter how much she/he was appreciated and revered by the people till recently, has remained untouched by corruption of one form or other. They all had exercised undue influence upon the state to benefit themselves or their family members. If there is any single most serious threat to democracy in Nepal, it is largely the corruption at political level.

Parliament and Government Business

The parliament of Nepal meets twice annually. The budget session is normally held at the end of June and continues till August. Special session of the House of Representatives may be convened for specific purpose on the petition of one-fourth of the members.

After the restoration of multiparty democracy in 1990 and subsequent elections, the process of building efficient and accountable system of governance has been initiated in Nepal. The most challenging task before the government was to make a thorough reorientation and resetting of the course of public affairs consistent with democratic governance. It was equally challenging to redefine the role of the state, for that matter, those of the government, for public benefit.

As per the established parliamentary tradition and the constitutional provisions, the parliament in Nepal has a wide-ranging role with respect to governance. The budget session of the parliament starts with the address by His Majesty the King to the joint sitting of both the Houses. It has been the convention that the treasury bench proposes a motion of thanks, i.e., the expression of approval by the parliament. Failure to pass it means the government has no confidence of the parliament.

Next important agenda of the government before the parliament is the annual budget. The government proposes estimates of revenues and expenditures before a joint sitting of the Parliament every year which is discussed in each House in detail and requires to be passed by each House. However, the role of National Assembly with regard to money bill is a matter of ritual.

The parliament has many more areas where it can exert its influence in the functioning of the government. They include question-answer, call-attention motion, urgent issues of public importance, adoption of resolutions, etc. These are the steps and strategies that parliament can apply to make the goverment accountable and transparent in its day to day business. Besides, the parliament consists of various standing committees, sub-committees, etc. The House of Representatives has seven and the National Assembly two of such committees. These committees, aside from going though a clause-wise scrutiny of the bill concerned, can make enquiry of state of affairs within the scope of it's subject. Public Accounts Committee, and the State Affairs Committee in the House of Representatives seem relatively active trying to make the government accountable. These committees have consistently drawn the attention of the government regarding irregularities particularly in civil service and financial affairs. Separate committee or joint committees may also be formed to deal with issues felt appropriate by the parliament.

Government by the majority and censorship against its excesses by the minority are the basic rules of the parliamentary politics. The majority holds the treasury i.e., the seats of the government and the minority constitutes the legitimate opposition in the houses of parliament. After the May (1991) parliamentary elections, the NC controlled the treasury till July 1994 and the UML constituted major opposition in the parliament. Although there were a few more other minor parties it was primarily the pattern of interactions between the government and the UML that determined the course of parliament in particular and politics of the country in general. Although there was a substantive change of party position in the second parliament after 1994 mid-term polls, the NC and the UML remained the major actors within the house.

Normally speaking, the government does not have any serious obstacle to get its routine business done through the houses of the parliament. Its mandate to rule is generally followed. However, the floor of the parliament is often used for "politicking rather legislative work" (Pandey, 1998). The legislative works do not seem to receive priority. Bills affecting the nation are often passed without debate. Ministers also give minimum time to the parliament. Although there are instances of commonality of views between the treasury and opposition benches regarding certain bills, in most cases the MPs are divided according to their party-line and behave accordingly. Most of the time, houses are preoccupied by political issues frequently causing tension between the treasury and the opposition which causes interruptions and delay in the proceedings of the House. When the treasury and opposition can reach an understanding, the legislative agenda turn to be a matter of formality which also undermines the quality of legislation.

Nepal Human Development Report, 1998, has succinctly summed up the state of politics in the following words:

> The government apparatus continues in tradition of centralization and remains far too remote from the people. The state is equated with central government and the central government with the executive... The parliament itself is regularly molested by the prime minister, a would-be prime minister or party bosses retain or capture power through amoral adventures and apolitical interventions. (Nepal Human Development Report, 1998)

Bureaucracy and Governance

Bureaucracy is the major arm of the government to execute its policies and programmes. It was expected that after the restoration of multi-party democracy, the Nepali bureaucracy would be reformed to meet the challenges of the time. Nepal's bureaucracy had long remained patrimonial based on family ties, loyalty to the ruling elites and social connection rather than competitive merit and achievement. Legacy of such a tradition continues to hinder the growth of modern bureaucracy based on professionalism and political neutrality. Each of the succeeding governments after 1990 had spoken about the administrative reforms based on professionalism, political neutrality, efficiency, and responsiveness as its basic policy commitment. But each government merely started with reshuffle in the bureaucracy.

Administrative Reforms Commission headed by Prime Minister G.P. Koirala constituted in September 1991, recommended changes in organizational structure, simplification of procedure and work, decentralization and delegation of authority, management of public enterprises, civil service reform, career development, control of corruption, etc. Recently, a new Civil Service Act has been passed by the parliament to bring stability in the civil service and enhance political neutrality and professionalism.

Despite changes and attempts at reform, the administration in general has remained shaky, inefficient, and least responsive to the public problems. Political connections of civil employees through various employee organizations or other linkages continue to be active, and influence the functioning of the administration. Party preferences and priorities are also conspicuous in recruiting and changing the executives and managing boards of the public enterprises. Reports of the State Affairs Committee of the House of Representatives reveal that a lot of administrative irregularities continue to exist in the handling of civil service in Nepal (Report of Reform Commission, 1992).

Decentralization and Local Governance

Decentralization of power to the local units of governments aims at bringing larger masses of the people into closer approximation of the governing process. The concept of local government is thus "linked to the delivery of services and goods within certain territorial jurisdiction" which is possible only through decentralization of power and resources from the central state structure to the local units (Shrestha, 1996).

The 1990 constitution has specifically mentioned that the responsibility of the state lies in maintaining "conditions suitable to the enjoyment of the fruits of democracy through wider participation of the people in the governance of the country and by way of decentralization ..." [Article 25 (4)]. The institution of local government in Nepal, has thus found the constitutional justification and are accordingly established through the parliamentary legislation.

Village Development Committee (VDC), Municipality and District Development Committee (DDC) constitute the institutions of local governance. It is a two-layer system: VDCs and municipalities operate at the bottom and DDCs as intermediary institutions between the central administration and the local government. These bodies are representative units of the people. VDCs and municipalities are elected through direct adult franchise and DDCs by the vote of those elected to VDCs and municipalities. The local bodies have a tenure of five years. His Majesty's Govt. (HMG) is authorized to suspend or dissolve them after conducting inquiries if they are engaged in corruption, irregularities or any other unlawful activities, and fresh elections is to be held immediately. Likewise, it can also extend their tenure by a maximum of one year in special circumstances.

The first local election was held in May 1992 through which nearly fifty thousand elected representatives were recruited to the local governing bodies. All of them completed their full tenure in office without interference from the government. Donor agencies were involved in strengthening and capacity building of these units. Federations of DDCs, VDCs and municipalities were formed respectively which strengthened their bargaining capacity *vis-à-vis* the central government. Attempts were made to increase financial resources as well as grants of the local bodies. Seventy five per cent of the land revenue is made available to these bodies along with the central grants. They are also authorised to raise local taxes and levies. A new decentralization and local governance bill is under discussion in the parliament.

The implementation of decentralization and local self-governance is dependent on a number of factors. Clarity of the concept and sincere dedication at the leadership level are important requirements. A tendency to treat local bodies as the 'outpost' of the central power and 'capture' it by whatever means at hand during the elections persist among the major political parties, which has greatly undermined the spirit of local governance. Besides, centralized party structures and strict polarization of the society along the party lines have also worked as impediments to the effective implementation of the schemes related to the decentralization and local governance.

Management of Foreign Affairs

Management of foreign affairs is an important issue of governance which is not only related to the national security and independence but also to the economic affairs of a country. These considerations have equally influenced Nepal's foreign policy too. With the restoration of the multi-party democracy and the parliamentary system of government, the conduct of foreign affairs in Nepal have become more transparent and subject of public debate. Article 126 of the Constitution have put certain limitations upon the government that require the treaties it concludes with foreign countries particularly related to such subjects as (a) peace and friendship, (b) security and strategic relations, (c) border of the Kingdom, and (d) natural resources and distribution of its uses are to be ratified by a two-third majority of the parliament. Such a constitutional requirement demanded a broad consensus among political parties in the parliament.

There appears to be general consensus regarding the basic principles of foreign policy that Nepal has been pursuing. Peace and friendship; adherence to the non-alignment and UN Charters; regional co-operation, etc. constituted the consensus elements. In recent years, democracy and human rights also seemed to have assumed important consideration. All the major parties namely the NC, the UML and the RPP had promised closer understanding and amicable relations with the neighbouring countries, India and China. Accordingly, Nepal was able to manage foreign affairs without much problems.

However, certain aspects and issues of relations with India, mainly, security and sharing of water resources, have remained highly controversial. Public positions maintained by political parties in Nepal and debates between the government and opposition on these and several other issues appeared to have been greatly influenced by the domestic political considerations. Indeed, relations with India had been very much a domestic political issue in Nepal for quite a long time from 1950 when Nepal was just preparing for entry into the world community.

Nepal's perception of India varied from one party to another depending on their politico-ideological lines and priorities. The Nepali Congress (NC), while remaining committed to non-alignment in general and friendly ties with the neighbouring countries in particular, pleaded for closer understanding with India based on historical, cultural and religious ties that existed between the two countries. However, it called for developing a clear, well defined and long-lasting understanding with India based on the geopolitical reality (Nepali Congress, 1994). The communists on the other hand, built their perception of India in a different ideological perspective which portrayed India, particularly its ruling elite as being the agents of "Anglo-American imperialism" and following the 'expansionist' policy towards Nepal. The communists, in general, therefore, advocated scrapping of all the unequal treaties and agreements concluded with India by the 'reactionary' regimes of the past (Communist Party, 1993).

It was against this background that the government in Nepal has had to address several issues related to India. The relations between the two countries had reached the lowest ebb during the last days of the Panchayat regime. It deteriorated due to the import of Chinese arms by Nepal in 1988 leading to a 'bockade' by India in 1989 which was relaxed only after the fall of the Panchayat regime. Now treaties on trade and transit were signed between the two countries in December 1991.

However, controversy on a number of other issues continued to exist between Nepal and India. The Janakpur agreement which was signed by the two countries during Prime Minister G.P. Koirala's visit to India in December 1991, with regard to resolving the dispute over the barrage constructed by India on Mahakali river, had become highly controversial and remained stalemated in the Nepali parliament. The parliament could not decide on the modalities of ratification of this agreement whether by a simple majority or two-third majority of the joint sitting of the two houses. This issue was resolved when the two countries signed a treaty on the utilization of Mahakali river water. An all party consensus was reached before the government signed the treaty which was endorsed by the joint sitting of the parliament as well.

Influx of refugees from Bhutan, who are residing in the camps of Jhapa and Morang districts of eastern Nepal, whose number is estimated to be over 100,000, is another major area that Nepal has been facing both in foreign and domestic policy front since introduction of democracy. Although the United Nations High Commission for Refugees (UNHCR), since 1992, is involved in supporting the camps and providing humanitarian supports within its limits (UNCHR, 1996), the refugee problems has become a serious matter of concern in Nepal.

In the beginning, Nepal's response to the refugees was guided more by sentiment and reactions than the rational consideration of negotiating the problem. Political parties and the leaders had expressed their support and solidarity with the Bhutanese movement for democracy. It was only after the elected government took office in May 1991, that Nepal could address the refugee problem. Accordingly dialogue was initiated with Bhutan for resolving the problem bilaterally, called as "quite diplomacy". It also sought India's help in this regard. But India declined to be involved maintaining that it was a problem between Bhutan and Nepal. The official negotiation between Nepal and Bhutan started in July, 1993 when the Home Ministers of the two countries met at Thimpu and agreed to form a Ministerial Joint Committee, with a mandate to arrive at "a mutually acceptable agreement" and providing "the basis for the resolution of the problem." The joint committee has held a series of meetings both in Thimphu and Kathmandu. Because of governmental instability in Nepal, further negotiation could not be pursued seriously and the issue remained stalemated.

Prospects

Foregoing discussion on the problems related to parliament and governance in Nepal makes it clear that there is a need for address of these issues seriously and with long-term perspective. It is felt that even with the restoration of democracy and the parliamentary system of government, the process of "transferring power" to the people is incomplete. There is a need for reorienting and reforming the polity suitably to match the spirit of the present constitution. So far the constitution is concerned, it fulfils most of the requirements of a democratic polity. However, there is also a need on the basis of eight years' experiment, for reviewing such aspects as dissolution of the House of Representatives, provision for special session and no-trust motion, anti-defection, etc.

Much of today's political mis-match and problems of governance are related to the behaviour of political parties. The Constitution conceives of a separate legislation regulating the political parties. A comprehensive law to this effect can help to improve the functioning of political parties in the context of transparency and accountability. Political parties have yet to develop coherent policies and minimum consensus on matters affecting the nation and the parliamentary democracy. Political parties also need to address their institutional and leadership capability suitable to meet the changing aspirations of the people in general and re-orient their activities based on healthy parliamentary practice and norms. There is a need for a consensus among the major political parties on broader issues of governance such as parliamentary accountability, depoliticization of bureaucracy and state owned enterprises, major development agenda, providing clean and efficient administration, and major foreign policy issues, particularly related to India such as security, water resources and the like.

Despite several positive aspects of ongoing democratic exercise, there is a feeling among the people that political parties have not been able to properly address the basic issues concerning governance and to provide efficient and fair administration to the country. As a result, some radical communist groups have resorted to violence in the name of 'people's war' aimed at overthrowing the existing state and establishing a 'Maoist' republican system. Although such violent politics is not likely to survive in an open political environment of today's Nepal, it caused severe strains and destabilizing effect in the current parliamentary politics of the country.

Democracy has scope for self-correction. Political leaders, too, have realized that they need to reform the behaviour of political parties. Public pressure for reforms is also growing. Although weak, civil society is also asserting its intervention aimed at improving the behaviour of political parties and MPs. Its positive impact could be seen in the government's decision to scrap the vehicle import facilities given to MPs and the marked decline of expenses for medical treatment of MPs and politician.

TABLE 1

Party Position in the Parliament

Political Party	House of Representatives*	National Assembly**
Nepali Congress	83	27
Communist Party of Nepal (UML)	48	9
Communist Party of Nepal (ML)	40	6
Rastriya Prajatantra Party	10	2
Rastriya Prajatantra Party (Chand)	8	2
Nepal Sadbhavana Party	3	-
Nepal Workers and Peasants' Party***	4	-
Independents	7	-
Nominated	-	10

* Two seats remain vacant.

** Four seats remain vacant.

*** Two of NWPP members defected one each to NC and UML.

References

Election Manifesto of Nepali Congress, 1994.

Manifesto of the Communist Party of Nepal, 15 September, 1949, Declaration of CPN (M-L) December 1978, *Janatako Bahudaliya Janbad* (Madan Bhandari) adopted by the Forth National Convention of the CPN (UML) 1993.

Nepal Human Development Report 1998, (Kathmandu: Nepal South Asia Centre, 1998).

Pandey, Devendra Raj, "Transparency in the Context of Good Governance in Nepal". Nepal Administrative Staff College, 1998.

Shrestha, Tulsi Narayan, *Concept of Local Government and Decentralization*, Kathmandu: Ratna Pustak Bhandar, 1996, p.13.

The Report of the Administration Reform Commission 1992, Kathmandu, 1992.

UNHCR/Nepal Document, 06/1996.

LEGISLATURE AND GOOD GOVERNANCE

K.M. Subhan

Introduction

The continuous development of British Parliament over nine hundred years witnessed the beginning of the party system in parliament, the development of the principle of ministerial development and laying of the foundations of cabinet system. The relationship between the House of Commons and the House of Lords, and between Parliament and the other institutions of government were so modified as to ensure that the legal sovereignty of parliament is exercised in conformity with the wishes of the people.

The British constitution has not developed according to any preconceived plan; over the centuries it has developed in response to needs and circumstances. However, its foundations are based on two principles, accepted by the King and his subjects:

a. in important matters, such as the making of laws and the imposition of taxes, the King is not to act without first taking advice,

b. in summoning such counsellors the initiative should rest with the King who is to act on the advice of counsellors.

The recognition of this to a great extent precluded the possibility of a despotic government and from it emerged the idea: "no taxation without representation." This led finally to the theory of legal supremacy of parliament. The acceptance of the second principle put the responsibility for formulating policy squarely on the government. Parliament's task was to watch, criticize and whenever occasions arose, to control.

Successive wars put pressure upon the Kings to explore new sources of revenue. Additional taxes were levied on the barons and the basis of taxes was extended to include a new class, the freemen of the country. These necessitated the introduction of the principle of representation.

The partnership between monarch and parliament was more successful under Queen Elizabeth. She got a number of Privy Councillors to support her policies. She did not dissolve parliament as soon as a particular business was completed like her predecessors; thus parliament became more permanent, but she kept a firm hand on its powers. Disagreements were not uncommon, and at times the speaker was admonished whenever she considered that parliament had overstepped. Parliament on rare occasions proved particularly obstinate. Compromise was used to settle the issue. During the Tudor period the outlines of parliamentary procedures were settled, which became necessary, partly because orderly debate had to be maintained in a large assembly and partly because parliament had to be protected against the encroachments of the administration. At the same time both Houses began to keep their Journals. In 1547 during the reign of Elizabeth the Commons obtained their first permanent home.

The conciliatory attitude of monarch of the Tudor period was not to be seen during the Stuarts. A crippling price inflation forced them to summon parliament to make grant for their needs. A collision was inevitable. The Commons considered that control over finance was their fundamental right. The Sovereign had also many common law power under their royal prerogative. These included the powers to summon and dissolve parliament, the right to suspend or dispense with laws, the issue of Proclamation having the force of law, and the imposition of certain taxes, the continuance of an army. James I wanted to go further from that. He propounded the doctrine of "divine right" which put him above the law and consequently beyond parliament's authority. Legal sovereignty of parliament was settled once for all by the civil war.

Political sovereignty to electorate was given by the Reform Act, 1832. Such political sovereignty had to be reconciled with the supremacy of parliament. This was brought about by extending party system from parliament to the country. The parties were linked with cabinet system of government developing an Opposition to take over many of the traditional functions of parliament, formalising the relationship between the Commons and the Lords, and modifying parliamentary procedure to secure effective government in the face of determined obstruction.

A distinction is to be made between "parties" and the party system. Broadly speaking, a party consists of a relatively permanent division of people into a group, which on a particular matter or matters connected with politics is psychologically an entity. The party system, which forms the basis of parliamentary government, is far more comprehensive and elaborate. In Britain the parties have a much longer history than the party system for it was not until after the Reform Act of 1832 that they attained their full maturity by being integrated into to the process of government.

The recounting of the history of the development of the British legislature from its earliest days to the present times is considered necessary to understand the importance of the legislature in the governance of a country. The triumph of the people over the monarch which led to the founding of the House of Common's came over hundreds of years of struggle between the monarch and the people. What the people gained during the Tudors were lost during the Stuarts. Eventually the elected Members of Parliament of the majority party came to formulate, and control the policy of the Government. It does so through the party system.

Bangladesh Case

In Bangladesh the concept of governance still remains hazy and the term lacks a precise definition. The concept of governance cover various actions by the state and government. The plain meaning of governance means the act, manner or function of governing. Thus the act, manner or the function of governing would have components such as the form of political authority exercised in Bangladesh which has changed several times from the inception of the country. Political authority has been exercised at its inception by parliament which was formed on the basis of a democratic Constitution. The Constitution declares that, "it shall be a fundamental aim of the state to realise through the democratic process a socialist society, free from exploitation — a society in which the rule of law, fundamental human rights and freedom, equality and justice, political, economic and social will be secured for all citizens." Government of Bangladesh is a democracy where "all powers in the Republic belong to the people and their exercise on behalf of the people shall be effected only under, and by the authority of the constitution. One of the components that make democracy work is a strong civil society which enjoy autonomy from the state and aims at exerting influence on the state on behalf of the members. A civil society directly supports democratic participation and a policy of accountability. Democratic principles can promote good governance.

Bangladesh Constitution speaks of participatory process and accountability of Government's actions and transparency of decision making. Freedom of media is guaranteed. It also declares that there shall be respect for fundamental rights and the rule of law. Rights of individuals as well as of groups and security have been guaranteed. The Constitution has empowered the judiciary to exercise judicial control over the executive action of Government. The judiciary has no jurisdiction to exercise over the legislature. It can enforce the basic human rights enshrined in the Constitution as "Fundamental rights." If an attempt is made to examine few of the characteristics of good governance, one sees that the actions of Government are participatory and it operates by rule of law. The accountability of Government is to the people through the legislature.

The first Amendment of the Constitution reads as follows: 47(3) notwithstanding anything contained in this Constitution, no law nor any provision thereof providing for detention, prosecution or punishment of any person, who is a member of any armed or defence or auxiliary forces who is prisoner of war, for genocide, crimes against humanity or war crimes and other crimes under international law shall be deemed void or unlawful, or even to have become void or unlawful, on the ground that such law or provision of any such law is inconsistent with, or repugnant to, any of the provisions of this Constitution". It addressed the crimes committed during the liberation war. To this end a new provision was added as 47 (A) which reads: "47 (A) inapplicability of certain articles-1 the rights guaranteed under Article 31, clauses (1) and (3) of Article 35 and Article 44 shall not apply to any person to whom a law specified under the clause (3) of this Articles applies.

The second amendment of the Constitution permitted preventive detention allowing Government to arrest and detain mostly for political reasons. This gave handle to the executive to act in excess of its authority denying the people the freedom guaranteed under the constitution. This amendment also empowered the President to declare emergency. Shortly after this the draconian Special Powers Act was passed which gave almost free hand to the police to arrest people at will. Under this Act an arrested person is not entitled to bail. By this amendment and the Act fundamental rights guaranteed under the Constitution shrank, accountability and transparency of the executive acts also receded.

The Fourth amendment of the Constitution passed on January 1975 changed the state structure. From parliamentary form of Government the country got presidential form of Government. This empowered the President with executive authority. The powers of the Supreme Court was curtailed. Appointment of judges to the Supreme Court could be made by the executive without any consultation with the Chief Justice. Thus the Constitution framed by the elected Constituent Assembly changed its character from democracy to an all powerful Presidential form. The power of judicial control of executive acts and judicial review of enactments was reduced. In short the jurisdiction of the Supreme Court was restricted. Multiparty system was changed to one party, thus affecting pluralism. Previously by Second amendment of the Constitution the freedom of movement, freedom of assembly, freedom of thought and conscience, freedom of profession and occupation and right to property were suspended. Democracy was no longer a state policy.

Martial Law Regime

Whatever little fundamental rights remained were gone with the proclamation of Martial law in August 1975 after the massacre of the Father of the Nation with his family. Under the military rule power was concentrated in the Executive and thus the "participation of the people through their elected representatives in administration at all levels", passed into oblivion. The people were denied of the basic human rights. Political dissent, rather politics itself became a forbidden subject and repression replaced democratic governance. The democratic institutions stopped functioning and rampant corruption became synonymous with military rule. Under the military rule the judiciary remained clouded and its functions were usurped by the military courts. The jurisdiction of the superior courts was further curtailed. Under military rule the Constitution was amended more than fifteen times by martial law decrees. Trade unions and students unions were banned. Further, political rivals were terrorised with multiple criminal cases. Bureaucrats who could create obstruction to military dictatorship were purged. Persons serving in the defence services became the most privileged class in the country.

Military rule did not last long and the civil society started movements for change in the administration. Military oligarchy first suppressed these movements but subsequently gave way and granted limited democratic rule by legitimising the Proclamation of Martial Law by amendment of the Constitution and going through the facade of election through massive rigging. The civilianization of the military rulers began through the orchestrated process of forming political party of the military rulers in an attempt to create a political base for them. Commenting on the character of military rule the Human Rights Commission said:

> the institutionalization of the emergency regime was a process that began when military came to power and in order to prove that they too were democrats, made elaborate manipulation of Constitution which would inter alia, enable them to obtain international financial assistance.
>
> In many instances, the military rulers call themselves transitional to democratic rule, a very convenient way of indefinitely prolonging their rule by both duping the people and the international community and claiming the allegiance of the one, and economic aid from the other.

The military ruler through rigged election turned the legislature into a club where members danced to the tune of the military, there being no effective opposition, as the opposition political parties boycotted the election. The military ruler usurped the powers of the legislature and passed martial law decrees. Even the Constitution was amended at will by the same process. The same office combined the office of the highest executive with the chief martial law administrator the only authority to legislate. The special military courts set up by martial law authority in trying cases which came within the jurisdiction of the courts set-up under the Criminal Procedure Code carry out the wishes of the martial law authority. Virtually all the three state organs, the executive, the judiciary and the legislature were concentrated, in one person, the Chief Martial Law Authority and the President. This was a flagrant violation of good governance and democracy.

When it becomes hard to continue military rule the military dictator turns into a politician through rigged elections. He gets himself elected as the President. Between 1975 and 1979 Parliament did not exist as it was dissolved earlier in 1975. From 1982 to 1986 the same condition prevailed. An election was held in 1986 which was rejected by the people. Parliament started functioning since 1991 and it passed a major amendment of the Constitution by which structure of the state was reinstated to pre-1975 position, that is, parliamentary form of government. The amendment did not restore the powers of the Supreme Court that it enjoyed before 1975. A new parliament was elected in 1991 under a caretaker government. This provision, however, was incorporated later in 1996 by another amendment of the Constitution under popular demands and public pressure.

Restoration of Democracy

Parliament since 1991 has not been functioning properly. There have been frequent walkouts by the opposition, continuous boycott and finally resignation from parliament by all opposition members of Parliament except one. The present Parliament has also seen frequent walkouts, occasional boycotting by the opposition. It has been a common feature that the parliamentary sittings are delayed for lack of quorum in the House. There have been some unusual incidents in the Parliament which are contrary to parliamentary norms.*

---

*The paper was written in July, 1998.

Separation of the judiciary from the executive is a long standing demand based on the Fundamental Principles of State Policy of the Constitution. Law making according to the theory of the separation of powers should be a function of the legislature. In practice, however, Parliament confers powers on administrative authorities, to make what is virtually their own law.

Such delegated legislation, as it is known, is not new and has developed out of necessity; the demands of the state and modern emergencies make it indispensable. The function of the State are now so extensive, that if Parliament attempts to enact statutes in detail the legislative machines would break down. Delegation helps in dealing with the technical nature of many of the schemes. Delegation also meets the need of flexibility in the application of statute. Delegated legislation has been criticised as it violates fundamental requirements of the rule of law. The rule of law implies the follwing:

1. citizens should be able to ascertain easily what the law is on a particular matter,
2. in case of any possible breach of the law in its application to him by an official, a person should have the right of appeal to the courts.

These two requirements are infringed by delegated legislation. Delegated legislation can be controlled by Parliament, as well as, by courts. Administrative tribunals have been set up by the legislature which deal with disputes in which a government department or public authority is involved. Domestic tribunals are set up to enforce professional discipline such as the Bar Council, Medical Council, Press Council etc.

The reasons for the establishment of administrative tribunals are:

1. when decisions of a judicial nature have to be made in administering a public service, parliament has preferred that they should be given by specially constituted tribunal, rather than by the courts;
2. the type of cases are different from that normally heard in a court of law;

3. the number of cases to be decided would grossly overburden the courts;
4. the procedure of tribunals is more appropriate to the type of dispute;
5. tribunals are quicker and cheaper;
6. appeal procedure is shorter, quicker and cheaper;
7. technical knowledge is necessary for decisions;
8. flexibility of decisions is desirable.

For good governance the legislature must ensure democracy in the functioning of government. "Democracy" said Lord Baldwin:

> is a most difficult form of government — difficult because it requires for its perfect functioning the participation of all the people in the country. It cannot function — cannot function well — unless everyone, men and women alike, feel their responsibility, to their State, do their own duty, and try to choose the men who will do theirs. It is not a matter of party; it is common to all of us, because democracy wants constant guarding.

Participation in Governance

Democracy must produce a government which is voluntarily accepted by the majority of the people. To do this, it is necessary to effect a compromise between the wishes of the electorate. This implies that government rests on consent, public opinion ultimately determining the government and its policy. The relationship between the majority and the minority is one of the tests of democracy, for each must play a constructive part. Although the majority governs, it has to recognise that there are limits to the restraints it can impose on the minority and that beyond a certain point, as for example, when fundamental rights are threatened, people are not prepared to submit to the majority rule. The task of the minority is to make the majority justify its views and policies. As J.S. Mill observed:

> to assume infallibility in public affairs, in a healthy democracy, the arguments of opponents are tolerated. They may be correct; but even when they are not, or only partially so, they provide that controversy without which the ideas of the majority become stale. The absence of

> challenge engender mental laziness which causes people to lose the clearer perception and livelier impression of truth, produced by its collision with error. (Mill, Essay on Liberty)

Opposition groups accept majority decisions for both moral and practical reasons. Not only would it be wrong to resist the greater opinion and impose policy on a reluctant public, but under a democratic constitution, the Opposition hopes that one day it will become the majority. Should it so, it will then have power to implement its own policy and in turn will be dependent upon the tolerance of its rivals. A wise opposition, therefore, sets a good precedent.

It is a common experience in Bangladesh that the respective roles of the Government and the Opposition are antagonistic to each other. The mutual respect between the majority and the minority has hardly been demonstrated in public. The majority and the minority are in constant verbal duel; at times punctuated by strikes and outbursts of violence. Such apathy between each other is detrimental to governance linked with development.

While the Government is accountable to the electorate as a whole, it must also consider group opinion. Pressure groups, however normally work unobtrusively. Professor S.E. Finer considers the phrase "pressure group" to be misleading since groups rarely exert pressure by applying sanctions or if they do so, not continuously. The position of the army and the police indicate the spirit in which a country is governed. The army from 1975 to 1990 has ruled the country directly or indirectly. But since December 1990 the army has restricted itself to the barracks and has not demonstrated any political ambition. The police however, has become a subject of bitter criticism as being highly inefficient, corrupt and extremely prone to torture and often acts in excess of their powers authorized by the laws.

The maintenance of democracy is dependent not only upon people having opportunity to participate but upon their willingness to do so. The legislature may legislate for good governance but its implementation is dependent upon the political commitment of the majority and the minority.

GOVERNANCE AND JUDICIARY

Ranganath Misra

Introduction

It is elementary to say that the basic ingredients to constitute a state are, a definite territory, population, a Government and sovereignty. India, prior to 1947, was a quasi state and as soon as independence came, it became a full-fledged State.

Though India became independent in 1947, it got her democratic constitution only in 1950. It got into three brief wars: one with China in 1962 and two with Pakistan: one in 1965 and the other in 1971. Jammu and Kashmir turned out to be an obstinate issue keeping the relationship overstrained in spite of India's vowed policy of friendliness with her neighbours.

In the early fifties, India adopted the model of Soviet planning system and set up a Planning Commission to plan and monitor Five Year Plans. India has achieved self-sufficiency in food, improved medi-care system and longevity of its population. More than half of her population have become literate. Her greatest handicap has, however, been the population explosion. At the time of independence it was around 250 million and in half a century it has grown in an uncontrolled manner and crossed the 980 million figure. It is likely to cross the incredible figure of 1000 million by the turn of the century.

Bangladesh and India — the two friendly neighbours perhaps differ in degrees of success in their onward march. The movement for containing population growth and the literacy drive in Bangladesh appear to have been more successful. Yet, both Bangladesh and India are still classed as developing countries of the South East Asia region.

Both India and Bangladesh are anxious that "Good Governance" is available to them and the people of the two countries have the benefit of participatory Parliamentary democracy. Good governance in a democratic system would require free participation of every citizen in the running of the Government. Such participation cannot be direct as was being done in the Greek city state. As of necessity it has to be through election and by choosing a group as the people's choice to run the system. The Indian Constitution prescribes 'equality' as the foundation and, mandates the entire activity to be tested by the touch-stone of equality. Yet, there is an area where the principle does not operate. Though equality is the rule, activated by considerations of the peculiar prevailing situation, reservation has been allowed in limited fields in favour of women, children, backward classes and certain castes as specified in the Constitution.

Three pillars — namely, the Executive, the Legislature and the Judiciary are the three basic wings of Government. Governance has been divided and put into the hands of these three. Law-making is the job assigned to the Legislature; administration is in the hands of the Executive and dispensing justice has been placed in the hands of the Judiciary. The Superior Judiciary has the additional power of superintending the performance of inferior courts and tribunals as also of the other two wings with a view to keeping them within their limits, through the process of 'judicial review'. Yet, the division of power is not total. The Head of the Union Executive is the President who has limited Legislative power. When Parliament is not in session, the President is competent to bring forth a law which has the same force as one enacted by Parliament but its life is subject to certain limitation. Parliament has authority to rectify retrospectively any defect in a particular legislation which has been struck down by a competent court and thus revalidate the law and restore it to the Statute book, the result being vacation of the court decision. Similarly, the Superior Judiciary has authority to interpret the law and read its own views into the legislation and give a meaning and shape different from what the legislature had intended. The three wings are thus expected to move hand in hand with mutual respect coordinating their activities for the ultimate good of the country. No wing is superior to the other — this is the basic postulate.

With this background, it is time to turn attention to the theme of the paper: "Governance and the Judiciary". As already stated, governance is in the hands of the three wings. Administration is in the hands of the Executive and has to be done in accordance with the law. Parliament often authorises subordinate legislation and allows the Executive to legislate within the four corners of a Statute. The three wings acting in cohesion and together, however, are responsible for the governance of the polity. Good governance is possible, and perhaps done, only when the three wings understand well the ethos and spirit of the Constitution, maintain appropriate respect for each other and are alive to the ultimate purpose of governance being for the maximum good of the people and function in their respective fields within limits.

The basic function of the Judiciary is to resolve disputes between citizens in accordance with the laws in force and also to decide disputes between citizens and the State. In a Federation, the Judiciary has the additional duty of deciding disputes between the Union and the federating States or between one State and another. In a system where there is separation of power and the system is run on the basis of enumerated powers, the Judiciary takes the freedom of adjudicating if there has been transgression of authority or power under the inherent 'judicial review' jurisdiction.

Experience shows that when one wing becomes weak, one or both the remaining wings become powerful. In recent years this has happened in India. The Superior Courts have stepped in to ensure appropriate functioning of the Executive when they found that the Executive was not functioning in the right way.

The menace of corruption has entered into the system of Governance in many countries both developed and developing. The vice has entered into the system and taken deep roots. Corruption can be of various types and of different kinds. But when it becomes common and shakes the system, it becomes difficult to sustain the system any longer. In some of the European countries, instances of corruption in different forms have come to light. Corruption among politicians in Japan has led a Prime Minister and other ministers stepping down from office.

The level of corruption in India perhaps requires special mention. What is interesting to note is the role of the Judiciary in bringing the acts of corruption and the persons involved in the process to trial before the Judicial fora.

The Indian Judiciary has been criticized on the ground that it has exceeded its jurisdiction and has been playing a role beyond its charge. Dismal poverty, abysmal illiteracy and alarming inequalities are individually and collectively obstacles to proper functioning of the Indian polity. For many of the apparent maladies, the Constitution offers no answer. That is because no one realized in 1949-50, when the Constitution was shaped, that the nation would sink in corruption and make the provisions of the Constitution structured on the foundation of idealism and philosophy so tardy in such a short period.

Corruption in any society is in inverse proportion to its sense of values. If the national standard of ethics of a nation were high. it would be difficult — nay impossible for corruption to penetrate into the everyday life of the people. The question whether the price one has to pay for honesty is worthy of efforts depends on each individual's own sense of value, and it can only be inculcated and nourished in the home environment of one's family and the influence of educational institutions manned by capable teachers.

Corruption, many feel, is perhaps a temporary facet and society would be able to generate adequate capacity to combat it. In normal conditions, it is the constitutional mandate which the judicial system would be called upon to fulfil. But in particular circumstances, the judiciary looks beyond the screen of limitation of jurisdiction.

The Constitutional goal is very clearly revealed in the Preamble of the Indian Constitution. The Constitution is secular, socialist, democratic, and republican in character. In interpreting the Constitutional provisions, the Preamble has its due role to play. The Indian Constitution has a set of fundamental rights guaranteed to its citizens. The right to move the Supreme Court for relief as prescribed in Article 32 is a sacrosanct right not to be suspended even in a state of emergency. The apex Court is entitled to entertain grievances of citizens and make appropriate directions. Fundamental rights are substantially pervasive and enforceable. The Directive Principles were not intended to be enforceable by courts but the Supreme

Court, has over the years, enforced them in part from time to time. The polity being a welfare state, and the Directive Principles having been aimed at guiding the state to turn its policies towards citizens' welfare, many or most of the Directive Principles have been enforced through the judicial process and the bar in Article 37 has vanished.

The Indian Constitution in its original form was right-oriented. It was realized at the end of the first quarter of the century that society was getting too much right-conscious and, as a result, everyone was taking from society without contributing anything in return. In 1976, by an amendment, 'Fundamental Duties' were inserted into the Constitution. The concept of Duty is wedded to 'Right' and both of them are complementary to each other. They co-exist and one cannot be there without the other.

India's culture has been to ensure performances of duties, and through such performance, to ensure fulfilment of one's right. By this process, every citizen's rights would stand protected by the act and performance of the rest of the citizens in the society. The provisions of Article 51A of the Indian Constitution are thus available to be worked out by requiring every claimant for relief by enforcement of his fundamental rights to satisfy the court that the corresponding duty has been satisfied or performed so as to entitle him to demand his right. The court can monitor this culture to grow and by this process, a right-oriented society can slowly be transformed to a duty-based one and as a result 'Good Governance' would be ensured and guaranteed for every citizen.

In the Indian Constitution, both the High Courts and the Supreme Court have been vested with powers to issue directions, order or writs in the nature of habeas corpus, mandamus, prohibition, quo warranto and certiorari. The exercise of this jurisdiction gives the superior courts the power of judicial review of executive action and in exercise of this power, not only executive actions including orders or directions made can be quashed but also positive directions can be mandated. The net result can be substitution of an enforceable order of the court replacing the executive order. Superior Courts in England at one point of time favoured quashing of unsustainable directions of the executive but were slow to substitute their own directions in place of executive action but later instances of one part or complete substitution have been plenty and can be taken as the prevailing practice. In India in the early years of constitutional functioning, the Superior Courts had exhibited their opinion against substitution but over the years the practice of remitting the matters to the appropriate executive authority to make a fresh proper order is no more considered necessary. For the sake of doing complete justice to the matter and the parties, the Superior Courts are now substituting their orders and directions in place of the quashed executive action.

Governance in the modern State often involves a lot of technical and complicated decision-making at the hands of the executive. Such matters also involve or have effect on international relations. These are matters where special expertise, on the one hand, and political responsibility, on the other, are involved. While exercising the power of judicial review, the courts should, therefore, be cautious enough not to get into complications and put the executive government and even the interest of the nation in jeopardy. Judicial review is an instrument to help the maintenance of the balance which is so much necessary to ensure proper working of the scheme of separation of powers, rule of business and the reviewing exercise of administrative discretion.

In recent years, the term 'Judicial activism' is often heard particularly in some of the developing countries of South-east Asia. Judicial review, as already stated, is an acknowledged power of the Superior Courts. As long as the exercise of the power is within known limits, it is legitimate exercise of jurisdiction. When judicial action is beyond the settled limits, such action is often referred to as judicial activism. When a politician in power is arraigned as an accused and is facing trial for corruption and the Court starts supervising the progress by taking control of the matter and regulating the progress, it is indeed not the power of the judicial review which is being exercised.

The term 'Judicial activism' is intended to refer to, and cover, the action of the court in excess of, and beyond the power of judicial review. From one angle it is said to be an act in excess of, or without, jurisdiction. The Constitution does not confer any authority or jurisdiction for 'activism' as such on the Court.

In course of the past decade, many instances of such action by the Supreme Court and the High Court have come to notice. In case of political corruption, such action of the courts has not been objected to; on the other hand, it has been welcomed. It must, however, be remembered that such action should be exceptional and not made a matter of routine in the anxiety to extend jurisdiction and make the court and its process move arbitrarily and disturb the balance provided by the Constitution.

Common law recognised the defence of *locus standi* and refused to entertain a litigation for adjudication if it was barred by this rule. In India, in 1982, the Supreme Court removed the bar in consideration of the prevailing situation which made it difficult for the poor and the under-privileged to litigate for their own rights. In public interest, any well-meaning citizen could fight out some one else's cause. The removal of the bar of *locus standi* soon gave rise to disputes of public issues being agitated in courts in the instance of individuals, groups or bodies having no personal cause of action to go to the court. Public interest litigation, as such cases have come to be classified, have spread their sphere and today every High Court and the Supreme Court, and even some of the Subordinate Courts are busy handling such litigations. As long as the limits are kept in view and not allowed to be transgressed, and private causes are not allowed to pass as public, perhaps this type of cases would contribute to proper up-keep of society.

The Judiciary is an indispensable part of Governance and an efficient and independent judiciary is the greatest guarantee of well-being of society.

Democracy is an edifice of trust. In a large state it is not possible for every citizen to directly participate in its governance. That is why by exercise of the ballot through the process of election a few are selected to run the Government. The courts which are the main prop of the Judiciary have their share in the process of Governance. Since the democratic process through the ballot creates a large trust — citizens' powers to govern being transferred to the group and as in the case of a trust, the trustees are accountable for their actions to the members of the trust. Those who run the 'Governance' have accountability for their actions to the citizens of the country. The

Judiciary which shares the power of governance too, is accountable for its actions. While the executive through the elected political supervisors is accountable to Parliament and through it to the people, the judiciary on account of its typical role and peculiar manner of functioning cannot be made responsible to Parliament as in the case of the executive. The hierarchical judicial system is accountable to the high tier and the apex forum is accountable to the oath taken and its conscience. Parliament has been vested with authority to remove a judge by following the prescribed procedure in certain eventualities. That is how the system of check and balance has been contemplated and evolved.

The twentieth century is running out and the twenty-first has started knocking at the door. Let us hope that participatory democracies has come to stay and become more acceptable; the judicial process would be appropriately geared and aim at contributing its best to good governance. The world is fast growing global and new challenges are appearing on the horizon.

GOVERNANCE AND JUDICIARY

M. Amir-Ul Islam

Introduction

From early times functions of the government could not be limited to trying the criminals or settling disputes between the subjects. It also included the business of law making and that of administration or regulation of public affairs and the conduct of public services — all of which took vast area of governance under the King or the Chief, as in ancient times that are also common in a modern state.

The modern state is however expected to deal also in the socio-economic area. Vast social problems are dealt either by direct intervention or by supervision of regulatory mechanism. In order to carry out this function the state must have agents or organs through which it is to operate. A state then not only has to establish such organization or agents, but it must also define their general function/power, their relations inter-se and between them and private citizens.

Montesquieu following the concept of Aristotle and Locke, divided these powers of the Government into Legislative, Executive and Judiciary.

Montesquieu was concerned with the preservation of political liberty, as he believed that:

> "Political liberty is to be found only when there is no abuse of power. But constant experience shows us that every man invested with power is liable to abuse it, and to carry his authority as far as it will go. ... To prevent this abuse, it is necessary from the nature of things that one power should be a check on another ... when the

> legislative and executive powers are united in the same person or body ... there can be no liberty. ... Again there is no liberty if the judicial power is not separated from the legislative and the executive. ... There would be an end of everything if the same person or body, whether of the nobles or of the people were to exercise all these powers." (Montesquieu)

Though a complete separation of powers without any overlapping or coordination may not be possible, the prime caution as contained in this doctrine remains valid. Consistent experience in all governments is that too much concentration of power on any person or body without any check of one power by another would give rise to tyranny.

During the 19th century the ruling political dogma was *laissez faire*, which envisaged minimum governmental control. State acted more like a police or a law and order state. Majority of people were poor and had less freedom.

"It came to appear that the unequals are never free and that without protective laws the free are only the strong. Against such destroying freedom men appealed to the society and the belief of Laissez Faire ceased" (McIver, 1964).

It came to be pleaded that the state should take more positive interest in ameliorating the conditions of the poor. In course of time, out of collectives emerged the concept of 'Social Welfare State' which laid state action as a vehicle for the socio-economic welfare of the people.

Friedman classified the functions of a modern state under 5 categories — the state as (i) a protector, (ii) a provider, (iii) a regulator, (iv) an entrepreneur and (v) and an umpire (Friedman). These roles of the state bring with it new problems. The state, then must have standard and institution which can ensure minimum fairness and reasonable balance between different economic and social groups in the community. As representative of the community as a whole the state has to administer justice between different sectors and the community.

Fundamental Principles

Bangladesh Constitution mandates the State to fulfill the detailed socio-economic programme for emancipation of people and for their social, cultural and economic uplift. They are known as fundamental principles of State policy. The principles so set out in part II have been made fundamental to the governance of Bangladesh.

The Appellate Division has taken due notice of the significance of the fundamental principles of the state policy:

> "Part II of it embodies the Fundamental Principles of State Policy. Article 8(2) mandates that the principles set out in this Part shall be fundamental to the governance of Bangladesh, shall be applied by the state in the making of laws, shall be a guide to the interpretation of the Constitution and of the other laws, but shall not be judicially enforceable. Among other things, Article 11 is to the effect that the Republic shall be a democracy in which fundamental human rights and freedoms and respect for the dignity and worth of the human person shall be guaranteed. Article 14 states that it shall be a fundamental responsibility of the State to emancipate the toiling masses — the peasants and workers — and through planned economic growth, a constant increase of productive forces and a steady improvement in the material and cultural standard of living of the people, with a view to securing to its citizens the provision of the basic necessities of life, including food, clothing, shelter, education and medical care; the right to social security, that is to say, to public assistance in cases of undeserved want arising from unemployment, illness or disablement, or suffered by widows or orphans or in old age, or in other such cases. Articles 16, 17, 18 and 19 likewise impose a duty upon the state to adopt effective measures for rural development and agricultural revolution, free and compulsory education, raising the level of public health and morality and ensuring equality of opportunity to all citizens. Under Article 21(1) it is obligatory for all citizens to perform public duties and to protect public property.
>
> They are not merely programmes for socio-economic development of the people, but much deeper in content. They firmly recognize human sensitivity for fellow-citizens and State responsibility for protection of human rights enshrined in Article 1 of the Universal Declaration of Human Rights (to which Bangladesh is a signatory) that "all human beings are born free and equal in dignity and rights. They are endowed with reason and conscience and should act towards one another in a spirit of brotherhood." (DLR, 49)

Justice Mustafa Kamal in the same case has held that:

> "The Supreme Court being a vehicle, a medium or mechanism devised by the Constitution for the exercise of the judicial power of the

> people on behalf of the people, the people will always remain the focal point of concern of the Supreme Court while disposing of justice or propounding any judicial theory or interpreting any provision of the of Constitution. ... In a capitalist *laissez faire* concept of private ownership of the instruments and means of production and distribution individual rights carry the only weight and the judiciary exists primarily to protect the capitalist rights of the individuals. But in our Constitution Article 13, a Fundamental Principle of state policy, provides the people shall own or control the instruments and means of production and distribution under three forms, namely (a) State ownership i.e. ownership by the state on behalf of the people, (b) Co-operative ownership i.e. ownership by cooperatives on behalf of the members and (c) Private ownership i.e. ownership by individuals." (DLR, 49)

In order to implement all these policies the government will need a vast administrative agency. It will need modern laws with more regulations, rules, by-laws to be administered by bureaucracy. In applying the laws or in making rules there would be exercise of wide discretions.

Administrative Laws

There are far too many problems of details, and far too many matters which can not be administratively decided in advance. Hence there is need for controls i.e.

1. Political control through Parliament.
2. Legal control through Court.

Equally, there must be control on legal power as to which there is normally no discretion. In this process of control there has emerged a new area known as Administrative Law. This branch of law relates to the control of the Governmental power:

> "The primary purpose of the administrative law, therefore, is to keep the powers of government within their legal bounds, so as to protect the citizens against their abuse. The powerful engines of authority must be prevented from running amock. ... Abuse is therefore inevitable and it is all the more necessary that the law should provide means to check it ... subject as it is to the vast empires of executive power that have been created, the public must be able to rely on the

> law to ensure that all this power may be used in a way comfortable to it's ideas of fair dealing and good administration." (Wade, 1994)

Law should provide means to check it. It is a common occurrence that an order of a Ministry is set aside by the court as unlawful. Detention order passed by the Deputy Commissioner or an order of land acquisition or compulsory purchase order may be set aside in the writ jurisdiction declaring them as unlawful. They are practical examples of Rules of Law. The Government must have legal warrant for what it does. If it acts unlawfully the citizen has an effective legal remedy. The question for administrative justice, therefore, is to find a way as to how the technique of government can be improved.

One of the objections to the Judicial Review of the actions of officers or Departments is on the ground that it is unnecessary because they are accountable to Parliament for the way they carry out their functions.

The power and the functions of the Governmental agencies are defined by law but the due performance thereof depends upon their official honesty, judgment and discretion. The repository of this power is given discretion whether to act and if so, how to act, as is described in Halsbury Law of England:

> "A discretionary Power is typically conferred by words and phrases such as "may", "it shall be lawful", "if it thinks fit" or "as it thinks fit". A statutory discretion is not, however, necessarily or indeed, usually absolute: it may be qualified by expressed and implied legal duties to comply with substantive and procedural requirements before a decision is taken, whether to act and how to act. Moreover, there may be a discretion whether to exercise a power, but no discretion as to the mode of its exercise; or a duty to act when certain conditions are present but a discretion how to act. Discretion may thus be coupled with duties. On the other hand, the duty unaccompanied by any discretion requires action in a prescribed manner and form to be taken when condition precedent exists; performance of such a duty is a mere ministerial act."

In public statute whether the words are only directory, or permissory, it may constitute a compulsory course where a thing to be done in order to accomplish an object of the law itself and this is to be done for public benefit or in advancement of public justice.

As said by Earl Cairns, "there may be something in the nature of the thing empowered to be done, something in the objective in it to be done, something in condition under which it is to be done, something in the title of person or persons for whose benefit the power is to be exercised, which may couple the power with a duty and make it the duty of the person in whom the power is deposed, to exercise the power when called upon to do so" (Cairns, 1880).

In exercise of this discretion, the statutory body or a governmental official has to act in accordance with law.

State activism and the increase of its functions in its quest to improve the physical, moral and economical welfare of the people lead inevitably to the assumptions of more and more powers by the state. Consequently, all the three organs of the state have a greater load to bear. State activism has meant increase of work for all these organs. Legislature is to enact more and more laws in order to initiate new socio-economic schemes and the courts have to interpret new laws and decide many more disputes generated by new laws. In order that the judiciary can cope with this new role, it needs to be ever so sensitive to the socio-economic issues and their dynamics in a changing society. It is only the pro-people and pro-active courts who may be able to meet this new challenge.

Executive-cum-Administrative organ becomes predominant in having the largest extension of function and the power. It makes policies, initiates legislations and even acts as guides in state's legislative function, executes and administers the law and makes manifold decisions. It also exercises legislative powers, issues rules, makes by-laws, orders and regulations, all of which are known as delegated and subsidiary legislation. This type of legislation is greater in volume than the laws made by the legislature. The truth is that, most of the laws enacted by the legislature often looks like a skeleton; it's details are to be filled-in through subsidiary legislation. The administration have acquired power of adjudication over disputes, not only between private individuals inter-se but also between it and private individuals in several areas. Thus the power of the court has been diluted specially at the initial stage of adjudication. As a result, the administration has secured extensive discretionary powers. Discretionary powers have been granted in the area of liberty, property and even in case of livelihood. Starting from the acquisition of property, allocation of favours, distribution of state largesse, it exercises discretion in case of arrest, seizure, enquiry and in maintenances of law and order and even taking away citizens' liberty under Special Powers, and in emergency.

As a result a proliferation of administrative bodies has taken place. Not only have bodies multiplied manifold, new administrative organs variously designed as Departments, Directorates, Committees, Commissions, Authorities, Tribunals, Officers, Bureaus, Boards have come into existence. In addition, there are statutory bodies created to manage public undertakings or to undertake specific regulatory functions. As has been observed by Lord Denning that the vast power of administration if exercised properly may lead to the welfare state but if misused, they may lead to administrative despotism and to a totalitarian state. While the administrative agency has capacity to do a lot of good it also has a capacity to do a lot of harm to the rights and interests of an individual. As Mr. Justice Douglas once said, "absolute discretion like corruption is the beginning of the end of liberty" (Justice Douglas).

Moreover, the uncontrolled administrative powers conferred on administrators have inherent seeds of corruption. In the absence of guiding norms to regulate the exercise of such power, there may be no way as to whether a particular decision arrived at by an administrator is bonafide or motivated by some corrupt consideration (Wheare, 1973).

Judiciary and Good Governance

The role of Judiciary *vis-à-vis* governance and particularly the paradigm for good governance becomes extremely relevant in this context. The question is: Can the executive power be controlled by laws? Can the procedural safeguards be ensured by the court? Can the judiciary help in implanting the legal ideas of fair procedure and just decision in the administrative power of the state?

Neither the Diceyan concept to Rule of Law nor the political control through parliamentary sovereignty, or the Montesquieu Doctrine of Separation of Power can provide today an adequate answer to these questions confronted by the citizens against the invasion by the administrative branch of the state in all walks of life.

A significant breach of the Doctrine of Separation of Powers occurs when the court conceded that legislative power could be conferred on administrative authority. But in order to bring back the same the court has developed the doctrine of excessive delegation. It cannot confer an unlimited legislative power on the administrative authority. The Parliament must lay down the basic policy which the delegatee has to follow while making the Rules. It must contain a framework within which the administrative delegate has to operate. The Doctrine of Separation of Powers was further diminished when adjudicative powers were also conferred on the executive. Administrative justice is now expanding in all directions.

There is a modern tendency to enforce the concept of Separation by having some sort of internal separation within the same agency separated by investigation and prosecution sub agencies. In a country with Parliamentary system, it has become quite common to set up statutory body having functions — Regulatory, Administrative, Legislative and Adjudicative. For example, in Bangladesh we have Security Exchange Commission, Registrar Joint Stock Company, Registrar Trade Mark, Board of Investment and regulatory role of Bangladesh Bank, The Board of Revenue, Tariff Commission so on and so forth in economic domain alone. In Singapore, many such bodies have been established — Board of Architecture, Tourist Promotion Board, Industrial Administrative Court, Monitory Authority of Singapore, Court of Singapore Authority etc.

Judicial control over the governance by the Executive-cum-Administrative authority can be through various means by the control of subsidiary legislation, by applying intra vires doctrine, by applying principle of natural justice, the fairness and reasonableness doctrine and by applying the Rule of Estoppel and legitimate expectations.

Firstly, our Courts can scrutinize as to whether the law itself is in conformity with the Constitution or whether it is ultra vires or violative of fundamental rights.

Secondly, it can also scrutinize as to whether the parent statutes which delegates subsidiary legislation is itself Constitutional or not.

Courts Scrutiny of Laws

Under our Constitution it is provided that "the Constitution is, as a solemn expression of the will of the people, the supreme law of the Republic, and if any other law is inconsistent with this Constitution that other law shall, to the extent of the inconsistency, be void" (Art. 7).

Reference may be made to a decision known as the Eighth Amendment Case, (16) (Anwar Hossain Vs. Bangladesh) whereby an amendment to the Constitution, bifurcating the integrated concept of the Supreme Court's High Court Division by diversifying it's territorial jurisdiction in various regional Benches was declared ultra vires.

Dr. Nurul Islam's case is another classic example of the role of the judiciary in scrutinizing the legislation. In Public Servant Retirement Rules, 1975 no principle or guideline was provided in the matter of retirement of government servant on completion of 25 years of his service, which in turn created the scope for discrimination. Section 9, Subsection 2 of the said Act was therefore, declared violative of the equality provision of the Constitution and hence declared ultra vires.

The Appellate Division of the Supreme Court while giving the Judgement in the case also relied upon certain principles enunciated by Indian Supreme Court in the case of Joyti Prashad Vs. Union Territory, (A.I.R. 1961 S.C. 1602) and adopted the following principles:

> "The enactment or the rule might not in terms enact a discriminatory rule of law but might enable an unequal or discriminatory treatment to be accorded to persons or things similarly situated. This would happen when the Legislature vests a discretion in an authority, be it the government or an administrative official acting either as an executive officer or even in a quasi-judicial capacity, by a legislation which does not lay down any policy or disclose any tangible or intangible purpose, thus clothing the authority with unguided and arbitrary power enabling it to discriminate. ... In such circumstances the very provision of the law, which enables or permits the authority to discriminate, offends the guarantee of equal protection afforded by Article 14." (AIR, 1961)

Our court also adopted the principles of a landmark case decided by the House of Lords known as Padfield case. In this case House of

Lords had the occasion to consider the limits of the exercise of the discretionary statutory powers by a Minister and the extent of the judicial control over such exercise.

"If the Minister does not, or refuses to give any reason for his decision what would be the consequence of his failure or refusal, or what was the duty of the Court? This would be to allow him to defeat the purposes of the Act. In such cases, the Court would intervene so as not to silently thwart the intention of Parliament."

It is said by Lord Denning that "a discretion of the statutory body is never unfettered. This is a discretion which is to be exercised according to law. That means at least this: the statutory body must be guided by relevant consideration and not by irrelevant consideration. If its decision is influenced by irrelevant consideration which it ought not to take into account, then the decision can not stand" (AER, 1971). Padfield Vs. Ministry of Agriculture, Fisheries and Food, have since been followed in series of cases in all common law jurisdiction.

Another potential aspect of the case was that the House of Lords refused to accept that the courts power is to be invaded by omitting the grounds of decision. The Privy Council held in an appeal from Malaysia that the decision of Malaysian Head of the States to revoke a proclamation of emergency is not entirely unfettered and the failure to revoke it after it is no longer considered necessary, therefore is an abuse of discretion.

Monitoring Discretionary Powers

The principle of Padfield Vs. Ministry of Agriculture is applied by our courts almost on a regular basis in case of detention under Special Powers Act. If the ground of detention contains consideration of something which is not covered under the definition of 'Prejudicial Act', then entire detention would be declared illegal. The courts are increasingly monitoring the discretionary powers of the executives and the statutory agencies and in monitoring the same courts take the view that the discretionary powers are to be wielded only by those to whom it is given and they should retain it unhampered by improper constraints and restrictions. The most significant principle of governance as determined by the court is that the power of the executives should be exercised in good faith and on proper grounds — in other words, they must not be abused. The other test applied is whether there was due compliance of natural justice and fair play. The Judiciary can thus control to a limited but important extent both the substance of the discretionary decision and the procedure under which they were made.

The Diceyan concept of Rule of Law has itself become dicey as Wade and Forsythe writes on Administrative Law, "it used to be considered as classical controlled doctrine — why discretionary power is incompatible to Rule of Law but this dogma can not be seriously taken today, and indeed it never contained much truth. What the Rule of Law demands is not that discriminatory power be eliminated but the law should be able to control its exercise. The requirement is that all powers has legal limit. The next requirement, no less vital, is that the Court should fix the limit in a way which will strike the most suitable balance between legislative efficiency and the legal protection of the citizen" (Wade and Forsythe, 1994).

Whatever may be the power given by the parliament which on the face might seem absolute and arbitrary the court has refused to countenance. They have woven a network of restrictive principle which requires statutory powers to be exercised in a reasonable manner and in good faith, for proper purpose only and in accord with their spirit and as well as the letter of the empowering Act.

The courts in this area while monitoring the powers of these statutory bodies, works within the familiar principles of ultra vires doctrine. The court assumes that the parliament could not have intended to authorize unreasonable actions which is, therefore, ultra vires and void.

Chief Justice Lord Russel said that, if a legislative authority is manifestly unjust and oppressive the court might well say, "Parliament never intended to give authority to make such rules; they are unreasonable and ultra vires".

Writs On Contracts

Our courts have been most reluctant to entertain judicial review in matters of awarding contract or giving settlement of land, and distributing state largesse. Traditionally, the courts are likely to view, as in the case of private parties, a tender as being merely an offer, and the government or corporation as having a discretion to choose whether to enter into a contract with any party, and have kept away from interfering into such executive discretion.

Our courts have, however, begun to recognize the need for intervention under the writ jurisdiction in matters of contractual relationships between the government and private parties. In cases of violation of the terms of a contract by the government with a malafide intention or where the government acts arbitrarily or in a discriminatory manner, the Court has protected the aggrieved party under the writ jurisdiction:

> 'Modern Government', as the Appellate Division of the Supreme Court acknowledges: "has multifarious activities. Some of its functions are governmental functions while exercising sovereign power and again some of the functions can be described as trading functions. ... When the Government grants of lease, privilege, settlement, etc.; the government acts and discharges a sovereign function "performing function in connection with affairs of the Republic or the local authority". Such function can best be appreciated in matters of settlement of hat, bazaar, fisheries, khas land, etc. The government acts in these affairs in pursuance of some statutory powers and any such contract when rooted in statute the government discharges its sovereign function. While doing so, if there is a breach of any statute or rule the same can be remedied by invoking writ jurisdiction." (DLR, 39)

In making this distinction between statutory functions and trading functions and placing the statutory/sovereign function on a higher pedestal by virtue of it being based in a statute, the Court has reiterated the accountability of the state in a court of law.

Yet, the decision begs further question as to what is the extent of sovereign function particularly in view of the fact that the modern government functions under a Constitution. The Constitution confers responsibility on the government for emancipation of peasants and workers, creating provisions of basic necessities, education, public health, rural development, agricultural revolution, rural electrification, development of cottage and other industries, improvement of education, communication and public health under the fundamental principles of state policy. There is, however, no statutory framework for the implementation of these principles. The government has undertaken massive programmes with large budgetary allocations to ensure the above objectives. These developmental activities can be seen as a reflection and realization of the fundamental principles of state policy. Consequently, such activities of the government could also be categorized as sovereign functions; this possibility needs to be further explored.

Many government actions, though not rooted in specific statutes, may nevertheless be considered as activities in exercise of sovereign powers under the Constitution. Thus, for example, the courts need to consider whether the government and state corporations should be subjected to a social audit under Article 102 of the Constitution when making purchases and floating tenders, often with foreign grants and loans.

Social Audit

Large amounts of public money are spent in matters of government expenditure, purchase, awarding contracts and floating tenders. Such awards and various grants and privileges, are often seen as state largesse. These are the sources of patronage distribution, giving rise to corruption and nepotism. These are also the sources of black money which in turn is the source of bribery and terrorism and contributes to the creation of a social and political mafia and in the process destabilises the socio-economic as well as the political and cultural environment of the society.

Until other effective mechanisms of accountability are developed, judicial review as a form of social audit and for policing the corridors of power could serve a useful public interest, particularly if it can be extended in matters of granting state largesse and in public finance.

In this area, there has been a significant change in India. Indian Supreme Court made timely departure from traditional concepts, as expounded by Justice Bhagwati in the Bombay Airport case:

> "It must therefore be taken to be the law that where the government is dealing with the public whether by way of giving jobs or entering into contracts or issuing quotas or licenses or granting other forms of

> largesse the government cannot act arbitrarily at its sweet will and, like a private individual, deal with standard or norms which is not arbitrary, irrational or irrelevant. The power of discretion of the government in the matter of grant of largesse including award of jobs, contracts, quotas, licenses, etc.; must be confirmed and structured by rational relevant and non-discriminatory standard or norm and if the government departs from such standard or norm in any particular case or cases the action of the government will '. liable to be struck down, unless it can be shown by the government that the departure was not arbitrary, but was based on some valid principle which in itself was not irrational, unreasonable or discriminatory." (Supreme Court, India, 1979)

Justice Desai in another case of government auctioning gave the following reasons for the Court's interference:

> The choice and the indicated path adopted by the court needs no justification because the end product justified interference.

A mineral quarry was auctioned, and Ram and Shyam Company offered the highest bid of Rs. 152,000 per annum which the State government refused to confirm. In the fresh auction, the company again offered the highest bid, raising it to Rs. 387,000. The bid was again not confirmed by the state government which was going to give it to another party offering Rs. 450,000 per year. Ram and Shyam Co. challenged the order of acceptance of the latest offer by the Chief Minister. The Supreme Court encouraged both the parties to increase their bid in the court room and the bid went up to 25 lakhs. Justice Desai narrated the shock and surprise which was, according to his Lordship, visible on the face of each one in the court room.

Their Lordships observed:

> "What happened in this case must open the eyes both of the government as well as the people at large. How an uncontrolled exercise of executive power to deal with socialist property in which an entire community's interest was sacrificed so as to cause huge loss to the public exchequer would have gone unnoticed but for the vigilance of the appellant who no doubt is not altruistic in its approach but its business interests goaded it to expose the unsavory deal. Conceding that on weighty and valid considerations, the

> highest bid can be rejected by the state, one such which can be foreseen is that the highest bid does not represent the adequate market price of the concession, yet before giving up the auction process and accepting a private offer if given in open would not be outmatched by the highest bidder." (AIR, 1985)

As for Bangladesh, the award of an oil exploration contract in Haripur, Sylhet and the consequent sale of gas below the international price; as reported in the press and revealed through investigations conducted by a people's enquiry commission, caused considerable public agitation. However, no attempt was made to test whether the Court would interfere in a situation in which public money was manifestly and grossly squandered or state property sold for a pittance or purchases made in violation of the rule of fair play.

Vigilance on Liberty

Our courts have been very vigilant in the question of liberty and the freedom of our citizens. There have been innumerable habeas corpus petitions entertained by our courts almost on regular basis and in most of the cases detinues are released after the determination that the detention is illegal. Our courts have also started monitoring the police excess. In the State Vs. Deputy Commissioner of Shatkhira the High Court Division issued a suo-moto Rule. A young detenu, Nazrul Islam, was produced in Court. Nazrul, who appeared in Court with chains on both his legs, had been arrested when he was 12 years old and twelve cases were filed against him between 1997 and 1983, some when he was already in prison. This case exposed the callousness, corruption, vindictiveness and inhuman and mindless prosecution of a young child at the instance of some interested quarters. The Court held that:

> "Since the alleged crimes were alleged to have been committed by this boy within the range from 8 to 12 years which is on the face of it malafide and void ab initio and since all the subsequent actions and proceedings were taken without legal authority and illegally, we are of the view that this court can rightly exercise its jurisdiction not only in declaring the detention of the detenu illegal, but also declaring the proceedings upon which the detenu was held in detention to be illegal and void."

Emphasizing the obligation of a judge to uphold constitutional values, Mr. Justice M.M. Huq issued directions as follows:

> "We are fully aware of our responsibility as regards enforcement of fundamental human rights as provided under Article 102(1) of the Constitution of Bangladesh and also of our solemn oath which we had taken under Article 148 of the Constitution. In a case like this, we also feel that we should give necessary directions to the relevant authorities for taking appropriate steps in order to take legal actions against them who are responsible for such negligence and also directing the authorities to inquire into the matter as to whether any other detenu or person is suffering in jail for no fault of his own like the present detenu.
>
> Let a copy of this judgement be sent to Begum Khaleda Zia, the Prime Minister of Bangladesh, and this Court earnestly desires that she should personally consider and feel as to how an ordinary citizen of her country being a poor minor boy of 8 to 12 years was put to such unspeakable suffering and inhuman torture for such a long period of 12 years, in fact, for no fault of his own, but because of malafide action of some interested person and of administrative negligence of different agencies of the government, while the Constitution of Bangladesh with all its fundamental rights is functioning, the Rule of law is being claimed to have been established in the country and democracy is marching forward with fame."

This judgement raised public awareness of and created checks against the abuse of the process of law. It exposed the extent of such abuse in the place where justice is supposed to be administered. This case is a significant example of judicial activism by the High Court Division of the Supreme Court of Bangladesh and may help poor juvenile prisoners to seek redress against the state's dereliction of its duty.

The same judge only last week issued a suo-moto Rule in respect of a young child of six years of age against whom a charge sheet has been submitted involving an incident when a mob snatched away arms from Akhaura Railway Police. The unlawful arrest and prosecution and the torture in the police custody and detention of young women under so-called judicial and safe custody has aroused much concern. Custodian rape, death and violence is another area where there is gross abuse of police power coupled with perverse and wanton criminalization of police power which pose a challenge for the judiciary. Our courts are yet to find a way how to effectively protect the human rights against such abuse of police power.

Equal Justice for All

One of the aspiration of our people, and the major goals of our Constitution, is to secure "a society in which the rule of law, fundamental human rights and freedom, equality and justice — political, economic and social will be secured for all citizens." Our Constitution while giving emphasis on equal justice social, political and economic justice as to be ensured has in no unclear terms set it's goals. This is further elaborated in fundamental principles of state policy contained in Part II of the Constitution followed by the fundamental rights guaranteed under Chapter III. In fact the Constitutional postulate for equal justice, social, political and economic is based on the concept of distributive justice as envisaged by Aristotle coupled with the new vision of welfare state. According to Aristotle, distributive justice is based on the principle of equal distribution among equals, while corrective justice is to restore when it is disturbed. In the modern governance if we are speaking of this distribution on the basis of equality, question is raised as to who decides the equality in what is to be distributed and unequal cases will have to be treated differently according to a given criteria of discretion. Unless criterion of inequality is chosen correctly it can not be called just.

If equal justice, in the social, political and economic life is to be achieved for the pursuit of happiness then such criteria and norms should not be confined to court rooms only nor be kept restricted within some judgements published in some law reports.

Concern is not so much because of the extension of the Executive domain as long as that Executive discretion is within the domain of law. Resistance against the Executive action and preference for the dispensation of justice by the judiciary is not because of special trappings of the court but because the executives have not yet had the discipline for adopting a judicial mind in exercising its discretion, and it is not easy to acquire it, as the discretions which our administrators use in their daily exercise and in the manner it is exercised, they are antithetic to Rule of Law.

"Prof. Morgan writes as though the legislative and judicature were perceived as riparian owners bargaining over a strip of land or Executive Power curving on an African Colony. What the court is trying to monitor and inject, is a judicial mind and the due process as it is said that without a judicial mind to apply law or a body of law would disintegrate our society in a year and the society will relapse into savagery" (Robson).

Judicial Spirit

The role of the judiciary is, therefore, not only limited to the reliefs it gives in terms of setting aside an order and/or declaring an action ultra vires but in the long term view the role of the court is to inject the judicial idea not merely in regard to question which come before the courts of law but also in reference to the executive and administrative action covering a vast area, nearly all the rational activities of the human race.

For the predominant virtue of the judicature lies only in the fact that it thinks and acts judicially and is recognized in doing so: "That and that alone, is the essence of its merit. "What society needs is the operation of a judicial spirit far more, than an insistence upon mere outward features of a formal court, though as we may discover, some of those outward characteristics are necessary before the judicial spirit can emerge or flourish with any guarantee of stability (Robson).

We are inclined to say that the whole modern conceptualization of economical and social democracy involves the execution of discretion which shall be judicial in that they are not to depend upon individual caprice and shall be free from personal favour, individual self-interest; and this may imply and extend in certain respect of the judicial mind and application of mental habits common among those who administer law, and exercise power of any kind over other citizens including the judicial process.

This judicial spirit has close links towards the concept of equality. Inequality before the law as a principle existed in ancient time. There were differences of liability varying with the rank, age and sex of the offender. But the marks of justice according to law in the modern sense are the generality and equality. Continuous mental efforts to suppress or to exclude rigidly all subjective consideration of an emotional type tend to fall into an order — a method of reasoning which is artificial, in the sense that it demands an unnatural objectivity and the suppression of a large number of important impulsive instincts.

Whether such artificial reasoning can be adopted in the execution of discretion by the executive Administrators may be of doubtful validity today. What might be useful is that the state agencies may evolve as a separate discipline by adopting a separation specifying who would be doing adjudicative function within itself while applying law to a citizen by way of exercising discretion under any law or authority.

In order to meet the challenge of the next century and to accomplish the Constitutional goal, to secure equal justice in economic, political and social life, it is important to extend the judicial mind and the due process in all spheres of administrative dealings with the affairs of men and society.

The role of the judiciary in governance is a coordinate role along with other two organs of the State. It's role is not limited, therefore, merely in settling disputes within the court room between two disputants, though one of whom may often be state or its agent. The judiciary can not be oblivious of the social consequence that may follow from what it decides and how it decides.

In the modern welfare state having a constitution which is to be upheld by a Judge under an oath to do so he can not be unmindful of his responsibility to ensure all the values that the Constitution stands for and to protect the "Fundamental Human Rights and freedoms and respect for the dignity and the worth of the human person" as guaranteed under our Constitution and to ensure the distributive justice as the final outcome of this role in ensuring social, political and economic justice as the sacred Constitutional pledge of the entire people.

References

AIR, 1961 S.C. 1602.

Breen Vs. Amalgamated Engineering Union (1971) 1 All. E.R. 1148.

Earl Cairns in Julius Vs. Bishop of Oxford 1880 (5) A.C. 214, 222, 223.

Friedman, *Rule of Law and the Welfare State*.

Ibid.

Ibid.

Justice and Administrative Law, by Prof. William Robson (Page 37).

Justice Douglas in New York vs. United States (342 U.S. 882, 884).

McIver, *The Modern State*, pp.460, 1964.

Mohiuddin Farooq Vs. Government of Bangladesh, 49, DLR (A.D.) pp.1 (Para 93, 94).

Montesquieu, L' Espirit des Lois, *The Spirit of Law*, Chapter XI, pp.3-6.

Ram and Shyam Co. Vs. State of Haryana, AIR (1985) S.C. 1147.

Rama Dayaram Shethy Vs. International Airport Authority 1979 (3) SCC 489.

Sharping Motshajibi Shamabaya Samity Vs. Bangladesh, 39 DLR (A.D.) 85 at 94.

Wade, *Administrative Law*, 4 (1994).

Wade and Forsythe on Administrtive Law (7th edition) 1994.

Wheare, *Mal-Administrative Functions —Its Remedies*, pp.7, (1973).

GOOD GOVERNANCE AND JUDICIARY: EQUAL RIGHTS OF WOMEN

Salma Khan

Introduction

Judiciary with the system of laws and institutions being responsible to protect the rights of individuals to live, work and enjoy fundamental freedom forms the foundation of social justice and equality. The legal system of a country therefore, must uphold the equal rights and inherent human dignity of women and men as an essential pre-condition of democracy and good governance. The existence of any body of law within the legal system that in any manner makes distinction, exclusion or restriction which has the effect or purpose of impairing or nullifying the recognition, enjoyment or exercise by women of their rights in political, economic, social, cultural, civil or any other fields constitutes discrimination against them and is therefore, contrary to the ideals of good governance.

The Constitution of the People's Republic of Bangladesh in its fundamental principle of state policy guarantees fundamental freedom and human rights of all citizens without any distinction. Corresponding to that, the Constitution ensures equal participation of women in national life and equal right of women with men in all spheres of state and public life. However, the constitution remains silent regarding the rights of individuals in the personal sphere which is governed by the personal law of each community or religious groups. Accordingly, Muslim population of Bangladesh are governed by the Muslim Personal Law in private sphere of their life.

The objective of this paper is to analyze briefly the two sets of laws — the Muslim Personal Law and Special Laws enacted as a provision to protect women and children in Bangladesh and how far these laws comply with the concept of non-discrimination and protection of human rights of women.

Muslim Personal Law

In Bangladesh the Muslim Personal Law which governs the critically important areas of the individual's life like marriage, dissolution of marriage, inheritance to property, child custody etc. are widely discriminatory to women. It is noted that equality which is accorded to women by the Constitution of Bangladesh in public sphere and in Civil Law are outweighed by application of Muslim Personal Law which adversely affects women's enjoyment of equal rights in personal sphere. It further contradicts Article 27 of the Constitution which guarantees equality of all citizens before the law. As the personal laws are applied differently on the basis of religion and sex, the fundamental rights and principles enshrined in our Constitution remain contemplative.

The national law of Bangladesh gives women and men the same right to contract marriage and legal impediments to contracting a marriage are not gender specific. However, the practice of personal law in this field has important bearing on status of women. According to Muslim Personal Law men enjoy the right to polygamy allowing them to contract marriages with more than one wife without dissolving a previous marriage.

The Muslim Family Law Ordinance 1961, which is considered as a milestone in its attempt to award better rights to women in personal sphere of life restricted polygamy upto four wives and under the amendment to the act in 1982, the husband is required to seek permission of the Chairman of the Arbitration Council in writing and forward a copy of the same to the existing wife/wives if he wants to take an additional wife. Violation of this provision is a ground for divorce by the existing wife under the Dissolution of Muslim Marriage Act (1939) although in reality such rights are rarely exercised by women due to existing socio-economic condition and non-compliance of men with the legal requirements. A major loophole of the law is that a marriage contracted without the consent of the existing wife and in the absence of conditions affecting normal conjugal life with the existing wife do not make the later marriage invalid. A marriage is also not declared invalid if it is not registered under the Muslim Marriage and Divorce Registration Act (1974) which constitutes additional impediment to punish the violator of the law. As in the case of marriage, women are also at a disadvantaged situation with regard to dissolution of marriage. There are 9 specified grounds for a Muslim woman to obtain a decree for the dissolution of her marriage but the conditions attached to a decree on any such grounds is difficult to prove by the wife due to socio-cultural situation and non-registration of marriages. The situation is made more difficult for women as husbands enjoy unilateral right to divorce. Under the Muslim Family Law Ordinance (1961), to exercise divorce right, the husband has to give notice to the chairman of the Union Council and a copy of the same forwarded to the wife. The divorce (talaq) pronounced will be effective on the expiry of 90 days after the notice is served. The husband can revoke the divorce at any time before it becomes effective. A wife may enjoy the right to divorce only if such power is delegated to her in the contract of the marriage.

In case of de facto separation or divorce, the exercise of personal authority over the children is the responsibility of the father after the ages of 7 and 11 for sons and daughters respectively. Another major discrimination faced by women under the Muslim Personal Law is unequal inheritance right both in parental property and marital property upon dissolution of a marriage or death of husband. From paternal property a daughter inherits half of the brother's share and wife inherits half of what a husband would inherit from his deceased wife. In case of dissolution of a marriage, although a wife is entitled to receive maintenance and dowry money, in reality such practices are few and far between.

It is apparent from the above analysis that persistent inequalities in the Muslim Personal Law institute grave obstacles to women's advancement in the context of the present reality. Furthermore, the weak procedure of the enforcement of the law deprives women whatever the laws intended to offer them.

Special Provision for Women's and Children's Rights

Besides a number of laws enacted since the early part of this century to codify the rights under the Muslim Personal Law and later amended Special Laws were enacted in Bangladesh, to protect women against gender based violence. It is commendable to note that all governments in Bangladesh recognized violence against women and children as one of the most insidious forms of discrimination which impair their ability to participate in family and public life on equal basis with men. With this approach respective governments have initiated legal measures to address the issue. The Cruelty to Women (deterrent punishment) Ordinance 1983 which was the first law in this direction basically addresses the issues of kidnapping, dowry deaths, rape and trafficking in women.

However, oppression of child or child abuse were not covered under the ordinance, it also did not include acid throwing or similar grievous crimes against women. With the change of government in 1990, the Ordinance was repealed and Oppression of Women and Children (special enactment) Act 1995 was introduced.

The 1995 Act although covered wider range of issues relating to violence against women and children, suffered from definitional and procedural limitations. The present government has repealed the act and formulated a replacement — "Women and Child Repression Act 1998" — which is considered to be too broad in scope as it also includes measures to address anti-terrorist activities and other crimes. The draft also suffers from procedural weaknesses and other loopholes.

It may be noted in this connection that although subsequent governments have attached importance to address the issue of violence against women through legal measures, in all instances the law was drafted without a public debate or consultation with women's organizations working in this field. Furthermore, during this period, no reform was brought about for effective enforcement of the law. The present government must be commended for providing with opportunities to various women's organizations to review the bill before it is finalized. *Sammilito Nari Samaj*, *Ain-o-Salish Kendra, Nari Pakhkho*, CEDAW FORUM and other organizations have reviewed the bill and made suggestions for modification of the draft to make it more effective.

Effectiveness of the Laws

Judiciary forms the basic element of the statehood shaped by deliberate policies to establish social justice and equality of all citizens. In a modern society it must, therefore, reflect the fundamental principle of state policy as well as universal value and ethics of international human rights regime which are not fundamentally altered by cultural or class differences.

The government of Bangladesh has ratified major international human rights instruments including the Convention on the Elimination of all forms of Discriminations Against Women (CEDAW) which obligate the government to remove all forms of discriminations against women and ensure participation of women, on equal terms with men in the political, social, economic and cultural life of their country.

How effective is the legal system of Bangladesh to meet these requirements? The Muslim Personal Law practiced in Bangladesh is derived from Sharia which includes both doctrine or belief and practice or law based on explicit or implicit command of God. It must be mentioned here that at various stages Islamic laws have gone through changes and modifications in the light of interpretations of various schools of thought. Since the 18th century there has been a general upsurge of reform in the entire Islamic world, the forerunner of which was the Wahabi movement in Arabia. The major characteristics of the movement was emphasis on the social content of Islam rather than on the purely spiritual side of the doctrine. These reforms, although, were important to enunciate the principles of reinterpretations of Islam in the light of changing situations — especially relating to social institutions of family and slavery, the liberal modernists failed to deal with issues relating to women's rights in the family and society. However, during the early part of the 20th century, some remarkable reforms in the Muslim

Personal Laws were introduced which particularly addressed the disadvantageous status of women in family relations. Countries like Turkey and Tunisia used ijtehad (reinterpretation) as a method for reform — particularly with regard to talaq, restitution of conjugal rights, child custody, polygamy and inheritance rights of women upon dissolution of marriage and other instances. Most Islamic countries although did not follow this, nor introduced reforms in the law itself but contemporary courts of those countries including Bangladesh have often tried to reflect the social needs and principle of justice and equality while dealing with specific issues in personal sphere of individual's life.

Sisters in Islam — an organization in Malaysia studying and researching on the status of women in Islam holds the view that Islam is a liberating religion that uplifted the status of women and gave them rights without difference and both men and women must participate as equal partners in all aspects of life as in the Koran there is no difference in the value given to the creation of women and men (verse 51:49). The Sisters in Islam further argue that it is essential to understand that a passage or verse from the Koran can not be taken out of a context or in isolation as the role and status of women in Islam have been defined in a particular setting. Although Islamic interpretations with respect to male behavior and way of life have taken into account contemporary realities, interpretations of laws that concern women having limited relevance to day has remained unchanged.

It is noteworthy that the Muslim Family Law Ordinance 1961 was the first law which introduced important reforms in the application of the personal laws but in no way equalized women's right to those enjoyed by men under the law. However, there were some attempts to overcome such legal discriminations through rational judgements.

Promulgation of special acts by various governments to address the issue of violence against women, although a clear manifestation of efforts to better protect women's and children's rights, suffered from many loopholes both in the law and in enforcement mechanism. Consequently legal and *de facto* equality was far from being achieved.

Conclusion

As the structure of society is going through changes in Bangladesh, reforms in Muslim Personal Law is crucially important. The fact must be emphasized that true spirit of Islam as reflected in the Quran is not to oppress women but to grant them equality and human dignity. The lawmakers must understand that Islam being a comprehensive way of life need to take into consideration the contemporary requirements.

Alternately, the Constitution of the country which is the solemn expression of the will of the people should be the basis of all laws both in public and private spheres. As a practical policy, duality in the legal system may be discarded and a single civil code may be introduced to harmonize the different aspects of life.

In 1989, Bangladesh Mohila Parishad suggested introduction of an uniform Family Code aiming at establishing equal rights of men and women which can form the basis for legal reform in that direction.

Government of Bangladesh is a signatory to the Universal Declaration of Human Rights and UN Convention on the Elimination of All Forms of Discrimination Against Women (CEDAW) both of which set standards of non-discrimination on the basis of sex and obligate the government to fully implement the provisions of these instruments. The women's organizations have also made long standing demand for full implementation of CEDAW in Bangladesh by establishing legal equality of women and men. In the given socio-cultural milieu in Bangladesh special measures are needed to protect and promote the rights of women and children which will necessitate promulgation of special laws. While drafting new laws, more emphasis should be given on practical application of the law in terms of sound investigation and prompt judgement rather than enhancing the penalty of the perpetrators. As a matter of principle of universal human rights, death penalty should be discouraged as it is more important to punish all perpetrators rather than awarding examplary death penalty to a few. Sound law and effective enforcement mechanism are the best deterrent against all crimes.

It may also be emphasized that a strong civil society and representative democracy are pre-conditions to initiate needed reforms in the legal system to disallow practices validating discrimination against women. The NGOs in Bangladesh are playing a growing role as advocates of social reform and progress and are often key collaborators of government and local authorities in social developments. The NGOs and civil society therefore, should play a pre-defined role with respect to achieving gender equality and interface between the state and other actors for full realization of human rights of women.

GOVERNANCE AND JUDICIARY

Mizanur Rahman

Introduction

The perennial problems of orderly and good governments were aptly discussed by Madison in The Federalist:

> "In framing a government which is to be administered by men over men, the great difficulty lies in this: you must first enable the government to control the governed; and in the next place oblige it to control itself." (Meadison)

The great difficulty mentioned by Madison confronts every civilized society which ensures by written or unwritten law fundamental freedoms, and civil liberties to its citizens, and respects the rule of law, and the independence of the Judiciary.

It is the responsibility of the judicial branch to determine what the law is, and to provide a public forum — courts for resolving legal disputes. In every case the court must determine the facts and their legal significance; if the court determines their legal significance by applying an existing rule of law unchanged (binding law) it is engaged in pure dispute resolution. "But to resolve the dispute if the court must create a new rule or modify an old one, that is law creation" (Posner, 1985). Both activities involve the courts i.e. the Judiciary in policy-making.

It is believed that one of the primary objects for which a state was established in the society was the creation and protection of individual's rights. But an independent organ, as the means through which this object might be accomplished, has been recognized and existed from early times. This independent organ is the Judiciary

The existence of Judiciary does not depend on the existence of a legislature. Even in the absence of legislative organs the courts might apply rule derived from other sources like from their own previous decisions or from customs and thereby recognize rights of individuals. 'A society without a legislative organ is conceivable, and indeed fully developed legislative organs did not make their appearance in the life of the state until modern times, but a civilized state without Judicial organs is hardly conceivable' (Halim, 1998).

Independence of Judiciary

Good governance necessarily demands and requires an independent Judiciary. 'A sound and independent Judiciary is the *sine qua non* of a healthy society' (Halim, 1998). James Bryce aptly says "There is no better test of the excellence of a government than the efficiency of its judicial system, for nothing more nearly touches the welfare and security of the average citizen than his sense that he can rely on the certain and prompt administration of justice. But if the law be dishonestly administered, the salt has lost its savour, if it be weakly or fitfully enforced, the guarantees or order fail, for it is more by the certainty than by the severity of punishment that offences are repressed. If the lamp of justice goes out in darkness, how great is that darkness! (Bryce, 1929).

Independence of the Judiciary truly means that the judges are in a position to render justice in accordance with their oath of office and only in accordance with their own sense of justice without submitting to any kind of pressure or influence.

The concept of judicial independence has broadened over the years. It has now many facets. Recent international efforts have particularly led to four meanings of judicial independence.

a. *Substantive independence* which is also referred to as functional or decisional independence meaning the independence of judges to arrive at their decisions without submitting to any inside or outside pressures;

b. *Personal independence* meaning that judges are not dependent on governments in any way which might influence them in reaching at decisions in particular cases;

c. *Collective independence* of judges meaning institutional, administrative and financial independence of the Judiciary as a whole *vis-à-vis* other branches of the government namely the executive and the legislative; and

d. *Internal independence* meaning independence of a judge from his judicial superiors and colleagues. It refers to, in other words, independence of a judge or a judicial officer from any kind of order, indication or pressure from his judicial superiors and colleagues in deciding cases (Bari).

Independence of the Judiciary depends on certain conditions like mode of appointment of the judges, security of their tenure in the office and adequate remuneration and privileges. Satisfactory implementation of these conditions enables the Judiciary to perform its due role in the society thus inviting public confidence in it. "Independence of the Judiciary", it is maintained, "lends prestige to the office of a judge and inspires confidence in the general public" (Robson, 1971).

The Constitution of Bangladesh in its original form devised a scheme of completely independent Judiciary. Part VI of the Constitution deals with the Judiciary. Art. 7 provides that all powers in the Republic shall be effected only under and by authority of the Constitution. The responsibility of seeing that no functionary of the state oversteps the limit of his power is, of, necessity, on the Judiciary. "This", as quite rightly put by Mahmudul Islam, "does not render the Judiciary a superior organ of the state, it remains as a coordinate and co-equal organ with the other two organs of the state, though it has to perform the delicate task of ensuring compliance with the provisions of the Constitution by all the organs of the State (Islam, 1995).

Our Constitution vests the executive power of the Republic in the Prime Minister and the legislative power of the Republic in the parliament. But it is silent about the vesting of the judicial power of the Republic. The Constitution may omit any express provision conferring judicial power on the Judiciary. Even then the judicial power is exercisable by the Judiciary (All ER, 1976).

Article 95(1) of our constitution provided that "the Chief Justice shall be appointed by the President, and the other judges shall be appointed by the President after consultation with the Chief Justice." The Constitution (Fourth amendment) Act, 1975 took away the provision of consultation. As it stands now, "the Chief Justice and other judges shall be appointed by the President." The element of consultation in the selection of other judges was a major safeguard against political and expedient appointments.

The original Article 95(1) contained a constitutional acknowledgement of the role of the Chief Justice in the matter of the appointment of the Judges of the Supreme Court. It implied a tacit recognition of the premises that appointments to the highest Judiciary need to be above political considerations and that the Chief Justice being head of the Judiciary is the most competent person to opine who is most suitable for such appointment. Consultation with him was therefore, made a constitutional imperative. The withdrawal of consultation is tantamount to a negation of that premise. However, in spite of this constitutional change in 1974, all appointments as judges of the Supreme Court have been made in consultation with the Chief Justice. One departure was made in February, 1994 when the Government appointed 9 Additional Judges to the High Court Division without consultation with the Chief Justice. The Chief Justice objected to such a method of appointment. The executive government denied any constitutional requirement of consultation. It was pointed out from the Bar that the process of consultation has been followed consistently from the time of the British Rule even though there was no constitutional or legal requirement of consultation. Such consultation is absolutely necessary for the independence of the Judiciary which is one of the basic features of the Constitution. As such, the convention of consultation is a part of the constitutional law of the country (Islam, 1996)[1]. The government ultimately had to accept the contention of the Chief Justice and the Bar.

Constitutional Provision

In order to maintain independence of the Judges of the Supreme Court, the framers of the constitution not only provided under Art. 147 that the, remuneration, privileges and other terms and conditions of their service shall be not varied to their disadvantage during their term of office[2] but also expressly declared in Art. 94(4) that the Chief Justice and the other Judges of the Supreme Court shall be independent in the exercise of their judicial functions. "It therefore, naturally follows," concludes Mahmudul Islam, "that the conduct of the Judges of the Supreme Court can not be discussed by the executive government or by the members of the parliament. The immunity under Article 78 of the members of parliament in respect of what they say in parliament can not be construed as allowing them to make any statement or comment which may directly or indirectly undermine the independence of the Judges of the Supreme Court. Article 94(4) is an implied limitation on the freedom of speech of the members of the parliament" (42 DLR).

Along with the Supreme Court the subordinate courts of the country wield the judicial power of the Republic. Officers in the judicial service or magistrates exercising judicial functions never had any constitutional protection in so far as their security of tenure, salary and other privileges, superannuanation and control and discipline are concerned. Those were governed by statutory rules, but the original constitution bestowed upon the subordinate courts a status and entity which was aptly commensurate with their assigned role as the wielder of judicial power of the Republic. The original Art. 115 conferred the power of appointment of judicial officers and magistrates exercising judicial functions upon the President, but he had to appoint district judges on the recommendation of the Supreme Court and in the case of any other person, in accordance with rules made by him in that behalf after consulting the appropriate public service commission and the Supreme Court. The Original Art. 116 vested the control (including the power of posting, promotion and grant of leave) and discipline of persons employed in the judicial service and magistrates exercising judicial functions in the Supreme Court.

The Supreme Court had thus a demonstrably consultative role in the appointment of district judges and in framing rules for the appointment of other persons in the judicial service. After appointment, however, the Supreme Court controlled the career and discipline of judicial officers and magistrates exercising judicial functions. The constitutional provisions in themselves constituted a built-in safeguard for the independence of the lower Judiciary.

The interference with the original scheme came from the Fourth Amendment in 1975. Article 115 was substituted making appointment of judicial officers and magistrates an exclusive preserve of the President in accordance with rules made by him in that behalf. The Supreme Court lost its consultative role. Art. 116 was also substituted. The control and discipline of judicial officers and magistrates are now vested in the President. The Supreme Court lost all vestige of connection with the subordinate court. However, during the martial law regime in 1978, by Second Proclamation Order No. IV of 1978, an improvement was made. The control and discipline of judicial officers and magistrates continued to be vested in the President, but the power "shall be exercised by him in consultation with the Supreme Court" (Islam, 1996). Articles 115 and 116 remain in this substituted and changed form till today.

Ironically, the Constitution (Fourth Amendment) Act, 1975 which made a drastic inroad into the independence of subordinate courts introduced a novel article 116A in the Constitution, namely, "Subject to the Provisions of the Constitution, all persons employed in the judicial service and all magistrates shall be independent in the exercise of their judicial functions", which provision remains unchanged to date.

Independence of the Judiciary, therefore, as a principle of good governance, emanates from another fundamental principle that, in a democracy, all powers of government and administration including that of the Judiciary must be conducted in accordance with the law — and that every holder of public office is subject to the law.

The principle of 'government according to law' operates at two levels. First, at the level of constitutional law. In Bangladesh, like in many other countries, the constitution is placed in a position of supremacy over all other forms of law, including the laws made by the parliament itself. If there is any conflict between the terms of the Constitution and the contents of an Act or Ordinance, the courts must give priority to the Constitution.

The second level at which the principle 'government according to law' operates is that of administrative law. This branch of law applies where powers have been granted by legislation to local government, or to other public bodies whether to provide services needed for the benefit of the whole community or to place under public control (by means of regulation) economic activities of private persons or companies.

Just as legislation by Parliament must itself conform with the Constitution, so too what parliament has laid down must be observed by public authorities. In respect of public administration, it is the task of the courts to ensure that the terms of legislation are carried out and enforced by public bodies.

Accountable Government

Good governance undeniably cherishes an Accountable government. The principle that public affairs must be dealt with on the basis of legality applies in an important way to the day-to-day conduct of government and administration. At the heart of the 'rule of law' doctrine, the principle of legality is one of several principles which promote accountable government. For accountability to be achieved, a public agency must be accountable to other public bodies which are able to scrutinize that agency's work from an independent position.

What accountability requires, however, is that the powers given to government are neither absolute nor without limits. One of these limits on government is that these powers are exercised in accordance with principles of good administration. These principles require that public administration:

a. Must be honest and not corrupt,
b. Must be conducted to serve the public at large, not the private interests of those in the public service,
c. Must observe the rules of good financial practice,
d. Must be efficient, responsive to the needs of the public, and conducted without undue delay or inconvenience to citizens.[3]

Both internal and external systems of supervision and control are essential for enforcement of accountability. These include:

a. Financial audit e.g. by the Auditor General,
b. An ombudsman or a citizen's protector or a Presidential Commission of inquiry to investigate injustice and maladministration

and propose a remedy for the citizen whose complaint is justified,

c. Parliamentary supervision and control, for example in relation to delegated legislation, or by the use of the parliamentary standing committees,
d. Courts and specialized tribunals,
e. Human Rights Commissions, which may, depending on their mandate, investigate alleged violations of human rights and recommend appropriate remedies,
f. Integrity Commissions, whose mandate may be to maintain proper standards of public life and to enforce codes of conduct for politicians and administrations.

These forms of scrutiny serve two-broad purposes. First, they help to redress grievances of the public, by giving individual citizens a remedy for an injury done to them or by assisting them to obtain a remedy. Second, they provide a means of ensuring improvements in administration of the future.

Control by the Courts

In the process of protecting the rights of the people under lawful and just administration, the courts, exercising their powers, especially in administrative law, play a crucially important role. Their duty is to ensure adequate legal standards in the conduct of government. They operate by granting remedies to individuals and their power to do this can lead to lessons being drawn which assist in improving governance.

The means by which the courts perform this function range widely. The criminal law (including anti-corruption laws) enforces minimum standards of honesty in public administration and governance. In the civil courts, actions can be brought to enforce contracts entered into by governmental bodies, or to claim damages for injuries caused by the unlawful acts of public servants.

In many countries, individuals may exercise statutory rights of appeal against certain categories of administrative decision. Such appeals may go direct to the ordinary courts or they may go instead to tribunals, boards or committees established to hear particular types of appeals.

Judicial Review

Still another way of seeking redress is through what is known as 'Judicial review'. In the sense in which judicial review is understood in England, "it is the power of a Court to hold illegal and hence unenforceable any action by a public official or any judicial or quasi-judicial act or proceedings of Subordinate Courts and tribunals or other administrative bodies and to enforce their performance of statutory duty." The principle has been extended in written constitutions to cover the power of a court to declare a law and even a constitutional amendment unconstitutional on the ground of its inconsistency with or repugnance to the constitution. In later years, judicial review has come to embrace the power of a court to enforce the fundamental rights guaranteed by the constitution and also to declare a law or an official action to be invalid if it contravenes a fundamental right.

Case Law

One of the salutary doctrines recently evolved by the courts is that decisions of statutory authorities and pubic bodies must be informed by reason and must not have any element of arbitrariness. A fascinating body of case law has developed around the concept of reasonableness. By invoking the doctrine of reasonableness the courts have examined and in appropriate cases controlled the substance of an administrative decision and provided relief to the parties aggrieved by the decision.

Courts have also laid down important rules which must be observed by statutory authorities and bodies in arriving at their decisions. For example, the principle of *audi alteram partem* requires that a person must be given a fair hearing before passing an order or arriving at a decision which adversely affects the rights or legitimate expectations of that person. Another rule evolved by courts is *Nemo Judex in re sua:* No person should be a judge in his own case. Soli Sorabjee, the Attorney General for India states that "The rationale of these rules is to vouchsafe fairness to the affected person and this is sought to be achieved by casting an obligation on the statutory authorities to observe fair procedure and thus control the exercise of their power. ..." (Commonwealth Secretariat, 1996).

Another development in this direction is about the requirement to give reasons in support of a decision. Where reasons are required to be given by virtue of a statutory provision and the concerned authority fails to do so the order will be struck down for non-compliance with the statute. The interesting and vexed question is whether in the absence of a statutory provision it is obligatory upon an adjudicator or decision-maker to assign reasons for its decisions.

Different views have been expressed. The legal position in UK appears to be that whilst it is desirable that reasons should be given, the failure to do so would not by itself invalidate the decision in the absence of a statutory requirement. Lord Denning in Breen V. AEU emphasized that "the giving of reasons is one of the fundamentals of good administration (read 'good governance' - M.R.).

The Judicial attitude in the USA is of strict compliance with the obligation to give reasons and is exemplified in the celebrated dictum of Justice Cardozo in United States V. Chicago etc. Rly Co.:

> "We must know what a decision means before the duty becomes ours to say whether it is right or wrong." (Sorabjee, 1993)

In India, in the early years the traditional thinking prevailed and there was no recognition of any common law obligation to give reasons. In 1967, the Supreme Court reversed the trend in the leading, case of Bhogat Raja V. Union of India (AII ER, 1995).

Since then the obligation to give reasons has been finally established in Indian Jurisprudence and Courts have uniformly held that absence of reasons would invalidate the order. The Supreme Court of India referred to the right to reasons as the "third principle of natural justice" and concluded that the 'obligation to give reasons is demanded by our national sense of justice" (Sorabjee, 1993).

According to the Supreme Court of India absence of reasons leads to denial of justice because "the rule requiring reasons to be given in support of an order is, like the principle of audi alteram partem, a basic principle of natural justice which must inform every quasi-judicial process and this rule must be observed in its proper spirit and mere pretence of compliance with it would not satisfy the requirement of law" (AIR, 1967).

Inspired by the ideals of good governance and attained through the concept of independence of the Judiciary, separation of powers etc., developed democracies have evolved sophisticated systems of checking the whims and arbitrariness of both the executive and the legislative.

Judicial Accountability

But who controls the Judiciary? How can it be controlled? How to avert situations when the Judiciary exercising its immense powers in controlling and regulating the acts of other organs, does not itself become 'uncontrollable' and usurp to a great extent executive and legislative powers what is dubbed by many as 'judicial dictatorship'?[4] (Sorabjee, 1993). Good governance necessarily requires a Judiciary which is restrained in the exercise of its powers and is at the same time accountable.

Traditionally the Judiciary is the "least dangerous branch" having no powers of enforcement beyond that offered by the other branches of government. It is common knowledge that the effect of most court decisions can be nullified by subsequent legislation. Even decisions based on the Constitution can be nullified, albeit with great difficulty, by constitutional amendment (Sorabjee, 1993). Thus the Judiciary is dependent on a perception of legitimacy surrounding its decisions.

The Judiciary, under the common law system should always bear in mind that it is not free to impose its own version of social arrangements, instead it is constrained by four fundamental principles (AIR, 1976).

a. **Objectivity:** The courts derive their legitimacy in large measure from a perceived adherence to objectivity. That is, judges will be impartial and devoid of ties to disputants. Objectivity also requires that a court avoid ad hoc justice, that disputes be resolved not through the application of rules that are peculiar to the case at hand but according to universal rules applicable to all similarly situated cases.

b. **Support:** The universal rules applied by a court must be supported by general societal standards or the particular standards of the legal system.

   This is necessary so that claimants can utilize the courts to uphold a claim of a right based on existing standards. Changes in existing standards are the province of legislative bodies whose enactments govern the future and may be deliberately designed to alter existing standards.

c. **Replicability:** In a complex society, it is desirable that lawyers be able to apply their skills of judicial reasoning in order to predict the likely outcome of a particular dispute. This enables legal advice to substitute for litigation. Disputes can be settled without recourse to formal judicial proceedings and the costs they can incur. This facilitates transactions since the parties involved acting on "sound legal advice," can anticipate the likely outcome of any disputes arising out of the transaction.

d. **Responsiveness:** The courts are obligated to be responsive not to the citizenry at large but to the legal profession. Responsive to but not obliged to follow, briefs and oral arguments, materials in law reviews, treatises and monographs, decisions of sister courts, addresses by legal scholars and practicing lawyers at bar associations and other professional conferences.

To the extent that courts fail to adhere to these principles, they undermine a rational system of law and move in the direction of **crude** justice, and they erode the legitimacy of the judicial decision (Quirk, 1994).

Judicial Responsibility

Judicial accountability, therefore, becomes all but indispensable. The issue, therefore, is not as to whether there should be accountability, but as to the kind of accountability that is appropriate.

Professor Cappalletti constructed three models of judicial responsibility (Cappalletti). The first was a situation of dependency or subservience of the Judiciary, or the individual judge, in which a judicial decision could be overruled by the executive, or a judge could be dismissed for making an unacceptable decision. It was this kind or relationship between the king and the Judiciary that gave rise to some of the conflicts leading upto the English Act of settlement. The second was a model of autonomy in which the Judiciary was totally separated from government and society. The author contended that such a situation existed, for a time, in post-war Italy (Cappalletti). The third model was described as "responsive" or "consumer oriented," involving a balance between independence and accountability. This model, it was said, reflected the central ideal of a democratic system, "an ideal which frequently goes under the name of classes and balances — that power should never go uncontrolled and that even controlling power should not be irresponsible, that is, itself uncontrolled" (Abadinsky, 1993).

Accountability of the Judiciary presupposes integrity of the decision-making process. The method by which decisions are made must be, and be seen to be, just. The decision maker must be impartial, and the decision making process must be transparent and fair. This is because the acceptability of judicial-decision-making is essential to the stability of the community. Courts deal with the prosecution of offenders, and with the resolution of civil disputes between citizen and citizen, or between citizen and government. In the case of almost every judicial decision, there is at least one loser. Judicial decisions may provoke serious disagreement, but the peace and security of the community depend upon there being a general willingness to abide by them.

At the level of political philosophy, democracy demands that all forms of governmental institutions are, in an appropriate manner, and to a sufficient degree, responsible and ultimately answerable to the citizens.

The matter needs to be considered, not only in terms of position of individual judges, but also in terms of the courts of which they are members and of the Judiciary as a collective body or institution. "For courts, effectiveness includes dealing with the business of the court with due dispatch and by procedures which are fair and which serve the ends of justice, and which allow for reasonable access to the courts by citizens. For the Judiciary as an institution, effectiveness includes the maintenance of the rule of law and the preservation of a just society" (Gleason). Acknowledging the significance of judicial accountability, many authors differentiate among various kinds of accountability: adjudicative, administrative and institutional.

Evidently, there is a continuous tension between judicial independence and judicial accountability. Tensions between the three branches of government will certainly involve, amongst other things, demands for increased judicial accountability. Where those demands are considered rationally, attention will need to be directed to the objects of accountability. How will a particular proposal promote effective decision-making of an adjudicative or administrative kind? How will it affect the acceptability to the public of the judicial process or the court-system? How, for example, it will affect the impartiality of the judge and the judicial process? How does it relate to our political theories of what is constitutionally appropriate?

Responsive Accountability

The Judiciary's best answer to pressure for accountability involving control of the Judiciary lies in embracing that form of accountability which involves responsiveness. The community accepts, and insists upon, adjudicative independence, so long as judges function openly and explain their decisions. Similarly the community will allow, and come to demand, administrative independence, but only so long as judges function in that area with the same openness. It should never be forgotten that "it is a collective responsibility of the Judiciary to see that the community values judicial independence and, at the same time, to meet the legitimate expectation that judges, in appropriate ways, give an account of themselves" (Gleason).

And in so doing, the Judiciary, especially in Bangladesh, has to depart from some of its traditional concepts, notions and values, and rearm itself to meet the challenges of the present day society. The following provides a random sampling of some of these traditional behaviours and attitudes:

a. The Judiciary must not pretend that it is composed of infallible persons of unquestionable integrity — moral, financial or otherwise. When the Head of the State referring to findings to Transparency International makes a public statement regarding corrupt practices of some judges we need to make a pause, take a deep breath and probably embark on definite actions to identify corrupt judicial officers and judges and take legal actions against them. An offensive on the part of the Judiciary, Judicial Officer's Association or the Ministry of Law, Justice & Parliamentary Affairs directed against the corrupt practices of some NGOs is hardly a response deserving any support. Will it be inappropriate to ask: How many proceedings have been drawn against corrupt Judges or Judicial Officers even after such a blatant statement from the Head of the State who happened to be the Chief Justice of the Republic"?

b. The Judiciary must shift away from its obsession with the concept of "Contempt of Court." Criticism of the Judges, the Courts and the Judiciary is, as if, taboo in our country. Healthy criticism aimed at modification of the institution has to be permitted because it helps in the development of the institution. In E.M. Sonkaran Naamboodiripad Vss. T.N. Nambiar though it was argued that the statement made by the defendant at the press conference was aimed at modification of the institution, Indian Supreme Court rejected the argument. The defendant did not mention any particular case pending before the court or any particular judge, but only stated the defects in the then existing judicial system. Nonetheless, the statement was said to constitute contempt of court (AIR, 1970).

   In S.C. Tyagi Vss. N.C. Gupta, a publication stated that wealthy persons could secure favourable verdicts by means of money, poor persons with no money could not expect any justice and that there is a conspiracy between the judges and the lawyers; and so it was held to constitute contempt of court. Now if I say that the picture depicted in S.C. Tyagi case is a reflection of the prevailing situation in the judicial system of Bangladesh, am I to be prosecuted for contempt of court? Will that be fair? Will not such proceedings be a slap on the face of the majority opinion in the society? (Criminal Law Journal).

c. The Court must shift away from the self-imposed assumption that it is the ultimate interpreter of the constitution. Such an assumption "would make the Judiciary a despotic branch" — remarked Abraham Lincoln.

Lessons can be drawn from US history. In 1820, Congress enacted the Missouri Compromise prohibiting slavery in any State formed from the Louisiana Territory. In Dred Scott V. Sanfor, the Court ruled the Compromise unconstitutional holding that Congress could not ban slave holding in the territory because the owner of the slave had a property interest in the slave which was a right protected by the Fifth Amendment.

Lincoln did not accept the Courts power. He conceded that the court had the power to dispose of the particular case before it but denied it could fix the meaning of the Constitution: "If the policy of the Government upon vital questions affecting the whole people is to be irrevocably fixed by decisions of the Supreme Court the instant they are made in ordinary litigation between parties in personal actions, the people will have ceased to be their own rulers, having to that extent practically resigned their Government into the hands of that eminent Tribunal." Dred Scott, despite Lincoln's opinion, nevertheless fixed the meaning of the Constitution. It destroyed the existing compromise and prevented any future political compromise. A war and the Fourteenth Amendment were needed to get the Dred Scott decision out of the system (US, 1956).

d. The Judiciary and the Judges must break the invisible knot that ties it to the conservative past, and be more human rights oriented. We have witnessed a number of encouraging decisions in matters of Public Interest Litigation (PIL). Some specific disputes have also been decided in a manner that has been acclaimed by the human-rights activists and women groups. The Hefzur Rahman case is but one such example, when the High Court Division opined that maintenance to a Muslim divorced wife be paid until her death or remarriage. As the appeal is now being heard at the Appellate Division, it is ominous to hear the remarks of one judges to the extent that such payment of maintenance would encourage the practice of 'Live together ' in our society (DLR, 1995).

e. Elsewhere it was mentioned that "our judges have fallen prey to either a vague sense of pride, or to money or to politics." Sometimes the Judges are prone to give more weight to political considerations (thus expressing more sympathies with the opposition political parties/leaders) as if to demonstrate their independence of the Government. Meanwhile, objectivity in decision-making becomes the casualty.

f. When the Judges make the law, and at times they do make the law, they need constantly bear in mind the boundary separating legitimate judicial development of law from impermissible legislation. In the words of Justice Cardozo:

> "The judge, even when he is free, is not wholly free. He is not to innovate at pleasure. He is not a knight-errant roaming at will in pursuit of his own ideal of beauty or of goodness. He is to draw his inspiration from consecrated principles. He is not to yield to spasmodic sentiment, to vague and irregulated benevolence. He is to exercise a discretion informed by tradition, methodized by analogy, disciplined by system, and subordinated to 'the primordial necessity of order in the social life.' Wide enough in all conscience is the field of discretion that remains." (Cardozo, 1921)

Judges should bear in mind that under the facade of independence, they are continuously dependent on public interest and well-being.

Therefore, judicial activism in our context, should encompass not only widening of certain concepts of law and procedure, but also judicial intervention in areas which traditionally were considered to be beyond the jurisdiction and accepted norms of behaviour of a common-law judge. Consequently, it is not sufficient that the court, on the ground of procedural flaws, frees the loan-defaulters, or political leaders accused of corruption, of all charges. It is expected that the Court, for purpose of good and rule-of-law governance, should direct the law-enforcers or the prosecutors office or the Attorney General's Office on what requires to be done to bring such perpetrators under the ambit of law.

Thus, we see that the relation between good governance and Judiciary is very intricate. The flaws in the Judiciary that have been mentioned in this paper, need to be eradicated. This demands adequate investment in the Judiciary. Promotion of good governance contemplates assurance of freedoms and rights, social justice and obviously, economic justice. It must not be forgotten that proportion of investment in Judiciary determines the quality of governance. While the USA spends 12% of the national budget on Judiciary, the UK spends 12%, Singapore spends 6%, India, for example, spends only .75%. What is the corresponding figure for Bangladesh?

Good governance depends on good and efficient Judiciary. For that to attain, the nation must make due investments in the Judiciary.

Are the policy-makers prepared to make such investments? Let us not delay in answering this question.

Notes

1. Mahmudul Islam opines that "The fact that the provision of consultation was omitted by the Fourth Amendment is not of great significance as notwithstanding the amendment the process of consultation was continued and what is more important is that the Fourth Amendment in this regard affecting the independence of the Judiciary is of doubtful validity." op. cit., g at p.363.
2. Commissioner of Taxes V. Justice S. Ahmed 42 DLR (AD) 163 (Salary of the Supreme Court Judge is exempted from income tax and this position cannot be affected by notification issued under the Income Tax Act).
3. See *Commonwealth Secretariat, Good Government and Administrative Law.* An Introductory Guide, 1996, pp.3-5.
4. The term was coined by Professor William J. Quirk in *Judicial Dictatorship.* Society, Vol.31, No.2, Jan-Feb., 1994, pp.34-38.

References

1971 (1)All ER 1148, 1154.

1974 Cri. L.J. (Allahabad High Court) 428.

294 US 499, 510-11 (1935) Cited in Sorabjee, S., op. cit., p.283.

60 U.S. 393 (1856).

Abadinsky, Howard. *Law and Justice: An Introduction to the American Legal System*, Chicago, 1993, p.132.

AIR 1967 SC 1606.

AIR 1970 S.C. 2015.

Art. 116, Constitution of Bangladesh.

Bryce, James, *Modern Democracies*, 1929, p.384.

Cappalletti. Who Watches the Watchman, *American Journal of Comparative Law*, p.1.

Cappalletti, "Who Watches the Watchman?" 31 *American Journal of Comparative Law*, p.1.

Cardozo, B.N., *The Nature of the Judicial Process*, 1921, p.141.

Cited in Sorabjee, S., op. cit., p.285.

Gleeson, Murray, *Justice: Judicial Accountability*. In AIJA, Courts in a Representative Society, 1994, p.167.

Gleeson, Murray Justice, op cit., p.182.

Halim, M.A., *Constitution, Constitutional Law and Politics: Bangladesh Perspective*, Dhaka, 1998, p.298.

Hefzur Rahman Vs. Shamsun Nahar Begum 47 D.L.R. (1995) 54.

Hindus V. The Queen, (976) 1 All ER. 353.

Ibid., p.298.

Ibid.

Ibid., p.60.

Islam, Mahmudul, *Constitutional Law of Bangladesh*, BILIA, 1995, p.361.

Islam, Mahmudul, op. cit., p.365.

Meadison, *The Federalist*, No.51.

Posner, R.A., *The Federal Courts: Crisis and Reform*, Harvard Univ. Press, 1985, p.3.

Robson, W.A., *Justice and Administrative Law*, 1951, p.47.

See more in, Bari, Dr. M.E., *Importance of an Independent Judiciary in a Democratic State*, Dhaka Univ. Studies, Part F, Vol.IV, No.1, pp.1-11.

Siemens Ltd. V. Union of India AIR 1976 SC. 1785, 1789.

Sorabjee, S.J., *Administrative Law: The Judicial Control of Government*, Conference papers, 10th Commonwealth Law Conference, Cyprus, 1993, p.282.

GOVERNANCE AND ADMINISTRATION: CHALLENGE OF NEW MILLENNIUM

Mizanur Rahman Shelley

Introduction

From time immemorial, a sound system of Public Administration has been a propelling force of good governance. Contemporary discussions on good governance have been working to evolve a new concept of development underscoring the centrality of people in the development process. "We are talking, of course, about basic needs: food, safe water, the elimination of widespread poverty and human misery. But we are also talking about human dignity, security, a feeling of belonging (Cloves, 1994).

In recent times several countries of the South and some even in the North have witnessed virtual disintegration of their societies. Lacking good governance that builds lively linkages between the society and the state, these societies have virtually broken-up. Illustrations of this phenomenon are manifest in present day Somalia, Angola, Haiti, Southern Sudan and Yugoslavia.

The gap between state and society, widened by the absence of good governance pose grave threat to many more societies struggling for peace, harmony and development. For the individual, the state is like a house, it provides shelter, a structure. But society is the home that provides the satisfaction of human needs (Cloves, 1994). "The state can hold great power, but the threat results from the disintegration of the social fabric. The challenge we now face is, how can we maintain pluralistic societies without a descent into social disintegration? It is certainly possible (Cloves, 1994).

Good Governance

Good governance, thus is more than mere sound and efficient public administration. It is the process of building enduring and consistently used bridges between the state and the society at large through an effective and people-oriented mechanism of administration.

It is a process dedicated to the achievement of the three great objectives of humankind in the present day world enshrined in the proclamation of the social development summit 1995:

(a) alleviation of poverty, (b) creation of productive employment, and (c) social integration.

In the post cold war world of the late nineties it involves fabricating and running efficient governing system capable of answering the exacting demand of pluralistic and participatory representative democracy and open-market economy. This is a daunting task posing formidable challenges to all actors: The politicians, the intellectuals, the administrators, the businessmen, corporate managers, media men and women, social welfare activists and opinion leaders. Ensuring good governance requires consensus and teamwork on the part of the leading components of societies and the state.

Sea-changes that have and still are taking place on a global scale add urgent and compelling dimensions to the demands of good governance. These relate to the changes fostered by the expanding processes of globalization, regionalism and regional co-operation in political, economic and commercial spheres.

On another plane, the resurgence of the wave of democracy and pluralism is strengthening the march towards a civil society where well organized and strong groups and associations are becoming increasingly resilient and important in the polity.

In business the near global acceptance of free-enterprise and open-market economy has heralded a new age where the role of government in business and economy is reduced to core regulatory functions.

Political Process

As a process, politics comprises interest — articulation and interest — aggregation of specific groups contained in a politically organized society. These varied groups represent different social forces.

Economically viewed, the social forces can be classified as lower class, middle class and the rich upper class. They can be identified on the basis of their work also. For example, there are weavers, farmers, fishermen etc. Other professional groups such as teachers, businessmen, industrialists, students and industrial labourers also exist in society. They are featured by group coherence and community of purpose and interests. They have to articulate their group interests,. before trying to achieve them. Social forces in those societies which try to identify these interests, do so with the help of politicians or political party activists so that they can place these before the larger society. But merely bringing these to light is not enough.

Political process needs to resolve the conflict of articulated group interests and complete the process in interest aggregation. This is also the task of politicians, the job of the political parties. The party which is able to perform this job successfully is likely to become popular and ascends to power. The articulation and reconciliation of interests of various social forces result in the formulation of social will.

Social (General) Will

In a politically organized society (state) the social will is manifest in government's policy. Every state has an administration or civil service or bureaucracy. The job of the civil administration is to implement the social will, which becomes transformed into policy — a decision from the political to the administrative tier. Adding up everybody's will, may not result in the welfare of all. The famous French Philosopher Rousseau defined it as "Will of all." But this will of all may not really be beneficial for the entire society. The social will ought to be "general will" which can reflect the common aspirations and aims at the common good.

The formulation of national will is the final result of the political process. And once such a will is formulated, it becomes the responsibility of administration or bureaucracy to implement or realize it.

Civil Administration

Civil administration, often critically described as "Bureaucracy", is inevitable in any society or state, an inseparable part of an organized society. Policy decisions and guidelines can be taken by the politicians. Heads of government with their fellow Ministers can take such decisions. The mechanism for implementing these happens to be a disciplined, well-trained and well-organized machinery which is described as administration. Therefore, civil service or bureaucracy is an essential element for a society or state. Such mechanisms are not a feature of the states of modern day world alone. Ancient Egypt, the land of the Pharaohs, Pyramids and Sphinx also had a strong bureaucracy.

Administrative Heritage in South Asia

The South Asian sub-continent, of which Bangladesh is a part, has a rich and continuous heritage of well developed civil administration. Elaborate bureaucracies, at imperial, central and provincial levels were in existence under such emperors as Changragupta Murya (322 B.C.-298 B.C.), Priyadarshi Ashoka (269 B.C.-232 B.C.), Samudragupta (320 A.D.-380 A.D.) etc. Later, during Turkomen-Afghan (1205 A.D.-1526 A.D.) and Mughal Imperial rule (1526 A.D.-1858 A.D.).

Akbar's Revenue administration, developed to a high degree of excellence by his able Revenue Minister Todarmalh, (one of the "nine gems" of Akbar's fabled court), eventually formed the basis of British colonial Revenue Administration and still lives in major features of South Asian Revenue laws, rules, procedures and practices.

The British Raj in India introduced a strong Civil Administrative institution called the Indian Civil Service (ICS). A highly trained, elitist and efficient machinery directed towards preservation and sustenance of the British imperial mission in South Asia, it was described as the "steel frame of the British empire".

With the end of the British Raj in 1947 India and Pakistan emerged as independent states but continued largely to maintain the pre-1947 structures of administration in the sub-continent, along with the elite cadre of top civil service on the model of the erstwhile ICS.

Until 1947 in India the elite's were the ICS officers who manned the field posts of Sub-Divisional Officers-cum-Magistrates, Collectors-cum-District Magistrates and the staff positions of provincial

Secretaries and Chief Secretary. From 1947 to 1971 the elite in the bureaucracy were manifest in the members of the Civil Service of Pakistan (CSP). They held the top posts in sub-divisions, districts and the secretariat. There were other specialized elite services. These included the Pakistan Foreign Service, Police Service, Audit and Accounts, Taxation, Customs and Excise, Military Accounts, Secretariat and Postal Services etc. The elite in each segment constituted the faster moving stream of administrative officials. Elitism permeated every sub-sector.

The elite civil service displayed distinctive characteristic features related to recruitment, structure, stratification, training and ethos.

Ethos and Code of Conduct

In all training institutions including the Civil Service Academy in Lahore, the values of services and the appropriate code of conduct were drilled into the consciousness of the new recruits along with training for their specific jobs. The total impact of the training tended to stimulate and strengthen self-confidence of the trainees on the basis of competent elitism. The method and manner of selection and recruitment, the nature of training — all contributed to setting the new top civil servants as a group apart, members of an "exclusive and superior tribe", earmarked and trained to administer their society.

A code of service conduct elaborately drawn up for the high civil servants stressed neutrality, detachment and objectivity in their work. Political bias was forbidden. Dispensation of justice and rendering of service were required to be done without fear and favour. The code of conduct and rules and regulations made corruption forbidden and punishable.

Self-Perception and Others' Perception

The result of the rigorous and exclusive processes of selection, recruitment, training and drilling of ethos were to promote the top Civil and Foreign Service cadres' perception of themselves as elite. Such was the force of heritage and continuation of inertia of momentum of that heritage in the immediate, post-colonial period that others in the society also perceived them, however grudgingly, as elite who were regarded as "arrogant, domineering and yet competent in their jobs". These important segments of the society including politicians, businessmen, landed aristocracy, teachers and academicians seemed generally to share the perception of the elite civil services.

Together, this self and others' perceptions reinforced the self estimation of the top civil servants in the post-colonial society as "better" than their political masters and leaders of other sections of the society.

Political Perspective and Bureaucracy

The legend of the "organized, competent and well-trained" bureaucracy in uneasy partnership with politicians lacking comprehension of the administrative processes was further strengthened in Pakistan and Bangladesh as a result of frequent and long intrusion of the military into the political arena.

The post-colonial countries of the South Asian sub-continent began their existence as independent states with parliamentary democracy of the British model. In the years following independence, India by and large succeeded in maintaining parliamentary-cabinet type of government both at the federal and state-levels. Despite great and complicated problems of ethnic, linguistic, cultural, religious and caste-related cleavages, the leaders of the Indian polity succeeded in continuing democracy.

By contrast, in post-1947 Pakistan parliamentary democracy was discontinued till 1958 when the military directly intruded in politics. Overt or covert military rule continued until 1971 when Pakistan was dismembered and Bangladesh freed as a result of the War of Liberation.

Thus as a province of the post-Colonial State of Pakistan, East Bengal (Bangladesh from 1971) also began with a Parliamentary-Cabinet form of Government. Bangladesh was liberated in 1971. Parliamentary democracy was introduced under the constitution of 1972. Political happenings transformed a system during early 1975 into a Presidential and single party polity. History seemed to repeat itself in the mid seventies as the military intruded in politics. Subsequent developments included civilianization of military rule under military leaders-turned-politicians. The multi-party system was revived but the form of government remained Presidential with an overwhelmingly strong executive. The end of this order came in the winter of 1990 when strong and widespread popular upsurge resulted in the fall of the existing regime and eventually in the resurrection of Parliamentary Democracy in Bangladesh.

In the territory now comprising Bangladesh, the relationship between the political and bureaucratic levels received further jolts in post-'75 Bangladesh. The takeover of the government by military leaders generally tended to strengthen the hold and influence of bureaucracy *vis-à-vis* the politicians. In the political and administrative processes during the "pure" Martial Law periods (1958 to 1962 and 1982-1986 in Bangladesh) bureaucracies, both civil and military had complete and dominant sway.

Such developments in public administration had salutary impact on the style and content of governance. The administrative system, dominated by military and civil bureaucrats, tended to turn the government's role into that of stern headmaster. The tutorial rather than the participatory style of governments became the order of the day. Combined with the paternalistic tradition of elite civil and military administration the autocratic element in military-dominated personal rule contributed to the isolation of authority from the people, excessive centralization of decision-making at higher levels and restriction of widespread popular participation in governments. These tendencies were manifest in the rules of business in force since 1975.

Rules of Business and the Changing Politico-Socio-Economic Contexts

For smooth and effective decision-making in public administration, 'The Rules of Business' constitute an essential document in which the sensitive areas are delineated and procedures are laid down for the disposal of business at the levels of the Secretaries to the Government, Ministers, the Prime Minister and the President. Each position is well defined so that conflicts, confusion and collision in sensitive areas are avoided and responsibility and authority properly identified and fixed. These also relate to allocation of business, (Ministry-wise), inter-Ministerial coordination, etc.

The Rules of Business introduced in 1975 largely remained unchanged, not only until the formal and substantive end of the Presidential system in the autumn of 1991, but even after the institution of a Parliamentary-Cabinet type of Government with the Prime Minister as the Chief Executive.

The Rules of Business that governed business and decision-making procedures and processes in the public administration sector in Bangladesh (during 1991-1996) were basically designed to serve a Presidential system with authoritarian orientations. In this design, the President, as the Chief Executive and head of both the State and Government, ruled mainly with the assistance of permanent civil servants at the senior-most positions: usually the Secretaries and the heads of vital agencies such as the Inspector General of Police and the Directors-General of Intelligence Agencies (who also, often enjoy the rank, status, pay and privileges of Secretaries).

The Ministers, though elected members of the Parliament were merely "Advisers to the President", holding office both formally and substantively at "the pleasure of the President". In such a dispensation, the permanent secretaries, civil administrative officials, and not the Ministers, were Executive Heads and Principal Accounting Officers of the Ministries. The Ministers however, were required to supervise the work of the Secretaries serving under them.

The amendments in 1991 to Rules of Business replaced the "President" by the "Prime Minister", who then became the Chief Executive of the government, as the focal point of executive authority and power.

These also sought to modify the position of Ministers' relation to the secretaries by underscoring their positions as Supervisors of Ministries. The result was that so far as the Rules of Business were concerned, the earlier dispensation continued while the character of the entire politico-administrative system at the top required change, following the ascent into power of an elected representative Government committed to bring forth a Parliamentary-Cabinet system of governance.

The stress given by the BNP government (1991-1996) on the role of Ministers as Supervisors of their respective Secretaries did not seem to have adequately addressed the problem. As executive Head and Principal Accounting Officer of the Ministry, the Secretary continued to bear the full responsibility for decisions taken with all their legal and financial implications and consequences. The supervisory role given to the Minister of a Parliamentary-Cabinet type of government, if too forcefully exerted by the Minister who was, in most cases, a popularly elected member of the parliament and one of the leaders of the ruling party, tended to cause embarrassing and potentially conflictful situations between the Minister and the Secretary.

Decision-making became complicated and slow in such a situation. The Secretaries might, as long as they could, tactfully avoid dissent and consequent conflict with the Ministers who might attempt to dominate and get decisions they wanted whether or not these were legally defensible or financially justifiable.

The other scenario could be more dangerous to the maintenance and further development of healthy public administration. In this one, a domineering Minister, corrupt or not, with inadequate knowledge and experience of government rules, procedures and practices might team up with a pliant, weak or corrupt Secretary. Such a situation would tend to lead to distortion of administration by corruption or unhealthy politicization.

The Ministers, especially those with greater political strength and influence and initiative, tended to stress their overall supervisory role to dominate and direct those in administration who served under them, from Secretaries downwards. In such situations the Ministers virtually inclined to act as Executive Heads of their Ministries, though they did not have to take (under the then existing dispensation) the responsibilities either of the Executive Head or the Principal Accounting Officer — responsibilities which still technically and substantially remained with the Secretaries.

Suitable amendments to the Rules of Business was ostensibly high on the agenda in the beginning of the second phase of Parliamentary-Cabinet government in Bangladesh as it began in June 1996.

The Awami League Government amended the Rules of Business and made the Ministers executive head of their Ministries (1996).

The impact of this change is not still very clear as the Secretaries continue to be Principal Accounting Officers of the ministries. It is likely that the difficulties and complications of relationship between politicians and bureaucrats in the government would continue unless comprehensive changes are conceived, planned, designed and implemented in a holistic manner.

Putting Matters Right

Defining the appropriate roles of the political leaders and civil servants and technocrats in a democratic set up is a comprehensive and continuous exercise which is essential for good governance. Central to the resolution of dichotomy and conflict is a clear perception of the respective responsibilities and functions of the two. The politicians ideally, should be concerned with the political process alone. As has been noted, the process consists of interest articulation and interest aggregation of social groups and forces. It ends with the formulation of the political will which is then manifested in policy. The task of the administrator-civil servant or technocrat begins where the work of the politicians end. The job of the former is to implement policy and to carry on the day to day administration within the framework of that policy without undue interference from the political superiors. This clear cut division of responsibilities and functions need comprehension and understanding by concerned parties.

Authoritarian rule, whether backed by populist or military forces, not only diminished the vitality of a participative and popular polity but also reduced the independence, objectivity, neutrality and efficiency of the public sector administrative services. Administration tended to become almost the fifth wheel of the carriage of government as the authoritarian rulers, civilian or military, made administration defer to their wishes. Whatever organization and efficiency it had inherited were destroyed and dissipated over the years.

The administrative services in the public sector as these stand now, are, however, unable to meet the public demands for making timely, prompt, accurate and fair decisions and their effective implementation, on account of constraints created by the totality of politico-administrative context. The problems issuing from the lack of comprehension and commitment at the political level along with those resulting from weaknesses in the organization and structure of government, civil service management, performance and accountability, human resources development, administrative culture and norms, policy development and analysis capacity, administrative challenges arising from the evolving context of government, and problems of reform implementation, strategies, approaches and institutions — all complicate the process of decision-making and policy implementation in public sector administration.

The areas of problems are inter-related. Like other social processes and mechanisms, public administration has organic features; its varied and many parts are interlinked and pathology in one tends to cause pathology in the others. The total socio-economic and political context of a "less-developed" society generally, and those of its public administration, in particular, need to be taken into account in pinpointing the problems of the sector and finding their solution.

As already noted, on account of overhang of populist or military authoritarian rule such rational and holistic approach was largely absent in the conduct of affairs in this sphere. This resulted in run-away *ad hoqism* in matters of recruitment to public services and in the training, posting and promotion of administrative officials and functionaries in the Public Administration Sector. Reform efforts were also not immune from *ad hoq* steps. All these have led to further erosion of strength and vitality of Civil Administrative Services and consequent disorder and confusion.

Reform Efforts

There have been several attempts, sometime still-born, to design and effect reforms in the Civil Service and Public Administration sector. In most cases these were inspired by pressure of circumstances faced by successive regimes. The pressures were both internal and external. For instance, the internal tensions generated by the evolving and increasing conflict between the generalist and specialists in Public

Administration compelled governments in the late seventies and early eighties to change and modify the whole system by increasing the number of cadre services manifold to include and satisfy various specialized professional groups as physicians, engineers, agricultural technocrats, economists etc. Designed and implemented without holistic comprehension and plan, these changes did not substantially satisfy the concerned groups.

External pressures such as those generated by donors and popular dissatisfaction with public services also led to foreign assisted efforts at analysis of problems and recommendations for reforms in the public sector. These too were mostly patchy and disjointed. Practically all of these awaited meaningful examination, approval and implementation. Apart from the usual Pay and Services Commissions that each Government appoints on assumption of power the studies and reports in this regard are:

1. Public Administration Efficiency Study, November 1989 (funded by USAID).
2. Public Administration Sector Study in Bangladesh, July 1993 (funded by UNDP).
3. Towards Better Government in Bangladesh, September 1993 (the so called Four Secretaries Report, emerging in the wake of an orientation trip by Four Secretaries to UK (funded by the British ODA).
4. Administrative Reorganizing Committee 1993-1996, popularly known as Nurun Nabi Committee (after the name of the Chairman who was a former Secretary to the Government).

In addition, in 1997 the World Bank fielded a document called "Government that works". The present government set up a Public Administration Reform Commission in January 1997. It is yet to submit it's final report.

The recommendations and suggestions emerging from various earlier reports and studies were considered by concerned governments but only few of these were accepted and moves were made to implement them partially.

It is clear that reform, to be effective in this sector, will need more serious efforts at integrated planning and implementation addressing the problems of Civil Service and Public Administration as a whole. Piecemeal measures have not been and will not be of substantial use.

Politics and Administration: Emerging Demands

Present and emerging times in Bangladesh, as in other developing countries, demand that the political and administrative levels of the societies work in tandem. This is necessary not only to ensure meaningful socio-economic development but also to build a secure and harmonious society free from violence and terror — a society that can be created and sustained only by good governance. If the rule of law, justice and fairplay are to be secured in the society there must be understanding and co-operation between the political leaders and the administrative officials. In such a situation reforms in the public administration sector in tune with truly democratic and participative politics are indispensable.

The initiative will have to come from the political top. Political leaders both within the government and without, will need to pool all political, intellectual and technical resources available, to start working seriously to respond to the crying need.

Meeting Challenges

As noted at the outset, the present and evolving times pose manifold challenges to the business of administration for good governance. Democratizing society and emerging open-market economy demand that the government acts as facilitator and encourager rather than controller and regulator. It, therefore, needs to be slim, sharp and effective. Democracy as participatory polity needs leaner government and stronger civil society. Similarly, market friendly or open-market economy needs strong and a sound private sector taking over most of the economic and commercial functions that used to be managed by the government through state owned enterprises or laws, rules and regulations suitable only for socialist economies.

We are facing a fast changing scenario in which there is an increasing role of private associations, groups, private sector business and industry. All this has made the need for right-sizing the government compelling.

On another plane, globalization and expanding role of multilateral, regional, bilateral organizations and multi-national companies are making the need for a new professionalism among the members of civil administration urgent and unavoidable.

Global Village: International Dimension

Good governance has acquired a new dimension and meaning in a globalizing context in which the world is fast becoming a global village. Bangladesh, as part of the globalizing and modernizing world cannot afford to ignore the challenges of the new evolving situation. It is geographically and traditionally a part of South Asia. Culturally and economically it is South Asia's gateway and land-bridge to South East Asia. It is an active member of the United Nations and its specialized agencies such as the UNDP, UNESCO, UNICEF, FAO, ILO, WHO, etc. Bangladesh is also the pioneer member of the South Asian Association of Regional Co-operation (SAARC) and newly created BISTEC (Bangladesh, India, Sri-Lanka and Thailand Economic Co-operation) and D-8 (Bangladesh, Egypt, Indonesia, Iran, Malaysia, Nigeria, Pakistan and Turkey) sub-regional organizations. It is also an active member of multinational organizations like the World Bank and has active dealings with other multilaterals such as IMF, ADB etc. Its relationships with distant regional organizations such as the European Union is also vibrant in the economic development and commercial fields. It is also a member of the Commonwealth of Nations — an organization to which it is bound by historical links. Government and governance in Bangladesh is thus, inescapably acquiring an expanding international dimension. This is creating inevitable impact and demand on public administration which need to be effectively addressed.

New Challenges: Domestic Dimension

In order that good governance has desirable impact on the international dealing in our modernizing and globalizing times, it is necessary to design, build and operate a sound and healthy public administration within the nation. Bangladesh today needs, more than anything else, a modern, effective and vigorous system of public administration responsive to the needs of present and future times. Public administration reforms, therefore, constitute a top item in the national agenda of priorities.

As is well known, administrative reforms are wider than and different from civil service reform. Though the two are interrelated, administrative reforms address the entire range of issues related to administrative process.

Administrative reforms have close and integral relations with "rightsizing" the government which is a context-specific exercise and takes place in a definite socio-political and economic milieu. It also takes place in the context of historical evolution as do administrative reforms.

We have already briefly reviewed the patchy, disjointed and non-integrated public administration reform efforts mounted by successive governments.

The recommendations made by various Committees and Commissions and studies by experts have so far remained, largely unimplemented. Many of these especially those contained in the reports of the Public Administration Sector Study (July 1993) and the so-called Four Secretaries report entitled towards a "Better Government" (September 1993), have continuing relevance and value in the still unrealized process of securing an appropriate public administration that would contribute meaningfully to good governance in Bangladesh.

Public Administration Sector Study: Recommendations

The Public Administration Sector Study in Bangladesh, prepared by an independent team of experts sponsored by UNDP for the government of Bangladesh in 1993,[1] recommended overall reform of public administration particularly in the following areas:

- Performance and Accountability;
- Policy and Decision-Making;
- Organization and Structure;
- Civil Service Management;

- Human Resources Development and Training;
- Technological Infrastructure.

The recommendations of the Public Administration Sector Study, if accepted and implemented by the government can go a long way in reforming public administration in Bangladesh and making it more capable to secure good governance.

Some of the pragmatic recommendations of the report called "Towards A Better Government in Bangladesh" prepared by four Secretaries in September 1993,[2] are also relevant and useful in this context.

Towards A Better Government

The report suggested revamping the core government administrative system. Thus it recommended:

- Creation of Task Force by Ministry of Home for efficient police administration;
- Revival and strengthening of performance standard for Deputy Commissioners (chief civil functionary in the district);
- Initiation by other Ministries of measures to link performance with incentives;
- Installation of an Efficiency Unit in the cabinet division.

It also recommended improvement of efficiency through financial management.

The report further suggested measures for greater accountability and transparency in administration and suggested steps for strengthening human resources. The report especially focused on measures to combat corruption in the Public Administration Sector.

Concluding Remarks

Recent past shows a lot of efforts in studying the problems of public administration in relation to good governance and recommending clearcut measures in this regard. A National Public Administration Commission headed by a former civil servant is now seized with a new phase of the efforts. While all these are laudable ventures, time is fast running out as many relevant and useful recommendations lie unheeded and unimplemented. Bangladesh would do well to seriously examine and accept the implementable portions of the recommendations of the studies and exercises in the Public Administration Sector Reforms. This should be relatively easy as all of these harp on common themes: restructuring and rationalizing Public Administration and Civil Service, modernizing and training the public sector administrators in ways appropriate to a democratizing order accompanied by expanding open-market economy, creating strong and smooth understanding between the politicians and public sector administrators and strengthening transparency, accountability and performance of the core government systems.

Society in Bangladesh is in a flux. Profound and far-reaching changes are taking place for both good and bad in a changing milieu. The government has to be in step with the fast changes of the society so that it can foster that which is good and arrest that which is bad for the society. It needs to move in tandem with the society at large so that state and society harmonize their movements. A sound and competent public administration dedicated to and capable of good governance can alone secure this much needed-harmony.

Notes

1. For details see — "Report on Public Administration Sector Study in Bangladesh, UNDP, United Nations Department of Development Support and Management Services, July 1993.
2. For further details see — "Towards a Better Government in Bangladesh", — A report prepared by Mr. Ayubur Rahman, then Cabinet Secretary, Dr. AMM Shawkat Ali, then Secretary, Telephones & Telegraphs, Mr. Hasinur Rahman, then Secretary, Establishment and Dr. Kamal Siddiqui then Secretary, Prime Minister's office, September, 1993.

References

Cloves, Maksoud, Introduction, "Social Summit, Copenhagen — Expectations of the Global South", Conference Proceedings, Washington DC American University (Centre for the Study of the Global South, School of International Service), October 12-13, 1994, p.6.

Ibid.

Ibid., p.7.

Ibid., p.174.

Public Administration Sector Study, Bangladesh. Decision-Making: Issues, Problems and Recommendations. Dr. Mizanur Rahman Shelley, Dhaka. July 3, 1993, p.2.

The Last Two Million Years. London, New York: Readers Digest Association 1973, p.172.

The Men Who Ruled India: The Founders, the Guardians. (1965 Jonathan Cape).

The New Nation, March 13, 1993.

The Public Adm. Reform Commission, Dhaka 1998.

World Bank, Dhaka. *The Govt that Works*.

GOVERNANCE AND PUBLIC ADMINISTRATION

Robert LaPorte, Jr.

Introduction

Good governance, as defined within the context of a democratically based political system, was the public rationale for US involvement in three global conflicts in the 20th Century. US political leadership maintained that the reason for US involvement in World War I was to "make the world safe for democracy." The public goals enunciated by the US in World War II included the unconditional defeat of fascism in Germany, Italy and Japan and the triumph of democracy. The "Cold War" pitted the "Free World" (led by the United States) against Communism and the "Evil Empire" of the Union of Soviet Socialist Republics. The relationship of public administration to good governance had not been systematically explored, but it was assumed, in the United States, that good governance could only exist when good public administration was present.

Theoretical and Conceptual Aspects

In theory and in practice, governance and public administration are indelibly linked. However, the formal study of governance (as the study of political institutions) has a much longer history. In western civilization, its origins lie in ancient Greece and Greek political theory. Plato (428-348 BC) is credited with developing the concept of the "philosopher king" as the ideal ruler (Plato). The "father" of the comparative study of government, Aristotle (384-322 BC), was perhaps the first political theorist to deal with the term 'governance' when he classified political organizations by indicating the manner in which they were ruled — a kind of numerical count of rule by one (dictatorship), a few (autocracy), or many (democracy) (Sinclair, 1962).[1]

On the other hand, the study of public administration in Western world is of a more recent vintage. It was not until the 19th century that what might be termed modern civil services began to emerge. One of the first was the Indian Civil Service that came into being in the 1830s. However, it was not until the 1880s that articles in professional journals in the United States began to advocate the systematic study of public administration.

Theory and Concepts of Public Administration

With public administration, we have the case of practice preceding theoretical developments. In the 19th century, the first theories of public administration were espoused and these took the form of organization theory. The concerns of the classical theorists were simple: how to design public organizations that would be both efficient and economical. The two goals, efficiency and economy, captured what both theorists and practitioners desired at that time.

Woodrow Wilson (1856-1924) is credited with being the first US scholar to advocate the scientific study of public administration. Although not a theorist, Wilson maintained that changes in public administration in the United States had to be undertaken to improve the way government conduct the people's business.

The first major contribution to public organization theory was by the German scholar Max Weber (1864-1920), a contemporary of Woodrow Wilson. Based on his observations of the 19th Century Prussian state, he developed his famous ideal-type bureaucracy whose purpose was to pursue efficiency in the conduct of the business of the state (Weber, trans. Henderson and Parsons, 1947).

Both Wilson and Weber viewed public administration as a positive force in governance. The antithesis to Wislon and Weber, of course, was Karl Marx (1818-1883). With Friedrich Engels (1820-1895), he proclaimed that:

> The executive of the modern state is but a committee for managing the common affairs of the whole bourgeoisie. (Marx, 1848)

In his critique of Hegelian philosophy, Marx predicted the withering away of bureaucracy (actually, the absorption by society as a whole of bureaucracy) with the advent of the proletarian revolution (Mouzelis, 1968). To Marx, then, bureaucracy (and public administration by inference) was a negative force in governance.

By the end of the 20th century, some standard text book[2] defined public administration, as all processes, organizations, and individuals acting in official positions associated with carrying out laws and other rules adopted or issued by legislatures, executives, and courts (many activities are also concerned with formulation of these rules), and public management as an important component of public administration and public policy as the component that drives public administration (Gordon and Milakovich, 1998).

Regardless of the emphases that might be placed on these terms, public administration, public management and public policy are all tied inextricably to governance.

Concept of Governance

One of the first international organizations to use this term was the World Bank, which defined governance in the following fashion:

> Governance, in general, has three distinct aspects: (a) the form of a political regime (parliamentary or presidential, military or civilian, and authoritarian or democratic); (b) the processes by which authority is exercised in the management of a country's economic and social resources; and (c) the capacity of governments to design, formulate, and implement policies, and, in general, to discharge governmental functions. (World Bank, 1992)

Governance is explicitly and by consensus accepted to be the "process of managing public affairs (Boyer, 1990).[3] Under "governance" the question of how to manage public affairs becomes analytical rather than normative. There are, historically and theoretically, many kinds of governance: monarchies, aristocracies, oligarchies, despotisms, theocracies, single-party systems and military-rule, to indicate a few. These systems can be compared and evaluated on their performance in "managing public affairs" and on the fundamental values they exemplify and sustain in that management (LaPorte, 1995).

"Good governance" is an even more value-loaded term than governance. In late 19th and early 20th Century United States, good governance was thought to involve the separation of politics from administration and the improvement of the management of government institutions so as to better serve the people. But even the science of administration was seen as being subservient to the values of a particular society as expressed in its fundamental legal document.

Evolution of Public Administration

Public administration has evolved to include not only the concerns expressed in policy implementation and public management (see the definitions given above) but also to facilitate "participation," "transparency," "accountability," "rule of law," and "decentralization." Governments are being required not only to provide goods and services that are effective, efficient and economical in their delivery but also to monitor/regulate and/or support the delivery of goods and services provided by non-government organizations (the private and non-profit, or non-government sectors). Governments are encouraged to be "market friendly" in their relationships with their private sectors. This evolution of public administration (and governance) has led to the downsizing, restructuring and, in some cases, elimination of government operations.

The causes of this evolution over the past two decades are many and varied. In the United States, the restructuring and rethinking of governance and public administration resulted from citizen unhappiness with the *status quo*. Voters perceived that the costs of government outweighed the benefits received. In developing societies, the restructuring and rethinking of governance and public administration resulted, both internal and external pressures. Internally, although governance has changed in most developing societies over the past five decades, there is little perception of change on the part of citizens of these societies. Public administrative systems still contain elements of the colonial past. Although the "steel frames" of colonial-type administrative systems have become somewhat more "elastic" in Bangladesh, India, Pakistan and Sri Lanka, they are still quite rigid in overall form. Externally, the international assistance community has promoted economic liberalization and all that this term means and engenders. Whereas in the past donor agencies worked solely with government organizations (although they sometimes asked governments to create new ones for them to work with), donor agencies now seem to prefer working with non-government entities. Further, the rules of the game in terms of functioning effectively in the global economy have changed. We now have "marxist entrepreneurs" in the People's Republic of China and "state capitalists" in other East Asian countries. No longer are "developing" societies producers only of raw materials. They are now quite often the manufacturers and exporters of high technology products.

As a result of the above, by the 1990s, the role of public administration required rethinking. This rethinking as it may apply to Bangladesh is the subject of the following section.

Rethinking on Public Administration in Bangladesh

Both internal (developing societies) and external (the international development assistance community) demands for increased "participation," "transparency," "accountability," "rule of law," and "decentralization" have been the stimuli for rethinking the role of public administration in good governance globally and specifically in Bangladesh. These demands have reached such proportions that political leadership in developing societies must no longer ignore them. But what are the specific items that are part of the good governance and public administration agenda? For specifics, we will examine attempts at rethinking the role of public administration in Bangladesh.

A. Political Framework for Rethinking[4]

Each successive government in Bangladesh established administrative review bodies commissioned to recommend ways and means to make the public administrative system more productive and efficient. But to understand these proposed as well as realized reforms, they have to be placed in the broader context of the political developments which occurred from 1972 to the present. Political developments and changes and their impact on the public administrative system may be placed in the following four phases.

1. Civilian Political Control of the Civil and Military Bureaucracies (1972-75)

Initially after independence (1972-75), political leadership did not follow the administrative norm of appointing personnel on the basis of seniority and status. Senior level administrative positions traditionally held by members of the higher civil service were given to junior civil servants, non-civil service personnel or political activists. Examples of this included the appointment of an academician to the Planning Commission and the appointments of business executives and politicians to head nationalized industries, financial institutions (commercial banks and development finance institutions) and most major public enterprises. The desire of political leadership during this time period was to secure control over both the military and the civil service and, wherever possible, to use government employment to establish and maintain a support base for the government in power.

Political leadership also destabilized the public administrative system by not following the traditional method of recruitment and appointment to the civil service at the entry level through competitive examination. A large number of appointments were made on the basis of patronage. Rewards for political service greatly influenced appointment, placement and promotion decisions. Even when a more formalized system of recruitment and appointment was put in place, a system was developed whereby 40 per cent of the new appointees came from those selected on merit, 30 per cent entered from those in the "freedom fighter" category and 10 per cent were inducted into the civil service because of gender (in this case, women). Tension generated through these appointment practices continue to plague the civil service today.

2. Military Control of Political System and Civil Bureaucracy (1976-81)

Depoliticalization of society marked the beginning of the second phase (1976-81) of political change in Bangladesh. Civilian political leaders lost their pre-eminent position to the military and the military emerged as the major power broker in Bangladesh.

This phase is characterized by major structural changes in the administrative system. First, a unified civil service structure was created to replace the disjointed multiple layered structure of administration that Bangladesh had inherited at the time of independence. The main purpose of the new unified civil service structure was to eliminate the positional, status, and reward differentials between different service groups and levels. A "Senior Service Pool" was established to increase the probability of access to the highest administrative and managerial positions by different levels of service and types of services. Second, the two separate public service commissions, which during the Pakistan period recruited and examined candidates for central and provincial government service, and which immediately after the independence of Bangladesh dealt with the higher and the lower levels of management, were merged into one. One consequence of this merger was the regularization of recruitment through the standardization of examinations, although the quota system of the first phase (1972-75) remained in force. A third major structural change is seen in the attempt to strengthen the pre and in-service training of the civil service. Toward this goal, a number of training institutions were established or revived, renamed, and upgraded including the Administrative Staff College, the National Institute of Public Administration, the Civil Officers Training Academy and the Staff Training Institute.

As the administrative and economic system stabilized, the Government of Bangladesh directed its attention not to the civil service structure but to the broader issue of the appropriate unit of administration for national development. During the latter part of the first phase (1972-75), the Government attempted to increase the number of administrative units (districts) immediately below the centre government from 19 to 61 units. During the British Period in India, district administration was key to British control and consolidation of the empire; the reach of government in what was then East Bengal was limited (Govt. of Bengal, 1915).[5]

The chief executive officer of the district had three titles. In his capacity of District Magistrate, he was in charge of civil dispute resolution and law and order. In his capacity of Deputy Commissioner, he was in charge of all other related matters of administrations. Finally, in his capacity as Collector, he was in charge of revenue collection. This British "steel frame" was built around district administration and was thereby relatively free to circumvent political pressure. In the second phase (1976-81), an attempt was made to move the central focus of administration from the level of the district to the level of the individual village. The Gram Sarkar, with elected officials responsible for development activities and receiving support from the public administrative system, was supposed to reshape the local government administrative system and redefine the role of administration in development. This was a major initiative on the part of the government. However, while the intentions were good, and parts of the plan were implemented, the overthrow of the regime effectively ended this effort.

Beyond the structural changes mentioned above, the public administrative system was fairly stable even while internal infighting between different groups continued. An emerging source of tension in public personnel management, however, had developed with the placement of military personnel in senior administrative and managerial positions. Concerns no longer focused on the role of the civil administrative system in development but rather on the role of military in the management of development.

3. *Military-Civil Service Partnership (1983-89)*

Besides the operational reform issues of pay and incentives, status and privileges, and efficiency and effectiveness of the public administrative system, the even more important strategic questions continued to revolve around what should be the most appropriate unit of administration for management of development, what should be the scope of its responsibilities, and how should it be held accountable. The Government of this period started as a military regime but transformed itself to a semi-democracy. In this process it made a number of operational changes in the administrative system. First, it implemented a new national pay scale system that had only 20 scales instead of hundreds of different scales and its ratio differential was 1:12. Second, the regime informally changed the balance of power between the military and civil bureaucracy. There were more military personnel in the public and semi autonomous (public enterprise) sectors than at any other point of time; but more subtly, whereas in the past the position of deputy commissioner was equivalent to that of a full colonel in the army, the same position now became equivalent to that of a major. This change effectively lowered both the status and power of the deputy commissioner.

The most critical strategic change, however, took place in the relationship between the people and government administration. Using the slogan "let's take the government to the people" and the recommendation of the Committee for Administrative Reorganization/ Reform, a decision was made to upgrade the *thana* or the administrative level below the district and above the village and use that unit as the focal point of the administrative system. The purpose was to provide the unit with power, resources, and independent decision-making capabilities. Unlike most other reform recommendations, this particular recommendation was based, to some extent, on systematic research and analysis (Ali, Rahman and Das, 1983).[6] It was recommended that Bangladesh be divided into 460 *upazillas*, each with an elected head with members of the civil service reporting and accountable to the elected representative. Each *upazilla* was assigned a lump sum grant for development activities. The basic framework of the system was implemented during this phase. With the overthrow of the Ershad government, however, the *upazilla* system was scrapped and the new government (under Begum Khaleda Zia) began the process of developing its own local government system.

In summary, the third phase (1983-89) can be characterized as a period during which the military bureaucracy as the "senior partner" dominated the civilian bureaucracy and the two together dominated the political system. The role played by the civil service during this phase is most important to understand the mind-set of many senior civil servants.

4. *Elected Civilian Political System Control of the Civil and Military Bureaucracies (1991-present)*

Since 1991, we have witnessed the efforts of two elected governments. Each government has had its share of issues to deal with including working with a public administrative system which had spent most of its existence as a captive or partner with the military or an authoritarian leader. The transition from authoritarianism to democracy has been neither smooth nor swift.

After the initial state of euphoria that prevailed shortly after the 1991 elections, political crisis upon crisis emerged. By 1994, the major issues included: intransigence of both the ruling party (Bangladesh Nationalist Party) and the opposition (Awami League, Jatiya Party and Jamaat-e-Islami); the effects of an increase in Islamic fundamentalism on both politics and society; and campus violence (Hossain, 1995).[7]

By the end of 1995, the political impasse created by the opposition's boycott of the parliament continued. Elections held on February 15, 1996, were boycotted by the opposition.

The climax to this crisis came on March 25 "... when government officers and employees, including the senior-most secretaries, issued an ultimatum to the [Khaleda] government to resign and hold new elections or face an indefinite strike of all of the civil bureaucracy" (Kochanek, 1997). A Neutral Caretaker Government (NCG) was formed and new elections were held on June 12. These elections resulted in the Sheikh Hasina-led Awami League capturing a plurality (147) of the 300 seats in the National Assembly. The BNP won 116 seats and became the principal opposition party.

The Awami League's political honeymoon "... lasted a little over a year and came to an end in the closing months of 1997 as Bangladesh's opposition parties once again took to the streets in an effort to topple the regime" (Kochanek, 1998). Although the opposition's hartal tactics have not caused the government to resign, this political "noise" in the system remains unsettling. The economy began to recover in 1997 after two years of political turmoil. However, according to business supporters of the government, Bangladesh's growth potential is limited by "... bureaucratic red tape, a credit crunch, poor plan implementation, the slow pace of privatization, infrastructure bottlenecks, and the need for political stability" (Dhaka Courier, 1997).

B. Internal Attempts at Rethinking

As the previous section reveals, the rethinking of public administration's role and reform attempts have been a part of Bangladesh's history as an independent nation. This rethinking has been the product of internal as well as external dynamics. Two internal public administration reform efforts are worth commenting upon.

1. Martial Law Committee on Organizational Set-up (1982)

Appointed by President Ziaur Rahman and chaired by Brigadier Enamul Huq Khan, the Martial Law Committee on Organizational Set-up inventoried Government of Bangladesh organizations and published its findings and recommendations in three volumes in 1982. It detailed government organizational structure from the ministries through divisions, departments, directorates and sub-directorate units. The Committee's findings initiated the organogram process whereby each government unit developed and maintained an organization chart for its unit. Some redundant government units were abolished and others were merged and consolidated with units with similar purposes. No radical change was made in either the relationship between political leadership and the civil service or civil service structure. For the fist time, the Government of Bangladesh knew how many organizations it had and what these organizations were in terms of title and organizational content.

2. The Task Forces on Bangladesh Development Strategies for the 1990s

With the downfall of President Ershad, a group of citizens organized themselves into task forces and developed a series of development strategies for Bangladesh as it entered the decade of the 1990s. They published their findings and recommendations in a series of volumes (Sobhan, 1991).[8] The areas examined included decentralization, poverty alleviation and the role of Non-Government Organizations (NGOs). The impact of this effort seems to have been limited, although the Government of Bangladesh produced a report on local government (Ministry of LGRD&C, 1993).[9] which may have been derived in part from the decentralization focus of the task force.

C. External Attempts at Rethinking

There are four donor-sponsored and initiated reform studies which should be examined.

1. USAID, "Public Administration Efficiency"

This study, conducted during the Ershad Period, was completed in November, 1989. It provided a thorough analysis of Bangladesh public management and involved both international and local consultants. Bangladesh government officials also participated in the study and advised the study team. When field work for the United Nations Public Administration Sector Study was begun in February 1993, the Government of Bangladesh (GoB) had not taken any steps to implement any of the Public Administration Efficiency study's recommendations.

2. British ODA, "Reforms in Budgeting and Expenditure Control"

The British ODA-funded effort was formed in response to a request by the Government of Bangladesh to undertake an examination of its budgeting system and the means it employs to control expenditures. The starting point for this study was the report of the Committee on Reform on Budgeting and Expenditure Control (CORBEC). CORBEC was appointed after the crisis in 1989/90 when the Government of Bangladesh's recurrent budget was overshot and the GoB found itself in the position of not having any resources to contribute to the Annual Development Programme.

This report, submitted to the GOB in June 1993, offered 79 separate recommendations in three areas: (1) the allocation of resources; (2) the budget as a management tool; and (3) how to develop more effective means of controlling and monitoring public expenditures.

At the time the United Nations Public Administration Sector Study was completing its work in July 1993, the Government of Bangladesh had accepted the recommendations of the British consulting team and had begun to implement at least some of them.

3. *UNDESD/UNDP, "Public Administration Sector Study"*

The United Nations Public Administration Sector Study will be examined by analyzing (1) the study process and (2) the substance of the study. First, let us analyze the process.

On December 6, 1991, when power was transferred to the Chief Justice of the Supreme Court as Acting President, Bangladesh began making the transition from a authoritarian, presidential system of government to Westminster-type parliamentary democracy.

Following the elections of 1991 and the restoration of democracy in Bangladesh, the Government of Bangladesh in the personage of Begum Khaleda Zia reiterated the pledge to establish a transparent, and accountable system of public management. A major objective of the Fifth United Nations Development Programme Country Programme for Bangladesh, approved by the Government of Bangladesh and the Governing Council of the United Nations Development Programme, was "economic management and administrative restructuring" designed to assist the Government of Bangladesh to promote economic growth with equity. The Fifth Country Programme was approved in June, 1991.

A proposal was made by UNDP, Dhaka, to the Ministry of Establishment and the Planning Commission to field a Formulation Mission to develop the research design for the Pubic Administration Sector Study. This proposal was approved by government in September 1992.

The Formulation Mission was fielded in Bangladesh from October 8-29, 1992. This was a two member team from the Public Administration Branch of the United Nations Department of Development Support and Management Services (UNDDSMS). Based on interviews with more than 50 individuals in the public and private sectors of Bangladesh, the Mission developed the overall research design for the Study, the Terms of Reference for the local consultants and made initial contact with the local consultants.

As stated in the Formulation Mission Report (Rahman et al., 1992)[10] the purpose of the Study is:

> ... to assist the Government of Bangladesh in developing a performance-oriented neutral civil service and a responsive and

> accountable administrative system to support parliamentary democracy as well as sustainable development. The scope of the study will encompass the main administrative system, the civil service (personnel) system, and related topics.

After considerable thought and negotiation, eight local consultants were contracted to conduct the research.

The initial composition of the local consulting team included: four retired (at the level of Secretary) civil servants; one retired executive of a Bangladesh public enterprise; two university professors; and the director of a Bangladesh development research organization. Two additional researchers (who were serving civil servants) were provided by the Ministry of Establishment to work on the study in February, 1993.

The Terms of Reference for the local consultants stated that the Public Administration Sector Study would be distinct:

> ... from previous studies of the public administration sector in that the current study attempts to be comprehensive, to follow the suggestions of key Government officials, and to utilize credible and competent local consultants who are so much a part of the process that their participation will assist in the eventual acceptance and implementations of the final report ... this one will generate primary data, rather than overly rely on secondary sources. ["Public Administration Sector Study in Bangladesh: Formulation Mission Report."]

To assist the local consultants and to coordinate the total research efforts, a senior international consultant was fielded by UNDP, Dhaka and UNDDSMS, New York, for mid-February to mid-March, 1993.

The review by the Team and UNDP, Dhaka, and the final report were completed by the third week of July, 1993. Before officially submitting it to the Government of Bangladesh, the Study's findings and recommendations were to be reviewed by an Advisory Committee proposed by UNDDSMS/UNDP

One meeting between the Members and Advisors of the Public Administration Sector Team and the Advisory Committee took place. After the Minister of Establishment opened the meeting and asked the Team Leader to explain briefly the Study (but not the findings and recommendations), several of the senior civil servants present dominated the meeting, castigated the UNDDSMS/UNDP for undertaking such a study and maintained that the Government had never agreed to such a study and openly questioned the legitimacy of the Study. In essence, these senior civil servants condemned the Study before they had seen the findings and recommendations or examined the data upon which the findings and recommendations were based.

After the Final Report of the Study was submitted to the Government of Bangladesh (on or about July 31, 1993), copies of the Study were released to interested parties, the mass media as well as the public. Several news accounts reported on the Final Report and analyzed its contents. Since the areas examined in the Study were very topical, the newspaper coverage generated extensive discussion and debate in the newspapers.

The formulation Mission identified five key areas to be examined in the Study. These included: (1) organization and structure of government; (2) civil service management; (3) performance and accountability; (4) decision-making issues; and (5) human resources development, education and training. In addition, four contextual factors were also studied; (6) administrative culture and norms; (7) policy development and analysis capacity; (8) administrative challenges arising from the evolving context of government; and (9) reform implementation, strategies, approaches and institutions; (10) the role and status of women in government.

The completion of the Public Administration Sector Study was the catalyst for extensive public and private debate regarding which recommendations should be implemented and how they should be implemented. Since the submission of the Study Report in late July-early August 1993, close to a thousand copies of the Study Report have been distributed by UNDP/Dhaka to government officials, the mass media and the general public. No systematic analysis of the reactions of the mass media to the findings and recommendations of the Report has been undertaken but news coverage was intense.

4. *World Bank, "Public Sector Reform for Improved Economic Governance"*

This "rethinking" effort began in the spring of 1994 in support of revising the World Bank's Country Economic Memorandum for

Bangladesh. Among the areas and topics that were to be examined included: (1) the size, scope and resource use of Government; (2) a comparative analysis of efficient and inefficient public services; (3) the regulatory role of government; (4) a user survey of government provided services; (5) the rationale for government intervention; (6) the role of Non-Government Organizations; (7) local government; (8) policy and programme processes, improvements design to strengthen the capacity of government; (9) public enterprise reform; (10) civil service reform; and (11) judicial system reform. Both local and international consultants were to be used and field work was initially scheduled to be completed by late 1994. This condensed focus was to define the minimal role that government must play in Bangladesh.

The study was completed. A workshop involving the World Bank and Government of Bangladesh officials was held and some agreement was reached regarding what government would pursue in regard to the recommendations of this study.

D. Restructuring Public Administration

In essence, most of the critical rethinking regarding the role of public administration in good governance in Bangladesh has been done. Vast amount of both internal and external resources have been invested into rethinking the role of public administration in governance in Bangladesh. The resulting studies and reports provide a compelling agenda for the restructuring of public administration in Bangladesh.

Agenda for Restructuring

The logical next phase is for the present government to approach the restructuring of public administration in a non-partisan fashion. This phase would involve several steps, including:

1. a programme review of all existing central government functions for the purpose of determining which should be continued to be performed and which might be terminated;
2. an organizational review of all central government ministries, divisions, departments, wings, cells and autonomous bodies

from a zero-base budget perspective — each unit would have to justify its existence;

3. a systematic review of central government rules and regulations to update government manuals;
4. the restructuring of the civil service along the lines suggested in the Report on the Public Sector Administration Study, Dhaka: Public Administration Branch, United Nations Department of Development Support and Management Services, New York, July 1993;
5. the development of both internal and external government performance audit or evaluation units;
6. the development of a set of systematic data bases of government decision-making; and
7. the development of an up to date technical infrastructure for the central government.

A restructuring of governance and public administration must deal with a series of tensions and dissatisfactions that are present. For example, inter-service tensions:

> "... are a feature of relations between cadres, between different batches recruited into the civil service and between Class 1 officers and others. Survey results showed widespread dissatisfaction among both encadred and non-encadred civil servants with the cadre system based on rank-in-person. A move towards a rank-in-position system seems to be favoured by a majority of civil servants." (Rahman et al., 1992)

Dissatisfaction exists with the Annual Confidential Report system and the promotion and transfer systems were viewed by many Bangladesh Civil Service officers as unfair due to the absence of objective criteria. Senior government officials and executives in the private sector are dissatisfied with the performance of government, particularly in the implementation of policy and the present system of accountability (Rahman et al., 1992).

A restructuring of public administration along the lines indicated above would require great political will to accomplish even a fraction of what is proposed. There are vested interests in every area of the restructuring agenda. Nevertheless, these challenges must be met and actions must be taken to define and achieve good governance within the Bangladeshi context. The restructuring of public administration is essential to the creation of good governance in Bangladesh.

Notes

1. In fact, his study of governance was, in part, the result of his "consulting" work with the city-states of ancient Greece. According to T.A. Sinclair, Aristotle" ... is known to have written, probably with the aid of collaborators, historical and descriptive accounts of 158 city constitutions." See, T.A. Sinclair, 1962. Aristotle, *The Politics*, Baltimore: Penguin Books, p.18.
2. All three are drawn from George J. Gordon and Michael E. Milakovich, *Public Administration in America*, 6th Edition, New York: St. Martin's Press, 1998, p.493.
3. This is seen in a definition of governance by one political scientist: "We may define governance as the action of government plus its interaction with it nongovernment partners in the process of governing — in their collective relationship with the economy and public policy." William W. Boyer, "Political Science and the 21st Century: From Government to Governance," PS: Political Science & Politics 33:50-54, 1990, p.51.
4. This section is based on a paper written by Syedur Rahman entitled "Civil Service of Bangladesh: Is the System Still Colonial?", 1992. See also, Robert LaPorte, Jr., and Syedur Rahman, "Attempts to Improve the Governance of Bangladesh Through Public Administration Reform," a paper presented at the 23rd Annual Conference on South Asia. University of Wisconsin at Madison, Madison, Wisconsin, November 4, 1994.
5. A statement from the District Administration Committee Report of 1913-1914 summarized the administration of rural East Bengal during the British colonial period in the following fashion:

   ... The old Bengal, Bihar and Orissa Province was an impossible charge and the Eastern Districts [Bangladesh] were the least favoured portion thereof ... altogether this difficult country, the most thickly populated rural part of India was administratively starved.

   Source: Government of Bengal. (1915) District Administration Committee Report, 1913-1914, Calcutta: Bengal Secretariat Press, p.16. Cited in Badiur Rahman, "Local Level Planning in Bangladesh: Problems, Prospect and Dilemmas," A Background Concept Paper prepared for presentation in the discussion forum organized and sponsored jointly by United Nations Development Programme (UNDP) and Association of Development Agencies in Bangladesh (ADAB) and presented in August 1991 in Dhaka. The parenthesis around "Bangladesh" in the quotation were Badiur Rahman's.

6. See Shaikh Ali Maqsood, M. Saifur Rahman and Khsanda Mohan Das, *Decentralization and People's Participation in Bangladesh*, Dhaka: National Institute of Public Administration, 1983.
7. See Hossain, Golam, "Bangladesh in 1994: Democracy at Risk," *Asian Survey*, Vol.XXXV, No.2, (February 1995), pp.171-178.
8. See, Sobhan, Rehman, ed. (1991), *Report of the Task Forces on Bangladesh Development Strategies for the 1990s*. 4 volumes. Dhaka: University Press Limited.
9. See *Local Government Division*, (February 1993). New Local Government System in Bangladesh. Dhaka: Ministry of Local Government, Rural Development and Cooperatives, Government of Bangladesh, Dhaka.
10. See, Rahman, A.T.R. and Jeanne-Marie Col. *Public Administration Sector Study in Bangladesh: Formulation Mission Report*. Public Administration Branch, United Nations Department of Economic and Social Development, November 1992.

References

Dhaka Courier, May 9, 1997, pp.11-13, as cited in Stanley A. Kochanek, "Bangladesh in 1997," op. cit., p.139.

Ibid.

Kochanek, A., "Bangladesh in 1996: The 25th Year of Independence," *Asian Survey*, Vol.XXXVII, No.2 (February 1997), p.136.

Kochanek, Stanley A., "Bangladesh in 1997: The Honeymoon is Over," *Asian Survey*, Vol.XXXVIII, No.2, (February 1998), p.135.

Marx, Karl, *The Communist Manifesto*, 1848.

Mouzelis, Nicos P., *Organization and Bureaucracy: An Analysis of Modern Theories*, Chicago, Illinois: Aldine Publishing Company, 1968, pp.10-11.

Rahman, S. and Cole, J.M., Report on the Public Sector Administration Study, op. cit.

Robert LaPorte, Jr., and Wunsch, James S., *Democratic Governance: A Conceptual Base for United States Economic and Technical Assistance*, A Report submitted to the Center for Democracy and Governance, Global Bureau, US Agency for International Development, January 17, 1995.

The Republic by Plato.

Weber, Max, *The Theory of Social and Economic Organization*, translated by A. Henderson and T. Parsons, 1947.

World Bank, Governance and Development, Washington DC: The International Bank for Reconstruction and Development, April 1992, footnote 1, p.58.

GOVERNANCE AND ADMINISTRATION IN SRI LANKA

G.D. Cyril Gunapala

Introduction

At the time of independence, Sri Lanka was mainly an agricultural economy. Tea, rubber and coconut were the three main export crops which brought in the major share of foreign exchange. Domestic non-plantation sector mainly produced subsistence food crops of which rice was the most important.

Out of a total population of 7 million, more than half was dependent on agriculture for livelihood — contributing to 40 per cent of the national income in 1948.

During the five decades since independence, real income has increased by an annual rate of 4 per cent. Although additional employment opportunities were created, it was not sufficient to absorb all new entrants to the job market. The unemployment rate increased to 24 per cent in 1973, but declined to 10.2 per cent in 1997.

National reconstruction was at the top of the agenda of all the seven governments that came into power since 1948. Achieving a higher level of development in a situation of fluctuations in world trade, adverse effects of climatic changes and resolutions of insurgency and the ethnic conflict were the main issues confronting the governments during this period.

The provision of economic and social infrastructures and the educational and health facilities for the improvement of the living standards of the people formed the basics of the government policy. Except during a brief spell in the latter part of 1960s, government followed a policy of direct intervention in economic development. In the two decades beginning with 1960, the main emphasis was on redistribution of income. Despite differences in the political ideology of successive governments attempts were made towards the liberalization of the economy. Economic reforms were introduced from time to time with this objective in view.

During 1951-77 economic growth averaged 3.8 per cent. The highest growth was in the period 1966-70 when attempts were made to achieve partial economic liberalization. The real GDP grew at an average rate of 5.3 per cent during this period. From 1977 to 1988 the growth rate was 5 per cent and during 1989-93 it declined to 4.8 per cent. During the past four years it has registered a slight increase to a rate of 5.2 per cent creating a favourable climate for private investment. Private investment has increased from 11.4 per cent of the GDP during 1989-93 period to 18.9 per cent of the GDP during the last four years.

Certain specific policy initiatives taken during the 1956-59 period deserve special mention. Steps were taken to expand the role of the public sector in the economy. State Industrial Corporations Act was enacted in 1957 with a view to facilitating state-led industrial development. The cargo handling at the Port of Colombo were nationalized. The Paddy Lands Act was introduced in 1958 to give protection to the tenant farmers.

A ten year plan was prepared giving emphasis to the development of both agriculture and industry. However, due to resource constraints occasioned by declining export earnings, a more modest three year plan was adopted.

The period from 1977-1988 saw a complete turn around in the economic policies followed in the earlier years. Open and liberalized economic policies were introduced. Private sector-led development was relied on. An environment conducive to foreign and local investment with the objective of export-led growth was created. There was a progressive reduction in trade and exchange control and licensing. Privatization of government enterprises commenced and the policy of import substitution gave way to export-led growth.

Food subsidies were curtailed and targeted through a Food Stamps Scheme extended to the poor. The system of rice rationing was abolished. The Flour Price Scheme and the Fertilizer subsidy scheme were withdrawn. The rural credit programme expanded with the introduction of the new Comprehensive Rural Credit Scheme and several other medium and log term credit schemes aimed at small farmers and the self employed.

The post-1977 period was an era of economic liberalization policies which generated a wide range of new economic activities, resulting in an accumulation of profits in the upper income decile. The expansion of economic activities resulted in a higher rate of labour absorption and hence a rise in the wage level. However, domestic wage increases could not keep pace with the much higher earning of the business and entrepreneur class and the self employed where earnings came mainly in the form of profits. As a result relative share of the lower income groups decreased.

The trend of worsening economic inequality seems to have reversed in the 1990s, mainly due to the employment generation following relatively rapid economic growth. Since 1994, the government has offered incentives and improved the legal framework to encourage the development of the financial sector and the stock market. Containment of inflation was accepted as a major policy of the Government and a policy of reducing the fiscal deficit under a medium term (3 year) framework was adopted. The major welfare programme such as "Janasaviya" and "Food Stamp Scheme" were centralized under one poverty alleviation programme — "Samurdhi" to be extended to the whole island with improved targeting of benefits to the poor.

Since independence some headway has been made in industrial development. Policies however, changed from time to time according to the socio-political and economic ideologies of successive governments and the changes in international economic environment. During the period between 1960 and 1965 the emphasis was on import substition. Several institutions have been set up to assist the private sector industrialists. Three free trade zones have been established. Incentives have been offered to foreign entrepreneurs to invest in industrial ventures in Sri Lanka. The industrial sector has been diversified. With the promotion of export oriented industries the textile and apparel group has become the largest contributor to industrial production and a major foreign exchange earner.

The concept of welfare state has formed the basis of government policy in several important aspects of life e.g. education, health and social services. In fact Sri Lanka has a proud record of providing these facilities to the people since the winning of Independence despite some of the economic and financial constraints they had to face. Although Sri Lanka is a developing country with a low income, successive governments since independence have placed high priority on improvement of the quality of life of the people in terms of education, health, nutrition, housing and social amenities.

System of Government

With Independence, Ceylon (Sri Lanka) became a Dominion with the Governor General representing the British monarch as the Head of the state. A British type of parliamentary system with a bicameral legislature and a Cabinet form of government with the Prime Minister as the chief was established.

In 1972 Sri Lanka became a Republic with a President nominated by Parliament as the nominal head of state. The bicameral legislature was replaced by a unicameral legislature by the abolition of the Senate (Upper House). The House of Representatives became the National State Assembly. In 1978 the system was further modified by the institution of the executive President directly elected by people. The Sri Lanka Presidency exhibits some characteristics of the Presidential System operating in the USA and France. The present system is expected to provide greater political stability and facilitate the decision-making process to implement rapid economic reforms.

The first-past-the-post system that existed in Sri Lanka upto that time was replaced by a system of proportional representation. The political system at present is a multi-party system with two major parties in coalition with key minority parties holding power alternately.

Upto the year 1987, Sri Lanka had a highly centralized form of government. Consequent to the enactment of the Thirteenth Amendment in 1987, some of the powers exercised by the Central

Government were devolved to the newly established Provincial Councils. The devolution closely followed the Indian model grouping the powers in three lists viz. (1) Provincial Council List. (2) Reserved List and (3) Concurrent List. The devolution has two main objectives viz. taking government closer to the people and providing opportunities for people at lower spatial levels to play a more active role in the administration of their own areas. It was hoped that the second mentioned objective would contribute to the solution of the present ethnic problem.

Sri Lanka has a participatory democracy. The people have changed the Government seven times since 1948. Each time it was a democratic government and peaceful transfer of power took place without any political upheaval.

Governance

A publication bearing the title "Economic Progress of Independent Sri Lanka" compiled by the central bank on the occasion of the 50th Anniversary of Independence contains the following observation on the significance of "Governance": "After regaining independence, Sri Lanka had two major challenges, namely nation building and economic development. These two objectives were inter-dependent. The type of governance had a strong bearing on achieving these twin objectives. Governance broadly deals with the political process that attempts to raise the living standard of the people to create an environment for them to enjoy the benefits of freedom equally. The political philosophy and objectives of different governments, the economic policies, the internal and external security of the nation and the relationships with other nations are important aspects that shape the type of governance."

In this paper, an attempt has been made to discuss the manner in which the public service has been instrumental in bringing about the desired economic change, to see the extent it succeeded in its efforts and where it failed to achieve the objectives. The paper will also focus attention on the need for administrative reforms, particularly in the context of de-regulated and free market economy, role of the private sector, civil society and globalization of economic activities.

Sri Lanka inherited a well organized administrative structure. It was however, nurtured to perform certain functions of a regulatory nature, particularly the maintenance of law and order and collection of revenue. Obviously it was unsuited for the management of development.

Since independence the public service underwent a different type of experience as stated in Report 1 of the Administrative Reforms Committee (December, 1986). "The administrative system which is in operation in mid-eighties is quite different from what the country inherited in 1947. It has been heavily influenced by four decades of dynamic national politics: It has undergone the vicissitudes of two major changes of Constitution: it is manned and led by officials who are no longer from the colonial period, and it is directed by political elites with traditions significantly at variance with those of the immediate post-1947 period. It is therefore, appropriate that we ourselves accept responsibility for the situation that we find the administrative system today. This would be a fitting start to a process of administrative reform" (Report No. 1).

There are considerable demands made on the public service by the development policies and strategies government seeks to implement from time to time. With changes of governments or within the government itself the system has to cope with several changes in development policies, strategies and approaches. These changes in turn have demanded changes in attitudes, approaches and skills on the part of the Public Servants. But as Mohan Kaul has pointed out "within a few decades government services had acquired a reputation worldwide, with a few notable exceptions for poor products, services and attitudes" (Kaul).

Role of State in Development

In several countries of the world the role of the state in development has undergone a significant change. Sri Lanka is no exception. The change manifests itself in the following ways:

i. The preferred role of the government has changed from acting as the principal vehicle for socio economic development to that of guiding and facilitating that development.

ii. Economic liberalization, transfer of state owned enterprises to the private sector, reduction in the size of the state bureaucracies and contracting out work have been placed high on the agenda.

iii. Managerial focus has increasingly been directed away from formal process and towards results.

iv. Attempts are made to improve the context for private sector development. Traditionally government has been viewed as an obstacle to development. But now public private partnership is increasingly viewed as having a positive role to performance improvement.

v. Public sector has a significant role to play in ensuring the proper operation of market forces. In many countries a publicly provided infrastructure has been a foundation for the development of the private sector. In developing countries governments have to assume a major role particularly in the provision of necessary social, educational and economic support for the market.

It is appropriate to examine whether the different aspects of the change enumerated above have influenced the Sri Lankan context.

From 1950's onwards successive governments have formulated economic development plans with the twin objective of creating employment and reduction of inequality in income distribution. Though well formulated , these plans could not be implemented as scheduled due to a variety of the factors, non-availability of required capital and non existence of the appropriate manpower being the most important constraints.

Since Independence, all governments invested heavily in the provision of infrastructure and social services. Attempts were also made to achieve a certain level of economic development through direct intervention by initiating nationalized ventures.

A significant change took place in 1977. Far reaching policy reforms were introduced to shift the focus from inward looking development strategy to an outward economic strategy and free the economy from a series of controls. The two main political parties have come to accept the market oriented policies.

Sri Lanka has made significant advance towards privatization, which was announced as government policy in 1987. The objectives in view were the reduction of the burden on the national budget due to the operation of public enterprises and improvement of efficiency and profitability.

The shift from the state sector to the non-state sector reflect a basic change from the role of the bureaucracy — from that of the implementor, controller and doer to that of a planner, policy formulator, monitor and evaluator. But the attitudes and approaches of the bureaucracy remain unchanged causing a serious impediment to effective implementation of policies. Changing attitudes and approaches, in addition to the acquisition of new skills and techniques is urgently needed.

Public Service

The public service of Sri Lanka is widely considered to be over staffed and under compensated. Despite the shift towards the private sector, little headway has been made in the rationalization of staff. Redundancy itself causes several problems like low salary levels, failure to upgrade knowledge and skills of the employees and duplication of levels at which decisions are made. Certain steps have been taken by the government in recent years to orient the public service towards achievement of results. Performance appraisal of the public officers commencing with the assessment of the performance of officers at the highest levels is one such major effort.

Two years after the announcement that privatization was accepted as a major policy, a programme of rapid implementation was initiated. Some poorly performing industrial enterprises were selected for divesture. During the second stage some profit making enterprises were also transferred to the private sector. During the third stage commencing in 1994 several large public enterprises were included in the privatization programme.

The provision of the infrastructure, however, remains with the government. Even in this regard certain steps have been taken in the direction of deregulation, telecommunication services being one of the important areas. The challenge before the public service today is to work with the private sector and to provide regulatory frameworks supportive of competitive markets. The following passage from the World Development Report 1997 well illustrates the position in Sri Lanka prior to privatization. "... State and market remain fundamentally at odds. Private initiative is still held hostage to a legacy of antagonistic relations with the state. Rigid regulations inhibit private initiative and often buttressed by monopoly privileges, dominate economic terrain that could more fruitfully be given to a competitive market" (World Bank, 1997).

It is imperative that the public service should be alive to the changes that are rapidly brought about by the enhanced role of the private sector and the forces unleashed by a process of globalization. Competition within the economy is accompanied by forces of the international markets. It is necessary to acquire capacity to meet new challenges.

The society is becoming increasingly more educated and enlightened. People become more and more conscious of their rights, particularly to change government through the democratic process, as Sri Lankan society has demonstrated over the years. The awareness of the people of their rights and the obligations government is called upon to fulfil are further supported by the development of the civil society.

NGO Activities

In addition to the spread of literacy and education, access to media and the expansion of the number, the spatial spread of the activity range of Non Government Organizations have contributed to the new situation. There are currently some 30,000 NGOs including community organizations in Sri Lanka concerned with social welfare activities. The NGO movement has by now advanced to development activities, providing the citizens with training and identification of development needs at the grassroots level, in aggregating such needs at regional and national levels as well as planning and management of implementation.

The significance and growth of the NGOs and the rise in their capacity levels is a significant factor. They can be capable of.

participating with greater cost effectiveness in the delivery of public goods and services. This would help to reduce the size of, if not eliminate, public sector agencies in the same field of activity. They would also be effective instruments for public articulation of needs as well as for monitoring of administrative agencies at the local level. On both counts their presence should be a factor to be taken into account in the process of administrative reform and restructuring.

The increasing awareness of the people about the role expected of the government is clearly indicated in the mass media — the newspapers, the radio and television. It is encouraging to observe that the average citizens of the country are fully conscious of their rights in society, what is expected of the administration in the fulfillment of their needs and where the administrative machinery has failed in the delivery of goods and services.

A great need exists to bring the state closer to the people. Governments are more effective when they listen to businesses and citizens and work in partnership with them in deciding and implementing policy. When governments lack mechanisms to listen they are not responsible to people's interests, especially those of the minorities and the poor.

It is necessary to bring the voice of the poor and the marginalized groups into the centre of the policy-making process. Greater information and transparency are vital for informed public debate and for increasing popular trust and confidence in the state. The best established mechanism for giving citizens voice is the ballot. Since the winning of independence Sri Lanka used this as an effective means of transferring power from one party to another. As shown elsewhere Sri Lanka has maintained its basic democratic structure and values throughout the period.

Developing power at other spatial levels has been recognized as another effective way of securing greater participation of the people in government. This has been fully recognized in Sri Lanka where meaningful steps have already been taken towards devolution. The present policy declared by the government reflects a willingness of the people to devolve more power in order to secure national integration.

Reform of Public Service

At this stage it is relevant to examine how the public service in Sri Lanka should be reformed in order to meet the new challenges. As one expert has stated "... If anything it is now even clearer that the economic, political and social change process which Sri Lanka embarked on with considerable hope and enthusiasm will be unsustainable in the absence of effective reforms to the administrative system which underpins it. Hence, if Sri Lanka is to move consistently towards a market economy and a decentralized polity, the interrupted policy of administrative reforms must be resumed and implemented. If not, the continuing mismatch between the administrative system and the demands of the market economy and decentralized policy will lead to a systemic breakdown" (Wanasinghe, 1994).

Sri Lanka in fact embarked on a process of administrative reforms as early as 1986 with the constitution of a Presidential Administrative Reforms Committee (ARC). The then administrative system — designed, structured and staffed to serve the needs of a centralized polity directing an administered economy was proving it elf unable to cope with the emerging demands of a decentralized polity seeking to serve the needs of a market economy.

Though initiated with great enthusiasm the interest shown in the implementation of the recommendations was far below expectations. Only some of the recommendations were implemented and that too on an ad hoc basis, hence the statement that *"... the interrupted policy of administrative reforms must be resumed."*

In resuming the process of administrative reform as suggested, it is necessary to take a note of the changes which have occurred in Sri Lanka since the ARC completed its work in December 1987. In view of these changes it may be necessary to even modify some of the ARC recommendations.

Need for Effective Performance

The impediments that stand in the way of effective performance have been described at length by the ARC. For this reason some of the important factors are restated:

i. It is a generally accepted position that the public service is overstaffed. Not only are the officials and minor employees far in excess of the actual requirement, even the number of ministries are too many for a country of this size and population. Given that each ministerial position entails a bureaucratic retinue of secretaries, additional, senior assistant and assistant secretaries, private secretaries and co-ordination secretaries and security and minor staff it is an admittedly enormous burden on the state coffers. The size of the administrative system bears no relationship to the nature and size of the tasks which the different levels of government need really to perform, given the fact of devolution, deregulation and privatization.

ii. An administration with its focus on maintenance of law and order and collection of revenue is unsuited for management of development. It is ineffective in terms of the demands made on it, as the catalyst and facilitator of the development process.

iii. Public service is not highly motivated and adequately compensated. There is, as a result, a lack of leadership for the co-ordinated planning and execution of development programmes. The system lacks a management orientation at higher levels.

iv. The public service is subject to disproportionate levels of political considerations in its personnel management and decision-making lacks co-ordination due to the absence of central policy-making organs.

v. Procedural deficiencies embracing two main areas, viz.,

   a. Financial management and related procedures and problems,

   b. Work systems in government offices.

Some Current Issues

Certain political developments in the country having a bearing on the problems of governance deserve special mention at this point. One of the major issues facing the people in the ethnic conflict in the North and East of Sri Lanka. Civil riots broke out in 1983 after killing of 13 policemen in Jaffna by terrorists. The ethnic conflict which had complicated the problems of governance since independence took a serious term.

Presently the government of Sri Lanka is burdened with the enormous cost of continuing a war in the North and the East. Much of the effort that could have been directed towards economic development has to be diverted to the war effort.

The major issues raised by the present government at the elections four years ago were the restoration of peace, reduction of the cost of living, halting the deterioration of human rights, removing the widespread insecurity, need to eliminate corruption and erection of a sense of transparency in government. In other words good governance was promised.

The negotiations carried on with the LTTE, the most powerful Tamil separatist militant group did not bring about the desired results. After 1994 there has been a several political consensus among major parties to arrive at a political solution acceptable to all communities. The government has put forward a comprehensive set of proposals to promote ethnic harmony through a greater devolution of power by constitutional reforms.

References

Activating the Administrative Reform Process in Sri Lanka. Shelton Wanasinghe, Institute of Policy Studies, July 1994.

Economic Progress of Independent Sri Lanka (1948-1998), Central Bank of Sri Lanka.

Enhancing the Effectiveness of Public Policy Management: The Challenges of Sri Lanka, Shelton Wanasinghe and Harshitha Gunasekera, Institute of Policy Studies, Oct. 1996.

From Problem to Solution: Commonwealth Strategies for Reform. Mohan Kaul, Commonwealth Secretariat.

Reform of the Personnel System, Report No. 4 of the Administrative Reforms Committee, Sept. 1987.

The Shifting Boundaries of Government. Sanford Boins, March 1998.

The World Bank, The World Development Report, 1977.

MALAYSIAN EXPERIENCE WITH DEVELOPMENT ADMINISTRATION

Norma Mansor

Introduction

Malaysia's economic development is characterized by strong state planning and public sector's involvement in the economy. Pragmatic in its approach, the Malaysian government designed economic and industrial policies to incorporate both internal and external economic conditions. Internally it has to deal with disparity in equity, income and economic opportunities, and the feudal nature of the governmental system. The external forces faced such as prices of commodities, economic grouping and worldwide recession are inevitable due to the openness of the economy and the dependency nature of trade and investment.

Phases of Economic Development

Pre-1970 Period

The political independence in 1957 was followed by an increase in awareness among the majority of the population. The people expected more from the indigenous government and aspired for better economic condition. The government continued with a laissez faire approach with import-substituting industrialization, some agricultural diversification and greater rural development efforts. The role of the public sector was limited to providing the industrial, commercial and agricultural infrastructures of the economy.

The desire to be economically independent could be seen in the efforts to reduce the degree of dependence of the economy on external trade, and a move to a more inward looking approach. This import-substitution strategy seemed little better in the face of protectionism generally in the industrialized world for it seemed to infringe the principle of comparative advantage (Keizai Doyukai, 1966).

Crosson (1966) pointed out that for the entire period 1955-1964, gross investment averaged 15.2 per cent of GNP while domestic savings average was 17.0 per cent. Thus, for the period as a whole domestic savings were more than adequate to finance the nation's investment requirements. But during 1962-1964, the first three years of the Second Five Year Plan, investment averaged 18.8 per cent of GNP, while domestic savings averaged only 16.6 per cent. Most of the requirements for net capital inflow in the later period resulted not from a decline in the domestic savings rate but from a sharp increase in the rate of domestic investment.

Foreign investment was very important because of lack of indigenous capital. The government thus offered a number of financial and technical incentives to promote this programme. The Pioneer Industries Ordinance was enacted in 1958 to attract more foreign capital and technical resources to the manufacturing industries. Pioneer Status was granted to foreign and local firms, which exempted them from paying corporate income tax for specified periods, depending on the amount of capitalization. Also, although the federal government still has not aggressively used tariff protection against foreign competition at home, an increasing number of external protective tariffs were installed to effectively encourage a rapid growth in the manufacturing sector (Keizai Doyukai, 1966).

The government adopted a more positive style of investment finance; public investment was increased in the Second Five Year Plan to quicken the pace of industrialization. Furthermore, the federal and state governments, recognizing the importance of providing industrial estates at low cost with all the facilities available to intending manufacturers, developed or planned a number of such estates in Petaling Jaya, Tasek Industrial Estate

(378 acres) and others at Butterworth, Johor Bharu, Taiping and Seremban.

The efforts to diversify the economy were not confined only to the industrial sector but also affected the agricultural sector. During this time, the second front of the diversification strategy was to encourage the growth of other crops particularly oil palm. The share of natural rubber in the export products of Peninsular Malaysia fell from 62.6 per cent to 39.7 per cent and that of oil palm increased from 2.1 per cent to 5.9 per cent between 1960 and 1970, as a direct result of the dramatic expansion of oil palm production.

The third distinctive feature of economic development in this phase is the emphasis on growth using specifically the Harrod-Domar model whereby the rate of investment required to attain targeted rates of growth of income and employment was estimated. This was adopted with the presumption of the trickle down effect. If the GNP and per capita income was the target, this approach was successful in achieving growth in per capita income and GNP but the trickle down effect was not realized.

Development policies that overemphasize growth in GNP but neglect the distributional problems are principally responsible for the inequality among sectors. The rural sector is associated with agriculture and the urban sector is mostly involved in industries. Rural poverty has implications, especially related to racial and regional problems. Rural poverty was found largely among Malays and other indigenous people, commonly referred to as 'bumiputra', and in regions with heavy bumiputra concentrations.

Apart from income inequality, there was inequalities in the employment pattern, the state of regional development and the ownership of wealth. The Malays in 1957 accounted for only 21 per cent of the total urban population while the corresponding figure for the rural area was 60 per cent. Malay employment was far less modernized than the other ethnic groups; 69 per cent of employed Malay males and 88 per cent of the females worked in agriculture while non-agricultural employment for Malays was concentrated in administrative services.

The inequality among the regions was also evident. The state of Selangor had per capita GDP almost 63 per cent higher than the average for Malaysia as a whole while Kedah, Perlis, Trengganu and Kelantan had per capita GDP less than two-thirds of the Malaysian average.

Although a major source of concern has been the persistence of rural poverty, nevertheless, the rural population in Malaysia as a whole, has a standard of living markedly superior to that in most countries of Asia (Young, 1980). Rural residents enjoy a relatively large and growing range of social services, and many have been given improved income opportunities through agricultural development programmes. Hunger is almost non-existent, and malnutrition is not a national problem. However, there is considerable incidence of poverty when measured by incomes within both rural and urban sectors (Hon, 1978).

Unemployment was another problem faced by the government in this phase. There was a high rate of unemployment (approximately 7 per cent) and underemployment. During the First Malaysia Plan period (1966-70), the annual growth rate of the Malaysian labour force of 3 per cent outstripped that of employment rate of 2.8 per cent. As a result, unemployment rose from 6.5 per cent of the labour force at the start of the period, to about 8 per cent at its close in 1970.

During the Second Malaysia Plan period (1971-75) the labour force was expected to grow at 3.2 per cent and this placed an additional burden on the Malaysian capacity to create jobs. The plan envisaged a rapid economic growth through the policies of promoting the growth of the private sector and expansion of the public sector.

Underemployment was also an acute socio-economic problem. Large numbers of workers were in low productivity jobs, with both low intensity of work as well as low incomes. For example, in 1967 about 11 per cent of the workers classified as "employed' were reported to be working less than 25 hours per week. Again, this involves sectorial inequality as these underemployed groups were in predominantly rural occupations such as fishing and single crop rice cultivation and in the service sector.

Although the post-colonial government had clear objectives in its policies and programmes, the approach was basically conservative and cautious. The free market economy and growth strategy were impressive in some terms; the rise in per capita income: rising social indicators of school and the increasing ratio of doctors, clinics and hospital beds per thousand of population and life expectancy at birth. But the policies were very slow in addressing the racial economic imbalance in terms of income distribution, employment and ownership and control of wealth.

The New Economic Policy (1971-1990)

The ethnic violence in 1969 apparently brought to light some of the underlying issues and characteristics of socio-economic development in the 1960's. It was with these considerations in mind that the Government introduced the New Economic Policy (NEP), which represented a new strategy whereby national priorities were reassessed. In essence, the strategy was incorporated in the objectives of the Second Malaysian Plan (1971-75), the Third Malaysian Plan (1976-80), and the Fourth Malaysian Plan (1981-85) and the Fifth Malaysian Plan (1986-90).

The twin objectives of the NEP were to:

i. reduce and eventually eradicate poverty, by raising income levels and increasing employment opportunities for all Malaysians, irrespective of race.

ii. accelerate the process of restructuring Malaysian society and to correct economic imbalance, so as to reduce and eventually eliminate the ethnic division of labour.

The Second Malaysian Plan (1971-75) sought to achieve these objectives by raising income levels; increasing employment opportunities through the modernization of the rural economy; a rapid and balanced growth of urban activities; the creation of a Malay industrial entrepreneurial community so that the Malays and other indigenous groups would become full partners in all aspects of the economic life of the country. More specifically it was targeted that by the year 1990 at least 30 per cent of ownership and employment in all sectors of the corporate economy would be shared by the 'bumiputra' (indigenous people).

This attempt to promote development, although with significant reliance on the private sector, gave a greater role to the public sector in the economy. Public agencies were established in the 1970's, which now operate in almost every sector, usually in collaboration with the private sector.

Several public enterprises were set-up in the manufacturing and the less participated commercial sector, such as MARA, UDA, SEDC's, Development Bank, Bank Bumiputra and other public corporations.

The government started to look outward to foreign capital. These foreign direct investments were mainly export-oriented and also labour intensive industries. Export-oriented industries were promoted from 1970 onwards with incentives such as the Pioneer Industry Incentives (PII) which grants tax holidays of between two to five years to firms, depending on the value of their fixed capital investment, plus additional tax relief of one year each if they are established in a development area manufacturing priority products and have specified percentages of domestic content in their products.

The early eighties saw effort by the Malaysian government to plan for another stage of development by investing in heavy industries and high technology sector. The Off-Budget Agencies (OBAs) also known as Non-Financial Public Enterprise (NFPE) were formed. Government investment through OBAs are mainly in high technology industries. The support for high technology was a preparation for the next step towards industrialization and a long term strategy for the country.

Education was one of the main item during this period. It has always been the third largest, bigger than defence and security (first being rural development, second transport and communication) item in the development budget. In the Second Malaysian Plan, education and training was at RM 0.537 million which is about 63 per cent higher than the actual development spending during the last five years. The emphasis, however, was on providing basic education and upper secondary, post secondary and higher education levels.

However, during this decade national integration and national unity was central to government policy. Therefore, education policy shared the objectives of the New Economic Policy of improving the education level among the indigenous people without paying serious attention to their specialization. As a result, many students tend to pursue liberal arts degree. During the 1970's there was an oversupply of these graduates. Those who were not absorbed by the public sector remained unemployed.

Post-1985 Period

In mid-80s it was widely believed that there was a need for the government to revamp its economic policies. There was strong pressure for liberalization and deregulation of the economy. It was also required by the International Monetary Fund (IMF) under the Structural Adjustment Programme.

The government started the structural adjustment process by keeping NEP at abeyance. To encourage private investment and restore investor confidence some regulations were relaxed.

Fiscal Policy

The economic problems brought about the shift in government stance on public expenditure. The role of the public sector in the economy started to further deteriorate. The government announced a fiscal policy that sent out positive signals to the private sector. Increase in public expenditure (for both development and operations) was controlled. This trend was further continued in the Fifth Malaysian Development Plan (1985-90) whereby allocation for public expenditure was reduced from RM 78 billion to about RM 55 billion.

Among other things, the new fiscal policy reflected the reduced role of the government, moving away from the direct intervention practised in the 1970's, towards taking a guiding and facilitating role, with more reliance on the private sector to take the lead.

The government also made a serious effort to cut external borrowings. This was done through strict monitoring on the borrowings of the NFPE's and the close supervision on their performance and management. In addition, the government made prepayments of external loans in order to reduce the nation's exposures to exchange rates especially after the effects of the Plaza Accord of 1985.

Privatization

A policy of privatization of public enterprises was initiated to reduce the government's direct involvement in commercially related activities, and thus lessen competition with the private sector in various activities. The policy was also aimed at relieving the financial and administrative burden of the government.

There have been criticisms on the implementation of the policy and lack of control and monitoring of the privatized entities. In addition, there have been allegations that divestment of government interests favoured certain groups and of the monopolistic nature of the projects.

The Impact

The above measures had significant impact on the economy. The GDP expanded by 9 per cent in 1988 and 9.7 per cent in 1990. From 1988 onwards, the economy recorded an 8-9 per cent growth per annum. In 1993 the manufacturing sector expanded to 30.1 per cent of the GDP compared with 19.7 per cent in 1985. Conversely, the agricultural sector shrunk to 5.8 per cent from 20.9 per cent. Unemployment declined to below 3 per cent of labour force in 1993.

The all-out restoration and effort to lure foreign investment had prompted the loosening of the administrative procedures and regulations. In addition, the administrative procedures for investment applications were simplified. The Malaysian Industrial and Development Authority (MIDA) introduced the 'one-stop service' so that an investor does not have to obtain approvals of other government departments.

Before the 1980s little attention was given to Small Medium Industries (SMIs) which as demonstrated by Japan, Taiwan and Singapore, are an important component in the industrial linkages. Since the Fourth, and especially Seventh Malaysian Plan (1996-2000) SMIs were given special attention. Provision of soft loans and training programmes are among the supports given to this sector.

Overview of Policy-Making

Policy-making in Malaysia is very systematic. The formulation of the Five Year Development Plans demonstrated a comprehensive and methodical process. The history of development planning in Malaysia started with the preparation of the First Five Year Development Plan covering the period 1956-60. The plan was prepared by a small Economic Secretariat in the Prime Minister's Department. The Economic Planning Unit (EPU) was established in 1961 as the central staff unit of the government for planning national economic development.

The formal planning process is a two-way interactive process between the economic Planning Unit (EPU) outlining the macro parameters on the one hand and the line ministries and agencies on the other, which indicate the top-down and bottom-up process. Development planning is very much a Federal affairs. The states act mainly as implementing agencies.

The other agencies involved at the Federal level in the National Development Planning Committee (NDPC) are, the Implementation Co-ordination Unit (ICU), Malaysian Administrative and Modernization Planning Unit (MAMPU) and the Statistics Department under the Prime Ministers Department, the Treasury and the Central Bank as well as the planning unit of the various ministries and agencies. The Committee is chaired by the Chief Secretary to the government.

Technically the planning process is from the bottom up — that is, programmes and projects are to be initiated at the district, state and line ministries. Their projects and programmes are based on the macro-parameters set up by the central administration. It is formulated and discussed at the various levels and departments before reaching the EPU as the secretariat of the NDPC.

The National Planning Council (NPC) is the highest level of policy-making in major issues affecting economic and social affairs.

Development Plans

Development Plans are based on long term projections of the economy. There are three types of plans. The Outline Perspective Plan, which is a long term plan, the Five Year Development Plan as a medium plan and the annual budget which is a yearly plan outlining what the government sets out to do for that particular year.

The annual budget covers the detailed activities of the government expenditure. The budget is prepared by the Ministry of Finance and the EPU on economic matters. It is the government's statement of purposes and expenditures. Over the last few years the private sector has been consulted in the preparation of the budget. The Inter Agency Planning Groups (IAPGs) is the body through which the views of private sector and other central agencies are co-ordinated.

Sources of Policy-Input

Until recently, planning had been the autonomous function of the federal bureaucrats with EPU as the main agency. It was mostly the administrator-civil servants, drawing on administrative resources of information, analyses and expertise, who formulated new social and economic policies. Malaysia's pre-independence centralized bureaucratic state, from the start of the indigenous government and before the national political awareness and full development of political institutions, was in a position to take the initiative in diagnosing social and economic problems and proposing solutions for them.

However, since the mid-80s Prime Minister Dr. Mahathir Mohamad has envisioned Malaysia becoming an industrial nation in the next century. The Japanese concept of Japan Incorporated had the demonstration effect. Therefore, it was deemed necessary to incorporate the commercial voice into economic planning. A co-operate concept was formalized by establishing the Interagency Group (IAPG). The IAPG is the link between the administrative apparatus and the industry.

The Economic Planning Unit (EPU)

EPU plays a crucial role of acting as a secretariat to the IAPG. A similar framework has also been set up at the state and district levels. At these levels, consultation with the private sector for planning and the implementation of development projects is encouraged.

Implementation Co-Ordinate Unit (ICU)

The unit was established in 1970 to co-ordinate and monitor development projects. Under the New Economic Policy many public enterprises were formed both at the federal and state levels. Federal projects cut across state boundaries and often override state projects. The ICU plays the integrative role, co-ordinating, supervising and monitoring the implementation of policies and programmes of development. The ICU is responsible for ensuring the efficiency of the development projects.

Malaysia Administrative Modernization and Management Planning Unit (MAMPU)

MAMPU is a unit set up in the Prime Minister's Department to bring about reforms in the public service. The stated objective of MAMPU is to introduce reforms in the public service so as to increase quality, efficiency and effectiveness in administration. It acts as a catalyst in public sector management and to advise the government in the area of organizational management.

The Corporate Elites

Over the last few years, the private sector has played an increasingly important role in policy-making. Previously, in the 1950s, '60s and in the '70s the government relied entirely on the public service technocrats. They identified the issues of concern on export performance, output and employment and provided policy guidelines to the cabinet. However, with the economic problems faced in 1980s and the completion of the New Economic Policy, the government formed the National Economic Consultative Council (NECC) to provide policy input. Members of the private sector represented by business association, non-governmental organizations, academics and political parties were appointed to the Council.

The input base was broadened and more consultations were held with the private sector. In fact, it was said that the structural adjustment was undertaken together with the private sector. Among the forums are the Budget Dialogue, Ministry of International

Trade and Industry (MITI), Dialogue and Bank Negara Dialogue. There are others whereby the private sector is consulted. The most active association in these forums are the Federation of Malaysian Manufacturers (FMM) and the Malaysian Business Council (MBC).

Annual budget dialogue has become a feature in the Malaysian national planning. Once a year before the budget is formulated, the Ministry of Finance holds a discussion with members of industry such as the FMM, all chambers of commerce, the National and International Chamber of Commerce and Industry (NICCI). Also Non-governmental Organizations (NGOs) such as the Consumer Association of Penang (CAP), Federation of Malaysian Consumers Association (FOMCA), the Anti-Drug Abuse Task Force (PEMADAM) and World Wide Fund for Nature (WWF).

Another instrument that seemed quite successful is the public and private sector dialogue also referred to as Consultative Panels. The dialogue is part of the Malaysia Incorporated concept, that was launched by the Prime Minister in 1983. All government ministries were directed to set up Consultative Panels.

The Malaysian Business Council is another influence in policy-making. The Business Council has 40-50 captains of industry, who meet with the Prime Minister twice a year. The Council provides him the opportunity to listen to the private sector's concerns.

Various think tanks were established to provide inputs for policy-making. The idea was initiated by the Prime Minister for non-government opinion and ideas. Particularly the Institute of Strategic and International Studies (ISIS) and Malaysian Institute of Economic Research (MIER) were set up to provide another perspective, the private sectors perspective. A few others were launched addressing specific concerns such as social issues, and the Malaysian Strategic and Research Council (MSRC), a socio-political forum was established.

Conclusion

The National Development Policy (1991-2000) envisages less government intervention in the economy. The private sector is identified as the leading sector, however, the public sector will continue to play a complementary role. The Malaysian management of the economy is, however, still very centralized with the power concentrated at the federal executive branch of the government. Industrial Policies in Malaysia are largely being formulated at the top echelons of the government. Development Planning is macro-oriented, with little attention given to micro aspects of the economy.

References

Arrif, Mohamed (1991), "Managing Trade and Industry Reforms in Malaysia". In *Authority and Academic Scribblers, the Role of Research in East Asian Policy Reform*, ed. Sylvia Ostry; San Francisco: International Centre for Economic Growth.

Crosson, Piere R. (1966), *Economic Growth in Malaysia, Planning Method*, Series No.2 (Malaysia: Centre for Development Planning).

Faaland, Just, Parkinson, J.R., Saniman, Rais, "Growth and Ethnic Inequality, Malaysia's New Economic Policy" Hurst and Company, London, 1990.

Hitam, Shamsudin, "Development Planning in Malaysia", paper presented at Workshop on Development Planning in Asia 17-18 October 1991 Bangkok by Asia and Pacific Development Centre (APDC) Kuala Lumpur, Malaysia.

Hon, L.S. (1978), *Growth and Redistribution of the Industrial Sector in Malaysia*, Fifth Malaysian Economic Convention, Penang.

Ismail Md. Salleh, "Privatization: The Malaysian Experience" in *Malaysian Economy in Transition*, Hisashi Yokohama and Mokhtar Tamin (ed.), Institute of Developing Economies, Tokyo, 1991.

Keizai Doyukai (1966), *Economic Development of Malaysia: Its Achievements*, Characteristics and Problems, Japan Committee for Economic Development.

Mahbob Sulaiman, "Structural Adjustments and Economic Growth in Malaysia", 1985-93, paper presented at the Annual Conference of OECF, Japan 11 October 1994, Tokyo.

Masri. Badri Hj, Dato', "Understanding Malaysia Incorporated" and Other New Policies of the Government: A primary guide. Adabi Ltd. Publisher. Kuala Lumpur. 1984.

Government Publications

Economic Report 1990/91, Ministry of Finance. Kuala Lumpur. 1990.

Economic Report 1991/92, Ministry of Finance. Kuala Lumpur. 1991.

Economic Report 1996/97, Ministry of Finance. Kuala Lumpur. 1996.

The Second Outline Perspective Plan 1991-2000, Government Press Kuala Lumpur. 1991.

GOVERNANCE AND LOCAL GOVERNMENT SYSTEM

Syedur Rahman

Background

Social, political, and economic changes of the last four decades, globally, regionally, and nationally, coupled with the intensity and magnitude of these changes have resulted in many developing nations and countries in transition to be on the brink of administrative collapse; others to be increasingly cut-off from the main source of their existence — their citizens; and still others in states of atrophy, unable to deliver goods to the majority of their citizens (UN, 1998).

At the turn of the century, five global trends: (1) strategies for redesigning the state, (2) methods for managing rapid and rampant change; (3) accounting for widening and broadening leadership from all segments of society; (4) impact of technology and innovation; and (5) impact of global megatrends on both Government structure and functions and the process of governance.

These five factors are changing the ways the public administrative system in developing countries are functioning and in effect these factors should be instrumental in leading reorganization and reform efforts.

Redesigning State

While it is not the purpose of the paper to elaborate on the five broad trends, it is important to highlight the issue of redesigning of the State as it has the most direct impact on governance and local government system. The nature of the state is changing rapidly.

From the mid 1980s to the present time deliberate attempts have been made to change the nature of the state from a producer and provider of goods and services to one in which the state is organized and structured on the basis of private sector management practices. The state is becoming primarily a regulatory body and serves as a catalyst and facilitator for private sector development. In the coming century, the State can be viewed as a composite of four different perspectives (Guy Peters, 1996).

Market State

The driving force behind this metamorphosis of the state is the acceptance of the private sector model of management as inherently superior than the strategies and practices of the traditional public sector. Therefore market structures of efficiencies are incorporated into all activities of state operations.

Participatory State

In this variation of the state it is accepted that conventional bureaucracies are an impediment to good governance. The primary purpose of the participatory state is to harness the huge talent and energy that lie fallow and underutilized in the lower echelons of society. The participatory state calls for participatory management, street level bureaucracy, discursive democracy where the public is asked to decide on all matters of public policy, and communitarianism in which neither the individual nor the state but rather the community is deeply involved in governance.

Flexible State

The flexible state is one that is capable of responding effectively to new challenges of surviving in the face of change. The state has the capacity to make appropriate policy responses to all types and forms of environmental changes. Neither the individual nor the organization has a high level of permanence in this formulation of the state.

Deregulated State

In this iteration of the state, deregulation is not concerned with economic policy but with the internal management of the government itself. In the deregulated government the workers are liberated and their entrepreneurial energies are utilized. In the deregulated state, the constraints on individual action are eliminated and therefore, government is expected to perform its functions better.

The challenge of governance is to balance the contradictory aspects of the four perspectives and at the same time coalesce the strengths and advantages of each perspective to serve the purposes of the nation. Since Governments cannot undertake all activities of a modern state single-handedly, they must incorporate into their operation the widest possible, if not all, segments of society. Governance, in its broadest iteration (interface between society and Government) refers to a process through which all individuals and groups in society can participate in making social, cultural, economic, and political choices. It refers to a society-wide process which involves an opening up of core processes of Government to both public participation and public scrutiny. Critical to the sustainability of governance are the emergence of broad spectrum of leaderships in society and the evolution of highly energetic civil society with its concomitant self-organizing abilities.

Critical Factors for Good Governance

The current rebirth of 'governance' can be attributed to the macro-economic policy reform initiated through the structural adjustment programmes of the early 1980s. The structural adjustment programmes were intended to jump start development through sound economic policy-making. The outcome was not as successful as was initially expected. In addition, the social impact was much more negative than anticipated. The experiment with structural adjustment further confirmed that Governments cannot do everything themselves. Since then significant efforts are being made to identify partners who along with Governments can support and lead economic development and social justice.

Good governance, according to Martin Minogue (1998) is both a broad reform strategy, and a particular set of initiatives to strengthen the institutions of civil society with the objective of making government more accountable, more open, transparent, and more democratic.

Local Government

While there are large numbers of justifications for a strong and viable local governments some of the most recent justification includes the following.

Cheema (1996) who points out that there were three worldwide institutional transitions in the last decade which are having and will continue to have significant impact and change on governmental and economic systems. According to him, one of the transition is a rapidly growing interest in decentralization of previously highly centralized governments and a broadening and strengthening of local governance capacity. It is this transition which will sustain the other two transitions of (1) movement towards democratization including enhanced government accountability; and (2) increasing emphasis on free market solutions to economic problems.

In the Report of a Pilot Project on Profiles of Asian Countries, United Nations Department of Economic and Social Affairs points out that administrative reform initiatives during the decade of the 1990s include a strong emphasis on the importance of local government (UN, 1997). Korea, China, Japan and the Philippines are all pursuing pro-active policies for local autonomy as an intervention strategy for (a) promoting democratization and popular participation; (b) delivery of public services at the local level; and (c) efficient allocation of public resources.

Perhaps the most interesting case in support of a strong local government system is the system-wide reform taking place in South Africa's negotiated settlement and its transition from apartheid minority rule to a democratically elected government. Although strong local government is theoretically justified and in developed countries have played a critical role in economic development and social justice and in the institutionalization of democracy, in most developing countries local government suffers from neglect and is at most times lost in the shadow of national policies, practices, and efforts at economic growth and social and political development endeavours.

Local Government System in South Asia

The different countries of South Asia followed different paths towards political and economic development. India went the democratic route with import substitution economic policy; while Pakistan went the military route with an export-oriented economic policy.

Sri Lanka went the democratic route with great emphasis on social development. Bangladesh played with military rule but settled on a democratic political system with increasingly greater emphasis on exports and regional and global integration. Nation-building activities, economic development planning, economic stabilization and reform and pressure for improving the quality of life led these countries to largely neglect the local government system.

Despite some advances, both in terms of devolution and delegation in the local government system of South Asia, it can be stated with a fair degree of certainty that the local government systems are generally weak. They all lack managerial expertise, and adequate financial resources to undertake the activities within their domain. Dependence of grants from higher levels of government have increased over time instead of declining. They lack appropriate knowledge and information to carry out the functions. Micro-management and various types of interventions from higher levels of governments do not allow for local government growth and development.

A prime example of such micro-omanagement and intervention is the practice of deputized central administrators to the local government systems. There is also a general belief that local governments are not capable.

In India, for example, a 1978 Report of the Committee on Panchayati Raj Institutions (PRI) pointed out that local government institutions became weaker instead of becoming stronger as development activities were carried out with the use of specialized central agencies.

Sri Lanka experiment in local government in some ways moved forward in the 1980s. In 1980 the formation of the Development Council led the decentralization effort of the country although it also led to the demise of the town and village councils. In 1987, the provisions of the Thirteenth amendment to the Constitution further devolved the local government functioning from the central government to the newly created provincial councils which in turn led to the demise of the district development council. Despite such attempts, the current complex political condition in Sri Lanka makes it difficult for the local government to thrive and flourish (Siddiqui, 1992).

A recent study of local government system in Bangladesh concludes that although the constitution provides for an autonomous local government system these provisions have not been implemented resulting in a local government system that is not functioning properly. The local government system has been subject to many changes and experiments which has not only destabilized the system but caused the local government system to distance itself from the community it is supposed to serve (UNDDSMS, 1996). In the three countries India, Bangladesh and Sri Lanka, as well as in Pakistan the national political scenario as well as the national economic initiatives have generally tended to direct thinking away from local government contributing to a generally weak local government system.

Assessing Local Government of Bangladesh

A number of authoritative sources exists regarding decentralization and local governance and local government in Bangladesh (Ali Shaikh et al., 1983). Alamgir (1988) in assessing the development strategy for Bangladesh concludes that while there was a felt need for a strong local government by the developers of the first five year plan, many of the programmes of the first five year plan failed because there was no local government system which could bring about effective local participation need to formulate and implement the five year plan.

The Report of the Task Forces on Bangladesh Development Strategies for the 1990's in Volume II entitled "Managing the Development Process" (Task Force, 1991) also provides a review of decentralization initiatives. This report concludes that local government system is needed not only to fulfil the objective of training in political system but also to make national level bureaucracies operating at the levels responsible and responsive to the demands and sensitivities of the local people. More recent studies include the 1993 "New Local Government System in Bangladesh" sponsored by the Local Government Division (GOB, 1993). This study outlines the salient features of the Union Parishad, and Zila Parishad and the Pourashava. The study also outlines the salient features of the Gram Unnayan Committee (Village Development Committee) and the

Thana Unnayan Samannaya Committee (Thana Development Co-ordination Committee). Finally, there is the 1996 co-sponsored study by the UNDP and the Government of Bangladesh entitled "Local Government in Bangladesh: An Agenda for Governance."

Brief Historical Overview

The current local government system in Bangladesh can be traced back to the Bengal Local Self Government Act of 1855 which established the three tier system — District Board, Local Board and Union Committee. The system showed differentials in number of members with a minimum of 9 at the district level, and differentials in elected and nominated as well as selection of Chairman. During the period 1885 and 1947 much of the development of the local government system in South Asia remained stunted due to undue role of the administrative system as controlling authority of the local government system.

Much later under the Basic Democracy (Pakistan period) the structure at the rural level was enlarged to four — Union Council, Thana Council, District Council and Divisional Council. This system was based on indirect democracy. Direct citizens participation took place only at the union level. The tier's above the Union Council consisted of representatives from the immediate lower level. Units higher than the Union Council also had appointed members. The role of controlling authority remaind the source of stunting a local government system already limited by the concept of "guided democracy".

The first Bangladesh Government of Sheikh Mujibur Rahman changed the name of the local body at the lowest level to Union Panchayet and then to Union Parishad, the Thana Council to Thana Development Committee and the District Council to Zila Board. Total membership of each Union Parishad was 11 members, with the Chairman and Vice-Chairman directly elected from the entire Union, and 3 members each from three separate wards of the Union. Union Parishad elections were held in 1973. Although plans were announced for further changes in the local government system resulting from the introduction of a presidential form of government, these changes were abandoned due to forced change in the governance of the country.

The Government of Ziaur Rahman reverted back to the Union Parishad, Thana Parishad and Zila Parishad structure and also attempted to restructure the member component but kept the role of the prescribed authority equally stringent. A Swanirvar Gram Sarkar at the village level was introduced in 1980 with the purpose of co-opting different functional and interest groups at the village level. Earlier in 1978, a parallel organization to the Thana Parishad was established called the Thana Development Committee. Once again forced change in the governance of the country created system-wide disruption.

The Government of Ershad also utilized the three tier system of Union Parishad, an Upazila Parishad which replaced the Thana Parishad and the Zila Parishad. A central factor guiding the reorganization of the local government system was the separation between all development activities of local level and national/regional development activities. The Upazila was selected as the most appropriate level and began to co-ordinate some of the activities of national level field offices and take over some of the functions carried out at the district level.

Following the Ershad period, the Government of Begum Ziaur Rahman formally dissolved the Upazila system and undertook a re-examination of the local government system. The proposed new structures included the Zila Parishad and the Union Parishad. A structure below the Union Parishad was also proposed called the Gram Shabha along with the development of a Thana Development and Co-ordination Committee. However, lack of full implementation and a democratic change of government left the local government system in a state of doldrum.

Structural Context

A structural profile of the size/population and revenue/expenditure variable of the existing state of local government system in Bangladesh shows that variation among the size of a district is nine time. Variation among thana is approximately 925 times between the largest and the smallest. Similarly the variation at the union level is 952 times. The lower the unit the higher the variation. In terms of population variation at the district level is 25 times. Variation at the thana and union levels are 42 times and 111 times respectively. The revenue and expenditure picture shows that per capita income at the union level is only 4 taka. Although higher, the average per capita revenue is only Taka 85 at Class A pourashava. Per capita expenditure at the union level is only Taka 27 with the highest being at Class A Pourashava of Taka 215. Government grant seems to be more focused towards Class C Pourashava where the average grants is 77 per cent of total revenue. Union level receives government grant of only 36 per cent.

The profile above does not present a very rosy picture for a local government system and leads to the conclusion that the system is structurally weak.

Process Context

Among the findings of most studies on decentralization and local government reviewed, conclusion which states that most local government systems are unable to conduct all their assigned responsibilities is common. The formal responsibilities currently assigned to local governments are numerous and varied. Rural local governments are formally allocated 38 separate functions. Realistically, they are able to undertake five to six of these activities and even then in a very limited manner. Urban local government have 22 assigned activities of which they carry out in some fashion approximately fifty per cent of these tasks.

Further conclusions identify lack of managerial capacity, inability to deliver services, poor record-keeping, concealment of decision-making, as well as lack of inclusivity of stakeholders also confirm the structural weakness of the system. Another major conclusion is the impact of historical layering and its negative impacts. Successive governments have impacted local government system or attempted to with such initiatives as the district governship, the Gram Sarker, the upazila system resulting in various forms of interfaces at the local level. Statutory local government shared its physical boundary, work and power base with national field agencies, the development committees, the national officials at the local level, national officials deputized to the local level, as well as elected national legislative members. They also are facing increasingly aggressive international, and national non-government organizations. This overall system at the local level have generally tended to weaken local government by dissipating the power and authority structure.

While the formal local government system is weak, there are many players at the local level and partnering among all the different players provide Bangladesh an opportunity to significantly reshape governance at the local level.

Enabling Conditions: Megatrends

Enhanced institutionalization of democracy at the national level in Bangladesh makes it imperative that the local government system is re-analyzed and re-engineered to fit the new political realities of Bangladesh. While assessment of Bangladesh are generally mired in negatives, two internal megatrends are changing the overall political and economic dynamics of Bangladesh and in a very positive way that bode well for the strengthening of a local government system. The first is the institutionalization of national elections as a means of power sharing in a democratic society. In the last 25 years thirteen national elections were held in Bangladesh of which seven were parliamentary, three presidential and three were referendum. The intermittent holding of elections and the negotiated process for holding each election resulted in the development of an election process which is both free and fair. No government in Bangladesh can any longer rule without the consent of the people. Local governments too must be based on the consent of the people.

The second megatrend is the intensive and extensive formation of self-governing groups initially instigated by the development of the 'no collateral' lending developed by the Grameen Bank. In Bangladesh today there are over 500 women's organizations with a total membership of over 2 million. It is estimated that there are over 13,000 non-governmental organization (UN, 1996). Within two decades, the formation of community and local groups in Bangladesh is viewed as a major factor changing the composition of life in not only the rural but also the urban areas. The proliferation of groups and group formation is not only advancing changes but can serve as instrumental in innovation of all kinds as well as become partners of the public sectors programmes for economic growth and development.

These two very positive trends provide the enabling conditions for a strong local government system.

Operational Condition: Shaping Local Choices

While much is made of the weakness of local government system, not much is made of significant successes at the local level. An assessment of 12 best practices of home-grown practices at the local level found the following five variables as significant to successful local effort (UNDDSMS, 1996). These variables together form the operational conditions for the development of a sound local government system.

Motivation and Leadership: Successful local endeavour is usually internally generated and leadership, the ability to convince and encourage the local community to get going, sets the tone for innovation and change.

Mobilization of Resources: In most successful cases resources were generated from a multiplicity of sources.

Good Management: Key to the success of the best home-grown cases was the recruitment of skilled management personnel but also the development of sound management practices including accountability of financial resources and responsiveness to all stakeholders.

Impact and Multiplier Effect: In successful cases, the impact of the local endeavour is not only felt by the immediate beneficiaries but the larger community. Successful project also have the ability to generate supportive projects and add-on projects to the main project.

Sustainability: Successful projects at the local level lead to the development of individual, group, or community self-confidence and independence. In addition, lessons learned from the effort is institutionalized and regularly practiced.

Collaboration and Co-optation: A sixth variable, one which is not derived from the analysis of the 12 best home-grown practices but nevertheless a strong indicator of successful local endeavour, is co-operation and co-optation between local government and other community and other non-governmental agencies and international assistance programmes.

The megatrends provide the enabling conditions and the analysis of best home grown practices indicate the operational conditions which provide ample supportive evidence of existence of good governance at the local level in Bangladesh.

A Vision for Local Government

What is missing is a general societal acceptance and a broad consensus for developing a strong local government system in Bangladesh. This consensus can be based on current local and national development and international trends. To develop this consensus, a local government system must be framed within a broad vision. In two articles of the Constitution of Bangladesh an administrative vision of local government is provided:

> **Article 59**
>
> (1) Local Government in every administrative unit of the republic shall be entrusted to bodies, composed of persons elected in accordance with law.
>
> (2) Every body such as is referred to in clause (1) shall subject to the Constitution and any other law, perform within the appropriate administrative unit such function as shall be prescribed by Act of Parliament, which may include functions relating to: (a) administration and the work of public officers; (b) the maintenance of public order; and (c) the preparation and implementation of plans relating to public services and economic development.
>
> **Article 60**
>
> For the purpose of giving full effect to the provisions of article 59 Parliament shall by law, confer powers on the local government bodies referred to in that article, including power to impose taxes for local purposes, to prepare their budgets and to maintain funds.

The 1996 UNDP study on local government system also provides a vision statement which can form the basis of developing a consensus on the issue of governance at the local level. Supporting the intent of the Constitution of Bangladesh, the UNDP study prepared for the Government of Bangladesh suggests four fundamental vision statement. These are:

1. The individual Bangladeshi is capable and resilient, despite adversities, and is deserving of trust and management of public goods and services.
2. Self-governance is possible and is a desirable outcome of democratic institution-building.
3. The inclusion of all social groups is a fundamental necessity for autonomous local government.
4. Local government is an integral part of a comprehensive national governance vision of partnership between central government units and local government units.

The UNDP study goes on to suggest challenges for implementing a system based on these four vision statement. First, people at all levels in Bangladesh are organizing themselves. Second, governments at all levels should be cognizant of this fact and must respond to the needs of the people or the people are likely to withdraw their consent. Third, the apparent complexity of local conditions will require re-thinking local government not as a single uniform entity but a broad framework which can show many different shapes and configurations. Finally, different levels of local governments can have completely different functions, or that the same function can be performed at different levels. For example, the study notes that from an organizational perspective, the Union can serve as the focal point for economic development and local planning, the village or ward may be the appropriate place for community decision-making, participation and local leadership, while resource mobilization and allocation may be at a higher level than the union and the district may serve as the training ground for national political leadership.

Building A New Local Government System

There is enough evidence to clearly show what has not worked at the local level in Bangladesh. Three factors that stand out include:

(1) process tinkering and tweaking the existing system, (2) uniformity and standardization of structure, (3) reforming structures, (4) utilization for partisan strategic and political alliance, and (5) micro-management from the top. On the other hand, there are some clear indications of what may work. These include: (1) the adherence to the concept of elected representatives at the local level, (2) facilitating the process which foster the development of local choice and decision-making process, and (3) enhancing the process of linking community private economic and social organizations with statutory local government as an essential element for good local governance.

The prime focus for building a new local government system should be on purpose and functions and not on structures and administrative control from the higher levels. The national legislature should in accordance with the Constitution provide the guiding principles. An example of a guiding principle is the direct election of members at all levels. Let the levels decide how many members and the format of the election, the position of the Chairman, the process of removal etc. that the local govt. system should have.

Another guiding principle may be that elections will be held every five years and all local elections will be managed by an independent local government election commission. All levels will therefore, prepare for election every five years and the levels should decide how they prepare for local election. Another guiding principle may be the accountability of public funds and annual audit by independent auditors. Let the levels account for their use of public funds and audits will inform the community of how funds were expended. Still another guiding principle is the transparency of decision-making process. Let the communities and the local media and community group evolve their own process of transparency. The guiding principles can define in broad terms such aspects as the responsibilities of the different levels, the taxing authority, types and conditions of national level assistance programmes, and sources of technical assistance and training. Let each level and each unit of local government derive their own process, leadership and management style, responsibility and accountability to its citizens.

To conclude that the local government system in Bangladesh is weak is justifiable. However, not to undertake significant functional innovation and change in support of enhanced local governance and statutory local government is to deny the social, economic and political realities in Bangladesh today (Rahman, 1996). A local government, autonomous and able to advance community wishes and aspirations but strategically aligned with national economic development and social justice programmes and effort will require abandonment of the current uniform structure and process and designing of a multi-layered, locally designed local governance supported by a set of guiding principles which will allow communities to elect representative and make them accountable to the local people. Communities should be charged to provide the leadership for local government design and the national government should facilitate the development without controlling the process.

The 12th Meeting of Experts on Pubic Administration and Finance (UN Report, 1995) organized by the United Nations Department for Development Support and Management Service noted that the public administrative system of a country was the "thinking part" of Government. It viewed the public administration system at three levels. At the "grassroots level" the public administrative system is required to perceive and address changes in immediate needs and demands. At the sub-national level, the public administrative system is required to have the capacity to respond to the needs and demands at the "grassroots" level while anticipating changes at the national level. At the national level, the public administration system is required to respond to levels below it but must also operate within the global context. In designing a local government system, extensive emphasis on structure should be avoided. Building good governance around the critical functions at the three levels is challenging but is necessary for economic development and social justice.

References

Alamgir, Muhiuddin Khan. *Development Strategy for Bangladesh*, Dana Prokashoni. Dhaka. Bangladesh. Third Edition 1988.

Ali, Shaikh Maqsood et al., Decentralization and People's Participation in Bangladesh National Institute of Public Administration Dhaka, Bangladesh, 1983.

Cheema, G. Shabbir, *The Policy Framework: Decentralization and the Strengthening of Local Government in the Report of the United Nations Global Forum on Innovative Policies and Practices in Local Government*. Gothenburg, Sweden September 23-27 1996.

Government of Bangladesh, Ministry of Local Government, Rural Development and Cooperatives, Local Government Division, New Local Government System in Bangladesh, 1993.

Minogue, Martin, *The Principles and Practices of Good Governance*, Institute for Development Policy and Management, University of Manchester British Council 1997.

Peters, Guy B., *The Future of Governing*, The University of Kansas Press, Lawrence, KS., 1996.

Rahman, Syedur, *Optimistic Trends and Pessimistic Past: Bangladesh at Twenty-Five*, Presented at the 25th Annual Conference of the Mid-Atlantic Region, Association for Asian Studies. Seton Hall University, October 1996.

Report of the Task Forces on Bangladesh Development Strategies for the 1990s. Volume Two, University Press Limited, 1991.

Siddiqui, Kamal, Local Government in South Asia: A Comparative Study, University Press Limited Dhaka, Bangladesh 1992.

Siddiqui, Kamal, *Local Government in Bangladesh*, University Press Limited Dhaka, Bangladesh Second Edition 1994.

UN Department for Development Support and Management Services, Local Government of Bangladesh, New York 1996.

United Nations Department for Development Support and Management Services Local Government in Bangladesh: An Agenda for Governance, New York 1996.

United Nations Department for Development Support and Management Services Local Government in Bangladesh: An Agenda for Governance. New York 1996.

United Nations Department of Economic and Social Affairs. Background Paper No. 1 "Key Issues and Emerging Trends in Public Administration" Group of Experts on the United Nations Programme in Public Administration and Finance. Fourteenth Session May 4-8 1998 New York.

United Nations Department of Economic and Social Affairs. Report of a Pilot Study on Profiles of Asian Countries, Administrative Reforms: Country Profiles New York 1997.

United Nations Report of the Secretary General on Public Administration and Development. United Nations New York. November 1995.

LOCAL GOVERNMENT FOR GOOD GOVERNANCE: EXPERIENCE IN ANDHRA PRADESH

G.M. Ramesh Kumar

Background

India has a long tradition of self-help and self governance. In the past, the villages enjoyed considerable local autonomy and self-sufficiency which was manifest through the system of local self-government, which is as old as Indian civilisation. These local bodies of ancient and medieval eras of Indian history were however no more than communitarian institutions engaged in conflict resolution in spheres in which the successive political establishments were not directly involved. At best, such institutions reflected the prevailing socio-religious consensus which had no political overtones beyond the boundaries of a village or a cluster of adjacent villages (Venkataranggaya and Pattabhiram, 1970).

In the Constitution of India, wherein a provision for organisation of village Panchayats was incorporated as a direction to the State Governments in Article 40 reads as follows: "The State shall take steps to organize village Panchayats and endow them with such powers and authority as may be necessary to enable them to function as units of local self-government." As such, the type of governance in local bodies has been left to the wisdom of the State governments.

In the present context, good governance is a reform strategy and also an initiative to strengthen the institutions with the objective of making the government more accountable, more open and transparent and more democratic. The following are the parameters which are identified for promoting good governance (ODA, 1993; UNDP, 1995; World Bank, 1999).

1. Participation

Participation envisages participation of the entire society in governance through change in their subsidiary roles and direct involvement in areas hitherto kept exclusively in the public domain.

2. Legitimacy

Legitimacy emphasizes, the need for a system of governance which operates with the assent of the governed and so provides means to give or withhold their assent.

3. Accountability

Accountability involves the existence of mechanism which ensures that both politicians and officials are answerable for their actions, use of public resources and performance.

4. Open and Transparent

Openness and transparency emphasizes the need for public access to quality information and making public all the transactions in which public interest is involved.

5. Competence

Competence demonstrates the capacity to create effective policy and decision-making processes in order to achieve the efficient delivery of public services.

Though some of the provisions of the State Acts provide for the same, yet not much of an exercise has gone in implementing the provisions and the local bodies were made to fend for themselves with little or no popular participation. As a result of this, many discrepancies have crept into these grassroots institutions. Even where these institutions functioned they were dominated by economically and socially privileged sections of rural societies.

It has been found that in implementation of Acts and Rules in force on Panchayats, several factors are responsible for impeding the growth of a self-sustaining local institutional system and local governance, leave alone good governance. These factors include, absence of regular and periodic elections within the time stipulated, prolonged suppressions, variation in structure, powers and functions, insufficient representation of weaker section such as: scheduled castes, scheduled tribes, backward classes and women, inadequate devolution of powers, lack of financial resources and above all, lack of political will. Keeping in view all these factors and past experience it became imperative to provide Constitutional status to Panchayat Raj bodies so that they can subserve the needs of the teeming millions who live in the rural areas. As such, the Government has created an enabling environment through Seventy-Third Constitution amendment within which the people can influence the direction and conduct of their governing institutions.

Seventy-Third Constitution Amendment

The Seventy-Third Constitution amendment 1993 lays down certain ground rules with basic structural framework for Panchayat Raj Institutions, so that it can withstand external interference and can establish itself as an effective and strong people's institution and perpetuate good governance. However, some aspects have been left at the discretion of State Legislature to make suitable provisions in their State Acts.

The mandatory provisions Are:

i. Establishment of a 'Gram Sabha' at the village level comprising registered voters of the village (Article 243 A).

ii. Establishment of a three-tier system of Panchayat Raj; at the village, intermediate and the district levels (Article 243 B).

iii. All levels of Panchayats will consist of persons elected directly from the territorial constituencies. The territorial constituencies shall be carved out in such a manner that the ratio between the population of each constituency and the number of seats allotted to it should be uniform throughout the Panchayat area [Article 243 C (1) and (2)].

iv. The chairperson of a Panchayat at the intermediate level and district level shall be elected from among the directly elected members representing the territorial constituencies [Article 243 C (3)].

v. Reservation of seats for scheduled castes and scheduled tribes in proportion to their population and seats to be allotted by rotation [Article 243 D (1)].

vi. Reservation of offices of chairpersons for scheduled castes and scheduled tribes in proportion to their population and offices to be allotted by rotation [Article 243 D (4)].

vii. One third of the total number of seats and offices, both in the reserved and unreserved categories, shall be reserved for women and allotted by rotation [Article 243 D (2) and (4)].

viii. All members of the Panchayat whether or not directly elected shall have the right to vote in the meetings of the Panchayat [Article 243 C (4)].

ix. A tenure of five years of Panchayat is fixed from the date of its first meeting. The tenure cannot be extended and in case a Panchayat is dissolved it has to be reconstituted within six months (Article 243 E).

x. Devolution of powers, authority and responsibilities to Panchayats to enable them to function as institutions of self-Government (Article 243 G).

xi. Powers to impose taxes by the Panchayats (Article 243 H).

xii. Constitution of Finance Commission every five years to review the financial position of the Panchayats and recommend the principles on the basis of which taxes and non-taxes are to be apportioned between the Panchayats and the consolidated fund of the State (Article 243 I).

xiii. The legislative body of a State may, by law, make provisions with regard to the maintenance of accounts and auditing of such accounts (Article 243 J).

xiv. Constitution of a a State Election Commission for the superintendent, direction and control of the preparation of electoral rolls and conduct of elections to the Panchayats. The Governor shall appoint the State Election Commission (Article 243 K).

xv. Extension of the above provisions to the scheduled areas with such exceptions and modifications (Article 243 M).

xvi. Bar to interference by courts in the electoral matters with regard to validity of any law relating to the delimitation of constituencies and allotment of seats to such constituencies (Article 243 O).

Andhra Pradesh Panchayat Raj Act, 1994

In conformity with the Constitution's Seventy-Third Amendment, the Andhra Pradesh State Legislature has passed a new Andhra Pradesh Panchayat Raj Act, 1994 which has come into force with effect from 30th April, 1994. While providing for what is stipulated in the Constitution Seventy-Third Amendment, the Andhra Pradesh Panchayat Raj Act further provides for the following:

a. 34% reservation for the backward classes (Sections 9, 15, 152, 153, 180 and 181).

b. Direct election for the post of village president (Section 14).

c. Elections to the Panchayats at intermediate and district levels will be on political party basis (Sections 152, 153, 180 and 181).

d. The heads of lower bodies will be permanent invitees to the next higher body within their jurisdiction (Sections 158 and 188).

e. Co-option of members belonging to minorities on the board (Sections 149 and 177).

f. A candidate with more than two children will be disqualified from contesting election or from continuing as a member of any Panchayat Raj Institution (Section 19).

g. Only directly elected members can participate in election or moving no-confidence motion against the chairperson/president (Sections 153 and 181).

h. No-confidence motion could be moved against the chair-person/president only after two years from the commencement of his term and it can be moved against a person only once in the entire term of five years (Section 245).

i. Voting against the political party whip attracts disqualification (Sections 153 and 181).

J. Gram Sabha shall meet at least twice in a year with a break of 180 days in between two meetings (Section 6).

k. Inviting a specialist for any of the meetings of the Panchayat (Sections 159 and 189).

l. Cheque drawing powers given to the presidents of village Panchayats (Section 74).

As seen above, the Andhra Pradesh Panchayat Raj Act, 1994 supplements for the quality of governance which expresses itself through attributes such as, democratisation, accountability, transparency, efficiency, empowerment, participation and devolution.

Seventy-Third Amendment and Good Governance

The Seventy-Third Constitution amendment and the Andhra Pradesh Panchayat Raj Act, 1994, which has been passed in pursuance of the amendment has transformed the status of local bodies from the institutions that are being governed to that of institutions of governance and have thus become a part with the other formal organs of the State. The parameters which promote good governance viz., legitimacy, democratisation, participation, decentralisation, devolution and accountability are manifest in the Constitutional amendment and the State Act as shown below.

1. Legitimacy

The Seventy-Third Constitution amendment has given constitutional status to the Panchayats. Further, Article 243 B provides that there shall be constituted in every State, Panchayats at the village, intermediate and district levels. Furthermore, as per Article 243 E, every Panchayat shall continue for five years and no longer. Also, a Panchayat dissolved for any reasons has to be reconstituted within six months. These provisions ensure legitimacy and continuity to the elected bodies which operate with the assent of the governed.

2. Democratization

Democratization emphasizes that the governing body shall be elected by the people and represent the people. This concept is manifest in Article 243 C, wherein it is prescribed that all the seats in a Panchayat shall be filled by persons chosen by direct election from territorial constituencies in the Panchayat area. With an elected body at the village level responsible to the electorate, the will of the people will find larger reflection in the implementation of economic and social development programmes.

As can be seen, there is no scope for nomination to any elective post or seat. Further, even though there are provisions to co-opt minorities on the board, yet they are also required to be indirectly elected by the directly elected members.

Furthermore, the Constitution amendment contemplates that each tier has to be independent of the other. This minimizes the hegemony of the higher level tier over the lower level tier and provides for the democratic institutions to act independently.

Above all, Article 243 K provides that the superintendence, direction and control of the preparation of electoral rolls and conduct of all elections to the Panchayats shall be vested in a State Election Commission consisting of a State Election Commissioner to be appointed by the governor.

3. Participation

Involvement of people at the grassroots level has been considered as the most effective means through which economic development can meet the aspirations of the people and to ensure that the benefits really percolate down to the lower strata of the society.

The Constitutional amendment ensures participation of all sections of people in governance. Article 243 C, provides that all seats in a Panchayat shall be filled by persons chosen by direct election. Further, Article 243 D, provides for reservation of seats and offices to scheduled castes, scheduled tribes in proportion to their population. Furthermore, reservation of one third of seats and offices has been made in all categories for women. This is supplemented by the Andhra Pradesh Panchayat Raj Act, 1994, which provides thirty-four per cent reservation for backward classes. Also, the reservation by rotation ensures involvement of all sections in the entire rural areas over a period of time.

As regards greater participation of the people in governance, Article 243 A, supplemented by provisions of Section 6 of the Andhra Pradesh Panchayat Raj Act, 1994 provides for the establishment of the Gram Sabha[1] which is the only statutory forum at the village level. All the voters in the village are the members of the Gram Sabha and the Gram Sabha meets at least twice in a year. Issues like annual statements of accounts, administrative reports, programmes of works, proposals for fresh taxation, selection of schemes, beneficiaries and locations are discussed in Gram Sabha. The importance of Gram Sabha has been further enhanced by instructions issued requiring that selection of beneficiaries in all centrally sponsored schemes shall be made by the Gram Sabha. Furthermore, the accounts of centrally sponsored schemes are to be placed before Gram Sabha for approval.

4. Decentralization

The factors of decentralization is manifest in Article 243 G, which contemplates that States are required to endow the Panchayats with such powers and authority to enable them to function as institutions of self-government. The provisions also contemplates preparation of plans for economic development and social justice, and the implementation of schemes for economic development and social justice.

Further, Article 243 ZD (Seventy-Fourth Constitution Amendment), contemplates that a District Planning Committee is to be constituted for every district to prepare schemes covering special plans, sharing water and other natural resources, development of infrastructure, environment conservation etc. These activities which remained under State domain all along, now percolates down to the district level.

5. Devolution

Article 243 G of the Constitution envisages devolution of powers and responsibilities upon Panchayats at the appropriate level with respect to the preparation of plans for economic development and social justice and implementation of plans for economic development and social justice in relation to the subjects included in the Eleventh Schedule to the Constitution. As can be seen twenty-nine subjects included in the Eleventh Schedule (Annexure-V) are exhaustive and take within its ambit all developmental functions at the district, intermediary and village levels.

State Government used to exercise arbitrary control over allocation of funds to the local self-governing institutions. This malady is sought to be rectified by the role of State Finance Commission. Article 243 I provides that a Finance Commission shall be constituted at the State level every five years to make recommendations with regard to: (i) distribution between the State and the Panchayats of the net proceeds of the taxes, duties, tolls and fees that may be assigned to the Panchayat, (ii) the grants-in-aid to the Panchayats from the consolidated fund of the State and (iii) the measures needed to improve the financial position of the Panchayats.

Furthermore, the District Rural Development Agency (DRDA), an apex agency for rural development at the district level, is required to be integrated with the Panchayat Raj. With these devolutions the Panchayats will be economically independent units of self-government.

6. Accountability and Transparency

Accountability emphasizes the existence of built-in mechanism which ensures that both the elected representatives and functionaries are answerable for their actions, performance and use of public money. Further, transparency implies that the governed shall have access to all the information and records of public importance. Also, there should be a proper forum for discussing the issues wherein public interest is involved. Article 243 A and the provisions of the State Act provides for Gram Sabha with all the voters of the village as members. A Gram Sabha of a village is a permanent body and exists even if the Panchayat is dissolved.

Structure of Panchayat Raj Institutions

The Constitution provision prescribes a three-tier system of Panchayat Raj Institution, viz., at the district level, intermediary level and at the village level. In Andhra Pradesh the district level institution is called Zilla Parishad,[2] intermediary level institution is called Mandal Parishad[3] and the village level institution is called the Gram Panchayat. The institutions are headed by the elected persons namely, chairperson, president and Sarpanch respectively.

Each institution has a separate Governing body which has both elected members and ex-officio members. The elected members represent a particular constituency and are directly elected by the voters. Apart from the regular members, there is a provision for co-opting member from minorities. Also, there is a provision for permanent invitees and special invitees.

One of the basic change the Constitution amendment has brought in is that each institution will be an independent one without any organic link. This arrangement may in a way, weaken the system for there are several subjects and functions wherein these institutions have to function in close co-ordination. This shortfall, to some extent, is compensated by providing for permanent invitees.

Elections to Panchayat Raj Institutions

As per the Constitution Amendment the elections are required to be conducted within one year of the commencement of the Act. There are two types of elections: one direct elections whereat the voters directly elect their representatives. In the second type which is also called indirect elections, the voters in the first instance elect the members and the members so elected will, in turn, elect their leader to head the institution.

As per the provisions of the Act, elections to all territorial constituencies and the 'sarpanchas' will be held directly; whereas, elections to the posts of chairpersons of Zilla parishad and presidents of mandal parishads are conducted indirectly.

Areas of Concern

Despite the positive line of action emerging out of the Seventy-Third Constitution Amendment and the Andhra Pradesh Panchayat Raj Act, 1994 which has been enacted in pursuance of the Constitution Amendment there are a few grey areas, some of which are discussed below.

1. Powers and Functions of Panchayat Raj Institutions

As per the Article 243 G of the Constitution, the Legislature of a State is required to endow the Panchayats with such powers and authority as may be necessary to enable them to function as institutions of self-government. Further, the subjects with regard to which the functions, functionaries and funds are to be devolved onto the Panchayat ·Raj Institutions[4] have been listed in the Eleventh Schedule, Annexure-V. As seen almost all the developmental activities including the hub of development agencies, i.e., the functions of District Rural Development Agency are to be devolved to the Panchayat Raj Institutions. As such, raison d'être of these bodies consists in their ability to effectively and efficiently plan and implement programmes of economic development.

The experience is that in several states only a few functions are devolved on the Panchayat Raj Institutions, though it is stated that effective steps are being taken to devolve powers after a thorough examination of the issues involved and an in-depth study of existing field conditions so that the ultimate arrangement made is effective, durable and yields the desired results. Further, it is contended that before the transition is effected through devolution of powers and functions to the Panchayat Raj Institutions, necessary spade work should have to go in with regard to the empowerment of these institutions, deployment of field level functionaries, dovetailing of the activities of various agencies presently involved in the areas of Rural Development so that there is no let-up or slowing down of the process of development. This undue delay is striking at the roots of efficient governance.

2. Role and Powers of the Gram Sabha

The Gram Sabha which is the collective body of the adult members of the village has not been given sufficient importance in most State laws. The Andhra Pradesh Panchayat Raj Act provides for at least two meetings of the Gram Sabha in a year. The experience is that these Gram Sabhas are being conducted to avoid penal provisions of the Act, for these meetings are not well attended. In the State law, there is no provision for quorum for Gram Sabha which has resulted in conducting the Gram Sabha for formality's sake. Further, the reason of lack of enthusiasm is largely the ritualistic powers vested in the Gram Sabha. Apart from giving the Gram Sabha only a ritualistic role, the problem is compounded by having the meeting at a time of the day when the women and weaker sections are busy at home or in wage employment. This effectively marginalizes them. The role of the Gram Sabha in bringing about transparency in the functioning of the Gram Panchayat[5] is not being appreciated.

3. Problems Faced by Weaker Sections

Right from the start, that is registration as a voter, to the last stage that is running of regular administration of the institutions, the members belonging to weaker sections are facing the following problems.

i. For contesting the posts which are reserved for women, often a woman is made to contest because she is some body's wife, sister or daughter; she therefore, is becoming "a proxy candidate" and continuing to depend on the man who set her up for the election for her decisions.

ii. In most of the cases, where the 'Sarpanch' is elected from the weaker sections and more so if she is a woman, they find a sort of non-cooperation from the staff working in the Institutions who are still acting on the dictates of the ex-Sarpanchas wielding influence in the village. Several instances have come to the notice of the government where the Gram Panchayats are not taking any developmental activities because of non-cooperation from the other members. No doubt, the meetings are regularly being conducted every month, the members are also attending the meeting for attendance purpose, lest they should be disqualified. This is resulting in defamation of Sarpanchas belonging to weaker sections alleging that no developmental activities are being taken up. The Act provides for dissolution of the entire body wherein the sincere sarpanch also suffers along with recalcitrant members.

iii. In the case of Zilla Parishad and Mandal Parishad there is a provision that the chairperson/president could invite a person who is having a specialized knowledge as a special invitee to the meeting of that institute. Though no such cases have come to notice with regard to Zilla parishads, several instances have come to the notice of the government that the lady mandal presidents are inviting husband/father to the meeting as a special invitee. The special invitee sits on the dais and almost conducts the meeting defeating the very purpose of making woman as the president.

iv. Further, the Gram sabhas have become a power centre for those persons who have been the Sarpanchas since time immemorial but could not contest the election because the post has been reserved for other category. It is often noticed that these persons disturb the Gram Sabha with a vengeance.

v. The provisions of the Act prohibits a person with more than two children either to contest for election or to continue in the office and comes into effect after one year of commencement of the Act. Though this provision has been incorporated so that the elected person could become a standing example, yet it is noticed that the members are circumventing this provision. When a notice is being given to them about the birth of an additional child, immediately they are responding with an explanation saying that one of their children has been given for adoption and in effect the number of children are not increased.

4. Supervision and Control

As seen from the provisions of the Act, Panchayati Raj Institutions are oversupervised and controlled; these provisions run counter to good governance:

i. "Any officer or person whom the government may empower" may enter in and inspect any institution under the Gram Panchayat, Mandal Parishad or Zilla Parishad (Section 225).

ii. Government is empowered to cancel or suspend resolution of any Panchayati Raj Institution, either suo moto or on reference on certain grounds after an opportunity for explanation has been given (Section 246).

iii. If a Panchayat fails to perform any function or discharge any duty — government may direct the Panchayat to do it within a given period and if this is not complied with, government is competent to get it done through some other person (Section 247).

iv. Government has power to issue directions to the executive authority and he shall implement the same failing which he shall be liable for disciplinary action (Section 248).

v. Sarpanch of the Gram Panchayat, President of the Mandal Parishad and Chairman of the Zilla Parishad can be removed on grounds of omission and commission, abuse of the authority, misconduct and non-performance etc. by the collector/government after obtaining an explanation. They can also be suspended for a period of 3 months — extendable to six months (Section 249).

vi. Finally, government is empowered to dissolve a Gram Panchayat, Mandal Parishad or a Zilla Parishad, if it appears to Government that it is "not competent to perform its functions, or has failed to exercise its powers or perform its functions or has exceeded or abused any of the powers or perform its functions." In the first instance, the institution is directed to act in a particular way and if it does not comply, it can be dissolved (Section 250).

5. Personnel

The Act is characterized by over-presence of government and its functionaries.

i. When both Sarpanch and Up-Sarpanch are under suspension, or the offices are vacant or they are absent continuously on a period exceeding fifteen days, a member of the Panchayat is appointed temporarily until a new Sarpanch or Up-Sarpanch comes. The appointment is made by the Commissioner.

ii. The Executive Officer of the Gram Panchayat (GP) is appointed by the Commissioner. The Mandal Parishad Development Officer is appointed by the Government and so also the Chief Executive Officer of the Zilla Parishad.

iii. Other staff of the GP are appointed by the Commissioner. Posts of officers and other employees of the Mandal Parishad are created by the government "for carrying out the purpose of the Act". Appointments to the posts and transfer therefrom are made in accordance with government rules. They are paid from the consolidated fund of the State and their service condition is regulated by government rules.

6. Restructuring of DRDAs

Government of India has directed that consequent to the 73rd Constitutional Amendments, there is a need for closer linkage and effective coordination between the Zilla Parishads and DRDAs. They, therefore, suggested the following for adoption by the State Governments:

i. DRDA shall function under the overall supervision, control and guidance of the Zilla Parishads. The Chairman Zilla Parishad will be the Ex-Officio Chairman of the Governing Body of DRDA and will preside over its meetings.

ii. The Chief Executive Officer of the Zilla Parishad will be the Member Convenor of the DRDA.

iii. All the proposals/schemes will be initiated and formulated by the Gram Panchayat and sent to the DRDA through Panchayat Samithi. The DRDA will approve the scheme in their Governing Body.

iv. The Governing Body of the DRDA will provide policy direction, approve the annual plan as well as the schemes, both in physical and financial terms. It will also review and monitor the implementation of the plan.

v. The Executive Committee headed by the Chief Executive Officer/Executive Director of the DRDA will execute the annual plan as approved by the Governing Body. However, before final approval and sanction of any scheme, approval of the Chairman, wherever expedient, may be taken.

Several States have contended that the organisational structure got evolved over a period of time depending upon the local conditions and environment. The DRDA has to have an intensive interaction with several specialized agencies in implementing poverty alleviation programmes and as such there is a need to take a holistic approach to integrate all these development activities. Further, entrustment of all developmental activities and poverty alleviation programmes being implemented through DRDA to a single individual may not appear prudent, since it results in concentration of power in one single individual rather than an institution. Therefore, any change contemplated uniformly through the country cannot be brought in overnight, it is contended.

Areas of Intervention

The Panchayat Raj has been established in all the States in India and is now an integral part of politico-administrative structure of the country. Though there may be opinions about approaches, pace of growth, and the extent of commitment to the concept of the system, yet it cannot be denied that efforts are still to be made to further activate the Panchayat Raj Institutions to sustain the changes and utilize the same for furtherance of good governance. In this regard concerted action on the part of Central Government, the State Governments, the elected representatives, the officials, the NGOs and the people at large is imperative. The following are the areas wherein immediate attention is required to make Panchayat Raj Institutions vibrant bodies of good governance.

I. People's Participation

People's participation is a running thread throughout the process of planning, implementation, monitoring, evaluation and above all enjoying the benefits of development. As the Panchayat Raj Institutions have been constituted at different levels, the leaders elected through democratic process have taken positions as decision-makers. As a result, rural development programme, and State sponsored schemes are expected to get a boost in their implementation. The underlying principle of development process envisages that the Panchayats will be suitably empowered and will get assured funds and will decide on the schemes which are to be taken up in their respective villages. With an elected body at the village level responsible to the electorate, the will of the people will find larger reflection in the implementation of economic and social development programmes. The institution of Gram Sabha will result in greater transparency, accountability and involvement of the entire village in activities which concern them. However, a close observation of the working of Panchayats shows that the intentions behind the Constitution Amendment have not been fully met and more sincere efforts need to be made to make the Panchayats as institutions of good governance. Further, the term 'social audit' still appears to be very vague. Thus, it needs to be well articulated so that people will take cognizance of it.

Experience has shown that approach of community based rural development has received little or no attention as a result of which various programmes for rural development have not yielded desired results. The absence of element of community participation in terms of institutional affiliation of the people has affected the successful implementation of a number of rural development programmes. One aspect which does not find place in the Acts is integration of the local level institutions belonging to both formal and informal sectors which generally have very little interaction despite their common objectives.

II. Devolution of Functions, Functionaries and Funds

Article 243 G of the Constitution envisages devolution of powers and responsibilities upon Panchayats at the appropriate level with respect to preparation of plans and implementation of schemes for economic development and social justice. The subject included in the Eleventh Schedule to the Constitution will have within its ambit almost all the subjects which relate to rural development. The concern is now to ensure that the transition is through a process of proper linkages and integration of functions. The devolution of powers, delineation of functions and deployment of functionaries has to be done in different stages through a process of capacity building of the Panchayat Raj Institutions. In short, the devolution of powers to, and the capacity building of, Panchayat Raj Institutions at different levels should be in tandem.

Further, till now, almost all the developmental functions in the village were carried out by the government machinery and there was practically no opportunity for the village people to participate in the process. This has rather created a dependency syndrome in which people looked towards the government for every thing. This scenario is quite against good governance. Therefore, under these circumstances it is a challenging task to reverse the situation in which people are supposed to take the role of decision makers on the one hand and the government machinery as a helping hand to them, on the other.

As regards devolution of financial resources to the Panchayat Raj Institutions (PRIs), the entire issue has been left to the State Legislatures. As such, today the PRIs are totally dependent on the largesse received from the State Governments. Much more important action will have to be taken by the State Governments to broaden the tax base of the PRIs themselves and to assign and appropriate some lucrative State taxes to the PRIs. In case the tax base of the PRIs is broadened by the State Government, the responsibility for utilizing the tax sources to the maximum extent possible would devolve on the PRIs in the State. This would be the surest guarantee for the strength as well as the autonomy of the PRIs. As such, the recommendations of the State Finance Commissions must be implemented in right earnest forthwith.

III. Decentralized Planning

Under Article 243 ZD of 74th Constitution Amendment the District Planning Committee (DPC) is to be constituted. The DPC is expected to prepare schemes of local nature covering special planning, sharing water and other natural resources, development of infrastructures, environmental conservation, etc.

Many advantages are claimed for such planning process from below. Although, the idea of decentralized planning at the lower levels has been there for quite some time, yet the concept has not so far taken off. As such, it is necessary to understand the forces operating against decentralized planning.

Political and bureaucratic resistance at the State level to sharing power and resources with the local level institutions for planning from below, is often cited as the most important reason for the failure of decentralized planning to strike roots. As such, democratic decentralisation should involve a process wherein power is dispersed from one single centre to lower units. The Panchayat Raj Institutions played a very insignificant role so far, in the absence of adequate empowerment. Therefore, for effective and appropriate planning at district levels, the following pre-requisites must be ensured:

i. Constitution of District Planning Committee with sufficient technical support.

ii. Clear demarcation of planning functions between State and districts.

iii. Devolution of plan funds and financial power.

iv. Ensuring people's participation at all stages in the planning process.

v. Training the personnel associated with planning.

IV. Integration of Specialized Agencies with Panchayat Raj Institutions

There are several specialized agencies in the districts like DRDA, District Scheduled Castes Service Co-operative Society, the District BC Service Co-operative Society, the Minorities Service Co-operative Society and the Integrated Tribal Development Agency to implement poverty alleviation programme for the specified target groups. There has to be intensive interaction among all these agencies for the roles of these agencies are supportive and complementary to each other. For all these agencies, the District Collector is the Chairman and they function under his overall guidance. Keeping these agencies outside the control of Zilla Parishads is likely to be counter-productive. Apart from duplication of administrative machinery the possibilities of conflict of interest among these agencies and Panchayat Raj Institutions will always be there. As such, integrating these agencies with Panchayat Raj Institutions will result in more efficient use of available manpower besides reducing the cost of administration. Further, there is no direct social audit for the activities of these agencies. As such, it is incumbent that all activities relating to poverty alleviation, rural development, etc. should be brought within the ambit of Panchayat Raj Institutions.

V. Interface between Officials and Elected Representatives

The Constitution Seventy-Third Amendment has broken a distinctly new ground in the field of public governance in India. The intention of Parliament and the expectations of the public are that these Panchayat Raj Institutions must succeed not only as principal vehicles of rural development, but also as institutions of self-government and good governance. A great deal of responsibility will still rest on the political leaders at the national and the State levels to translate the spirit of the Constitution into reality, by suitably empowering the Panchayat Raj Institutions at all levels. Only with proper understanding and appreciation by both the polity and bureaucracy, can Panchayat Raj Institutions develop as vibrant institutions of local self-government and perpetuate good governance.

VI. Capacity Building of PR Functionaries

Effective implementation of the provisions of the 73rd Constitution Amendment will call for, among other things, empowering the elected functionaries at different levels of Panchayat Raj administration with necessary knowledge and skills in the management of Panchayati Raj bodies.

It is in this context that training of elected representatives, particularly the first time entrants and those belonging to the weaker sections, assumes significance. In other words, the second generation of Panchayat Raj leadership will have to be empowered to play their role effectively. Since the Panchayat Raj Institutions have been entrusted with 29 subjects under the Eleventh Schedule to the Constitution, the elected representatives will have to play a pivotal role in the management of development programme at lower levels, particularly in view of the fact that the Panchayat Raj Institutions have been Constitutionally entrusted with specific responsibilities of preparing plans and implementing various schemes for economic development and social justice. As such, an action plan for training of elected representatives of the Panchayat Raj Institutions has to be envisaged so as to provide them with the opportunity to acquire appropriate knowledge and skills in different aspects of management and decision-making process.

Conclusions

The Seventy-Third Constitution amendment and the Andhra Pradesh Raj Act 1994 which has been enacted in pursuance of the amendment provides for restructuring, reinforcing and revitalizing the institutions of grassroots and bring them within the ambit of the polity. To realize genuine development, local bodies are only suitable institutional vehicles for planning and implementation of programmes pertaining to economic development and social justice. The parameters of good governance viz., legitimacy, democratisation, participation, decentralisation, devolution, and accountability are manifest in the provisions. However, there are certain impediments with regard to devolution of functions, functionaries and the funds. The role of Gram Sabha is required to be further enhanced for ensuring social audit. The process of decentralisation is required to be accelerated. All the specialized agencies which have been constituted for the common cause of poverty alleviation should be integrated with the Panchayat Raj Institutions. A great responsibility lies with the State government to tie loose ends and issue instructions to expedite the process.

Notes

1. Gram Sabha means a body consisting of persons registered in the electoral rolls relating to a village.
2. "Zilla Parishad" means a local body at the district level.
3. "Mandal Parishad" means a local body at the intermidiate level.
4. Panchayat Raj Bodies means local bodies in rural areas.
5. "Gram Panchayat" means a local body at the village level.

References

Overseas Development Administration (ODA), *Taking Account of Good Government*, London, 1993.

UNDP, *Public Sector Management, Governance and Sustainable Human Development*, New York, 1995.

Venkataranggaya, M. 'and Pattaviram, M. (ed.), *Local Government in India*, Alfred Publishers, 1970.

World Bank, *The World Bank and Participation*, 1994.

URBAN GOVERNANCE IN DEVELOPING WORLD AND BANGLADESH

Nazrul Islam

Urbanization: A Global Overview

Right now we are experiencing a phase of transformation of the world from a "Global Village" to an "Urban Globe" (Ministry of Foreign Affairs, Netherlands, 1994), or to an "Urbanized World" (UN, 1996). By the year 2005 more people will live in urban areas than in the countrysides.

The process of urbanization and the growth of cities are inevitable and irresistible. It has also been very rapid during the last half century. In 1950 only 29.2% of the world's population lived in urban areas. The proportion increased to 37.1% in 1990 and to 42.1% in 1990. It will cross the 50% mark in 2005 and by the year 2025, the share will rise to 60% of the world's total population (Table A.1).

In 1950 the total urban population in the developed countries was nearly double that of the developing countries, with 447 million people in urban areas against only 227 million in the developing countries. The level of urbanization (percentage of total population living in urban areas) at that time was 53.8% in developed countries and only 17.0% in developing countries. But it did not take too long for the developing countries to out pace the developed countries in the number race. Already by 1990 there were more urban people in the developing countries than in the developed countries, with 966 million against 798 million. However, the level of urbanization was still very much higher in the developed world, with 70.2% against 29.2% in the developing world in 1980. The trend continues. The estimated total urban population in the year 2000 is 950 million for the developed world and 1904 million for the developing world. By 2025 the developing world will have 3845 million urban people, which will be nearly 4 times more than in the developed world (Table A.1).

While the developed world had achieved the 50% level in urbanization before 1950, the developing world will do so only by around 2015, and the whole world by 2005 when the global urban population will be over 3 billion.

There was a time when the desirability of urbanization was questioned but the current thinking is that urbanization can be positive. "As in richer countries, cities are contributing to growth by absorbing population increase, affording a base for more diffused productive activities and providing infrastructure and services required for marketing and exporting" (UNDP, 1991).

Contemporary Urban Problems

But urbanization is not an unmixed blessing. Managing the urban transition will require a better understanding of the characteristics of urbanization and of the major problems that are associated with it. These problems include overconcentration of population and economic activities in a few large cities, rise in the number of urban households living in poverty, enormous shortfalls in shelter and services, deterioration of the environment, increase in crime and violence and exploitation of women and child labour.

Overconcentration in Large Cities

Recent urbanization is characterized by overconcentration of population and economic activities in a few large cities. This has happened globally, regionally and even within individual countries.

Spectacular increase has taken place around the world in cities with more than 4 million inhabitants. In 1960 these numbered 19, with 10 in industrial countries. In 1980, cities with more than 4 million people had almost doubled in number to 35 with 22 in developing countries. Such major cities are projected to increase to 66 by the turn of the century and to 135 by 2025, with most of these rise in developing countries.

But cities with more than 10 million, or megacities, as they have come to be known are the focus of attention at present. By 2000 there will be 20 of these megacities in the world with Dhaka (11.5 million) being the 19th largest, just above Cairo, and Tokyo being the largest with 28 million people. Only 3 out of these 20 megacities are located in the developed world.

Increasing Poverty in Urban Areas

Urbanization has brought an alarming rise in the incidence of urban poverty. According to the World Bank, in 1998 about 330 million urban residents or about a quarter of the urban population were living in absolute poverty (World Bank, 1990 and UNDP, 1991). This number will swell with continuing rapid growth of urban population. In many regions or countries, even if the percentage share of urban population living in poverty may not rise, the absolute number of poor people will rise. This has been the case in many countries including Bangladesh where the number increased from only 5.6 million in 1973-74 to 10.8 million in 1988-89 and to over 14 million in 1997-98.

Growing Demands on Shelter and Urban Services

Rapid urbanization has led to more demands on low income housing and provision of basic utility services. Already more than 600 million people in developing countries are either homeless or live in extremely poor quality housing. In many large cities of the third world, 20-50% of the population live in slums and squatter settlements. The ratios are 52% for Bombay, 40% for Dhaka, 60% for Ankara, for example.

Many urban residents in developing countries have to live without electricity, piped water, hygienic sewerage facility and proper fuel.

Environmental Degradation

Due to rapid population growth, increased industrial activities, poverty and poor enforcement of regulations, quality of the urban environment in developing countries is declining fast. Given industrial export market orientation, further industrial pollution in large cities of developing countries is almost inevitable. Growing affluence in a section of urban population encourages growth in the number of automobiles, causing air pollution. Even secondary cities are no longer free from pollution.

Crime and Violence

Incidence of crime and violence has increased manifold in most cities of the developing world. Crime is no longer a big city monopoly, even secondary cities and small towns have also become vulnerable to criminal activities of organized mafia. A new dimension to urban crime is the direct involvement of the police in such activities, including drug dealing, sex crimes and violence.

Exploitation of Women and Children

Large cities, as industrial and manufacturing centres, exploit female and child labour rather harshly. Gender exploitation in developing country cities is rampant, in terms of wages, hours worked and physical and mental harassment. Child labour exploitation is common in informal sector enterprises, but also in many formal sector establishments. Sexual abuse of women and children also abound.

Urban Local Governance in the Developing World

The contemporary world is experiencing profound change in the field of governance and in this context many developing countries are undertaking extensive state reform including decentralization of state structures and functions, public administration reorganization, and transitional steps to democratization. As a result there is an increased emphasis on the need to address local government more specifically, since in many countries this has been a neglected tier of government in the development effort (McCarney, 1996).

Recent dynamics of globalization of economic and socio-cultural developments, urge for democratization, decentralization and structural adjustments and market orientation in economy at the national level and the emergence of enormous problems of over population, poverty, environmental degradation, shortage of shelter and services, increase in violence, and gender and child exploitation at the local (city) level and the inability of urban local governments to combat these problems effectively, have all focused attention on the need for strengthening urban local government. A new form of urban local governance is the demand of the day. This governance is through a new 'state' which has been defined quite aptly by Hye in his paper on "Good Governance" written for the present international seminar (Hye, 1998). The new state, he schematizes, as one composed of a partnership of the Government (National) private sector, local government, civil society (which again is composed of a multitude of organizations or bodies), the judiciary and legislature (or parliament).

The need for a new type of local government is being felt by both the national governments and also pushed by the international development agencies (such as, the World Bank, the Asian Development Bank, European Commission and the UN System). The UN commitment to and insistence on encouraging local government was evident in the inclusion of mayors of cities and other stakeholders in human settlements issues, notably the private sector organizations and NGOs in the official delegations to the United Nations Second Conference on Human Settlements, otherwise referred to as Habitat II, or the "City Summit" held at Istanbul in June, 1996.

The international scholarly community also seems to favour stronger and more autonomous local (city/town etc.) level governance (McCarney, 1996b, p.16-17) of course, in the new sense of the term "governance".

In Hye's scheme of governance, "The New State" is the composite of the state and the rest (including the civil society). It is a kind of partnership between the state and the rest. To the group of governance researchers with the Global Urban Research Initiative (GURI), "Governance" refers to "the relationship between the state and the civil society, between the rulers and the ruled, the government and the governed" (McCarney, et al. 1995) and it is this relation of civil society to the state that distinguishes their idea of governance from other ideas of governance. It is the nature of partnership and not just partnership that matters in governance. This nature of partnership may range from tokenism to real or equal partnerships.

A short review of the nature of urban local governments and their relationship with the civil society and other actors in different parts of the developing world is presented in the following section.

Africa

Most African cities have been experiencing rapid population growth. This associated with dwindling urban services, has posed strong challenge to urban governance. Search for a proper form of governance is evident in different parts of Africa. Britain and France, as the major colonial powers on the continent for the late 19th century to the 1960s, provided the framework for two largely parallel approaches to local government. These two approaches overlapped to some degree by the 1990s, but their essential elements could still be distinguished. The pattern most common in Francophone countries may be called the communal structure while the pattern in Anglophone countries may be called the representative council structure (Stren, 1996).

In most of the Francophone countries, urban local governments provided for communes with mayors, municipal councils and specific revenue and expenditure powers and procedures. By the end of the colonial period in the late 1950s, the evolution of the municipal institutions was such that the municipal councils (the administrative organs of the communes) in the larger cities had become responsible for a relatively important range of local services, and were presided over by elected mayors. By the end of the 1980s more attention was placed on development of metropolitan government structures, with a more democratic and decentralized framework. Many of the major Francophone countries were organizing multiparty elections to city/metropolitan councils, as well as to national councils. In the process, the mayors in cities such as Abidjan in Ivory Coast, has come to play a pro-active role in local urban governance. They even go out to obtain additional resources from foreign embassies and international NGOs (Stren, 1996).

In the Anglophone African countries, the British laid a stronger thrust on introducing efficient and democratic system of local government but only at the end of their colonial period. They tried to position more autonomous local councils, as counterforce to the more broadly nationalist movements. However, partly as a result of both political and financial factors in most English speaking countries, the political autonomy and fiscal resource base of municipal governments was progressively restricted during the 1960s and 1970s. Exception was, Nigeria, where under military rule local governments were favoured (similarly in Pakistan and to some extent Bangladesh).

The 1970s largely saw little role of the local communities and civil society, while the reforms of 1950s and 1990s have shown more involvement of these other forces in the local urban governance in Anglophone cities. Zimbabwe boasts of a strong civil society participation, Uganda has a "Resistance Council" (Grassroots participatory ystem) working with the traditional department-based administrative structure (Stren, 1996). The most dramatic example of civil society's involvement in local governance (as well as national) is of course from South Africa since the end of apartheid days in 1994. Elsewhere in Africa, as highly centralized governments are getting weaker under the twin assaults of globalization and structural adjustments, local communities and interest group in the cities are beginning to assert themselves in the governance of their communities, towns and cities. A new form of governance is beginning to evolve (Stren, 1996).

Latin America

Latin American countries have been characterized by strong centralized political, administrative and economic systems and were not known for decentralization. It is only in the last couple of decades that the democratic process has become a little consolidated with elected governments in many countries. As a result local government has also gained some political importance as the institution most directly responsible for the resolution of urban problems and as a point of interaction between the state and the society (Mercondes, 1996).

In **Chile**, decentralization introduced changes in the management of urban and social services, modifying and strengthening the role and functions of Chilean municipalities. Democratic elections of mayor and town councillors were instituted together with community participation mechanisms. As a result Chilean municipalities enjoy local autonomy and a revenue redistribution mechanism (through the Municipal Common Fund) which provides them with financial resources (Mercondes, 1996).

In **Mexico**, municipalities are still highly dependent on and subordinated to the state and federal governments for financial resources and for the development and implementation of programmes. Civic participation is also often discouraged.

Urban local governments in many Latin American countries have a limited capacity to deal with new and increasing demands for social services and infrastructure. In some countries (such as Mexico) democratization and modernization of the political system has been slow, difficult and uneven (Missal, 1996).

NGO activities have been relatively limited to local level but their action have benefited the poorest sectors (McCarney, et al. 1995).

Asia

Being a vast region with diverse historical, political and economic backgrounds, the local government system in Asia is also very diverse. At least 3 major sub-regions have to be considered for Asia. The three Asian sub-regions are: (1) Northeast Asia, (2) Southeast Asia and (3) South Asia. (There could be a fourth one with Australia-New Zealand and the Pacific countries and a fifth, West Asia; these are excluded from this review.)

Northeast Asia: This includes China, Japan, Korea and others. **China** has a long history of local government. But modern China (or PRC) has now three types of local governments: main body type, autonomous governments of nationality regions and government of special administrative regions.

Japan also has very long history of local government, with a highly centralized system until the Second World War. After the war, democratization brought about changes in the local government structure also. The new constitution of 1947 viewed local self-government as an indispensable element of democracy and a Local Autonomy Law was enacted in 1947 for the purpose. The latest revision (in 1994) of the Local Autonomy Law provides scope for new system for urban local bodies to be more efficient with "Core City System" and "Wide area cooperative system" (Kim, 1998).

Participatory planning in urban areas is a common practice. In this process even university teachers and students work very closely with the community and the local authority (UNCHS-CITYNET, 1997).

Malaysia has a three tier administrative hierarchy, the federal, state and local levels. Within the local level there used to be four urban councils before 1976. These being: (1) City Hall of Kuala Lumpur, (2) Municipal Council, (3) Town Council and (4) Town Board and rural councils e.g. (1) Rural district and (2) Local council. After restructuring the 1976 Act provides for a total of four councils, in 1997 these are (1) City Halls (Numbering 2), City Council (3) Municipal councils (16) and (4) district councils (113). Civil Society participation in Malaysian cities is a common practice.

The **Philippines**, with 327 years of Spanish rule saw a highly centralized political administrative system. Since independence, decentralization has progressed significantly. Finally, the Local Government Code of 1997 strengthened local governments. At present there are 78 provinces, 67 cities, 1600 municipalities and 42,000 barangays (villages). There are also special units such as Metropolitan Manila Development Authority (MMDA). Autonomous Region of Muslim Mindanao (ARMM) and Cordillera Administrative Region (CAR). Urban local governments in the Philippines now enjoy considerable autonomy, with one of the liveliest mechanisms for people's participation in local governance, The law mandates that 25 per cent of membership in Local Development Councils at the municipal, city authority and other local levels be reserved for NGOs (McCarney, 1996: p.217).

Thailand maintains a European style parliamentary system within Monarchy since 1932. Local Government in Thailand is organized at six levels, 3 for urban and 3 for rural. For urban areas there are: (1) the Bangkok Metropolitan Administration, (2) Municipalities (governing urban centres in the provinces) and (3) the city of Pattaya (in the form of City Manager). All these forms of local governments are subjected to considerable degree of control by the central government through the Ministry of Interior (McCarney, 1996).

Thai local governments suffer from low level of people's participation and inefficiency, among other limitations. NGO participation and involvement is also limited. However, in Bangkok some instances of NGO activism (as in housing rights of the poor) can be seen.

South Asia: Unlike Northeast Asia and Southeast Asia, South Asia is somewhat more homogenous in terms of local government system, particularly in the three large countries, India, Pakistan and Bangladesh, because of their historical political common tradition. All these three have long history of local government, evolving from the times of the Mughals, through the British and then through post colonial independent governments. A more modern form of urban local government began with the establishment of municipal administration in three presidency towns of Madras, Bombay and Calcutta (all in present day India) in the 1860s.

In **India** today, local governments are basically of two types: rural and urban. Generally rural governments consist of three tiers, namely, Village Panchayats, the Panchayat Samity and the Zila Parishad. Urban local governments can be divided into five types: City corporations (numbering about 70), the Municipality or Municipal Council which number (700), the Cantonment Boards, the Notified Area Committees, and the Town Committees.

The City Corporations as the highest level of urban local governments enjoy more autonomy and functions compared with other types of local governments.

The Municipal administration is typically responsible for the provision of basic public goods falling into four broad categories; public health, public safety, public work and public order. They also perform important regulatory functions. (These responsibilities of municipalities is common in almost all major South-Asian countries.) The other common feature is the dominance of property taxes in the fiscal domain of municipalities.

The 74th Constitutional Amendment Act, 1992 in India provides greater autonomy to Indian municipalities, in which their supersession by state governments can not be made for indefinite period and in which municipalities or corporations will have economic functions as well. Some cities are even floating bonds.

In **Pakistan**, the record of urban local government has not been good. Since its independence in 1947, Pakistan experienced many military take-overs and although at times the military dictators favoured the flourishing of local governments, there have been many ups and downs. In 1977, the military government of the time established the current local government system, which for urban areas, consists of three tiers: (1) Municipal Corporations for major metropolitan cities (500,000 or more), Municipal committee (in towns of 30,000-500,000) and towns (Nagar) Panchayats and over 36,000 Ward Committees. The Town Panchayat is the only urban body in **Nepal**. The urban centres should have minimum population of 10,000 to be a Town Panchayat. The Executive Committee of the Town Panchayat consists of a Chairman and Vice Chairman directly elected by the people with a 5 year term. Under the Integrated Action Plan (IAP) participatory action planning and development are seen in Nepalese towns. IAP provides for development work jointly by municipal representatives, sectoral departmental representatives, NGOs, communities and IAP planners. Democratic participation is the present trend in local governance in Nepal.

Urban Governance in Bangladesh

Bangladesh experienced more or less similar tradition in local government system like India or Pakistan, in the distant past, it had the same system as Pakistan's (during 1947-51) and a system of its own since 1971. The latest developments in local government restructuring took place as recently as 1997. In the overall structure in the local government in Bangladesh there is a four tier system, with Zila Parishad, Upazila Parishad, Union Parishad and the Gram Parishad. The latter two have already been brought under legal coverage while the other two await such coverage. Parallel to these are the urban local governments, with City Corporations (for the 4 large metropolitan areas) and Pourashavas for the municipalities (over 140 in number). Rest of urban centres (numbering nearly 382) are run under Union Parishad structure. The 140 municipalities are again divided into 3 class categories, based on their tax income level.

Local government in Bangladesh has a democratic character, as all mayors, chairmen and council members or commissioners are directly elected by the people for a 5 year term. Even seats reserved for women will now be directly elected at Gram and Union Parishad level and hopefully later also at the other levels. People participate in corporation and municipal elections with great enthusiasm.

The urban local governments enjoy more or less similar functional responsibilities as in India (Table A.2).

Corporation and municipalities are however heavily dependent on central government for funds and even personnel. Property tax is the main source of revenue of local bodies.

Large cities, like Dhaka, Chittagong and Khulna, face all the typical problems of contemporary major cities, such as those of over-population, poverty, shortage of housing and services, environmental degradation, crime and gender exploitation. Efficient management of cities has become difficult due to poor human resource quality of the authorities, their lack of commitment and integrity, shortage of financial resources, lack of coordination amongst the city authorities and other government agencies and the other actors.

The local authorities also suffer from too much control from central government, two little participation of the people in the local body's planning and development activities (NGOs operate parallel to city authority and in isolation) and lack of accountability and transparency. Ultimately, the urban local bodies are known to be characterized by weak administrative capacity, a limited financial and human resource base, and little public participation (Ahmed, 1997).

Central Government and Parastatal Bodies

A large number of central government departments and autonomous bodies have been assigned responsibilities in providing services in urban areas. The number of such agencies is greater in city corporation than in municipalities. In Dhaka, for example, more than 40 governmental departments/autonomous bodies are involved (Table A.3). These are involved in planning, physical development, infrastructure, land and housing, slum improvement, water supply and sewerage, electricity, gas supply, environmental control, law and order, traffic and transportation, roads, education, health, population and welfare, culture and sports etc.

Private Sector

The private sector is composed of the formal private sector and the informal private sector. In terms of employment generation the ratio between the two varies between 30:70 in large cities and to 20:80 (or even lower) in small municipalities, with larger share contributed by the informal sector. In terms of gross city product the ratios will be perhaps 50:50 for large cities and 40:60 or 30:70 in smaller towns.

Besides employment, the private sector provides for land supply, housing, transport, shopping, health, education, recreation, religious services and others. The private sector is now also involved in telecommunications.

The private sector is increasingly becoming more significant. In the process, the sector is also causing many problems in urban development and governance, as it frequently disregards statutory restrictions.

NGOs and Civil Society

In urban areas NGO involvement has increased significantly in the last few years (although these are not as extensive as in rural areas). Urban NGOs have brought about noticeable improvement in the living conditions of many of the urban poor by providing credit, skill training, and by building awareness about their rights, and about health and education.

In Dhaka city alone, there are now over 100 large and small NGOs working; similarly in all other cities and secondary towns some NGOs are found active. However, unlike in the Philippines, NGOs are not yet an official participant in local government sponsored planning and development programmes, although in some specific projects, they are invited to participate. Normally, NGOs work parallel to the local government and central government programmes.

Besides registered NGOs, a number of civil society groups, social organizations, citizens forums, women's groups, association of professional groups, research organization like the Centre for Urban

Studies, the media and the others have become increasingly active in raising issues of governance in cities.

The environmental concern of Dhaka, has forced organizations like Bangladesh Lawyers' Association (BELA) to take Dhaka City Corporation or the Department of Environment to the court. The newly formed citizens forum have been mobilizing public opinion against some RAJUK/GOB decision which could threaten environmental balance in the city, by filling up lakes and by other developments.

Donors

International donor agencies are important actors in urban governance. Through funding and technical support they can and often insist on sustainable and participatory urban governance and urban development, UNDP-UNCHS, UNICEF, WHO, World Bank, ADB, the European Commission and many industrial-developed countries have intervened in urban planning, urban development, infrastructure, water, sewerage, electricity, flood control, transportation, poverty alleviation, health and education in urban areas.

Search for an Appropriate Local Government System

In response to some recent crises in governance of the cities in Bangladesh, a solution was deemed appropriate. All the four city corporations have complained of central government's excessive control over them, and city corporation's lack of adequate authority or power over government or autonomous bodies.

The present government formed a 16-member Coordination Committee for Dhaka City Corporation, with the Minister for Local Government, Rural Development and Cooperatives (LRGD & C) as its convenor and the Mayor as its co-convenor. Similar committees were also formed for other cities also with minister as convenor. The committee failed to be effective for several reasons. But most basically, it cannot work unless the Mayor (who officially has a cabinet status) is made the convenor with appropriate authority and power vested in him (if necessary by amending existing legal provisions).

Secondly, the Co-ordination Committee (CC) only comprises 16 governmental bodies although there are many more with development or service activities in the city. They should be made members of Co-ordination Committee (CC). The private sector, NGOs and other members of the civil society should also be assured representation in the Co-ordination Committee (CC). (In the Philippines, participation of NGOs has been made constitutionally obligatory). Participation of women should be adequately ensured.

In addition to the Coordination Committee, an Advisory/Consultative Committee for the City Corporation should be considered. This committee should include professional and technical people, among others. Similar arrangements can be made for all cities and towns.

The problems of physical planning, architectural and housing development in Dhaka prompted the Ministry of Housing and Public Works to form an Advisory Committee for the Ministry, with the Minister as the Chairman, and with technical and professional people as some of the members. This committee should have close liaison with the Coordination Committee of DCC, otherwise there will be unnecessary duplication of work.

The World Bank is supporting the Dhaka City Corporation and the Bangladesh Road Transport Authority to develop an improved urban transportation system for Dhaka. It has provided for some degree of citizen's and concerned group's participation in the planning and implementation process. This is laudable and should be followed in all projects.

The World Health Organization (WHO) is supporting a programme of healthy City Development in four cities, namely Chittagong, Rajshahi, Cox's Bazar and Sylhet. In each of these a Coordination Committee has been formed with the Mayor/Chairman as the Convenor or Chairman and appropriate representatives of all governmental/parastatal bodies working in those cities, as well as representatives of the private sector, NGOs, civil society groups and distinguished persons. The system seems to be acceptable to the people. In each city a number of sectoral/zonal Task Forces have been formed to identify problems and initiate development activities, Frequent meetings are held to perform these tasks.

A participatory process of urban governance appears to be taking shape. However, the effectiveness of this process will significantly depend on the personality, commitment and leadership of the key person, the Mayor/Chairman.

A demand of the Mayor of Dhaka (and also some other City Corporation) is for establishment of Metropolitan Governments in the City Corporation. A review of the urban local government system in the countries of the developing world (Africa, Latin America and Asia) does not convince us that a Metropolitan Government is the ideal solution to problems of good governance in our cities, or even in Dhaka. There are very few examples of Metro-Government in the Developing World. Our political culture is also not yet ready for such a system. On the other hand, City Corporations and municipalities can be made more autonomous and powerful. Local bodies should have economic developmental functions in addition to service and regulatory functions. More specifically, as suggested earlier, the Dhaka City Corporation Committee should be headed by the City Mayor, with adequate power.

The problem of governance of Capital cities is always complex and serious thinking needs to be devoted to its solution. Governance in Dhaka deserves full attention of experts and all concerned people.

TABLE A.1

Urban Population in Developed and Developing Countries, 1950-2025

Year (est)	Developed Countries		Developing Countries		World Total	
	Urban Popn (m)	% of Total Popn	Urban Popn (m)	% of Total Popn	Urban Popn (m)	% of Total Popn
1950	447	53.8	287	17.0	734	29.2
1960	571	60.5	460	22.2	1032	34.2
1970	698	66.6	673	25.4	1371	37.1
1980	798	70.2	966	29.2	1764	39.6
1990 (est)	877 (est)	72.5	1357 (est)	33.6	2234	42.6
2000 (est)	950 (est)	74.4	1904 (est)	39.3	2854	46.6
2010 (est)	1011 (est)	76 0	26.12 (est)	46.2	3623	51.8
2020 (est)	1063 (est)	77.2	3425 (est)	53.1	4488	57.4
2025 (est)	1087 (est)	77.8	3845 (est)	56.5	4932	60.1

Source : Richard E. Stren and P. McCarney, 1992, (based on various UN Sources).

TABLE A.2

Urban Local Government Functions, Bangladesh

Compulsory Functions

- construction and maintenance of roads, bridges and culverts;
- removal, collection and disposal of refuse;
- provision and maintenance of street lighting;
- maintenance of public streets, provision of street watering;
- provision and regulation of water supply;
- establishment and maintenance of public markets;
- plantation and trees of road rides;
- regulation and insanitary buildings;
- prevention of infectious diseases and epidemics;
- registration of births, deaths and marriages;
- provision and maintenance of slaughter houses;
- provision and maintenance of drainage;
- control over erection and re-erection of buildings;
- provision and maintenance of graveyards and burning places; and
- control over traffic and public vehicles.

Optional Functions

- checking adulteration of food products;
- control over private markets;
- maintenance of educational institutions & provision of stipends to meritorious students;
- provision of flood and famine relief;
- provision and maintenance of parks and gardens;
- establishment of welfare homes, orphanages, prevention of begging and organization of voluntary social welfare services;
- establishment of public dispensaries, provision of public urinals and latrines;
- establishment of veterinary hospitals, registration of cattle sale, improvement of livestock;
- celebration of national holidays;
- reception of distinguished visitors;
- establishment of public libraries and reading rooms;
- promotion of community development schemes; and
- naming of roads and numbering of houses.

TABLE A.3

Agencies for Urban Development in Dhaka City: Their Status and Major Functions

Sl. No.	Name of Agency	Administrative Ministry/Agency	Major Functions
01.	National Economic Council (NEC)	National Council	Investment in Metropolitan Areas.
02.	Planning Commission	Ministry of Planning	National Development Planning, Policies and Strategies.
03.	Urban Development Directorate	Ministry of Works	Nation-Wide Urban and Regional Planning.
04.	Rajdhani Unnayan Kartripakhya (RAJUK)	Ministry of Works	Development Planning: Dhaka Metropolitan Area.
05.	Housing and Settlement Directorate (HSD)	Ministry of Works	Provision of Public Housing in Urban Areas.
06.	Public Works Department (PWD)	Ministry of Works	Construction of Public Buildings and Maintenance.
07.	Deputy Commissioner of Settlements (DCS)	Ministry of Works	Land Lease, Title Transfer.
08.	Dhaka Water and Sewerage Authority (DWASA)	Ministry of Works	Provision of Water Supply and Sewerage Disposal.
09.	Dept. of Public Health Engineering (DPHE)	Ministry of Works	Sanitation and Drainage.
10.	Registrar Cooperative Societies (Housing Sector)	Ministry of Works	Registration of Housing Cooperative Societies.
11.	Dept. of Environment and Pollution Control	Ministry of Environment and Forest	Control of Air and Water Pollution.
12.	Telegraph and Telephone Board (T & T)	Ministry of Post and Telecommunication	Provision of Telephone and Telegraph Services.
13.	Power Development Board (PDB)/DESA	Ministry of Energy and Mineral Resources	Generation and Supply of Electric Power.
14.	Titas Gas	Ministry of Energy and Mineral Resources	Supply of Fuel Gas.
15.	Roads and Highway Department (R & H)	Ministry of Communication	Construction and Improvement of Highways, Major Roads, Bridges and Related Works.
16.	Bangladesh Road Transport Corporation (BRTC)	Ministry of Communication	Provision of Public Transport (BUS) Services.
17.	Bangladesh Railway (BR)	Ministry of Communication	Expansion and Maintenance of Rail Transport.

(Contd.)

(Continued Table A.3)

Sl. No.	Name of Agency	Administrative Ministry/Agency	Major Functions
18.	Civil Aviation Authority	Ministry of Civil Aviation and Tourism	Development and Maintenance of Airports
19.	Bangladesh Parjatan Corporation (BPC)	Ministry of Civil Aviation and Tourism	Provision of Facilities for Tourists (Parks, Restaurants).
20.	Inland Water Transport Authority (BITA)	Ministry of Port, Shipping and Inland Water Transport	Expansion and Maintenance of Water Transport.
21.	Dhaka Metropolitan Police (DMP)	Ministry of Home Affairs	Control Traffic, Collection of Road Tax and Licensing of Vehicles.
22.	Fire Service and Civil Defence	Ministry of Home Affairs	Fire Fighting and Ambulance Services.
23.	Cantonment Board	Ministry of Defence	Provision and Maintenance of Services in Cantonment Areas.
24.	Survey of Bangladesh (SOB)	Ministry of Defence	Land Records and Areal Photography.
25.	Space Research and Remote Sensing Organization (SPARRSO)	Ministry of Defence	Collection and Analysis of Satellite Data.
26.	Board of Investment (BOI)	President's Secretariat	Approval of Industrial Projects.
27.	Small and Cottage Industry Corporation	Ministry of Industries	Development of Small and Cottage Industry.
28.	Directorates of Primary, Secondary and Technical Education	Ministry of Education	Construction, Maintenance and Supervision of Schools and Educational Institutes.
29.	Universities	Ministry of Education	Higher Education and Research Services.
30.	Bangladesh Water Development Board (BWRDB)	Ministry of Irrigation, Water Development and Flood Control	Embankment for Flood Protection.
31.	House Building Finance Corporation (HBFC)	Ministry of Finance	Provision of Loans for Housing Construction in the Private Sector.
32.	Bangladesh Agricultural Development Corporation (BADC)	Ministry of Agriculture	Provision for Marketing Facilities.
33.	Uddayan Unnayan Board	Ministry of Agriculture	Development of Horticulture.

(Contd.)

(Continued Table A.3)

Sl. No.	Name of Agency	Administrative Ministry/Agency	Major Functions
34.	Sports Federation	Ministry of Youth and Sports	Promotion and Provision for Facilities for Games and Sports
35.	Housing Estates (HE)	Ministry of Commerce	Provision for Land and Housing.
36.	NGO Affairs Bureau	Prime Ministers Secretariat	Construction and Maintenance of Local Urban Services.
37.	Ministry of Land	Ministry of Land	Khas Land.
38.	Directorate of Health	Ministry of Health	Health Facilities.
39.	Department Social Welfare	Ministry of Social Welfare and Women Affairs	Community Development and Services, Income Generating Activities, Literacy Programme.
40.	Department of Women Affairs	Ministry of Social Welfare and Women Affairs	Protection of Women's Rights, Upliftment of Women's Development.

References

Hye, H.A., 1998. "Good Governance", Concept paper for International Seminar, Dhaka, 4-6 August 1998.

Islam, N. and M.M. Khan, 1997. *Urban Governance in Bangladesh and Pakistan*, Dhaka: Centre for Urban Studies.

Islam, N., et al. 1998. *Reforming Governance in Dhaka*, Bangladesh. Paper for the Global Urban Research Initiative (GURI), Dhaka: Centre for Urban Studies.

Kakpol, O., 1996. "Thailand: Governance", in McCarney, 1996b.

Kim. B-J, and Suns Gul Hong, 1998. *A Summary Report on the Local Governments in the Asia Pacific Region*, (Unpublished Report for IULA, based on 14 country Reports).

McCarney, P.L., 1996a. *Cities and Governance: New Directions in Latin America*. Asia and Africa. Toronto: Centre for Urban and Community Studies, University of Toronto.

McCarney, P.L., 1996b. *The Changing Nature of Local Government in Developing Countries*, Toronto: Centre for Urban and Community Studies, University of Toronto.

McCarney, P.L., M. Halfani and A. Rodrignez, 1995. "Towards an Understanding of Governance: The Governance of an Idea and Its Implications for Urban Research in Developing Countries", 1995 in R. Stren and J.K. Bell (eds.) 1995, Perspectives on the City. Toronto: Centre for urban and Community Studies University of Toronto.

Massalo, A., 1996. "Mexico: Governance", in McCarney, 1996b.

Mercondes, C., 1996. "Latin America: Introduction" (Governance), in McCarney, 1996b.

Ministry of Foreign Affairs Netherlands, 1994. Sectoral Policy Document of Development Cooperation: Poverty Alleviation, The Hague.

Siddiqui, K., 1992. *Local Government in South Asia: A Comparative Perspective*, Dhaka: University Press Limited.

Stren, R., 1996, "Africa: Introduction" (Governance), in McCarney, 1996b.

Tapales, P.D., 1996. *Philippines* (Governance). In McCarney, 1996b.

UNCHS-CITYNET, 1997. Partnership for Local Action: A Sourcebook on Participatory Planning to Shelter and Human Settlements Improvement for Local Government Officials. Bangkok and Yokohama: UNCHS (Habitat) and CITY NET.

UNCHS (Habitat), 1996. An Urbanizing World: Global Report on Human Settlements, 1996.

Oxford: Oxford University Press for UNCHS (Habitat).

UNDP, 1991. *Cities, People and Poverty: Urban Development Cooperation for the 1990s*. A UNDP Strategy Paper, New York: UNDP.

Zaidi, S.A., 1997. "Urban Local Governance in Pakistan", in N. Islam and M.M. Khan (eds.).

Urban Governance in Bangladesh and Pakistan, Dhaka: Centre for Urban Studies.

ROLE OF CITY GOVERNMENT IN GOOD GOVERNANCE

K.C. Sivaramakrishnan

In the past two decades the world's urban population has increased by about a billion people, from 1.35 to 2.28 billion. About 60 per cent of this increase has come from Asia and most of it, from the five countries of China, Indonesia, Bangladesh, India and Pakistan. Within South Asia the total population has increased from 718 million in 1971 to about 1.11 billion by 1991. The percentage of people living in urban areas has also gone up from 19 to 26: more in some countries like Bangladesh (from 8 to 20 per cent) and less in others like Sri Lanka (from 21 to 22 per cent). Absolute numbers of people living in cities have risen from 136 million to 286. Current estimates are closer to 400 million and in twenty years, more than 880 million people will be living in the towns and cities of South Asia, a number larger than the total population of numerous countries in the world (Table 1).

This vast and dramatic change in the South Asian landscape is a manifestation of the economic change in all the 5 countries of the sub-continent.

Large city growth is a prominent feature of South Asia's urbanization. There are 23 cities in India with a million people or more, 7 in Pakistan and 3 in Bangladesh. The proportion of urban population living in these large cities is indicated in Table 2. But urbanization is not limited to the large cities: growth is taking place across the board and the number of towns, small and medium, of various size classes, is increasing (Table 3).

Tasks of Governance

a. Alleviating Poverty

For those who can afford, city life in south Asia may indeed be attractive but for a large number of urban dwellers poverty is a stark reality. The UNDP's Human Development Report of 1991 offers a cross-country comparison (Table 4). While the number below the absolute poverty line is quite high in rural areas, the percentage of urban population below that line is about the same in Nepal and Pakistan while it is less, but very significant in India and Bangladesh.

Poverty thresholds are usually based on minimum calorific intake. If the gross inequities in access to basic sources like water and sanitation, and morbidity characteristics are considered, the prevalence and deepening of urban poverty may be more pronounced. In almost all South Asian cities excepting Sri Lanka, slums account for 20 to 40 per cent of urban residence.

b. Infrastructures

In most South Asian cities, urban infrastructures, built slowly over several decades is under severe strain. Running out of water is a recurrent problem in many. Karachi, Hyderabad (India) or Bangalore have to draw their water from distant sources through expensive conveyance systems. Madras (Chinnai) has faced three water famines in the past forty years prompting fears of evacuation. In medium and smaller towns water supply is tenuous, to say the least. At the same time it is true that almost all cities in the region have invested and implemented water supply augmentation schemes. However, rising demand, poor pricing practices, inadequate maintenance, leakages robbing the water supply system of 20 to 35 per cent in all South Asian cities and increasing contamination of water sources and distribution system have rendered drinking water supply into a perennial problem.

c. Sanitation

Sanitation and solid waste management are other serious problems. Sewerage systems covering both conveyance and treatment exist only in 20 out of 300 class I cities in India. Disaggregated and community-based systems as demonstrated in the Orangi project in Karachi, slum improvement schemes in India and the low cost pour flush latrines have been promising initiatives but have not been scaled up. Per capita solid waste generation is about half kg. per day in the urban areas. Collection and organized disposal rarely cover the total volume, with the result of indiscriminate dumping in low lands, water bodies and hill slopes is rampant.

d. Transport

Faced with distortions in road pricing and taxation and irrational allocation of road space, public transport has been steadily loosing ground in most South Asian cities though the demand for it continues to be pressing. In the circumstances a variety of motorized and non-motorized, safe and unsafe vehicles collectively dubbed as 'pare transit' have virtually invaded the South Asian city. The 200,000 cycle rickshaws and 40,000 three-wheelers in Dhaka, the extended three-wheelers called 'tempo' or 'vikram' in north India, the mini-buses in Karachi or Lahore are all examples of the bewildering public transport scene in South Asia. Between national ministries of transport, roads, energy, industry or urban development on the one hand and the police, road transport regulators and municipal authorities on the other, provision of public transport is a subject lost in the institutional interstices. Only Sri Lanka has a semblance of an integrated institutional arrangement.

e. Environment

Inadequacies in infrastructures and the failure to provide basic services has had its impact on the environment. Air and water pollution affect most cities in the region particularly the metropolitan areas, like Dhaka, Calcutta, Delhi, Bangalore, Karachi or Kathmandu. To this already formidable list of problems are to be added the pressures of globalization and the need to maintain the competitiveness of cities. It is also to be realized that what is perceived as an economic advantage by some section of the society are rendering some others more vulnerable to an increasingly competitive environment,within and between countries. These are some of the many complex issues in the context of governance in South Asian city.

Structures of Urban Governance

As against these growing and complex tasks, the structures of urban governance have remained rather static over the years. Though the first municipal corporation was established in Madras in 1688 by the East India Company and sanitary committees, or Conservancy Boards were established in Karachi, Lahore and Rawalpindi as early as 1804s, it was Lord Ripon's resolution of 1882 which proclaimed that a major political purpose of local self government would be to serve as the schools for democracy. Forty years later the Montague-Chelmisford Reforms of 1917 declared local self governing institutions as the first step in the progressive realization of responsible government in India. The 1935 Government of India Act allowed provincial autonomy and permitted provincial governments to frame laws on local government systems. This Act has been the basis for the municipal set-up in India, Pakistan and Bangladesh since then and well into the period since independence. The provincial set-up and the formation of municipal councils in Sri Lanka have been more or less on similar lines. Municipal councils for Colombo, Kandy and Galle were established in 1965-66. However, in Nepal the Rana regime for over a century from 1946 to 1951 did not take any initiative for local self-government.

Whatever be the lofty sentiments of the Ripon Resolution and Montague-Chelmsford reforms, a few provisions pernicious to local self-governance have endured in most municipal Acts. One is the power of the District and Provincial governments to approve the municipal budgets and exercise various supervisory powers over municipal functioning, Another is the power of the provincial government to supercede an elected municipal council or a corporation on various grounds of impropriety and non-performance.

From time to time, the spectre of supervision has loomed large over the municipal horizon. In India, at any time after independence, about half of the municipal councils and corporations have been under supercession, irrespective of the political parties in power in the States. The Madras corporation was superceded in 1973 which lasted for 24 years. In Pakistan municipalities in the north-western province were set aside in 1991, Sindh in 1992 and Punjab in 1993 for the ostensible purpose of ensuring free national elections without being influenced by incumbent local government leaders. In Bangladesh, the municipalities have had an uncertain existence during both the East Pakistan and post liberation periods. In Nepal municipal autonomy was insignificant during the national panchayat system.

Contrary to expectations, independence from colonial rule did not really lead to a flourishing of local self-governance or consolidation of autonomy. Some scholars like Akbar Zaidi have pointed out that with democratic participation at the provincial and national levels becoming a reality, municipal government has lost its value as the only platform available for public participation during the colonial period.

Urban Development Authorities is another South Asian arrangement, which has reduced the functional domain of municipalities. Originating from the concept of City Improvement Trusts (the one for Calcutta was set up in 1911) which undertook redevelopment and city extension schemes on a self-financing basis and by adding some features of British New Town Corporations and the statutory master planning and enforcement functions, Development Authorities have been created in almost all metropolitan cities. Apart from taking away town planning from the domain of the municipalities, these development authorities became in due course powerful behemoths combining planning, regulation, real estate development, housing and public works functions. It was also felt that such authorities would be efficient and technocratic and be able to attract external assistance. The first came in Delhi in 1952 and was given the monopoly for land acquisition and development in the union territory. It became a big land bank and moneyspinner in its early years and thus an attractive model in the region. Development Authorities for Karachi and Lahore were set up in the 1970s. The one for Calcutta, called the CMDA, was established in 1970 mainly to mobilize funds for a metropolitan wide rescue programme and coordinate implementation functions. Very soon it took over execution of works as well. Similar authorities followed in Madras and Bombay and in most of the 23 'million plus' cities in India. In many cases the elected municipalities in the respective cities were under supercession which no doubt, facilitated the creation of these parallel organization. In Bangladesh, the Capital Development Authority or RAJUK was set up in 1987, a successor to the Improvement Trust created in 1956. Similar bodies for Chittagong, Khulna and Rajshahi followed. In Sri Lanka an Urban Development Authority was created in 1978 with nationwide jurisdiction,similar to the Singapore model.

Apart from these Development Authorities, special purpose agencies, particularly for water supply and sewerage were also set up for many cities in the region. Technical imperatives of single control from source to tap, operational efficiency and cost recovery uninfluenced by municipal politics were cited as the rationale for these bodies. In many cases these were supported by the World Bank and other external assistance agencies. Metropolitan wide water and sanitation boards or authorities were set up in Karachi, Lahore, Delhi, Madras, Dhaka, Chittagong etc., and state-wide boards in U.P., Bihar, Maharastra, Tamil Nadu, Kerala and so on. Bombay and Calcutta are two exceptions where the corporation still has the responsibility for handling water supply and sanitation as basic municipal functions.

Decentralization

To the currently world-wide phenomenon of decentralization, South Asian countries are no exception. As elsewhere the motivations are numerous and varied. The rising aspirations of an increasing population and the inability of central governments to meet them is one important factor. Ethnic, linguistic, communal, caste or cultural diversities are a reality in each of the South Asian countries. The struggle for freedom from colonial rule provided an unifying force where these diversities were sub-merged, but in the past three decades the forces have surfaced and sub-regional, sub-national identities are now a major political factor. To preserve their polity South Asian countries have to accept a measure of decentralization.

So far as India and Pakistan are concerned, there has been significant devolution of functions, powers and resources to the provincial level, though the process has had its ups and downs. In Sri Lanka, Municipal Councils have had a long and fairly stable existence. Bangladesh and Nepal have a more unitary structure but here again initiatives for decentralization to sub-national levels have been taken. In Bangladesh a four tier set up with Gram Parishad, Union Parishad, Upzila Parishad and Zila Parishad is in the process of being set up as recommended by the local Government Commission in 1997. In urban areas the Mayors of Dhaka, Chittagong, Khulna and Rajshahi are directly elected and have been accorded the rank and status of Ministers and State Ministers. In Nepal the municipal mayors are also directly elected while the functional domain of the municipalities has been significantly enlarged. In Pakistan after a long gap, elections have been held very recently in May '98 for the metropolitan council of Lahore and other corporations/municipalities in the province of Punjab.

The 73rd and 74th Amendments to the Indian Constitution has been an extensive exercise of decentralization in the sub-continent as far as rural and urban local governments are concerned. When the amendment exercise began during Rajiv Gandhi's time there was much opposition from the States. Those run by non-congress parties felt that since local self-government was a State subject, the exercise was an encroachment into the State domain. After extensive modification in the joint parliamentary committees, the 73rd and 74th amendments were passed by the parliament in 1992, ratified by the States and came into force in 1993.

The salient features of these two Constitutional Amendments are:

— The establishment of a three tier 'panchayat' system at village, intermediate and district level panchayats in the rural areas and nagar panchayats, municipalities or municipal corporations in urban areas, both comprising principally representatives elected from territorial constituencies.

— Mandatory elections for the panchayats and the municipalities ordinarily once in five years, to be conducted by state Election Commission.

— Supercession of elected local bodies only in exceptional circumstances and not to exceed six months within which elections have to be held again.

— One third of the seats in all local bodies to be reserved for women.

— Mandatory State Finance Commissions to review the finances of rural and urban local bodies and recommend assignment of tax revenues, grants in aid etc.

— Mandatory District Planning Committees and Metropolitan Planning Committees and

— Illustrative lists of functions to be entrusted to urban and rural local bodies.

It will be useful to compare certain other aspects of the decentralization process and structure among the South Asian countries.

Position of MPs and MLAs in the Local Bodies

i. The constitutional Amendment in India specifically authorises state governments to make laws for the representation of the Members of Parliament and Members of Legislative Assemblies/Councils in Nagar Panchayats, Municipalities and Corporations. However in 6 States, Gujarat, Maharastra, Orissa, Punjab, Kerala and West Bengal no provision has been made for the MPs or MLA's to be such members. This variance between the 73rd and 74th Amendments and the divergent arrangements in the States is an indication of the ambivalence on this issue.

ii. Pakistan, India and Nepal have a scheme of financial allocation for MPs/MLAs which can be spent at their discretion within their constituencies by-passing the panchayats/municipalities therein. The functioning of the scheme and the poor utilization of funds has also been strongly criticized in a recent report of India's Comptroller and Auditor General.

iii. **Representation of Women:** Both India and Bangladesh have made specific provisions for such representation. In India 1/3rd of the seats are reserved for women at all levels of rural and urban local bodies. In Bangladesh 3 seats in each of the 4276 Gram Parishads are reserved for women. In both countries there has been no shortage of candidates. The Punjab government in Pakistan is reported to be considering an increase for representation by women in the local councils from 10 to 20%.

iv. **Proximity to People:** In India the Constitution specifically enjoins the setting up of Wards Committees, for each municipal ward or group of wards, in all cities with a population of 3 lakhs or more, Many states have set up such committees for groups of wards such as Bombay or Madras. Some like West Bengal, Kerala and Gujarat have set up committees for each ward. None of these states has provided for election of the ward committee members. Representation from community groups, welfare organization etc. are on the basis of nomination, In the other countries of the region such arrangements have been made in large cities like Karachi, Lahore, Dhaka or Colombo as administrative measures rather than as legal requirements. Co-option of community group rather than election appears to be the preferred approach. In the other countries of the region, participation of community based groups at the neighbourhood level continues to be informal.

v. **Adult Franchise:** All countries in the region have accepted adult franchise as the basis for local body elections and restrictions limiting such franchise to rate payers no longer apply. However, in Bangladesh and Pakistan, local body elections are supposed to be held on a non party basis. In Bangladesh this appears to be only in theory and not in practice. Similarly, in Pakistan in the elections to local bodies held in Punjab in May '98, political parties chose candidates and actively campaigned, though in theory the elections were supposed to be non partisan.

Management Problems

The decentralization initiatives in South Asian countries have, no doubt, helped in reviving interest in the issues of urban governance. Some major problems however, persist. One is the management of large cities, particularly the multi-municipal metropolitan areas. Multi-municipal situations have also aggravated the problem. The Calcutta Metropolitan Area comprises 2 corporations, 33 municipalities and as many non-municipal urban areas. Madras consists of more than a dozen municipal authorities. Even Greater Bombay does not cover all of the metropolitan area. Karachi and Lahore were multi-municipal but have been brought together within a metropolitan framework. So is the Colombo metropolitan area. During the 1940s and 50s consolidation of smaller municipalities was attempted and also accomplished in some cities but in recent years the municipal boundaries have remained frozen. This is not to say that a metropolitan view or perspective does not exist: indeed they have been cultivated over the years but as yet confined to planning, organizations and professional groups. Single metropolitan-wide governments have been politically unwelcome especially in national and provincial capital cities, whether Dhaka, Calcutta, Bombay or Karachi.

Managing growth in the metropolitan cities of the region is not merely an inter municipal issue but also involves several departments and agencies of national and provincial governments. Transport is an apt illustration involving railways, river traffic, different kinds of motorized and non-motorized transport regulated by different agencies, roads and highways, policing etc. It is impossible to gather all these vast variety of tasks in one single organization. South Asian cities have been experimenting with Inter departmental, Inter municipal Planning and Coordintion bodies for such purposes. The recent creation of the Greater Dhaka Transport Planning and Coordination Board is a promising initiative.

Within large cities, the municipal structure also needs to provide for sharing of powers. The Mayor-in-Council system introduced in Calcutta in 1980 has been a major improvement in this regard. Patterned after the Cabinet system, the Mayor-in-Council comprises the Mayor, elected by the Corporation Council from among its members for a 5 year term, a specified number of Councillors appointed by the Mayor and assigned portfolios and the Corporation Commissioner, a civil servant appointed by the state functioning as the secretary and executive officer of the council.

Fiscal domain is another largely unanswered issue in many South Asian cities. Expenditure in major items of infrastructure is usually met by higher levels of government but in comparison to the needs, funds provided have been woefully short. Overall outlays on urban development activities has been 6 to 8 per cent in Pakistan (1993-98), 3 per cent in Bangladesh (1990-95) and 3 per cent in India. Of the combined revenue base of the Centre, States and Municipalities, the share of the last category is less than 3 per cent. Municipalities in this region have an extremely narrow and unelastic tax base and have to rely on high rates of taxation which in turn leads to large scale evasion.

As cities expand and spill over traditional boundaries they are no longer homogenous societies. Indeed social heterogeneity is considered to be a positive feature of cities. In the face of liberalization of the economies and globalization of trade and investment, this heterogeneity will be further accentuated. Cities will need to perceive and define their roles at the macro as well as at the micro levels. Communities and neighbourhoods will have to devise ways of coping with daily pressures. This needs a framework which is flexible and participatory but which will not at the same time, succumb to the pressures of fragmentation. Participation and accountability are thus essential ingredients of good governance at both the city and neighbourhood levels.

TABLE 1

Urbanization in Five South Asian Countries (Existing)

(Population in Millions)

	Nepal	Sri Lanka	Bangladesh	Pakistan	India	Total
1971						
Total Population	11.48	12.51	76.39	69.37	548.16	717.91
Urban Population	0.46	2.74	6.00	18.09	109.11	136.40
%	4	21	8	26	20	19
1981						
Total Population	14.30	14.80	18.20	86.90	684.50	888.70
Urban Population	0.95	3.20	13.56	23.80	159.67	201.18
%	7	22	15	27	23	23
1991						
Total Population	19.14	17.21	109.90	120.70	844.32	1111.27
Urban Population	1.68	3.68	21.60	42.25	217.18	286.39
%	9	22	20	35	26	26
2000						
Total Population	24.08	19.42	150.58	162.41	1014.54	1371.03
Urban Population	3.37	4.66	34.63	61.72	324.65	429.03
%	14	24	23	38	32	31
2010						
Total Population	28.90	21.52	188.20	205.49	1223.48	1667.59
Urban Population	5.78	6.61	57.02	93.23	480.83	643.53
%	20	31	30	45	39	39
2020						
Total Population	33.08	23.66	220.12	248.12	1371.76	1896.74
Urban Population	8.87	9.13	84.09	131.75	648.84	882.68
%	27	39	38	53	47	47

Source : United Nations (1991) World Urbanization Prospect 1990, New York.

TABLE 2

Proportion of Urban Population in Large cities

Country	Total Urban Population	Number of Million-plus cities	Their Total Population	Percentage of Urban Population (4/2)
Bangladesh	21.55	3	9.9	46%
Pakistan	42.25	7	18.2	43%
India	217.18	23	71	33%

Source : 1990/1991 Population Figures.

TABLE 3

Growth of Towns in South Asia

Size class	5 to 10.000	10 to 25.000	25 to 50.000	50 to 100.000	100.000+
India					
1961	711	719	437	129	102
1981	758	1059	743	270	218
1991	725	1135	927	341	296
Pakistan					
1961	173		30	10	12
1981	246		65	34	26
Bangladesh					
1961	21	23	15	5	4
1981	129	114	45	23	13

Source : Population Figures.

TABLE 4

Absolute Poverty Line Estimates (Rural and Urban)

Sl.	Country	India	Pakistan	Bangladesh	Nepal
01.	Rural Population	627	78	88	18
02.	Number below Poverty Line	320	24	83	10
03.	Percentage	51	30	94	57
04.	Urban Population	217	42	22	17
05.	Number Below Poverty Line	90	12	16	1
06.	Percentage	41	30	75	60

Source : UNDP Human Development Report 1991.

CITIES: PERSPECTIVE ON LOCAL GOVERNANCE IN PAKISTAN

Tasneem Ahmed Siddique

Hyper-urbanization in developing countries has no parallel in history. It is a mass exodus of epic proportions. The rapid transformation from rural to a heavily urbanized world of today and the consequent development of a way of life have been more dramatic and spectacular than the population explosion itself.

Cities are bursting at the seams. Pollution, congestion, lack of basic infrastructure, 'pathological' growth of slums, unemployment and high rate of crime have made the life of the people miserable. 25-30 years ago people could enjoy their life in cities like Karachi, Lahore, Peshawar, Quetta, Hyderabad and Rawalpindi. In Sindh, district towns like Mirpurkhas, Nawabshah, Sukkur and Larkana were liveable places. Today, they are heaps of debris, almost a garbage dump where even the rudimentary urban facilities are not available.

Today, the position in urban centres of Pakistan is as follows:

— 30% people live in squatters' settlements, another 20% in unserviced areas

— about 50% of Pakistan's population (both urban and rural) live in one room tenements where congestion can be as high as 8-12 persons

— 50% have no access to piped water

— 70% lack sanitation

— unemployment rate is as high as 20%

— public transport system/mass transit does not exist at all

The poor are surviving in the cities because of the emergence of a powerful 'informal sector'. Some surveys show that in Karachi, 70%

population is dependent on parallel economy. Most of the services to the low income people are provided by the unorganized sector.

Bigger cities like Karachi and Lahore have additional problems of homelessness, pollution, environmental degradation, lack of open spaces, solid waste management and increasing crime against life and property.

The phenomenon of rapid urbanization in Pakistan cannot be stopped, reversed or altered. At best it can be regulated, that too to a small extent, provided there is change in attitude and development strategy.

One can argue that urbanization *per se* is not bad. People would be drawn into cities because they offer diversity of career and lifestyle options; economic activities would be attracted into cities because of the advantages associated with concentration, Cities, thus, are centres of activities and focal points of the transport network; location of superior accessibility at which firms can most easily reap economies of scale and at which industrial complexes can obtain the maximization of their profits. But urbanization has to be a gradual phenomenon, and to be problem free, cities have to expand keeping pace with availability of more jobs. In Pakistan, alongside mass migration to big urban centres, two phenomena have also taken place: (i) due to high growth rate of population, there has been a process of densification in the old cities. Therefore, urban centres like Karachi, Lahore and Peshawar engulfed the old villages and agricultural land at the periphery; (ii) with changes from barter to cash economy, and infusion of money from abroad, big villages along main highways have been converted into agricultural markets, thus giving rise to mandi towns in Punjab and parts of Sindh. This urbanization has been part of natural growth and has caused least problems. The problem in most developing countries (and Pakistan is no exception) is the development strategy foisted from above and political priorities *which did not follow the logical sequence of transformation from agriculture to industrial economy.*

Apart from mindless application of urban-industrial model of development, if one were to give one major reason for this paradox, it would be this: lack of a regularly elected local government. What is seen today in cities — big, medium or small is the direct consequence of the absence of a responsible local-self government. In other countries, governments at the national level come and go, but the local government continues to work. At least the ordinary citizens are assured of the basic amenities of life, and therefore, are not bothered about political shenanigans.

Whenever any discussion about the decay of cities and absence of basic urban service takes place, most people naively believe or argue that the main problem is lack of money. Yes, it can be one of the reasons in some cases, but the real problem now is that there are no structures on the ground which can deliver the services. There is an institutional vacuum — a systemic failure. Questions of mis-management and mis-allocation of resources are in addition. In the recent past, huge funds were made available to Karachi, Hyderabad, Sukkur and Larkana under PM's Special Packages. Apart from Karachi, where some showpieces were completed, in Hyderabad, Sukkur and Larkana this money couldn't even be fully utilized.

Institutional Decline

There has been an institutional exhaustion in Pakistan during the last three decades, and local-self government is the worst sufferer. At the time of independence in 1947, the performance of these institutions could be compared with those of any other country. But since then this vital link in the hierarchy of government has been neglected and its potential stifled, never allowing it to grow. Attention has always been focused on making the central government more powerful perhaps because historically everyone believed in a strong centre and charismatic personalities.

No wonder with each passing year, the size of federal government has increased manifold and it has expanded in all directions. It is now a mammoth, unwieldy organization and has assumed a number of functions which are either provincial or local in nature. It controls all the productive resources of the state, and collects all the major taxes, and then doles out the money to the provinces. All administrative and technical capability is also concentrated at the apex level.

Then, there are provincial governments which have a large number of departments, autonomous and semi-autonomous organizations and development authorities. These have mostly arrogated the powers and functions of the local government institutions to themselves. These departments are over-centralized and are answerable only to the chief executive. Line departments of the provincial government undertake development projects in municipal areas (without even consulting them) and on completion, hand them over to these bodies for operation and maintenance.

At the bottom is the local government, which is supposed to tackle problems people face in their day to day life. Initially, this institution was able to deal with these problems adequately because it had the financial, administrative and technical capacity to do so. But soon after Pakistan's creation, politicians started tinkering with local institutions, and succeeded in stifling their potentials in the most glaring manner. They have been mostly run by bureaucrats or nominated administrators. Local self-government was thus never allowed to take roots and develop organically. At best it functioned as a handmaiden of the bureaucracy. Elections were held off and on, but never on a regular basis.

It is also an interesting fact that democratically elected governments have always been averse to the concept of local government. On the other hand, 'long ruling' military dictators were afraid of an elected parliament, but loved grassroot institutions. The reasons were obvious.

What is the result? Unlike the developed world, countries like Pakistan have ended up with an inverted pyramid, an upside down power structure:

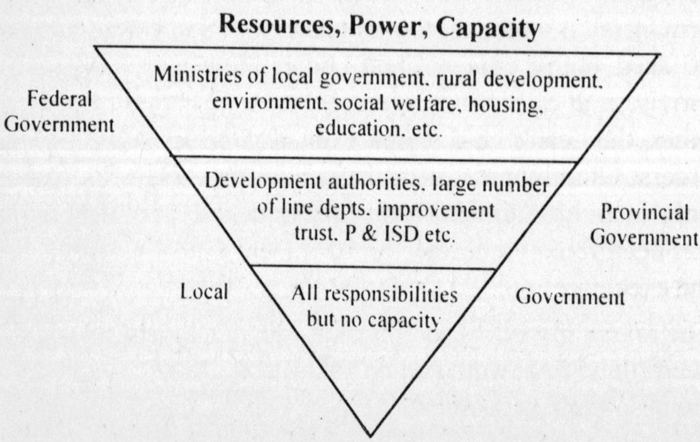

Similar was the case with the elected municipal committees/ corporations that managed the cities. 90% problems people face in their day to day existence are local in nature. As a matter of fact; as one American statesman said, 'ALL POLITICS IS LOCAL'. If the grassroot institutions are elected on a continuing basis, and perform their duties well, people don't feel alienated. They are also ready to share some of the responsibilities. This participation reduces the burden of government institutions to a large extent.

The problems of local-self government have to be seen at three levels: (a) cities having a population of three million or more, (b) smaller towns which have manageable populations, and (c) rural areas which have union councils. Needless to say that the only way to deal with the problems of bigger cities is to have an elected city government which in addition to discharging usual municipal functions, can effectively deal with the problems of mass transit, traffic management, policing, pollution, housing etc.

There are areas which need immediate attention of the ruling elite, provided they have the political will to reform the system. Major issues include:

1. Pakistan's 1973 constitution has only two lists: federal and the concurrent. The provinces take their authority from the concurrent list. Local Government has neither been given any constitutional protection nor there is any 'local list'. Local bodies are at the mercy of the provincial government. Another interesting point is that in case of dissolution of national and provincial assemblies, the mandatory period for re-election is 90 days, but in case of local bodies there is no constitutional provision at all. If they are superseded, for one reason or the other, they can't be restored even if superior judiciary passes orders. Other countries in the region face the same problem, only in India, through 74th Amendment a period of 90 days has been fixed for re-election if a local body is superseded by the executive.
2. The role of ministries and divisions dealing with urban services needs to be reviewed, and only those should be retained which are absolutely necessary.

3. As there is proliferation of land-owning agencies in major urban centres, federal government should set up a committee comprising secretaries of the concerned federal ministries to work with representatives of the provincial governments of Sindh and Punjab to devise permanent institutional arrangements, working under the local government institutions at co-ordinated management of urban services in Karachi, Lahore etc.
4. Development authorities in most urban areas (created under separate legislation) operate directly under the control of the provincial government. This is in conflict with the idea that elected local government is the prime urban institution to deal with urban services. It is therefore, necessary that after down-sizing these development authorities, the provincial government should declare them as 'development wings' of the local government institutions.
5. Current mode of allocation of resources to local government institutions is arbitrary, ad hoc and totally at the discretion of the provincial governments. It is necessary that a mechanism at the provincial level be created for transfer of resources to local government along the lines of the National Finance Commission which provides for sharing of resources between the provinces.
6. Provincial governments exercise a large degree of discretionary and arbitrary powers in matters pertaining to the local government institutions and provisions of urban services. In so far as possible, these powers should be abolished.
7. Mobilization of resources can improve, once provincial and local government roles are clearly defined, and steps are taken to strengthen the local tax base by making it broader, more responsive to changes and more equitable. The objectives should be:

   i.. to diversify and broaden the tax base;

   ii. to link changes more closely to costs of services and to design taxes which are not adjusted by inflation (indexation);

   iii. to make tax incidence progressive; and

iv. to strengthen tax administration including procedural reforms to increase coverage, valuation accuracy and collection efficiency.

These reforms will take time, but for immediate improvement in the existing situation, following steps can be taken:

1. The possibility of contracting-out aspects of urban services (such as solid waste and garbage collection) should be considered and the scope of contracted-out services gradually be extended overtime. Guidance in preparation of contract specifications, terms of contract, tender evaluation, and award and supervision would be required.
2. At present, management capacity of the urban local councils is limited and it is not possible to put into effect regulatory systems which are needed to allow greater private sector provision of services. The challenge is to find medium-term policy options that compromise between two extremes of inefficiency and the non-performing public sector, and costly private sector provision by individual firms and households.
3. There is ample evidence from all urban areas in Pakistan that users are willing to pay more for reliable services when available. Regulatory audit to assess the costs, benefits and distributional consequences of specific regulations will need to be carried out.
4. In terms of policy and priorities for urban infrastructures, the emphasis should be on short term actions in the development of infrastructural elements which will have the most immediate, positive impact on economic growth, productivity and efficiency and on improving shelter conditions for the lowest income groups.
5. Greater emphasis on technical and managerial human resource development must be a key aspect of the provision and maintenance of urban services.
6. Particular attention should be paid to regulations that tend to prevent the growth of productivity of urban entrepreneurs, particularly in the urban 'informal sector' (for example

regulations that limit the access of the small scale entrepreneurs to urban services, credit and markets).

7. The efforts of communities and NGOs to provide services in their neighbourhoods should be supported. The local government institutions need to establish strong information and community relations units to work with the planning and implementation machinery for dissemination of information to the public and seek community involvement in the decision-making and development process.
8. Master Plans for future development, land use and provision of urban services acceptable to local residents should be prepared and implemented.
9. Co-operation, and where required technical and financial support, should be extended to community groups; and although their activities have local political significance, enabling them to meet community needs can generate positive political relationships.
10. Technocrats or civil servants can only succeed if they become true professionals and develop expertise in different fields. For that, their orientation will have to be completely changed and all those notions discarded which are taught to them in the universities, civil service academies, training and staff colleges.
11. For improved access by the poor to basic urban services, shelter and upgrading low serviced settlements (to ensure security of tenure), successful projects like OPP, HDA's incremental development scheme in Hyderabad, SKAA's Regularization and Improvement Programme, should be closely scrutinized for replication.

Now we will briefly discuss the model of incremental housing development for the poor known as 'Khuda Ki Basti' which has been developed by Hyderabad Development Authority (HDA) with major input from "Saiban"

The Model

A group of committed professionals and administrators working in Hyderabad Development Authority launched a housing scheme at

Kotri in November, 1986. The scheme is based on the idea that people should settle before houses and infrastructure are constructed and that once settled, they can develop their housing and infrastructure incrementally, as and when they have the resources.

Experience in many Latin American and African countries have shown that for the lowest income groups, neither the modern approach whereby a fully serviced plot with a complete house is provided to the allottees:

Land → Infrastructure → Housing → People

nor the site and services approach, whereby a fully serviced plot is provided but the house has to be constructed by the allottee:

Land → Infrastructure → People → Housing

is an appropriate sequence.

For housing the low-income groups, it is necessary to return to the traditional sequence of human settlement whereby people settle on unserviced land and develop their housing and infrastructure incrementally, as they feel the need for the facilities and accumulate the funds to pay for them in the following sequence:

Land → People → Housing → Infrastructure

The HDA scheme popularly known as Khuda Ki Basti, focused its attention on this traditional sequence and other important issues which had not received appropriate attention in government housing schemes: targeting and affordability, the procedure of allotment, ease of entry, immediate delivery of the plot (i.e. no time-lag between allotment and possession of plot) and incremental development of the houses and infrastructure.

In this scheme, through a process of trial and error, a new approach has been developed which is capable of overcoming the common weaknesses of site and services schemes to an amazing degree. Basic in the new approach is the option offered affordable to the target group. Therefore, a very low down payment (Rs. 1,000) is required. Development of the scheme is incremental. Initial services are limited to the absolute minimum: at the start, only communal supply and public transport are provided. Only in the longer run, house-to-house water supply, sewerage, road paving, electricity, and gas will be provided as the allottees pay their monthly instalments ranging between Rs. 50 to Rs. 100. Also standards prescribed pertain only to items that cannot be changed later. Thus, only the lay-out of the scheme is fixed; otherwise absolutely no standards are prescribed as to the quality or plan of the house. The allottees are rather encouraged to innovate and improvise.

The critical factor is the guaranteed and assured title to the land. Once people have that, it is amazing how resources are pooled by the family to invest and gradually make a respectable structure. Secondly, just as in the case of illegal developments, the time-lag between allotment and occupation has been eliminated. Development takes place while the allottees are residing in the scheme. In order to achieve all this, the allotment procedure is crucial. It is especially in this respect that new ways have been developed to reach the target group and to exclude those who do not intend to live in the scheme after acquiring the plot.

A reception area has been provided at the site where the shelterless family is registered for the allotment of a plot, only if it brings all its members and entire belongings with it. A regular plot is allocated if they stay in the reception area for about a week.

The allottees have freedom to build. But they must live on their plot from the first day otherwise it can be cancelled and given to somebody else. As soon as the first 50 families have occupied their plots, supply of water through tankers and transport is arranged. Soon after mosque, schools, and mobile vans for primary health care are organized through NGOs.

Replicability

The scheme has all the possibilities and potential of replicability because:

a. It is entirely self-financing. There is no element of subsidy, formal or non-formal. The entire cost of the developed plot (which is Rs. 9,600/-) is being borne by the beneficiaries in easy instalments spread over a period of eight years.

b. It is simple in approach and all procedures are transparent — no paper work is involved — no expert is needed; only 3-4 junior officials manage the entire scheme.

c. It is highly flexible from planning to execution; modifications and adjustments can be made keeping local conditions in view — only the basic concept has to be adhered to.

d. Provision of services has been linked with cost recovery. Therefore, there is no risk of losing the money which generally happens in public housing schemes.

e. Cheap technology is used for construction of houses, keeping in view the local climatic conditions and socio-economic status of the allottees who are encouraged to innovate and improvise. (As a matter of fact, a learning atmosphere has been created for other activities as well, like income generating schemes, home schools etc.).

f. Flexible planning and building control standards are used: no restrictions are imposed on autonomy to build.

URBAN GOVERNANCE: LESSONS FROM ASIA

Dinesh Mehta

Introduction

Over the past two decades, many countries in Asia have experienced rapid economic growth. This has led to a rapid rise in their urban population. It is estimated that by the turn of this century, nearly half of Asia's population will reside in urban areas. However, in spite of significant increase in national wealth and personal incomes, the quality of life of an average urban resident is quite poor. Squalor, slums, traffic congestion, and shortages of water and power characterize urban centers in Asia. While the national governments pursue the goals of economic development, it is generally left to the local governments to manage rapidly growing urban areas, and provide for basic services to its residents.

Urban governance has assumed increasing importance as the capacity of a nation to pursue its economic goals is contingent upon its ability to govern the cities. This is largely due to the significant contribution that urban centers make in the national income. In fact, it is often said that 'cities are the engines of growth of the national economy'. Economic liberalization and decentralization of government have been the most common feature of developmental policies of most countries in the past decade. Nations have evolved policies aimed at achieving high economic growth rates, integrating the national economy with the global economy and increasing economic efficiency through greater competition. The interdependency of national economic development, globalization and urban development is clearly seen in the recent economic crisis in East and Southeast Asian countries. This has affected the cities in these countries more adversely and has resulted in increased poverty, unemployment and violence.

The emergence of these trends has profound implications on urban governance. In the general discussion of macro-economic policies, the role of urban economies is not well recognised. The macro-economic policies often have an anti-urban bias and programmes restricting the growth of large cities, reducing migration to cities, and achieving a 'balanced urban pattern' have been pursued by the national governments. It is only in recent years that the role of city economies in national development has been recognized. It is seen that in a global economy, there is an increasing competition among cities to attract cross-border investments. The ability of a city to attract the global investments largely determines the extent of investments in a nation.

The flight of international capital from Asian cities in recent months and the rapid erosion of economic base of these cities have necessitated readjustments of local priorities. The close link of national economic development and urban growth now requires that 'bail-out' packages for cities of East and Southeast Asia will also need to be considered. National and local governments in these countries would need to evolve policy frameworks within which participatory urban development could be achieved. The strategy of city consultation of the Urban Management Programme of UNDP/UNCHS provides an extremely relevant framework for identifying national and local priorities and action programmes that can be implemented in a participatory mode.

Decentralization programmes initiated for local government in many Asian countries are expected to provide an adequate infrastructure base to attract domestic and international investments as well as ensure that a minimum level of basic services is available to all its residents. New forms of urban government structure and decentralization policies of some kind have been implemented in most South Asian countries in recent years (e.g. Nepal, India, Pakistan and Bangladesh). In many countries, this has been associated with a move to democratic rule or a return to democracy.

The rapidly changing macro-economic environment and the return to democracy pose enormous challenges to the elected representatives and municipal officers. The ushering of local democracy has inducted a new cadre and skills for local level decision-making. For the municipal staff, the process of local democracy and the problems of rapid urban growth have necessitated an improved managerial, technical and financial capacity. There is now a perceived need for a major shift away from the traditional methods of urban governance.

In many Asian countries, in spite of the decentralization programme, local governments that have most of the responsibilities for managing urban change and growth often lack the power and resources to fulfil them. The balance of power and distribution of functions between national and local governments is still evolving.

However, the national governments in South Asia are as yet not inclined to invoke the principle of subsidiarity and devolve greater power to the local authorities. For effective urban governance, it is necessary to ensure that adequate powers and responsibilities are granted local governments. At present the success of these decentralized efforts in South Asia have been varied.

On the positive side, it is important to recognise that for the first time in many decades, democratically elected urban local governments are in place in all the South Asian countries. Though these local democracies are in a nascent stage, and their specific functional and fiscal domains are not well defined, there are examples of a few urban local governments that have adopted innovative approaches of urban governance to meet the new challenges. These 'successful' urban authorities provide useful lessons to others to embark upon a new mode of governance.

From Governing to Participatory Development

Governance is a term that has been used in development literature only in recent years. It is, therefore, used by various authors and agencies to describe very different phenomenon and processes. Most of the earlier uses of this term relate to its narrow dictionary meaning of 'action or manner of governing.' The World Bank (1992) defined it as the "manner in which power is exercised in the management of a country's economic and social resources for development." It identifies three distinct aspects of governance: (i) the form of political regime, (ii) the process by which authority is exercised in the management of country's economic and social resources; and (iii) the capacity of the government to design, formulate and implement policies and programmes and discharge its functions.

From this very narrow meaning of the term, it has now begun to mean more than government or its management. It now refers to the relationship, not only between governments and state agencies, but also between government, communities and social groups.

The OECD links governance to participatory development, human rights and democratization. It advocates the member states to link governance issues to: legitimacy of government (degree of democratization), accountability of political and official elements of government (media freedom, transparency of decision-making, accountability mechanisms), competence of governments to formulate policies and deliver services, respect for human rights and rule of law (individual and group rights and security, framework for economic and social activity and participation).

The UNCHS (1996) 'Global Report on Human Settlements', identified three critical factors that have led to a focus on urban governance. These were:

1. The elaboration and implementation of decentralization policies including the emergence and acceptance of the concept of subsidiarity,
2. The introduction of or return to democratic principle of government in many countries, both at the national and local level,
3. The increased importance that citizen and community pressure, as well as urban social movements, combined with concerns for economic development and environmental degradation, have helped place on local control and involvement in decision-making.

The preparatory process of Habitat II Conference at Istanbul in June 1996 defined governance as broader than "government." It said that governance concerns not only the public administrations and official State, regional and municipal institutions that formally manage public affairs, but also encompasses the activities of many other political and social groups.

A UNDP policy document 'Governance for Sustainable Human Development' (Jan. 1997), states that, "governance includes the State, but transcends it by taking in the private sector and civil society. All three are critical for sustaining human development. The State creates a conducive political and legal environment. The private sector generates jobs and income. And civil society facilitates political and social interaction — mobilising groups to participate in economic, social and political activities.

UNDP's description of the process of governance however, takes the more narrow view of the term. The process of governance is described as the exercise of economic, political and administrative authority to manage a country's affairs at all levels. This comprises the mechanisms, processes and institutions through which citizens and groups articulate their interests, exercise their legal rights, meet their obligations and mediate their differences.

In its definition of the state, private sector and the civil society, the UNDP (1997) has adopted an inclusionary approach. It states, "what constitutes the state is widely debated. Here, the state is defined to include political and public sector institutions. ... The private sector covers private enterprises (manufacturing, trade, banking, cooperatives and so on) and the informal sector in the marketplace. Civil society, lying between the individual and the state, comprises individuals and groups (organised or unorganised) interacting socially, politically and economically — regulated by formal and informal rules and laws. Civil society organizations are the host of associations around which society voluntarily organises. They include trade unions; non-governmental organizations; gender, language, cultural and religious groups; charities; business associations; social and sports clubs; co-operatives and community development organizations; environmental groups; professional associations;

academic and policy institutions; and media outlets. Political parties are also included, although they straddle civil society and the state if they are represented in parliament."

Elements of Good Governance

Just as there are differences in the use of the term governance, there are various ways in which good governance is defined. The phrase 'Good governance' is epitomized by the World Bank in its recent literature as,

> "Predictable, open, and enlightened policy making, a bureaucracy imbued with a professional ethos acting in furtherance of public good, the rule of law, transparent processes, and a strong civil society participating in public affairs. Poor governance, on the other hand, is characterized by arbitrary policy making, unaccountable bureaucracies, unenforced or unjust legal systems, the abuse of executive power, a civil society unengaged in public life, and widespread corruption. Good governance fosters strong state capable of sustained economic and social development and institutional growth. Poor governance undermines all efforts to improve policy making and to create durable institutions. (World Bank, 1997).

Habitat II Preparatory Discussions Identified Good Governance as a Commonly Shared Goal. It Stated:

> Good governance requires accountability by public officials; both elected political leaders and civil servants. Their public functions must serve the community at large.
>
> Second, good governance requires transparency in public procedures, processes, investment decisions, contracts and appointment. It is not sufficient that information simply be available, it must also be reliable and presented in useful and understandable ways to facilitate accountability.
>
> Third, good governance requires wide participation in making public choices, such as policies and regulations (and even in the operation of markets).
>
> Major public choices demand wide participation and debate involving not just governmental agencies but also diverse, representative and accountable non-governmental organizations. A main

objective of good governance as it relates to participation is to encourage a political leadership that reflects and promotes ideals of good citizenship, such as informed participation, compassion and fairness.

Fourth, good governance is built on the **rule of law**. Modern societies, especially those in cities, are extremely complex. Those that remain organized and prosperous do so because rules and expectations closely correlate to how political procedures and markets function.

Fifth, public and private institutions, such as Government agencies and markets, must have some measure of predictability. The rule of law helps to protect against erratic and uneven enforcement and the whims of public officials. But the process of making and changing public rules and expectations must also be predictable (UNCHS, 1996).

According to the UNCHS, these five elements outline a workable and fair mode of governance. They imply the need for fiscal responsibility and sound management of national and local resources. They require building and utilizing the capacity for analysis and formulation of sound social and economic policies. They describe governance as a partnership between the public and private sectors — between Government and private citizens, management and labour.

The key elements of good governance as defined by UNDP are listed below:

Participation: All men and women should have a voice in decision-making either directly or through legitimate intermediate institutions that represent their interests. Such broad participation is built on freedom of association and speech, as well as capacities to participate constructively.

Rule of Law: Legal frameworks should be fair and enforced impartially, particularly the laws on human rights.

Transparency: Transparency is built on the free flow of information. Processes, institutions and information are directly accessible to those concerned with them, and enough information is provided to understand and monitor them.

Responsiveness: Institutions and processes try to serve all stakeholders.

Consensus Orientation: Good governance mediates differing interests to reach a broad consensus on what is in the best interests of the group and, where possible, on policies and procedures.

Equity: All men and women have opportunities to improve or maintain their well being.

Effectiveness and Efficiency: Processes and institutions produce results that meet needs while making the best use of resources.

Accountability: Dicision-makers in government, the private sector and civil society organizations are accountable to the public, as well as to institutional stakeholders. This accountability differs depending on the organization and whether the dicision is internal or external to an organization.

Strategic Vision: Leaders and the public have a broad and long-term perspective on good governance and human development, along with a sense of what is needed for such development. There is also an understanding of the historical, cultural and social complexities in which that perspective is grounded." (UNDP, 1997).

This policy document of UNDP further states that, "It needs to be recognised that these core characteristics are mutually reinforcing and cannot stand alone.

While there has been some general discussion of good governance in the international agencies' documents, few examples exist where these characteristics have been applied to the Urban Management Practices. In a very novel exercise, the Konrad Adenuer Stiftung attempted to identify better managed cities in Asia. The "Better Cities Network of East and South-East Asian Cities" used the following eight criteria for assessing the performance of urban local governments (KAS and LOGO DEF, 1997).

1. *Accountability* — Accountability flows from the concept of stewardship and rests on the consent of the governed. It also refers to adhering to an established set of criteria in measuring the performance of local government officials to estimate the economic and financial performance of local government.
2. *Responsiveness* — It is a measure of accountability wherein leaders and public servants address the needs of the public. It can be indicated "by a deliberate citizen and customer-orientation policy being consistently espoused by the local

administration" or by "the presence of mechanisms and procedures for swift recourse on unfair practices and avenues for the community to articulate issues requiring local government assistance."

3. *Management Innovation* — This refers to reforms successfully implemented by local governance in various areas of local government administrations, e.g., administrative procedures, resource mobilization, political reforms, economic sustainability, environmental preservation, community participation, etc.
4. *Public-Private Partnership* — This suggests an active joint working arrangement between local government and the private sector in the programmes of local government.
5. *Local Government-Citizen Interaction* — This indicates open communication between the government, non-government organizations and the community as a whole.
6. *Decentralized Management* — This concerns the ability of the local management to delineate and delegate responsibilities to various responsibility centres and to ensure accurate reporting and monitoring of delegated responsibilities.
7. *Networking* — This refers to the ability of the local governments to forge co-operative relationships with other local governments and other entities to build infrastructural capacities.
8. *Human Resource Management* — This suggests the sustained implementation of a programme to recruit, train, motivate and develop a local work force to become more efficient, dedicated and effective members of the public service.

Innovative Urban Governance Experiences

One of the most significant contributions of Habitat II to good governance was by identifying and promoting examples of "**best practices**". These include success stories on local efforts to tackle problems of human settlement development. By showcasing such models and using them to inform debates over the future and opportunities of cities, the Habitat II process has initiated significant changes in the traditional ways in which national and local governments have dealt with habitat related problems. A sample of the Best Practices from Asia in the Habitat II database is in Annex II.

Some observers of the global urbanization process argue that the living conditions in world's cities are bad and will become worse even if the general economic situation improves. The global and national media also propagate such views. These observations are based on the apparent poor capacity of local governments to manage the present conditions. It must, however, be recognized that given the size of the urban population, the apathy of the national and sub-national government and the limited capacities of the local governments, cities in Asian have been able to cope with their problems remarkably well. In recent years, a few cities have, in fact, demonstrated that they are able to manage the existing problems as indicated by the 'best-practices' database. The fact that the 'best-practice' database has continued to grow over the years, suggests that in all parts of the world, urban local governments and the other stakeholders have been actively involved in improving the living conditions in their cities.

In India there have been many studies in the past few years of innovative urban management approaches. These studies in India and other countries and the 'best practice' database of UNCHS have demonstrated that there are important lessons to be learnt from them (Annex III).

Key Characteristics of Innovative Practices

While recognising that each "best-practice" case is unique and is rooted in the local context, it is important to examine the key characteristics of the successful innovative or good governance practices. This is necessary to identify a strategy for improved urban governance. These successful innovative practices provide lessons for other local governments to improve their management practices. For the list of innovative practices described in Annex III, there are certain common characteristics that have been identified and listed below:

a. *Internal Motivation:* Each of the innovative urban management experience was motivated from within the local government system. No external support agency was involved and no major plan of action was drawn up.

b. *Local Leadership (Change Initiator):* In each case, it is possible to identify an individual who played a keynote in initiating the changes.

c. *Institutional and Legal Context:* Another key feature is that there was no major change in the institutional and legal framework. All the efforts were directed towards improving the efficiency of the existing administration.

d. *Improved Credibility of Local Government:* A major impact of these practices has been a tremendous boost to the credibility of the municipal government among the local residents. The change in people's perception from a corrupt and inefficient municipal government to the one that 'means business' has had several fall-outs. The morale of municipal staff is high, as they have gained respect of the local residents. With increased compliance in payment of local taxes and charges, municipal finances have improved. This is also partly due to the feeling of the local residents that the municipal resources are being used for their welfare of the city. Access to capital market is also facilitated, as the credit rating of these cities for a potential municipal bond issue has been quite favourable.

The search for key characteristics of the successful best-practice examples continues. The UNCHS Best Practice database is being analyzed to identify the key characteristics of these success stories. A recently concluded Yale/UNDP Internet conference on public-private partnership for urban environmental management also discussed examples of successful and innovative partnerships. The conference summarised the key features of successful public-private partnerships from around the world. These are presented below.

Key Features of Successful Public Private Partnerships

Public-Private Partnerships Start with Either or Both

1. *A Widely Acknowledged Crisis:* Until there is a widely acknowledged crisis, seriously affecting the individual needs

of key stakeholders, and incapable of being solved by any one party, there are few incentives to develop collaborative solutions.

2. *Effective Champions:* One or more individual, with the credibility, stature, trustworthiness, drive and commitment to push through the partnership.

To Build the Foundation for the Partnership Based on

3. *Complimentary Goals:* Partnerships can only work to the extent that the goals of the major stakeholders are both (a) mutually compatible (acceptable services for acceptable prices and levels of return) and (b) articulated, understood and respected — and
4. *An Enabling Environment:* The collaborative effort needs to occur in a legislative, administrative, political and social environment that is supportive of both the process of developing the partnership, as well as the achievement of its objectives over time.

Using Processes that Generate Arrangements that are Durable Over Time, including

5. *Resource Commitments:* The major parties to the system must commit resources (financial, human, material) to give them a stake in ensuring its success.
6. *Participation and Transparency:* The interests of all the major stakeholders must be reflected in project development. Special attention should be paid to meeting the needs of the poor. Broad participation in the collaborative process must be sought at strategic points to maximize the acceptability and sustainability of the solution developed. Transparency on the basic features of the project (framework, fees and ownership) is necessary.
7. *Capacity Building:* Projects requiring substantial institutional change or large capital investments will require building the capacity of all stakeholders: (a) consumers on the nature of the

service they are receiving and the costs associated with its provision; (b) providers, particularly local organizations, on entrepreneurial skills; and (c) governments on adopting the frameworks for and overseeing the provision of the services.

8. *Patience:* In addition, projects requiring substantial institutional change or large capital investments require lots of time. Careful attention must be paid to the balance between responding rapidly to the most pressing crises and developing integrated solutions that will last.
9. *Flexibility:* All partnerships are context-based and locally embedded. Draw from experience elsewhere, but be opportunistic about exploiting the comparative advantage of local resources. For long-term, capital intensive projects, changes in investment plans, technology choices and priority actions will be necessary in response to unforeseen circumstances including clear procedures for making such changes over the life of the project (UNDP, 1997).

Lessons for Improved Urban Management

The recent experiences of a few cities provide some important lessons for improved Urban Governance. These lessons are:

a. Build credibility of local government through improved administration.
b. Make initial efforts in a few critical areas that are 'visible' and affect daily lives of most residents.
c. Changes have to come from within the system, not forced by state or national government.
d. Demonstration effects are important and more cities will learn from the few success stories. Dissemination and net-working of local governments is crucial.
e. State and national governments may not always support the initiation of changes, but will yield only when citizen support is received.
f. Responsive administration for citizen grievances is essential.

Strategy for Good Urban Governance

Given the few successful experiences of improved urban governance and the lessons derived from these examples, it is necessary to examine possible strategies for inculcating good governance in Asian cities. A tentative outline of such a strategy is presented below.

Strategy of Enablement

While supportive and enabling national and state level policies will be required for urban development, the major responsibilities to increase efficiency of the urban areas and improve its productivity, will remain with the local government. Within the notion of the 'subsidiary principle', the national and sub-national governments will have to empower the local governments. They will also have to provide a policy environment in which local governments can adopt and practice the participatory development process and pursue the key characteristics of good governance.

Strategy of Participation

Participatory development process requires that the present alienation of the civil society to the urban local government be eliminated. The present corruption and inefficiency in local government have led to a loss of faith in the system of governance by the common citizens. The government is seen as pursuing only its self-interests rather than larger societal interests. The local government, in addition to the crisis of institutional capacity, also suffers from a crisis of identity.

The partnership mode of governance requires that each stakeholder in the city has an adequate voice and that the partnership is built on the strengths and interests of each stakeholder — the local government, the private sector and the community. The present experience of such partnerships is limited but has provided many important lessons. (Mehta and *Mehta*, 1993).

Innovative models of financing urban development are also recently being attempted in India and other Asian countries. Here also, the critical realization has been that the government can no longer continue to provide and create urban services at highly subsidized rates. The emerging financial market discipline suggests that the present financing based on directed credits, subsidized prices and budgetary support will soon become obsolete, as it is inefficient and uncompetitive.

Financing of urban development will have to be integrated within a larger financial market. This implies that all land development related activities and all urban infrastructure and services would have to be financed through market based borrowing from financial institutions or the capital market. The market discipline would require that the services be priced appropriately to recover the full cost of capital and operations.

Strategy of Capacity Building

Achieving good governance requires building capacity as well as applying these principles to existing institutions. New capacity may be needed to help assure the rule of law and open access to public information. But "capacity building" is a broader concept as well. It includes the need to ensure that diverse social groups are able to get needed information and participate in the making of public policy. It includes the need for vibrant markets and a private sector that operates in partnership with Government, and for both to have sufficient stability and confidence that they make the investments needed for tomorrow's urban infrastructure.

Capacity building of local governments has traditionally been viewed as human resource development activity. It is, however, realized that efforts to train better urban managers are not sufficient without appropriate changes in the institutional environment. Capacity building is now referred to as improving the ability of the institutions — government private and community based groups — and individuals within these institutions, to perform appropriate tasks and fulfil their roles effectively, efficiently and sustainably. The dimensions of such capacity building exercise are human resource development, organizational development and the institutional and legal framework (Peltenberg et al., 1996).

Often the capacity of organizations is assessed on indicators of good governance. Grindle and Hildebrand (1994) provide a framework for building sustainable capacity of public sector organization. This approach is shown in Table below:

TABLE

Good Governance Indicators Based on Capacity

Capacity	Good Governance
1. Institutional Capacity	• accountability • transparency • adaptability • judicial independence
2. Technical Capacity	• Perspective planning and projecting future investment needs • Management of services and infrastructure • Financial management and accounting practice
3. Administrative Capacity	• Grievance redressal system • Personnel Policy • Flexible and decentralized decision-making • Performance evaluation
4. Political Capacity	• Articulation of local needs in the context of organizational capacity • Mechanism for participation of stakeholders • State-local relations in policy formulations and fiscal transfer.

Source : Adapted from Grindle and Hildebrand (1994) and Razon Abad (1997).

Conclusions

The description of successful examples in this paper suggests that there are many local initiatives of innovative urban governance that would be qualified as good governance practices. From these experiences one can derive some important lessons. Some of the key characteristics of these successful experiences are enumerated to demonstrate that it is possible for most urban local governments to adopt good governance practices. A strategy for improved urban governance is enumerated. This includes strategies of enablement, strategies of participation, and strategy of capacity building. Various programmes of the UN system, including the global programme on Urban Management, have been promoting these strategies. It is expected that with the successful implementation of these strategies, good governance practice will become widespread and lead to an appreciable increase in the quality of life of urban residents.

References

Basu, Dipankar (1994). *Decentralization and Municipal Finance: With Special Reference to Gujarat.* A dissertation submitted to the Indian Institute of Public Administration. New Delhi in partial fulfilment of the requirement of the Nineteenth Advanced Programme in Public Administration.

Dutta, Shyam. *Urban Management in India.* The Institutional Framework of Urban Government Case Study No.8, Development Administration Group, Institute of Local Government Studies, The University of Birmingham.

Grindle, M. and Hilderbrand, M. (1994). *Building Sustainable Capacity Challenges for the Public Sector.* Harvard Institute for International Development, Cambridge, USA.

Mehta, D. and Pathak (1994). *Economic Development, Globalization and Urban Governance in India.* Global Research Initiative, University of Toronto, Canada.

Mehta, Dinesh (1997). *Vision 2021: Urban Governance in India.* Paper presented at the Seminar on India's Urban Vision: 2021, Oct. 6-7, 1997, Ministry of Urban Development, Government of India.

Mehta, M. and Mehta, D. (1993). *"Privatization of Municipal Services"* in Urban India, July-Dec., 1993.

National Institute of Urban Affairs (1993). *Urban Development Strategy for the State of Gujarat*, Research Study Series Number 55.

National Institute of Urban Affairs (1997). *A Compendium of Municipal Legislation's in Conformity with Constitution (Seventy-Fourth) Amendment Act, 1992.*

Peltenberg, M. et al. (1991). *Building Capacity for Better Cities.* Institute for Housing and Urban Development Studies, Rotterdam.

Swamy, HMS and S Narang (1998). *Transformation of Surat — From Plague to Second-Cleanest City in India.* Urban Innovations Case Study No.1, UMP and AIILSG, New Delhi.

UNCHS (1996). *An Urbanizing World: Global Report on Human Settlements, 1996.* United Nations Center for Human Settlements (HABITAT), Oxford, New York.

UNDP (1995). *Public Sector Management, Governance, and Sustainable Human Development.* A discussion paper. Management Development and Governance Division, Bureau for Policy and Programme Support, UNDP, New York.

UNDP (1997). *Governance for Sustainable Growth and Equity.* Report of International Conference, United Nations, New York, 28-30 July 1997.

UNDP (1997). *Governance for Sustainable Human Development.* A UNDP policy document, New York.

UNDP (1997). *Participatory Urban Governance.* Technical Advisory Paper 1, Local Initiative Facility for Urban Environment. Management Development and Governance Division, UNDP, New York.

UNDP (1997). Public-Private Partnerships for the Urban Environment. UNDP, New York.

UNDP (1997). *Reconceptualising Governance.* Management Development and Governance Division, Bureau for Policy and Programme Support, UNDP, New York.

World Bank (1997). *The State in a Changing World: World Development Report, 1997,* Washington DC.

ANNEX 1

Criteria for Better Cities Network

1. ***Accountability***
   Indicators:
   a Regularity in the fiscal transactions and faithful compliance/adherence to legal requirements and administrative policies.
   b. Efficient and economical use of funds. property. manpower and other resources.
   c. Participatory and decentralized activities in the planning and implementation of programmes/projects.
   d. Systems in place which ensure that goals are clearly communicated to the constituents.
   e. Mechanisms are installed to evaluate economic performance.

2. ***Responsiveness***
   Indicators:
   a. Mechanisms are in place to determine that people's needs and wants, e.g., surveys. public forum. telephone hotline, etc.
   b. Mechanisms are installed to allow citizen participation in planning and implementation of plans, programmes and projects, e.g. consultative council meetings, public hearings, etc.
   c. Existence of a system for monitoring to determine that goals and desirable social ends of the programmes/projects are attained and delivered to targetted number of beneficiaries.
   d. Presence of simple procedures to ensure fair and swift action on suggestions. grievances. etc. by the public.
   e. Availability of information to the public to give feedback on how the local governments respond to demands articulated by the constituents.

3. ***Management Innovations***
   Indicators:
   a. Bureaucratic structures and procedures have been improved to conform to service standards such as efficiency. effectiveness, timeliness and economy.
   b. Presence of innovative or creative devices to deal with the public.
   c. Introduction of innovations in generating resources and in instituting cost-saving measures.
   d. Adoption of innovative concepts and practices that deal with local problems such as environmental degradation. land tenure. poverty incidence. etc.
   e. Application of new management techniques adopted such as total quality management (TQM). information technology and computerization.

4. ***Public Private Partnership***
   Indicators:
   a Implementation of policies incentive schemes to encourage private sector to participate in development.

(Contd.)

(Contd.)

b. Presence of business sector initiatives to improve efficiency of local government bureaucracy, e.g. technology improvement, training, etc.
c. Join involvement of public and private sector in planning, funding and implementation of programmes/projects.
d. Privatization of local government services.

5. ***Local Government-Citizen Interaction***
Indicators:

a. Presence and extent of cooperative efforts among local governments, non-governmental organizations.
b. Existence of mechanisms that allow consultation between the local government and the constituents on various local concerns.
c. Implementation and extent of projects as a result of LG/NGO/PVO collaboration.

6. ***Decentralized Management***
Indicators:

a. Presence of clear-cut guidelines on delegation.
b. Presence of a monitoring system to provide feedback on the implementation of delegated tasks.
c. Existence and extent of decisions made by officials to whom tasks are delegated.
d. Consistency between the organizational hierarchical structure and actual delegation of tasks.

7. ***Networking***
Indicators:

a. Extent (number) of inter-local government networks.
b. Extent (number) of regional (intra-local) networks.
c. Extent of international network (local unit in one country with various local units in other countries).
d. Scope of resource complementation in the network/networks.
e. Extent of technology interchange/collaboration.
f. Promotion of common interest and agenda.
g. Exchange of expertise and training.

8. ***Human Resource Management***
Indicators:

a. Presence and extent of the coverage of policies designed to improve the different aspects of human resource management.
b Existence of an adequate and sustained programme of recruitment and selection based on merit and fitness.
c. Presence of training programmes to improve the capabilities of local government personnel.
d Installation of a workable and responsive Position Classification and Pay Plan based on the principle of "equal pay for comparatively equal work."

Annex II

1. Comprehensive Development of Urban Infrastructure, Foshan City People's Republic of China

The People's Government of Foshan City of China has implemented the comprehensive development strategy for urban infrastructure, which is a forerunner on infrastructure construction and emphasis on housing construction. By adjusting the management system for urban infrastructure construction, reforming the investment system and price system of urban construction, and giving active play to functions of the non-government organizations, it has made the urban construction and the environment of residential districts develop coordinately.

2. Kaantabay sa Kauswagan, an Urban Poor Programme in Naga City, Philippines

The Kaantabay sa Kauswagan (or Partners in Development) Programme is a social amelioration programme primarily designed to empower squatters and slum dwellers which comprise some 25 per cent of the city population residing in 21 urban barangays of Naga City. So far, it has resettled 2,017 families to relocation sites with a combined area of 33 hectares; secured home-lots for 789 squatter families; and upgraded 27 urban poor communities, which host around 2,700 families.

Anchored on the belief that the urban poor is a vital sector in Naga's quest for total development, the programme addresses the sector's two main problems — (1) the absence of security of land tenure, and (2) the lack of basic infrastructure and facilities in their communities — primarily by adopting a "partner-beneficiary" perspective in dealing with clients. This approach sees the urban poor both as a programme partner and beneficiary, and as such is compelled to actively participate in every step of problem resolution.

In response to these major problems, the Programme focuses on two main components: (1) land acquisition which provides a sense of permanence to the urban poor's occupancy of a property, and (2) urban upgrading which provides decency, ease and comfort to daily life in the blighted areas. By institutionalizing a functional mechanism for permanently settling land tenurial problems between landowners and land occupants; elevating living conditions of the urban poor through on-site upgrading projects for blighted urban poor communities; establishing intra-city relocation sites for victims in extreme cases involving eviction and demolition; and providing them livelihood opportunities by introducing a livelihood component to the Programme, the Kaantabay sa Kauswagan was able to shape new strategies in cushioning negative impacts of urbanization. These strategies include accessing various modes of land acquisition — like direct purchase, land swapping, land sharing, community mortgage, and resettlement; institutionalizing a separate window catering specifically to urban poor clients of the lending arm of the local government; and evolving a financing scheme anchored on internally-generated resources of the beneficiaries.

3. *Partnerships for Poverty Alleviation in Cebu City, Philippines*

The City Government initiated the Cebu Urban Basic Services Programme in 1988 with the support of UNICEF; the Presidential Commission on the Urban Poor and the cooperation of several national government agencies programmes as well local and national NGOs. The programme was expanded to address land tenure and housing improvement by the development of the Community Mortgage Programme in 1990. The establishment of the Local Government Code in 1992 greatly increased the autonomy and authority of city government and laid the foundation for institutionalization and replication of the Cebu poverty alleviation policies and programmes in other cities.

4. *Khuda-Ki-Basti — Innovation and Success in Sheltering the Poor in Hyderabad, Sindh, Pakistan*

The former Director General of Hyderabad Development Authority (HDA) initiated this scheme in 1986. Restrictive governmental process such as allotment procedures, allocation of loan against land mortgages or land/property ownership provision for speculative purposes, were replaced with unconventional and innovative approaches. Some examples include: targeting needy households; simplification of bureaucratic procedures; optimising choice of relocation; providing urban basic services incrementally through community involvement; providing housing credit facilities to every household; creating direct rapport with the communities; and periodically monitoring the development process. The first incremental housing scheme (KKB) was developed at Gulshan-e-Shahbaz near Hyderabad and has since been followed by four similar schemes in various parts of Sindh Province including Karachi. This innovative approach of incremental housing by HDA has proved itself to be a viable alternative to the public sector's attempts to provide housing for urban poor. It represents a change in the World Bank administered sites and services housing programmes by allocating the service provisions in increments according to the land holder's need and their ability to pay.

5. *Effective Waste Reduction, Inchon, Korea*

The port city of Inchon has experienced rapid growth and is now facing a serious problem of increased solid waste production. The Inchon Metropolitan government enforced a solid waste control programme employing a Volume-based Collection Fee System (VCFS). Before the enforcement, the total quantity of solid wastes produced was 2,272 tones per day but after enforcement, 1,598 tonnes — a 30% decrease. The revenue from waste collection increased 195% from some 4 million US dollars to 11.6 million in 1995. Other supportive measures were also employed.

6. *Community Participation for Clean Surroundings — EXNORA, India*

EXNORA International is a broad-based voluntary, Non Governmental organization. It has created widespread environmental and civic awareness by promoting community/street directly involved in a voluntary effort in waste collection, removal, recycling and keeping their environment clean and green. The local units of EXNORA have made innovations to this scheme by adopting different methods of disposal, recycling, reuse and composting of waste, which reflects initiative and a conscious dicision-making process. The residents of each street/community manage the entire scheme. This sense of involvement in community work gives great satisfaction to all the participants.

Annex III

Innovative Urban Management Experiences in India

1. **Ahmedabad** (Pop. 3.5 million)	Financial revival through strict administrative measures. Improvements in civic information. Public-private partnership for road improvement project. Slum networking through public, private and community partnership. Accessing capital market through Municipal Bonds.
2. **Tirupur** (Pop. 3000,000)	Infrastructure improvement through private sector initiative. Parternership of state government, local govt., private industry and a financial institution for a major project.
3. **Surat** (Pop 1.8 million)	Declared as the second cleanest city in 1996 only two years after plague outbreak. Administrative decentralization and daily monitoring of routing municipal functions. Major investments in infrastructure through internal revenue surplus. Responsive administration to citizen complaints.
4. **Calcutta** (Pop. 10 million)	Removal of encroachment that were made two decades ago. Improved solid waste management. Responsive civic administration. Improvements in civil facilities.
5. **Pune** (Pop. 2.5 million)	Consistently good financial performance and sufficient revenue surpluses to self finance most capital investments. Public private partnership for proposed water supply and sewerage project.
6. **Jalgaon** (Pop. 350.000)	Revenue generation from real estate development for most of city's capital needs. Improved civic infrastructure. Vision to become a major urban centre in the country.
7. **Anand** (Pop. 150.00)	Efficient municipal administration for over two decades. Resource generation from land.

REPRIORITISING SOUTH ASIA'S DEVELOPMENT AGENDA: ROLE OF GOVERNANCE

Rehman Sobhan

Introduction

This paper argues that governance derives from an interplay of the nature of the state which in turn drives the sense of vision, along with the commitment and capacity to realize this vision. The development of such an autonomous vision serves to establish domestic ownership over the policymaking process in a particular country. Positive developmental outcomes originate from such a domestically owned vision and the capacity for its realization. The capacity for realizing this vision in turn derives from the interface between the management capacities of the state with the role of the political leadership and political parties in influencing the relationship between politics and development. To establish the interior logic of this argument it is useful to relate this discussion to the historical experience of particular countries in South Asia and to distinguish this experience from that of East/South East (SE) Asia.

The above arguments underlying this paper are structured under the following six heads; (i) The nature of the state and development; (ii) Vision, commitment and capacity; (iii) The role of aid donors in South Asia; (iv) The issue of transparency, accountability and development and their relation to governance in South Asia; (v) The role of politics in governance and development in South Asia; (vi) Conclusions on the extent to which governance influences South Asia's development compared to East/South East Asia.

State and Development

Regime Change and Effective Governance

In analysing the nature of the state in influencing the quality of governance we need to analyse the extent to which different state systems such as multi-party democracies, authoritarian/military regimes with political continuity as opposed to periodic regime changes, influence the quality of governance in South Asia through their impact on the vision, commitment and capacity of the state.

Within the South Asian scene authoritarian regimes originating in the cantonment have held office for long periods in both Pakistan and Bangladesh. In Nepal a state of autocratic rule prevailed, under a feudal and then a monarchial dispensation for most of its history and democratic governance in this mountain kingdom is of very recent origin.

It should however be kept in mind that under more democratic systems based on relatively free and fair elections held periodically, the Congress Party had ruled India for 30 years, 1947-77, then again from 1979-89 and from 1991-96. Similarly, in Sri Lanka power has oscillated between the UNP and the SLFP who have respectively alternated in fairly long tenures in office. It is therefore, by no means established that in South Asia it is only autocratic rule which coincides with long tenures in office. Thus, the longest tenure of any party in command of state power has been in India where the Congress Party has ruled the country for close to 45 years of its 50 years history.

To the extent that long tenures in office owe to contested elections rather than forceable occupation of power it is expected that such regimes will remain more accountable in their governance. However, it must be recognized that the behavioural patterns of regimes whether in power through an electoral mandate or more forceable arrangements, over long tenures, breeds autocratic tendencies, weak accountability and indifference to democratic pressures. The concept of *illiberal democracy* has derived from such a perversion of the democratic process. Thus it is arguable that only in Sri Lanka and more recently, in all other South Asian countries, have claims on national power been regularly exposed to democratic contestation where parties in office operated under a credible apprehension that they could be compelled to vacate office at the next election.

There is unfortunately no evidence that this exposure of all countries in South Asia, certainly over the last decade, to plural democracy, has noticeably improved the quality of governance, accelerated development or indeed encouraged more equitable distribution of its benefits. Indeed a more competitive political system has coincided with an increase in the importance of money and violence as instruments of electoral gain, the emergence of a highly confrontational parliamentary culture and a progressive degeneration in the morality of the political system. Thus, the causal links between political arrangements, tenures in office and positive development outcomes remain unproven in South Asia. This relationship obviously merits more rigorous comparative analysis than has hitherto been attempted by the scholars of South Asian development politics to understand what lies beyond the trappings of formal democracy to ensure better governance.

Concept of Embedded Autonomy and its Implications for Governance

To understand the causal links between the nature of the state and the quality of governance we need to know more about the capacity of the South Asian state to function as an autonomous agent, insulated from sectional and external pressures, in directing its development agenda. It has been argued by Peter Evan's in his pathbreaking work, *Embedded Autonomy*, that successful development outcomes originate in a strong state which can work in close intimacy, defined as *embeddedness*, with the business sector, whilst retaining their *autonomy* of governance from the pressures of special interest groups. There is, however, virtually no attempt to conceptualize this notion of *embedded autonomy* within a South Asian context and no empirical effort to assess its prevalence in any state of South Asia. Peter Evans, has used India along with the Republic of Korea (ROK) and Brazil, to test his hypothesis of *embedded autonomy* where he points to ROK as an effective example of such *embedded autonomy* compared to India and Brazil. It is not clear if Evans would feel as strongly about ROK today after the revelations emerging from their recent financial crisis about the malfeasant links between the state and the business sector.

Looking at the South Asian experience it appears this region inherited a relatively strong state at independence. This manifestation of state power originated in the all-powerful bureaucracy established by the British in the Indian subcontinent and Sri Lanka as a *steel frame* to sustain imperial rule. The legacy of the *steel frame* served to establish the ascendence of the state in South Asia, and enabled it to exercise considerable authority in their relations with civil society. In post-colonial South Asia, the authority of the state was used to empower particular fractions of the feudal elites and the bourgeoisie through dispensation of state patronage.

The once powerful state in other South Asian countries has, with the passage of time, been exposed to a process of downsizing under the pressure of externally driven economic reforms. Such a process of disempowerment has gradually eroded the autonomy of the state, compared to what it was in the post-independence period and indeed in relation to the East Asian states of South Korea, Taiwan, China, Indonesia, Malaysia and Singapore. It is arguable that in each of these East Asian and some South East Asian countries, the state has been far more powerful in relation to civil society in general and various fractions of the elite groups, than is evident in any South Asian state. This supremacy of state power in the East Asian state has given it greater autonomy in its dialogues with the business community and other elite groups in particular, as well as enabled the state to provide more decisive direction to the development process. By contrast, the over-regulated states of South Asia have remained much weaker in their capacity to influence development outcomes.

State-Business Relations in South Asia

In general, state-business relations in South Asia remain uneasy and far more contentious than in East Asia. This over-regulated but weak state in South Asia has encouraged the emergence of private rather than institutionalized state-business rent seeking coalitions. Such private rent-seeking coalitions have become pervasive in virtually every South Asian state and have led to the spread of corruption to the point where it extends to all levels of the state. This has contributed to delay in decision-making as well as inefficient implementation of such decisions.

The contemporary South Asian experience suggests that elements of embeddedness prevail in every country of the region, based on social and personalized financial ties. Politicians in every country today draw upon the business sector to finance their election campaigns and in the process incur political debts. The debts are repaid through patronage when in office or when in opposition by their failure to take business groups to task for particular acts of malfeasance. These symbiotic links between business and politics are increasingly manifest in the number of members of parliament who now show business as their primary source of livelihood. Thus we have the spectacle of rich businessmen buying nominations from the political parties and spending large sums of money in complete violation of electoral expenditure laws, to 'buy' electoral victories. In turn, sitting MPs from both the ruling and opposition parties use their access to the decision-makers to establish themselves or their family members, in business or become the closet partners of some business house.

This rent-seeking coalition between business and politics has served to fuel corruption and violence in the body politic of South Asia. Money is used to sustain a new class of armed mercenaries who remain immune from the forces of law enforcement because of their political connections. This class of mercenaries is now directly entering into the political arena where money and violence are becoming important variables in influencing the course of electoral politics. Thus, a new form of embeddedness is emerging between business, politicians, the criminal classes and the machinery of law and order. This is undermining the autonomy of the state by seriously compromising the rule of law.

Bureaucrats are caught up in this process particularly in the operational agencies which deal directly with the private sector. They enter into their own collusive transactions with business houses whilst in office or expect to join business houses on their retirement, fuelled by lucrative compensation packages. Bureaucrats socially interact with the business community and marry into each other's families. These bureaucrats, along with the politicians, and in particular cases the army, in association with a select class of businessmen constitute an exclusive ruling elite who draw benefit from the resources and patronage of the state.

This form of state embeddedness is, however, far from autonomous in the way that a state guided by its own vision create its embeddedness with business to realize the state's developmental goals. Thus in South Asia, in varying degrees, we have witnessed an evolution from the relatively autonomous post-colonial state bequeathed to at least three countries in South Asia, living in a relationship of dominance rather than embeddedness with the business community, to that of an embedded state, which has surrendered its autonomy to accommodate the appetites of specific interest group.

Vision and Commitment

It is central to the argument of this paper that a sense of vision backed by political commitment is essential to establish the autonomy of the state and to invest it with a capacity to direct the development agenda. It is useful to assess the extent to which the development project of various states in South Asia demonstrates a degree of autonomy in the exercise of state power which originates in such a vision, and political commitment. It would be then useful to evaluate this commitment by assessing the capacity of the various states to accumulate the political and administrative capacity to implement their vision.

Looking at South Asia today it would be difficult to identify any state which is driven by a clearly articulated vision of its leadership. If we were to look at the Prime Ministers/President's who have held office throughout South Asia, over the last decade none appears to be driven by a sense of mission to transform their societies in a particular direction. This is in marked contrast to some of the founding fathers of the South Asian post-colonial state such as Jawaharlal Nehru, Sheikh Mujibur Rahman, even Z.A. Bhutto who had definite agendas, about the direction they wanted to give to their countries, whatever may have been the merits of their vision. In contrast, East/SE Asian states were driven by the developmental vision of leaders such as Mao Tse-tung, then Deng Xiaping in PRC, Park Chung Hee in ROK, Lee Kuan Yew in Singapore, Mahathir Mohammed in Malaysia and Soeherto in Indonesia, who all enjoyed long tenures in office which enabled them to realize some, if not all of their vision.

In the absence of a clearly articulated vision prospective reformers, such as Dr. Manmohan Singh, in his capacity as Finance Minister of India, may have a notion to deregulate and liberalize the Indian economy but this vision tends to fall victim to a series of political compromises which erode the intensity of the mission. Such Finance Ministers who themselves usually tend to be unelected technocrats or bureaucrats remain dependent on the patronage of the political leadership.

In contrast to the South Asian experience, the East/SE Asian tradition has fostered a class of professionals who have been inducted into high political office, defined popularly as *technopols*, who have remained relatively insulated from political pressures, in their management of the economy often due to the backing of strong visionary leaders. However, the power of such unelected *technopols* remains open to question since their lack of accountability, except to their leader, is now held as partly responsible for the prevailing crisis in the region. If such leaders falter in their commitment to their vision this compromises the work of the *technopols*.

The lack of a developmental vision amongst the leadership in South Asia is compounded by their weak commitment to realize such a vision. Thus, we more often have evidence of a pseudo-vision where, for example, particular political leaders in South Asia commit themselves to eradicate poverty. However, a measure of commitment to realize the vision through a holistic, time bound, practical agenda for poverty eradication is absent in all South Asian states. Thus the statements on poverty eradication, including a declaration at the SAARC summit in Dhaka in 1993, to eliminate poverty in the region by 2005, has a hollow ring to it. What we are left with are a series of ad hoc anti-poverty programmes in most countries of the region, underwritten by a variety of donor sponsors.

Capacity

In the absence of any developmental vision or commitment to realize a clearly articulated developmental mission, capacity to implement the development agenda remains weak. Administrative capacity is already weak in every state of South Asia, being increasingly compromised by their growing embeddedness with particular interest groups. The growth of such predatory tendencies in the executive and legislative branches of the state, deprived of any motivation or direction from a leadership without vision, appears hardly capable of carrying through any developmental mission to a positive conclusion.

This bleak statement of the lack of vision and depreciated capacity of the executive does not preclude initiatives by particular executives driven by their own sense of mission, to realize a particular micro-objective. Thus ministers, senior bureaucrats, field executives have carried through their own private agendas such as reforming agricultural extension or building a bridge, accelerating infrastructure development, building a milk cooperative, delivering micro-credit within a particular programme where they have achieved visible results within a micro-area. But such micro-interventions in no way generate sufficient externalities which can motivate their cabinet or service colleagues to improve their own areas of work or transform the face of a particular area. It is not surprising that such micro-interventions are disappearing from within the state systems of South Asia and such initiatives are increasingly being led by visionary NGOs with a strong sense of mission and the administrative capacity to realize such micro-agendas.

Weak executive capacity in the South Asian states is compounded by weak political capacity. In every South Asian state the style of politics remains highly confrontational. This process precludes any effort at promoting political dialogues to build a consensus behind a development agenda. Parliament tends to be an arena for rhetorical exchanges rather than a vehicle for political consensus building. Parliamentary Committees tend to be under-used or undermined by the unilateral agendas of the executive in South Asia. Whilst some Ministers in some countries may be more cognizant of the importance of building a political constituency supportive of the reform process such initiatives are undermined by the generally confrontational political environment as well as the lack of support for such initiatives from the political leadership. Thus, as with the case of micro-administrative success, individual efforts at political capacity building generate few externalities.

The ultimate answer which emerges from our argument states that not only do the South Asian States lack the capacity to realize particular developmental goals but that there is little awareness for the need and hence no initiative is forthcoming to build such capacities.

Role of Donors in South Asia

Donors Influence on State Policy

Apart from India, the donors and particularly the *Bretton Woods Institution* (BWI), the *World Bank* and *International Monetary Fund* (IMF), have played a dominant role in the policymaking process of every South Asian country. Thus, successive administrations in Pakistan have pursued the BWI agenda without any hesitation and have made very little effort to assert any ownership over these agendas either through domestic professional inputs or through attempts to build political support behind the BWI agenda. The Pakistani experience with the BWI has been replicated in Bangladesh through successive regimes. The same *Policy Framework Paper* (PFP) negotiated by the bureaucrats of the Ershad regime with the IMF in August 1990 has been directing the policy agendas without modification, of successive elected regimes of the BNP in 1991 and the Awami League in 1996. A similar continuity in a BWI designed policy agenda put in place in Sri Lanka in 1977 by the newly elected UNP regime through negotiations with the IMF, continued without modification, through the entire tenure of this regime and has since been inherited by the successor SLFP regime without modification. In Nepal the BWI agenda put in place in the 1980's under the monarchial regime has been continued though successive regimes under the Congress, the Panchayat parties and even the Communists.

In India, when the first loan was negotiated by the regime of Indira Gandhi with the IMF in the early 1980's a reform process influenced by the IMF was put in place. This policy regime has persisted through the regimes of Rajiv Gandhi and the Janata Dal, has been accelerated under the Congress regime of Narshimhha Rao under the leadership of Dr. Manmohan Singh and has been perpetuated under the United Front coalition. The BJP appears to be maintaining continuity in this BWI influenced policy regime.

It is arguable that in India the change in policy direction in the early 1980s and its acceleration in the 1990s, derived from domestic compulsions and were designed by India's own highly competent policy professionals who happen to share the views of the BWI. This view of domestic ownership over India's reform process has been contested by the critics of these policy reforms.

Donors and Domestic Politics

This pervasive influence by donors over policymaking in at least 4 South Asian countries derives from the high degree of aid dependence of each country in financing the development process. This high degree of aid dependence has to some extent been reduced in Pakistan and Bangladesh in the 1990s compared to the 1970s and 80s, but still remains high compared to India. Since 1982, when the process of structural adjustment reforms (SAR) was initiated by the World Bank, policy lending through programme loans has been increasingly used to promote particular reforms.

This heavy dependence on aid is to some extent tied to the importance of aid in assuring the political survival of particular regimes. It is arguable that over the last 20 years, no political regime, including the Martial Law regimes in Pakistan and Bangladesh, could have survived in office without such an inflow of aid. The extent of this political necessity for aid may again be arguable. But there is little doubt that every regime which held office in each of these countries actually believed that a regular inflow of aid was needed for their political survival. This conviction about the importance of the aid donors has remained a binding constraint in the response of each regime to the policy advise of the donors.

It has, in practise, been far from certain that gestures of contradiction would have invoked a cut-off in their aid. Nor is it testable if aid cut-offs would have been threatening to regime. Martial Law regimes, surprisingly, appear highly insecure in their exercise of authority and are particularly sensitive to the advise of donors. The perpetuation of military regimes in power in Pakistan and Bangladesh for over a decade must owe in considerable measure to the patronage of their aid donors who made little effort to use their disproportionate leverage over these military regimes to nudge them towards democracy.

In contrast to the military regimes, elected regimes appear no less genuflective to the donors even where such donor-driven policies expose them to electoral risk. Rather, in South Asia elected regimes have been quite willing to give greater attention to the concerns of aid donors than to those of their electorate.

Degrees of Ownership

It would be no exaggeration to argue that such a donor-driven reform process remains totally without official ownership. Many of the policy agendas promoted by the donors originate in long standing problems which have remained inadequately addressed by successive goverments in South Asia. It is generally accepted even amongst critics of the BWI reform agenda, that in South Asia economic activity has been over-regulated, is too insular in its orientation and that a degree of liberalization in trade policy was in order. The point at issue was the pace of liberalization and its sequencing. It was, thus, argued that other aspects of the reform process, such as creating an appropriate environment of investment and production which would have moved to, at least partially, level the playing field for domestic industries to compete with freer imports, should have been, *ab initio*, put in place. It has been observed that in Bangladesh, Nepal and Pakistan, possibly Sri Lanka, a more graduated import liberalization process, compatible with the slower pace of liberalization actually adopted in India, would have enjoyed more ready domestic acceptance.

It is arguable that externally driven reform agendas, however meritorious and indeed acceptable to particular ministers, will fall victim to weak implementation in the concerned country. No policy initiative, unless backed by firm conviction which translates into a strong commitment manifest in a willingness to develop capacity, is likely to be sustainable. Thus weak governance originates in lack of commitment which in turn derives from weak ownership. Developmental failures originating in weak governance thus originate further upstream in the donor driven reform process.

Few governments in South Asia have made such externally driven reform agendas the basis of political mobilization to seek support for such reforms. Little attempt is made to expose the plethora of aid agreements annexed with numerous policy conditionalities, which impact on the daily lives of South Asia's citizens, to parliamentary debate. Nor have these regimes made the donor driven reform process into the piece of their election campaign. Even the Congress Party was loathe to put Dr. Manmohan Singh's liberalization agenda at the forefront of their election campaign in 1996 and had already begun distancing themselves from the reform agenda at least 2 years before the election in 1996. Neither did the United Front government project the reform agenda of its Finance Minister. Mr. P. Chidambaram, during the 1998 election campaign.

It is similarly evident that sitting Finance Ministers elsewhere in South Asia make only a limited effort to reach out to civil society to sell their reforms, whilst their colleagues in the line Ministries usually tend to distance themselves from the reform process. Again this weak effort at political mobilization originates in weak ownership. Weak political support for any policy is one of the measures of weak governance and accounts for poor developmental outcomes.

Issues of Transparency, Accountability and Development and their Relation to Governance is South Asia

Instruments for Regulation and Scrutiny

Transparency and accountability are generally recognized as important aspects of good governance. They expose the state to regulation and public scrutiny. It is argued that a system of accountability to the people reinforced by top-down accountability will ensure that policy reforms are being implemented and that malfeasance will be discouraged through exposure to public scrutiny. Transparency in all government transactions, through full public disclosure before the parliament and in the press serves as an instrument of accountability for the government before the people.

Accountability

Traditionally South Asia's lines of accountability from the executive to the legislative and beyond to their citizens, has remained weak. This was part of the colonial legacy where during imperial rule, the Government of India (GOI) was accountable to Whitehall and not the people of India.

In states such as Pakistan, Bangladesh and Nepal with a long tradition of autocracy, originating in the unchallenged power of the Chief Executive, there were no institutional mechanisms of accountability where Parliament itself functioned at the will of the Chief Executive. Even during episodes of electoral democracy the tradition of the all powerful chief executive, with no civic accountability and little accountability to parliament, has persisted. In India and Sri Lanka, chief executives have been rather more accountable to their Parliaments, though in Sri Lanka, the move to a Presidential system, during the UNP regime led by Julius Jayawardena, has certainly weakened the accountability of the Chief Executive to parliament. In India too, even within a more tested system of parliamentary democracy, we have witnessed the rise of the all powerful chief executive in the person of Indira Gandhi, with a far weaker degree of accountability either to her cabinet or to the legislature, compared to her father, Jawaharlal Nehru. Her successors did not have either her authority or her will to sustain such a distance from parliament but there is a general acceptance that even in the post-Indira Gandhi era accountability to the legislature remains far weaker than was envisaged by the authors of the Indian constitution.

In countries where accountability to the legislature remains weak, the confrontational posture of the opposition has itself been far from conducive to promoting Westminster style accountability through sober parliamentary debate and pro-active parliamentary committees. Again country variations in the functioning of the respective parliaments and parliamentary committees merit study to enable us to gauge the extent to which the executive remains accountable to its legislature.

Parliament's accountability to its electorate remains to disemploy successive regimes throughout South Asia. The political tradition of electorates taking their sitting MPs to task for failures of governance has not been strong except on election day where many 'failed' MPs throughout the region have been voted out of office by their electorate. In turn, sitting MPs seek to keep faith with their electorate by lobbying for locating items of public expenditure in their respective constituencies and measure their parliamentary achievements by their success in securing public funding for their constituents. This appears to be seen by MPs as compensation for being unable to serve their constituents in securing relief from administrative oppression and mis-governance or to play a creative role in parliament by taking the executive to task for its failures of governance. It is arguable that the weak degree of accountability of the executive to the legislature and of the parliamentarians to the electorate has both promoted and compounded weak governance.

The inherited imperial tradition of lack of accountability to the people was, however, compensated by a much more serviceable system of bottom-up accountability. The British did put in place a mechanism where every official from the local *patwary* upto the Viceroy of India, was accountable to a superior power. Institutional mechanisms of reporting up and surveillance of subordinates was the hallmark of the imperial system. This tradition persisted into the post-colonial state where the inherited administrative structures maintained this tradition of bottom-up accountability. However, it is writ large in the post-colonial history of each South Asian country how these systems of bottom-up accountability progressively weakened to the point, where at least in such states as Pakistan and Bangladesh, this system of accountability has all but disappeared.

It remains arguable that the weak capacity to implement development programmes leading to weak developmental outcomes, in large measure originates in the virtual absence of executive accountability either to the people or to their superiors so that in the end no one really remains accountable to anyone or for anything. This process both perpetuates corruption, mal-distributes its benefits and raises the costs of development.

Transparency

Weak accountability in a system discourages transparency in their dealings with their citizens. In South Asia parliament was the ultimate pressure point on the government to remain transparent in their dealings with their citizens. However, only India and Sri Lanka has a functioning parliament, served as an effective vehicle for bringing to light the failures of governance in their country. Here again both the weak capacity of parliamentarians to exercise their custodial function and the skills of administration in minimizing the degree of information they would share with Parliament, weaken the role of the legislature in promoting transparency. In those countries with long traditions of subordinated legislatures the executive met their reporting obligations to parliament on a need to know basis. This tendency was encouraged by the poor calibre of the MPs, their lack of curiosity and willingness to be fobbed-off with inadequate or even misleading information by the executive. Tradition of the parliamentary committee has served the process of transparency somewhat better than has parliament. But this again has depended on the pro-active role of particular MPs rather than the good intentions of the government. It is also recognized that an investigative press and a pro-active judiciary remain a vital resource for a parliament in enforcing accountability on the executive.

However, the best instrument for ensuring transparency remains a free media serving an alert civil society. In South Asia, compared to East/SE Asia, the press has remained relatively free, at least whenever military rule has not sought to curb the press as it did in Pakistan and Bangladesh and in India during the emergency declared by Indira Gandhi in the mid-1970s. However, the daily press in most countries of the region tends to be owned by big business houses, some of whom have their own political and policy agendas which may come into conflict with editorial independence. In contrast, the electronic media in most countries of South Asia, has remained subservient to the state which has compromised both its independence as well as its quality. It is only with the arrival of satellite television that, in India at least, a highly independent form of discourse on television, manifest in a variety of talk shows such as Ap Ki Adalat, is exposing acts of mis-governance to a high degree of transparency.

To sustain such a process of transparency demands more than a free media. It demands an alert civil society anxious to take the state to task for its acts of mis-governance. Such a conscious civil society remains the strongest pressure point to make governments both accountable and transparent since the natural tendency of the state in South Asia is to minimize the exposure of its governance to public scrutiny.

Leadership's Accountability

Within South Asia the struggle for making the national leadership and executive accountable to the people has been part of an on-going process pre-dating independence. However, the struggle to establish accountability whether from the imperial power or from military junta's has no corresponding spin-off in demanding accountability of the political leadership within the participants in the democratic struggle. Most of the political parties which led the struggle for independence in South Asia were elitist by their composition and led by charismatic leaders whose authority was rarely questioned within their respective parties.

This tendency to vest absolute power in such party leaders, without accountability to their rank and file, perpetuates their lack of accountability within their party when such leaders assume state power and accounts for the weak foundations of the democratic system in South Asia. Thus, leaders who have enjoyed absolute power within their party, as and when they assume power, remain less inclined to be collegial in the running of their administration. The resultant weakening of the cabinet system of government and emergence of a viceregal tradition with executive power being monopolized in the office of the chief executive, emerges as the outcome of a tradition of weak accountability within the political party system itself.

This move towards absolutist leadership, even within a working democratic system, in turn contributes to the weakening of any system of accountability within the system of governance. The emergence of such fiefdoms throughout the hierarchy of government, originates in the assumption of absolute power by the respective political leaders throughout South Asia and their increasing reluctance to devolve this leadership both to their colleagues and beyond this to lower echelons of a federated polity. Such a system breeds weak governance not just within the administration but within political parties, who remain organizationally weak and financially non-transparent in their practices.

The hazard posed by strong leaders to good governance lies in the complete dependence on such a leader to articulate the vision and demonstrate the commitment to realize their vision. If the leader's vision is weak or defective this permeates both the direction of party politics as well as the quality of governance when the leader is in office. When such a leader passes on it is rare for their vision to be bequeathed to a successor even to their genetic heirs. The departed leader's vision thus lives on in the slogans and rhetoric of their heirs.

Role of Politics in the Governance and Development of South Asia

Building a Political Consensus

To understand the role of politics in development we need to diagnose the political culture of a country to establish whether it is consensual or confrontational, since this tendency impacts on governance and development.

In virtually every country in South Asia democratic politics is becoming increasingly confrontational. An earlier tradition of sober consensual political debate, depended in no small measure on the absolute immunity of the ruling regime from political challenge, as in the case of the Congress Party in India and the stature of its leaders who enjoyed high public esteem. As Indian politics moved to incorporate a wider spectrum of social forces, through the struggle of these forces to assert themselves within a more plural system, parliament became a more contentious arena. This process has culminated in the decline of the Congress and the emergence of local and caste based parties more representative of the pluralism of Indian politics.

Whilst such a process of democratic assertion is part of a process of widening the representative base of politics it has not only made Indian politics more confrontational but has helped to destabilize the national governance, which is increasingly dependent on a coalition of dispirate political elements built around a coalition of regional and caste interests. Indian politics today appears to increasingly depend on coalitions built around the ambitions, whims and appetites of particular leaders, who remain unmoved by issues. Within such a system, politics degenerates as much into a clash of egos as it does of irreconcilable political forces.

In the remaining South Asian countries the political system remains far less plural and hence more manageable. Bangladesh and Sri Lanka have effectively built a two-party system, as indeed has Pakistan, at least at the national level; so too has Nepal, though its two party system is now being exposed to a process of sub-division which is exposing it to serious instability. Even in Pakistan loyalities within the dominant parties remain ephemeral so that the coherence of these parties remains far from assured, given the opportunism of the individual party members. Similarly, in Sri Lanka their two party system has not been able to accommodate the demands of the Tamil minority which has served to perpetuate one of the most durable insurgencies in contemporary Asia.

Bangladesh is perhaps the only country in South Asia today which has two major political parties, the Awami League and BNP, evenly matched and capable of ousting the incumbent regime through elections. However, in Bangladesh and indeed in all other South Asian countries, to the extent that such a two-party system prevails, it has become highly confrontational where the principal parties remain disinclined to agree on the rules of the game. This not only leads to sharp divisions over parliamentary procedure, but makes discourse particularly incendiary, replete with walkouts and boycotts by the opposition. There is a temptation to run a parallel process of politics on the street even where a parliament with reasonably impeccable electoral credentials is in session.

It is not surprising that such a confrontational political system diverts attention from development and prejudices good governance by making it difficult for any government to build a consensus behind its development agenda. In such a system opposition for opposition's sake is commonplace in the political process. Thus political parties which have themselves initiated a process of economic reform demonstrate no compunction in opposing these same policies when they are perpetuated by the successor regime. In turn, it must be recognized that particular government's have, themselves, shown no great enthusiasm to seek out their opponents to include them within a process of consensual policymaking.

Problems of Regime Stability

The logic of this confrontational system is for the opposition to seek to unseat a sitting government before it completes its scheduled term in office. In most of these countries attempts to prematurely terminate the life of the regime draw upon a variety of tactics such as encouraging defection, (Pakistan, India, Nepal) or where this is not feasible by street agitation (Bangladesh, Pakistan, Nepal) and even through conspiracy with the armed forces (Pakistan). In response, sitting governments are becoming increasingly repressive in the treatment of their political opponents and less mindful of the legitimate rights of a parliamentary opposition.

Over the last three decades, such a confrontational political environment had been virtually unthinkable in most of East and South East Asia, where governments, in office could expect to remain there undisturbed for fairly long tenures. The only unstable polity in the region was Thailand, where, however, unstable parliaments were underwritten by continuity in policies as well as a unifying highly revered, monarchy, a stable and powerful bureaucracy, military and business establishment who together constituted the steel frame of the Thai state.

Regime stability in East/SE Asia has encouraged continuity in policies, risk taking to push through reforms in the knowledge that this would not threaten the political life of the regime and a more consensual approach to politics. Some of this consensus was obviously artificial, built around suppression of dissent. But this frustration of dissent was to some extent compensated by a more inclusive development agenda. However, the political explosions in ROK and Indonesia and the upsurge at *Tiananmen Square* in Beijing, indicate that successful development outcomes, including the reduction of poverty, are not sufficient compensation for frustrating the urge for democratic expression in a country.

In contrast, South Asia has sacrificed some of positive features of democracy because of its confrontational approach to politics which has bred a sense of uncertainty in the style of governance. Even where governments, as in Pakistan, Bangladesh and Sri Lanka, have been elected with clear mandates to rule for five year tenures, their approach to policymaking and administration tends to remain predicated on the impermanence of office. In contrast, in East/South East Asia most policies were designed on the assumption of the durability in office of the policymaker and the lack of challenge to the implementation of such policies. Such a political culture, built upon the impermanence of office has, at least in South Asia, proved inimical to good governance.

Unfortunately, rather than move towards improving transparency in governance and make the executive more accountable, regimes throughout South Asia have become more defensive in their political responses leading to intolerance of criticism not just from their opponents but even from civil society where all criticisms are seen to be politically motivated. Competitive politics also contributes to a tendency to politicize the bureaucracy leading to political nepotism in administration, where loyal bureaucrats are used to play a partisan role in the service of the ruling party rather than the people. Such a system, perpetuates a politics of patronage and corruption where it subordinates the forces of law and order to overlook the indiscretions of the party faithful whilst persecuting the opposition.

In such a political environment, built around using the administration for political gain, there is a tendency to propitiate the bureaucracy. This political patronization of the bureaucracy is largely responsible for the failure of most South Asian regimes to downsize the government and reduce the share of current expenditure in GDP even where such an oversized state machine is manifestly dysfunctional.

Not even donor conditionalities have managed to downsize the central bureaucracy of South Asia due to the political indispensability of these bureaucrats to successive regimes.

Conclusions: Putting Governance in Perspective

State of Governance in South Asia

The available evidence points to the importance of governance in influencing developmental outcomes in South Asia as indeed in any country. Every South Asian state is seen to suffer from a lack of vision, commitment and political capacity to give clear direction to their respective development agendas. In most countries of the region, outside perhaps India, donors have played a major role in influencing policy agendas which has led to weak ownership over the direction of development. In every country, bureaucracies have become increasingly politicized so that the quality of administration has deteriorated, in relation to the tasks before it. Thus, transparency in governance has remained poor and accountability remains weak.

The resultant growth of corruption has added to the costs of development. The growing tendency to accommodate special interest groups and the weakening of state autonomy over decision-making has made governance in South Asia into an increasingly predatory process. This monetarization of governance has extended into politics so that the dynamics of South Asian politics increasingly appears to be driven by money and violence which are used to influence governance in the pursuit of private gain.

In contrast to other developing countries, South Asia has two of the oldest, continuous democracies in the Third world, in India and Sri Lanka. In the last decade all five states in South Asia have graduated to functioning democracies, made credible by the contestation of political power and the replacement of incumbent regimes through relatively free and fair elections. A relatively free press, and increasingly pro-active civil society have given depth and sustainability to the democratic process. These positive political tendencies have however, not been potent enough to counter the negative influences.

Comparisons with East/South East Asia

The East/SE Asian states have over a long period of time, performed far better than South Asia under a variety of development measures. The regimes in these regions have had longer tenures in office, which have allowed for greater predictability in policies and stability in administration. This stability has undoubtedly influenced investors at home and abroad in ways that have never been evident in South Asia except in India in the first two decade after independence. Thus, whatever may be the revisionist view today about the state of governance in East/SE Asia we must either recognize that this coincided with a superior development performance or that our conventional understanding of the nature of the link between governance and development needs rethinking.

However, East/SE Asia has always been and remains a much less transparent society with lower levels of popular accountability than in most South Asian states. In East/SE Asia their system of top down accountability has, if anything, been more coherent and capable of extracting effective performance from public functionaries than has been evident in South Asia. We have observed that the increasing politicization of administration in South Asia has made public employees less amenable to discipline and accountability. Greater electoral accountability in South Asia has thus not compensated for the absence of an effective system of supervision over the various tiers of administration.

The lack of transparency in East/SE Asia and lack of public accountability have clearly not been inimical to their remarkable growth and structural transformation over the last three decades. Today lack of transparency is seen as the source of the financial crisis in the region. But this same lack of transparency was evident for three decades and was not seen as being prejudicial to attracting foreign investment, or in compromising the quality of financial intermediation. Unless more evidence can be accumulated to establish causality between transparency and good governance, the significance of transparency in explaining differential performance as between East/South East and South Asia remains at best anecdotal without sufficient empirical foundations to provide a satisfactory explanation of the East/SE Asia crisis. Nor is there enough evidence to indicate whether South Asia, because of weak transparency and accountability, is more or less corrupt than say Thailand, Indonesia or the Philippines. Whilst we may hypothesize about the merits of a more stable, predictable corruption, as compared to a more anarchic system of corruption, we have no robust theory or body of evidence to establish causality between governance and corruption or indeed to establish whether some forms of corruption as opposed to others are indeed more development friendly.

This leaves us with an assumption that the structure, management and oversight of the administration has been more conducive to good governance in East/SE Asia. We have seen the limitations in the administrative system of South Asia but do not know enough about the corresponding role and quality of administration in East/SE Asia to warrant a meaningful comparison.

There is however robust evidence of the greater degree of institutional intimacy between state and business in East/SE Asia associated with embeddedness. This embeddedness is of course viewed today as a source of the SE Asia crisis where once it was seen as a developmental virtue compared to a more adversarial relationship in South Asia. It is not clear if embeddedness is indeed more evident in SE Asia. Not enough current empirical evidence is at hand to support this hypothesis. Today, however South Asia is witness to close intimacy between the state, business and politics where the authority of the state is perhaps far less evident than that of the East/SE Asia state. Here again the crisis in ROK/Thailand/Indonesia/Malaysia suggest that this autonomy may have been weaker than was once believed. It is possible that the degree of embeddedness between state and business in East/SE Asia may have prejudiced the regulation of business malpractice, whilst doling out favours to special interest groups. The state patronized the Chaebols in ROK, the Suharto family and its cronies in Indonesia. privileged Malay elite in Malaysia and a broad cross-section of the Thai and Filipino business elite. To the extent that this practise persisted over three decades and was co-terminous with the East Asia miracle, crony capitalism could hardly provide a comprehensive explanation of the crisis in East/SE Asia. In contrast, exposure of South Asia, to multi-party democracy and a free press do not appear to have made its governments more transparent or accountable than in East/SE Asia or less liable to promote its own local variant of crony capitalism.

To the extent that South Asia has a multi-party competitive political system, compared to East/SE Asia, politics has been a more dominant factor in influencing policies and their implementation in the former region. This proposition may be less valid for Thailand and the Philippines where the importance of both money and violence on politics reflect their more contentious political system compared to People's Republic of China (PRC), Taiwan, Republic of Korea (ROK, until the last 5 years), Indonesia or Vietnam. However, in the largely one party states of Singapore, Malaysia or Indonesia, parliamentarians remain more dependent on the patronage of the state and ruling party to pursue their political careers than to their capacity to get elected to office. Once in parliament the politicians of East/SE Asia are quite active in using this vantage point to promote business interests for themselves and/or their friends. Thus, politics as business is as pervasive in East/SE Asia as it is in South Asia today.

Points of Departure

What then remain the points of departure between the governance of East/SE Asia and South Asia? The main features of governance in East/SE Asia which differentiate them from South Asia are summarized below:

1. A more purposeful leadership with a more focused developmental vision
2. Regime longevity and policy continuity
3. Lack of democratic contestation
4. A more development oriented administration
5. A more effective machinery of law and order
6. A more comfortable relation between state and business
7. With the exception of the Philippines, a weaker Civil Society.

It is worth pointing out that lack of democratic contestation, state business intimacy and a weak civil society are today being projected as the source of the East/SE Asian crisis and are being proclaimed as important ingredients of good governance needed to promote development. This revisionist view of governance in East/South/East Asia is a reflection of the weaknesses in the new received wisdom on good governance and points to the sensitivity of these ideas to the levels of development performance. The evolving theory of governance has yet to satisfactorily weigh the relative importance of the above variables in explaining their contribution to variations in developmental outcomes. Furthermore, how far differences in governance in turn explain the extent of differentiations in developmental outcomes between E/SE Asia and South Asia and within South Asia will need to factor in the policy regimes of the respective country. This remains part of another exercise.

GOVERNANCE AND ECONOMY

Yousuf Abdullah Harun

Introduction

Bangladesh is passing through a difficult phase of transition. The development strategy has undergone a sea change marked by a fundamental shift from public-sector dominance to a private sector-led growth. The principal objective behind this change is to accelerate the growth process so as to make a significant break-through in poverty alleviation. The task of spearheading the growth process has been assigned to the private sector. This change in development strategy has taken place at a time when the global scenario is marked by spectacular events. These are: collapse of communism, end of cold-war; relaxation of East-West tension; emergence of a new World Trade Organization (WTO); establishing a rule-based free-trade regime; proliferation in the formation of various regional and sub-regional blocs like NAFTA, APEC, EU, ASEAN, SAARC etc; erosion of the philosophy of command economies and interventionism; and emergence of a global consensus for reliance on market forces and private initiatives for promoting socio-economic development. As a result, a new economic order has emerged.

Global Competitive Environment

The rule-based WTO regime is now a reality for Bangladesh as we are signatory to the Marrakesh Agreement that gave birth to it. In keeping with it, the economy has extensively been liberalized, perhaps rather too soon. The private sector of Bangladesh has to play its assigned role under this new and competitive global environment. It must fully comprehend the challenges and opportunities that WTO system has posed and opened. As a business community of an LDC, private sector of Bangladesh has to perform a formidable task in rising to the requirements of meeting the challenges and exploiting the opportunities. The required enabling environment and the level-playing field are largely lacking in Bangladesh. Liberalization is no doubt good and well-intended but in the absence of reforms in deregulation, facilitation and provision of physical and social infrastructure services, the survival of the business enterprises are gravely threatened in the home market. And as unequal partners it is difficult to have access to the global market that WTO system has opened up.

An Emerging Private Sector

The leading role assigned to the private sector is pragmatically based on the performance records of the private sector. The utilization of private sector allocation in the preceding period of Fifth Plan has been 16% higher, while public sector could utilize only 88% of ADP allocation. Private sector has also demonstrated its capability and buoyancy in the economy. A new generation of private entrepreneurs has emerged who are well-educated, hard-working, capable and eager to face challenges of the globalized competitive market. They have proven their mettle in a few sectors where they had opportunities to work with freedom and where government played the role more of a facilitator than a controller. The booming industries in ready-made-garments, knitwear, shrimps and ceramics are clear indicators of the latent capabilities of the private sector and these also act as pointers to what the government should do to capture these potentials.

Role of Government in Changed Policy Environment

The change in policy for private sector and market-led growth does in no way mean marginalization of the role of the Government. The Government has to continue to facilitate and promote private initiative providing enabling environment and level-playing field through development of social and physical infrastructure and support services. The critical point to consider here is: whether the government institutions as they exist now can deliver what is expected of them. There is now clear world-wide evidence that there is significant and positive correlation between efficiency of the governmental institutions and economic growth. It is also increasingly becoming clear that the inability of Bangladesh to get out of the low growth trap is largely due to the weak implementation capacity and inefficiencies of public institutions, the government's inability to plan and manage key reforms and its predilections to manage economic activities at the micro-level. Bangladesh needs a jump-start in efficiency and effectiveness of the government, if she has to accelerate and sustain growth, reduce poverty, harness opportunities and face challenges of the upcoming new millennium.

High Cost, Poor Service Delivery

In Bangladesh the staffing cost of government works out to 4.5% of GDP. In Korea and Singapore the cost of government staff is similar to that in Bangladesh in terms of GDP share, but the efficiency and quality of services these governments provide are far superior to those in Bangladesh. How seriously inefficiency deters business and investment initiatives can be seen from some examples taken from a World Bank study (1996). It takes 12 days (with a maximum 30 days) to have customs clearance of imported inputs for export, 9 days (with a maximum 75 days) for customs clearance for export, 7 days (with a maximum of 30 days) to complete all documents required for export, 58 days (with a maximum of 120 days) and 6% additional expenditure to get a refund cheque from DEDO.* Another example of public institutions' glaring inefficiency is the loss incurred in the state-owned-enterprises (SOE). The total losses of all SOEs amounts to about 26% of ADP, 45% of external aid disbursement and 2% of the GDP.

Despite Bangladesh's big strides in economic and policy reforms for private sector-led growth and liberalization for a market economy

---

* DEDO = Duty Exemption and Drawback Office.

no significant break-through in accelerating growth rate has yet taken place. Private investment which is a critical factor to foster growth has not yet responded to these changes. Both domestic and foreign direct investment (FDI) continue to remain shy. Unless the government institutions are reformed and made people friendly, economic and policy reforms will yield little results. The issue of governance must be addressed to create the right environment for investment and the government must introduce and implement a regulatory framework conducive to the market economy. Failure to undertake effective institutional reforms in the judiciary, administration, SOEs, public utilities, tax administration and the financial sector is breeding inefficiency, apathy, harassment and corruption. There is need for an efficient administration and improvement in the quality of services. Economic policy reforms will not work unless institutional reforms are made.

Legacy of Colonial Era

From the period of the British Raj, we had inherited an administrative structure which was established to serve the interest of the colonial rulers on the basis of patron-client relationship. The civil bureaucracy, the legal and judicial system, administrative system were all attuned to serve the colonial and exploitative interests. The people had little part in governance.

In the absence of building up a true democratic system, the civil bureaucracy continued to play an upper hand in running the affairs of the state after 1947 (except for some short breaks). The mistrust between the people and the government still continues. Corruption in bureaucracy has added to this feeling of mistrust.

Agenda of Actions

The Federation of Bangladesh Chambers of Commerce and Industry (FBCCI) as the apex body of the private sector business has been deeply involved in advocating to the Government to pursue appropriate policy reforms and their meaningful implementation so that the private sector can play its due role in contributing to the growth of the economy.

In recent years FBCCI found that there was lot to be gained by all concerned if the Government functionaries could be persuaded to come closer to the business community and look objectively at the latter's problems. A meaningful dialogue between the two parties could help remove much of the distrust and allow opportunities to work together to find solutions that would be good for both the businessmen and the Government. It is well known that close working relations and synergies between the Government and the private sector in certain countries in East Asia worked wonders for the economies of those countries and Bangladesh should take lessons from that. It has been seen that many good policies of the Government are not owned up by all Ministries and agencies who are involved in implementing the same. As a result, the administrative Ministry which spearheads that policy finds itself rather helpless. In many instances of policy formulation or proposed reforms, the views of the private sector are either not obtained at all or they are not given due importance. FBCCI, therefore, thought that it would be appropriate to make some fresh attempts to identify some important issues which needed to be dealt with urgently for paving the ways for rapid increase in private sector investment, both domestic and foreign, which remained very low even after commencement of the liberalization process.

FBCCI conducted in-depth studies through eminent consultants on various issues that affect trade and industry especially the Small and Medium Enterprises (SMEs). It identified the major issues and made recommendations. In the present context, these seem relevant to take into consideration. These are:

Deregulation and Regulatory Reform

Despite easing of controls on investment, certain features of the regulatory framework remain a problem. Outdated, irrelevant and ineffective controls create both distortions and due to cumbersome and discretionary bureaucratic processes — unnecessary delays. The SMEs feel fettered by extensive and intrusive regulations, while the GOB remains deeply skeptical both of the willingness of private entrepreneurs to abide by rules set in the public interest, and the ability of the private sector associations to enforce desirable standards of commercial behaviour. Discussions were conducted on the identification of specific areas where regulatory reforms were needed.

Recommendations

In order to create an institutional forum a permanent Regulatory Reforms Commission (RRC) should be set up with representatives from the Government, its relevant agencies and the private sector. The proposed RRC should review the existing regulatory measures related to investment and trade and take appropriate steps for initiating the reforms. It should be a high powered body working under the Prime Minister.

Government Sector Institution (GSI) and Private Sector Institution (PSI) Collaboration

The East Asian economies have demonstrated how strong GSI-PSI partnership can boost investment, improve resource allocation and assist business to meet the competitive challenges of the international market place. In sharp contrast, GSI-PSI consultation in Bangladesh remains sporadic and limited in coverage.

Recommendations

Joint Coordination Committees should be set up both at National and District levels with representation from both Government Sector Institutions (GSI) and Private Sector Institutions (PSI) headed by respective local Departmental Chiefs covering the areas like customs clearance at the sea and airports and inland container terminals, income tax collection, telecom, electricity, gas, water supply etc. It should be mandatory to have meetings of such Committees at specified regular intervals, the minutes of which should be widely circulated.

Credit Policies

This complicated issue presents different choices for policy makers. The critical trade-off appears to be between the need to allow market forces full freedom to allocate credit and the need to check against the 'insider lending' and the emergence of credit approval procedures which discriminate against SMEs. Failures in regulations appear to have led to the introduction of distortionery controls over lending.

Most financial institutions in the country are suffering from various kinds of fund crisis. Investments needed for restructuring of the existing industries to remain competitive in the new liberalized regime as well as for setting up new industries especially by the SMEs are badly constrained due to shortage of funds. Whereas the commercial banks are unable to grant any significant term loans, the DFIs are also passing through severe shortage of funds.

Recommendations

a. The DFI should be revamped and provided with adequate credit lines.
b. In order to reduce financial outlay and minimize the risks for any single institution as well as to benefit from the experience of others, several financial institutions should join hands for co-financing industries. One of the co-financiers should act as the lead agency to carry out the appraisal and if needed, suitably revise the project proposal to make it viable, and determine simultaneously the requirements of bridge financing, term loan and working capital for the project which the members of the financing consortium should undertake to provide obviating the need for multiple appraisals.
c. Credit operations of banks and other financial institutions should be free from any outside interference and all kinds of directed lending should be avoided.
d. Interest rate on lending should be lowered corresponding to the reduction of deposit rate. Contracted interest rate for SMEs should be kept stable.
e. Tangible equity should be insisted upon but collateral conditions should be relaxed. Except for footloose industries, assets created out of loan and equity funds viz., land, building, machinery etc. should be considered sufficient security for financing industrial projects. In order to improve end-use supervision, financing institutions should be encouraged to take up some equity position in the projects to be disinvested later, if desired.

Credit Guarantee Scheme

The Small Industries Credit Guarantee Scheme should be made functional and availability of credit for all export-oriented industries as well as the SMEs should be made easier. If this cannot be done, a Credit Guarantee Corporation may be set up to help the SMEs. Special Credit Programme under which SMEs are supposed to get industrial loans at 2% lower rate of interest should be made operative.

Legal Framework

The linchpin of all efficient systems of economic governance is a properly functioning legal system. Deficiencies in the legal system in Bangladesh — in terms of outdated laws and slow and unpredictable courts — raise transaction costs as contractual risks are magnified by the absence of any means of legal redress. These deficiencie also circumscribe SME's ability to challenge arbitrary bureaucratic decisions, something which is vital to ensure accountability.

Recommendations

Code of Civil Procedure (1908) encourages frivolous appeals and baseless adjournments as it does not provide for any mechanism for imposing costs for delays relating to appeals.

a. Recently formed Legal Reform Commission (LRC) should be made operational immediately. The LRC should take early action to update the business and trade related laws. Operations of the courts need to be vastly improved and time limits need to be set for disposal of cases.
b. For reinforcing the arbitration and other Alternative Dispute Resolution (ADR) mechanism currently operated by the FBCCI and other chambers and for imposition of penalties for judicial appeals following the decision of an Arbitration Council whose jurisdiction was originally accepted by mutual agreement by legal measures should be provided.

Customs Clearance

The efforts by the NBR in consultation with the business community to reduce customs formalities have been welcome. Yet irksome problems remain and it may be useful to draw on the experience of other countries in the region which have successfully dealt with this issue. Without compromising compliance targets discretionary powers may be reduced. Spot checks should be limited in number and only initiated and authorized at the highest levels, in order to prevent harassment and damage of goods during inspection. A standing committee for customs appeals — levying costs to discourage frivolous complaints — involving the NBR and relevant PSIs may be instituted to provide quick redress. Also it may be desirable to form a joint PSI/GSI committee to recommend changes to the present system.

Recommendations

Customs Clearance and DEDO — SMEs suffer mostly due to delays in assessment and dilatory tactics adopted in completing cumbersome documentation procedures, discretion applied in the valuation of goods since most SMEs cannot afford costly pre-shipment inspection and also imposing arbitrary penalties on technical grounds.

Procedural simplification, limiting powers and prescribing time limits for customs clearance should be arranged. In case of exhorbitant tariff value, appeals should be disposed of with orders for refund within a prescribed time limit. Duty draw back should be ensured within scheduled time frame. Private Sector (PSIs) should be directly involved in the work of streamlining procedures.

Promotional Agencies

The GOB promotional agencies have difficulties in demonstrating that they are making much of an impact in terms of supporting investment or exports. The possibilities of private sector involvement in these agencies and of shifting some of their functions to PSIs may be considered. The case of all promotional agencies and not just the most visible ones should be taken into account.

Recommendations

a. The possibility of private sector participation in the management of promotional agencies may be considered to enhance their performance.

b To minimize the problems caused by the high degree of overlapping functions, regular inter-agency coordination meetings should be held in which representatives of PSIs should be invited to attend.

c. In order that the promotional agencies e.g. BOI (Board of Investment), EPB (Export Promotion Bureau), BEPZA (Bangladesh Export Processing Zones Authority), training institutions etc. can be made more effective, they should be supplied with trade information by the PSIs on a regular basis.

d. A centralized Centre of Information on the services and facilities provided by the different promotional agencies may be developed for which FBCCI may perhaps function as a focal pint.

Labour Relations

The approved Labour Code is expected to introduce greater flexibility in the labour market. However, the overriding problem in this area appears to be the Government's predilection for suddenly announcing blanket pay increases for employees of the State Owned Enterprises (SOEs) sector. These increases invariably get reflected in private sector wage levels. The principle of linking wage increases to productivity gains needs to be established in order to protect competitiveness. Measures to increase flexibility in hiring and firing decisions will lead to further widening of the efficiency differential between the state and private enterprises.

Recommendations

Wage Policies and depolitization of Industrial Labour — to keep private sector free form the adverse effects of sudden pay increases for the SOEs, Government should have prior consultation with the FBCCI and related Member Bodies before they announce any award of pay increase. Industrial labour must be depoliticized. Wages should not be determined centrally but left to individual enterprises which should hold consultation with the employee.

Power Sector and Related Matters

The GOB has approved an Energy Policy under which a much larger role is to be given to the private sector in developing infrastructure in this sector. The issues here relate to providing conditions attractive enough for the large scale private foreign investment that holds out the best prospect for developing this sector, while at the same time ensuring that modern and least-cost power sources are developed.

Recommendations

Power Sector — To attract more foreign private investment in power generation constraints related to tariff issues, cost of fuel and credit ratings as well as workforce related issues on the distribution side should be solved. Privatization initiative by contracting out meter reading, billing and collection as well as maintenance of plant and equipment should be started as early as feasible.

Centralized Information System — A Centralized Information Repository with all facilities and access to information provided to the different promotional agencies should be developed for which FBCCI should function as the focal point of the private sector with necessary financial support from the Government.

Attitudinal Changes — As attitudinal and behaviourial changes to lend ungrudging assistance to the private sector are needed to be brought about for the Government functionaries at all levels, constant persuasion and supervision by the political leadership particularly by the Prime Minister and the Ministers would be required to achieve the objective. Interchange of officials from public sector to private sector and vice versa for more interaction among the public and private sector in the areas of trade promotion, investment, consultancy and market promotion can be arranged.

Technology Transfer & Human Resource Development — The Government should pursue a vigorous policy for facilitating acquisition, adaptation and development of appropriate and modern technology to increase productivity and enable the SMEs to face global competition. Human Resource Development programmes should also be undertaken to upgrade skill and ensure availability of requisite manpower for the SMEs.

[illegible] the unorganised sector [illegible] should be [illegible]

[illegible] of information on the [illegible]

[illegible] Relations

[illegible] expected [illegible] in the labour market. However, [illegible] productivity [illegible] pay increases [illegible] employees [illegible] wage levels [illegible] productivity [illegible] to make it more competitive. Measures [illegible] in hiring and firing [illegible] will lead to [illegible] between the State and private sector.

[illegible] Industry and development of Industrial Labour [illegible]

[illegible] Search and Related Matters

[illegible]

WASHINGTON CONSENSUS AND ECONOMIC GOVERNANCE IN BANGLADESH

Zaidi Sattar

Introduction

There has been a noticeable paradigm shift in the objective of development strategies in the past two decades. For the developing countries, the collective wisdom of the 1950s and 1960s emphasizing state-directed investment planning and import-substituting industrial growth has slowly given way to the notion of synergy and partnership between the state and markets — a partnership in which markets have a primacy in the production and allocation of goods and services. In parallel, the obsession with growth of GDP per capita as a development objective has been replaced with more broad-based concepts of development which Joseph Stiglitz describes as "raising living standards" and Amartya Sen, in a social choice perspective, sees as a strategy for "enhancing human capabilities". In either case, there is a recognition of the state's role in the provision of health care, education, social security, environmental protection and social development. And there is an appreciation of the state's catalytic role in making markets function efficiently. The essence is a minimal but effective state.

This paradigm shift in our understanding of development strategies presents formidable challenges for the organizational design of the state as policymaker and for framing the rules of governance that makes for a fruitful state-market interaction. Key to this interplay of statecraft and market forces is the appreciation that it is ultimately a dynamic but co-operative game, where markets are allowed to operate freely and effectively so that all segments of society benefit from the outcome.

Today's economic reforms reflect this shift in the development paradigm. And Bangladesh has embraced, in principle, the core instruments of economic reforms. But the reform process, which gained momentum and intensity during the 1990s, has faced resistance from various quarters. Questions have been raised about the adequacy and applicability of the reform agenda in all circumstances and under given state of institutional development. In particular, strong reservations have been expressed about the universality of reform instruments and what is perceived as one-size-fits-all nature of the reform agenda often espoused by international agencies.

Unacceptability of the Status Quo

It is fair to say that the Bangladesh economy continues to perform below its potential — that is, the economy and society functions well inside its production possibilities frontier at any given time. Averaging 4.5 per cent annual GDP growth in the 1990s is a modest improvement over past performance, but this can hardly be characterized as the high performance necessary to create a significant dent on poverty and raise living standards of Bangladeshis perceptibly. At this rate of growth, in 25 years time, the country will not have moved out of the low income group of underdeveloped economies of the world. And no amount of income redistribution under this scenario will have any appreciable impact on poverty either. High growth is a necessary, albeit not a sufficient condition, for alleviation of the kind of widespread poverty with which Bangladesh is afflicted.

But high growth, of the 7-8 per cent variety, does not come easy. Given large scale unemployment and under-employment and the impossibility of full employment — neo-classical growth theories prove inadequate in explaining how the desired rates of high growth could be achieved. To achieve high performance on a long-term sustainable basis, the prospect lies in capital accumulation (via domestic savings and foreign capital inflows) as well as gains in productive efficiency from technological innovation and absorption and, what is now becoming increasingly clear, from improvements in the economic organization of production — through changes in the policy environment and streamlining of the process of economic governance. In this frame of things, good governance augments productive efficiency both in the micro-economic sense — at the enterprise level — and in the aggregate macro-economic sense of national economic performance. Bad governance, on the other hand, acts as a drag on production outcomes.

Case for Reforms

The pursuit of high growth and the need for poverty alleviation should be enough to seal the case for economic reforms. The existing order is failing to deliver and the current outcome in terms of economic performance and living standards are quite unacceptable. Consider the following telling statistics: Over half the population of Bangladesh is illiterate; another half still lives in poverty, after twenty-five years of independence. Economic reforms, which gathered momentum early in the 1990s, remain half done. It is often said that reforms half done are worse than no reforms. Undeniably, there are short-term costs. While Bangladesh has not derived the full benefits of whatever part of the reform agenda that has been implemented, the human and material costs such as displacement of workers, elimination of subsidies, closure of inefficient public enterprises, strengthen the voice of protest and encourage resistance of further reforms by vested groups.

In recent times, increasing global competition and the debilitating consequences of a failure of governance in the domestic scene has convinced even the critiques of the need for fundamental reforms in the way we manage our economy, govern markets and regulate society. Doubts and debates are more about the pace and sequencing of reforms rather than the substance. There is hardly anyone who would disagree with the notion that so many of the disruptive symptoms that are observed in our daily lives — a dysfunctional public service delivery system, chaos in the ports, telephones, power system and utilities that don't work, almost complete absence of the rule of law, hartals, toll taking, abuse of the law, arming of students — clearly undermine much of the efforts at national development. In the economic scene, the financial sector appears to be in chaos with most banks burdened with non-performing loans, loss-making state-owned enterprises drain the national exchequer annually to the tune of $200-$300 million, and a general lack of institutional capacity for economic policymaking remains while the economy continues to maintain a tenuous macro-economic balance with a critical level of foreign exchange reserves and modest economic growth. To top this all, there is a growing public perception that nothing moves. The energy sector is still in crisis in spite of abundant private sector interest. Power shortages are costing the economy crores of taka each month and system losses remain almost as high as ever. Chittagong port is still chaotic. Bangladesh Telephone and Telecommunications Board (BTTB), unable to provide effective telecommunications services, is nonetheless opposed to privatization and is still obstructing private sector investment. Little progress has been made in reducing the level of loan default. Few State Owned Enterprises (SOEs) have actually been transferred to private owners. Toll taking is reportedly rampant. The recommendations of the Nurunnabi Committee and the Four Secretaries Report on the reform of government remains unattended. The public still awaits the appointment of an Ombudsman. All of these and other necessary reforms require hard choices to be made and ultimately create the justifications for deep-rooted and wide-ranging reforms in overall economic governance.

Washington Consensus

During the past quarter century, economic reforms have been introduced not merely in developing countries of the world but even in some of the developed countries of Europe and Australia. The wide experience in reforms has generated discussion and debate on "how to do" reforms, what the "best practice" might be, how to sequence the various components of the reform agenda, and, most importantly, what should be the pace of reforms — gradualism or shock therapy? It is on the pace of reforms that disagreements are known to be the strongest.

Nevertheless, as a result of these debates, a broad consensus has evolved over time on what the core principles and key components of an agenda for economic reforms might be. The World Bank's World Development Report 1991: *The Challenge of Development* presented an authoritative summary of the main elements of a "market-friendly approach". Earlier, John Williamson (1990) made an attempt to synthesize the content of policy reforms being urged by the most influential Washington institutions (namely, the World Bank, IMF, US Treasury) in Latin American countries in the late 1980s. The result of his exercise was dubbed, perhaps unwisely, the "Washington Consensus",[1] and comprised ten core policies which could be summarized under the headings of *Stabilization, Liberalization* and *Opening Up*.

Stabilization

- **Fiscal Discipline**. Budget deficits, broadly defined to include the balance sheets of state enterprises, should be small enough to be financed without recourse to the inflation tax. For Bangladesh, it would mean a budget deficit (including losses of state-owned enterprises) of 4-5 per cent of GDP that has been considered to be sustainable for the long run with a strategy for keeping domestic bank financing of deficits within non-inflationary limits. (World Bank, 1997)
- **Public Expenditure Priorities**. Policy reform consists of redirecting expenditures from politically sensitive areas, which typically receive more resources than their economic return can justify, such as administration, defense, indiscriminate subsidies, and other 'white elephants,' towards neglected fields with high economic returns and the potential to improve income distribution, such as primary health and education, and infrastructure. This is an aspect of reform that has been highlighted in two recent World Bank's Public Expenditure Review for Bangladesh but no progress on expenditure prioritization, particularly relating to the Annual Development Programme, has been forthcoming.

- **Tax Reform**. Tax reform involves broadening the tax base and cutting marginal tax rates. The aim is to sharpen incentives and improve horizontal equity without lowering realized progressivity. Improving tax administration, broadening the tax base and preventing leakages in revenues are the principal areas of tax reform in Bangladesh.

Liberalization

- **Financial Liberalization.** The ultimate objective of financial liberalization is the elimination of financial repression and the achievement of market-determined interest rates. But experience has shown that, under conditions of a chronic lack of confidence, market-determined rates can be so high as to threaten the financial solvency of productive enterprises and government. Under the circumstances a sensible interim objective is the abolition of preferential interest rate for privileged borrowers and achievement of a moderately positive real interest rate. Financial liberalization in the above sense has been largely achieved in Bangladesh with some exceptions with regard to preferential rates on loans for agriculture, cottage industries and exports. But, as we all know, much more deep-rooted and fundamental reforms are needed in the financial sector to turn things around.
- **Exchange Rates**. Countries need a unified (at least for trade transactions) exchange rate set at a level sufficiently competitive to induce a rapid growth in non-traditional exports, and managed so as to assure exporters that this competitiveness will be maintained. Bangladesh resorted to the unified exchange rate system back in 1991 and has since maintained a managed but moderately flexible exchange rate system with an eye towards maintaining a competitive exchange rate with respect to competitor countries.
- **Trade Liberalization**. Quantitative trade restriction should be rapidly replaced by tariffs, and these should be progressively reduced until a uniform low tariff in the range of 10 per cent (or at most around 20 per cent) is achieved. There is, however,

some disagreement about the speed with which tariffs should be reduced (with recommendations falling in a band between 3 and 10 years), and about whether it is advisable to slow down the process of liberalization when macro-economic conditions are adverse (recession and payments deficit). Bangladesh made substantial progress in the removal of Quantitative Restriction (QRs) until the year 1995 but progress thereafter has stalled. While average tariffs were reduced from around 90 per cent in 1991 to 23 per cent today, progress in moving to a uniform rate faces stiff challenges from the domestic protectionist lobby quite apart from the concerns about revenue. The fact that a competitor country, India, is lagging behind in its trade liberalization, adds complexity to the whole issue of trade liberalization as an essential component of economic reforms.

Opening Up

- **Foreign Direct Investment:** Barriers impeding the entry of foreign firms should be abolished; foreign and domestic firms should be allowed to compete on equal terms. Bangladesh has made the greatest progress in this area of reform by opening up its entire economy to foreign investors with only a few activities reserved for national security reasons. There is at present neither any limit on the size of foreign investment nor any restriction on the repatriation of income and profits. Indeed, the capital account works as if it is fully convertible for foreign investors. As for overall incentives, foreign investors might even have a slight competitive edge over domestic producers.
- **Privatization:** State enterprises should be privatized. The lackluster progress in this area of reform in Bangladesh is too well documented to merit further comment.
- **Deregulation:** Governments should abolish regulations that impede the entry of new firms or restrict competition, and ensure that all regulations are justified by such criteria as safety, environmental protection, or prudential supervision of financial institutions. In principle, deregulation has taken place

in the industrial and service sectors of Bangladesh where substantial regulations existed in the past resulting in a "license and permit" regime. Vestiges of bureaucratic control still remain partly from the lack of an understanding of or commitment for a market-friendly approach to governance on the part of public functionaries.

- **Property Rights:** The legal system should provide secure property rights without excessive costs to the business and investor community. Bangladesh has a long way to go in this respect simply because the legal system lacks the institutional capacity to even ensure that the rule of law exists and is applied evenly to every citizen regardless of his/her financial standing. Under World Bank sponsorship, judicial reforms are under way but it will be long before the objective of this reform agenda can be satisfactorily achieved.

The Washington Consensus was not necessarily conceived in Washington. The convergence of policy principles evolved over a long period of research and professional debates and is the fruit of global experience with economic policymaking. But disagreements over many aspects of the reform package, particularly with the application of some constituent policies are many, and the following list merely gives a flavour of the many points of departures in the discourse:

- the desirability of maintaining capital controls;
- the need to target the current account;
- how rapidly and how far inflation should be reduced;
- the propriety of attempting to correct market failures through such techniques as compensatory taxation or subsidies;
- the proportion of GDP to be taken in taxation and spent by the public sector;
- whether and to what extent income should be deliberately redistributed in the interests of equity;
- whether there is a role for industrial policy;
- the model of the market economy to be sought; and
- the priority to be given to environmental preservation.

In all the above areas there appears to be a wide divergence of views and large scope for disagreements. Yet it leaves a substantial stock of economic wisdom to work with — consisting of empirically reliable generalizations about the nature of economic policies that can be expected to yield good results in due course.

Economic Reforms and the Governance Question

The divergence of views notwithstanding, the Washington Consensus still represents a policy package that most mainstream economists regard as constituting good economic policies under the altered paradigm of development strategies. Good economics would have been good politics had economic policies yielded quick and predictable outcomes. Because, in reality, there is often a divergence between desired and actual outcomes, and there are short-term human and material costs, political commitment to reforms do not come readily. The Latin American experience showed that when economists themselves assumed political leadership roles and had an active part in economic policymaking, reforms were speedily implemented and were largely successful. Such is unlikely to be the case in Bangladesh where economists are not known to seek political office. Thus, to succeed, economic reforms would have to take the state of governance as 'given' and work within that framework or make governance itself a central issue to be addressed by reforms.

This brings us closer to the theme of this seminar, "Good Governance", and the fresh conceptualization of an "inclusive State" — a nomenclature I suggest for Hye's (1998) re-defined state as a modern day extension of the "conventional State". The "inclusive state", following Hye's formulation, encompasses more than the conventional constituents, viz., Parliament, Judiciary and Executive Government to include the Private Sector, Civil Society and Local Government as collaborative partners in governance. Such a conceptualization fits well with the World Bank's own understanding of the evolving role of the state in today's world. (World Development Report, 1997) it recognizes the functioning of an effective state as critical to economic, social and sustainable development, but more as a partner and facilitator than as director. The state, in this scheme, is expected to complement, not supplant markets. One might add that the notion of the "effective" state is indistinguishable from the idea of "good governance".

Political Economy of Reforms

The case for reforms, given the pitiful state of governance reflected in a dysfunctional public service delivery system in almost all sectors of economic activity has already been documented. Few people will deny that reforms are needed except those few with direct vested interests. We all know what needs to be done. All of these matters have been repeatedly studied. Reports of experts abound including the Bank's own study, 'Government That Works' (World Bank, 1996). In June 1996, when a new government took office, the World Bank drew up a list of most urgently needed reform measures in its publication, An Agenda for Action. (World Bank, 1997) This list was nowhere challenged or disputed. Yet an update of this report in December 1997 showed that, with the exception of social sectors like health and education, critical progress in most other areas remained stalled.

The message clearly is that reforms don't get implemented without ownership and political commitment. Reforms involve making hard choices — both political and economic. In a democratic process, an elected government with a strong political mandate is likely to be more effective in implementing the reform agenda than, for instance, a government run on a weak coalition. Again, I allude to Williamson's (1994) schematic treatment of the conditions for the success of reforms giving rise to a number of hypotheses about when reforms work best:

- the "crisis hypothesis"[2] suggests that public perception of a crisis is needed to create the conditions under which it is politically possible to undertake extensive policy reforms. In the Bangladesh context what this means is that unless a fiscal or foreign exchange crisis (growing uncontrollable budget deficits and fast depleting foreign exchange reserves) is at hand, a debt default is imminent, inflation is beyond control or the economy suffers an external shock (rapid decline in exports or remittances), the crisis conditions are non-existent to create the compelling circumstances for wide-ranging reforms.

- the "mandate hypothesis" argues that a government may be able to introduce reforms if it campaigns on a programme of reforms in the preceding election. Economic reforms in Bangladesh have not been part of the election manifesto of any political party as yet. Hence, such reforms would lack the mandate of a campaign promise. To the extent that political parties endorse economic reforms in whole or in part in their political campaigns, this hypothesis could be put to the test in the not too distant future.
- the "honeymoon hypothesis" emphasizes that extensive reforms have to be implemented immediately after a government takes office. In a five-year political cycle, this hypothesis would suggest that the most difficult reforms (which might have high short-term costs) have a better chance of success if implemented in the first two to three years. In a political democracy, difficult decisions are unlikely to be forthcoming in the last years of office.

The above might be considered as the political conditions for the success of reforms. Some of the non-political but governance related conditions would include:

- the existence of a comprehensive programme (which could be developed around the Washington Consensus) for transformation of the economy and a rapid timetable for implementation;
- the will and ability to appeal directly to the public and bypass vested interests; and
- the existence in government of a team of economists with a common, coherent view of what is needed to be done and commanding the instruments of concentrated executive authority.

As mentioned earlier, a comprehensive agenda for urgently needed reforms was already available in the World Bank's Agenda For Action — a programme of action that was framed around the core ideas of the Washington Consensus. Although the proposals contained therein have not been disputed, the preference for a home-grown version of the agenda would be understandable. However, the absence of an in-house team of economists within the government make it difficult for them to come up with a comprehensive agenda on their own unless it is chosen to assign the task to a group of professional economists outside the government. Finally, concerns have been expressed about the human and other costs of IMF-World Bank structural adjustment policies. An exercise is under way through the SAPRI[3] initiative to carry out a systematic study of the impacts of these policies in Bangladesh. One would expect the results of the exercise to provide some answers to the questions usually posed by various groups in civil society.

Concluding Remarks

The pitiful state of our public service delivery system is widely regarded as the symptom of a deeper malaise — a failure of governance. Although the primary objective of economic reforms is to rapidly improve living standards by raising productive efficiency and eliminating the costs of resource misallocation, these reforms also form an integral part of 'good governance'. The Washington Consensus merely offers a common platform for formulating policy interventions on which there is broad agreement amongst mainstream economists and development practitioners. It does not necessarily rule out the scope for developing customized version of action programmes that fit the country characteristics better. The fundamental laws of market economics remain unchanged across national boundaries, which leads to the presumption of uniformity in the responses of rational economic agents to economic incentives. This is what gives a universal character to the core principles of economic reforms. But there is nothing static about a set of reform principles. As we move into the next millennium, 'good governance' as a focal point of reforms has become the quintessential need. This is because the success of reforms rests as much on a nation's institutional capacity to govern markets and manage change as it does on the quality of the reform agenda.

Notes

1. An Alternative expression that was put forth was "universal convergence", on the grounds that (a) there was really no complete consensus, and (b) that the real convergence extended well beyond Washington policy circles.
2. An analogous argument for poor economic performance, in the absence of crisis conditions, is to be found in Mancur Olson (1982). He explains the miracle growth performance of post-war Germany and Japan by arguing that vested groups and coalitions, which slow down progress, were unable to form under the totalitarian regimes and the crisis of a debilitating war. Countries like Britain and Sweden, which had long periods of peaceful democratic regimes experienced low growth since lobbying groups had all the time to organize for collective action.
3. Structural Adjustment Participatory Review Initiative of the World Bank is under way in seven countries of Asia, Africa and Latin America, including Bangladesh.

References

Hye, Hasnat A. 1998. Concept paper, International Seminar on Good Governance, Ministry of Local Government, Rural Development and Cooperatives.

Malinvaud, Edmond, Sen, Amartya K., Stiglitz, Joseph, Nabli, Mustapha, Sengupta, Arjun, Milleron, Jean-Claude. 1997. *Development Strategy and Management of the Market Economy*, Vol.1, London: Oxford University Press.

Olson, Mancur. 1982. *The Rise and Decline of Nations: Economic Growth, Stagflation and Social Rigidities*. Yale University Press.

Stiglitz, J. 1997. *An Agenda for Development for the Twenty-First Century*: Keynote address at the Ninth Annual Bank Conference on Development Economics. World Bank.

Williamson, John. 1990. *Latin American Adjustment: How Much Has Happened?* Washington: Institute for International Economics.

Williamson, John. 1994. *The Political Economy of Policy Reform*. Washington: International Institute for International Economics.

World Bank. 1996. *Government that Works: Reforming the Public Sector*. Dhaka: University Press Limited.

World Bank. South Asia Region. 1996. 1997. *An Agenda for Action*.

World Bank. South Asia Region. Bangladesh Public Expenditure Review 1997: *Making the Best Use of Public Resources*.

World Bank. World Development Report 1991: *The Challenge of Development*.

World Bank. World Development Report 1997: *The State in a Changing World*.

GOVERNANCE AND ECONOMY: BANGLADESH PERSPECTIVE

M. Kabir Hassan

Introduction

The central thesis of the paper is that good governance can only be achieved by "moral man and woman". This way a society can achieve the maximum output from scarce resources. A successful strategy to realize an optimum balance between efficiency and equity consists of three important elements: (a) a filter mechanism to enable individuals to choose between the unlimited use of resources in such a way that the aggregate claims do not exceed the supply, and the socio-economic goals of the system are also realized; (b) a motivating mechanism to induce individuals to put in their best in conformity with the dictates of such a filter mechanism; (c) socio-economic restructuring to help transfer scarce resources from one use to another until optimum efficiency and equity are realized. The proposed strategy cannot be equipped with these three indispensable elements without injecting a moral dimension in the economic system.

Governance and Development

The classical Marxist view of Government as merely a facade for the rule of the capitalist class and as entirely determined by the means of production, has long been abandoned. The neo-Marxists came to believe that the state of government is constrained more by the dominant ideology in the society than by the class structure or the means of production. The dominant class influences the structure and policy orientation of the state, which determine the structural properties of the economy. These, in turn, influence both growth and distribution.

The modernist school (Huntington, 1968) differentiates the developmental state, run by the elite and committed to modernization, from most other states with confused parochial and personal concerns. Peter Evan's more recent "Embedded Autonomy" theory of state measures embeddedness in terms of the density of links between the state and the business sector. Through such links the state is able to influence the business class to share the state's development designs and strategies. The East and South East Asian states come closest to Evan's model characterized by strong states driven by strong leadership and independent and effective bureaucracy with close links with the business class.

However, none of these and several other models of autonomous state explain the variation in the developmental outcomes of states with broadly similar characteristics. The South Asian countries have a strong tradition of competent and well-trained bureaucracy as that of East and South East Asian countries. Nevertheless, the developmental outcomes in the South Asian and African countries fall far short of those in East and South East Asia.

Thus "the concept of governance remains vague to the point of being dysfunctional as a guide to policy intervention" (Sobhan, 1998). World Bank's guidelines, when it comes to non-economic measures of governance, are tentative and too broad and general. None of the donor countries have made any systematic effort to identify the constituent elements of good governance and taken the care to explain why particular governance measures will produce the desired developmental outcome.

Governance and Globalization

Globalization generally refers to the greatly increased integration of markets for capital, labour, technology and services. Globalization, essentially, means the growing together of product markets across national borders. Globalization is shaping the industrial and trade structures of both developing and developed countries. Globalization, sustained by price and trade liberalization, has become the driving force of economic growth in many regions of the world, and at the same time, cause of concerns for many developing countries.

A globalized economy is an ideal type distinct from that of the international economy and can be developed by contrast with it. In such a global system distinct national economies are subsumed and rearticulated into the system by international processes and transactions. The international economy, on the contrary, is one in which processes that are determined at the level of national economies still dominate and international phenomena are outcomes that emerge from the distinct and differential performance of the national economies. The international economy is an aggregate of nationally located functions. Thus while there are in such an economy a wide and increasing range of international economic interactions (financial markets and trade in manufactured goods, for example) these tend to function as opportunities or constraints for nationally located economic actors and their public regulators.

The global economy raises these nationally based interactions to a new power. The international economics system becomes autonomized and socially disembedded, as markets and production become truly global. Domestic policies, whether of private corporations or public regulators, now have routinely to take account of the predominantly international determinants of their sphere of operations. As systemic interdependence grows, the national level is permeated and transformed by the international. In such a globalized economy the problem posed for public authorities is how to construct policies that coordinate and integrate their regulatory efforts in order to cope with the systematic interdependence between their economic actors.

The first major consequence of a globalized economy would thus be the fundamental problematicity of its governance. Global, socially decontextualized markets would be difficult to regulate, even supposing effective cooperation by the regulators and a coincidence of their interests. The principal difficulty is to construct both effective and integrated patterns of national and international public policy to cope with global market forces. The systematic economic interdependence of countries and markets would by no means necessarily result in a harmonious integration in which world consumers benefit from truly independent and allocatively efficient market mechanisms. On the contrary, it is more than plausible that the populations of even successful and advanced states and regions would be at the mercy, of autonomized and uncontrollable, global market forces. Interdependence would then readily promote disintegration — i.e.; competition add conflict — between regulatory agencies at different levels. Such conflict would further weaken effective public governance at the global level. Enthusiasts for the efficiency of free markets and the superiority of corporate control over that of public agencies would see this as a rational world order freed from the shackles of obsolete and ineffective national public interventions. Others, less sanguine but convinced that globalization is occurring, may see it as a world system in which there can be no generalized or sustained public reinsurance against the costs imposed on particular localities by unfavourable competitive outcomes or market failures.

A first consequence of the notion of a globalizing international economy would be the transformation of Multi-National Corporation (MNCs) into transnational corporations (TNCs) as the major players in the world economy. The TNC would be genuine footloose capital, without specific national identification and with an internationalized management, and at least potentially willing to locate and relocate anywhere in the globe to obtain either the most secure or the highest returns. In the financial sector this could be achieved at the touch of a button and in a truly globalized economy would be wholly dictated by market forces without reference to national monetary policies. In the case of primarily manufacturing companies the TNC would source, produce and market at the global level as strategy and opportunities dictate. Thus the TNC, unlike the MNC, could no longer be controlled or even constrained by the policies of particular national states.

A second consequence of globalization would be the further decline in the political influence and economic bargaining power of organized labour. Globalized markets and TNCs would tend to be mirrored by an open world labour market. This market would operate not primarily by actual labour mobility from country to country but by mobile capital selecting locations with the best deal in terms of labour costs and supply. Thus while companies requiring highly, skilled and productive labour might well continue to locate in the advanced countries, with all their advantages, rather than merely seek low wages, the trend of the global mobility of capital and the relative national fixity of labour would favour those advanced countries with the most tractable labour forces and the lowest social overheads relative to the benefits of labour competence and motivations.

A final and inevitable consequence of globalization is the growth in fundamental multi-polarity in the international political system. The hitherto hegemonic national power could no longer impose its own distinct regulatory objectives in either its own territories or elsewhere, and lesser agencies (whether public or private) would thus enjoy enhanced powers of denial and evasion *vis-à-vis* any aspirant 'hegemony'. A variety of bodies from international voluntary agencies to TNCs would thus gain in relative power at the expense of national governments and, using global markets and media, could appeal to and obtain legitimacy from consumers/citizens across national boundaries. Thus, the distinct disciplinary powers of national states would decline, even though the bulk of their citizens, especially in the advanced countries, remained nationally bound.

Public versus Private Goods

The state must provide defense, administration of justice and internal security to the public and undertakes macro-economic management and other policies, which are strictly in the public domain. What is debatable is the matter of public provision of "private goods" like textile and engineering products, and electricity generation, telecommunication, radio and TV programmes. A schematic presentation of what might be considered appropriate functions of the state may be seen in Table 1. It may be noted that nowhere in this scheme does it recognize public production of private goods such as textiles, steel and paper as appropriate functions of the state (The World Bank, 1997).

Market failure and equity considerations constitute the most cogent argument for public production of private goods. When market failure exists, the result is the non-supply of a good whose demand is there, but private pursuit of profit maximization does not justify production. The outcome is inefficient resource allocation, which can then be corrected through public production. Existence of increasing return to scale which gives rise to natural monopoly is also an instance of market failure prompting public production. It should be noted, however, that technology is slowly cutting at the roots of the natural monopoly argument. Equity considerations still justify public production in the transportation area where rail links are carried to remote corners of the country or public transports in urban centres are made available at off-peak hours (Sattar, 1997).

We would be missing the point if we were to ignore the fundamental economic value that formed the basis for a policy of nationalization of industries in the early 1970s. It is what Deepak Lal (1985) aptly describes as the Dirigiste dogma. The essential elements of this dogma is the belief that the price mechanism, or the working of a market economy, needs to be supplanted (and not merely supplemented) by various forms of direct government control to promote economic development. The essential task of government was seen as charting and implementing a 'strategy' for rapid and equitable growth which attaches prime importance to macro-economic aggregates such as savings, investments, and the balance between agriculture and industry. According to this view, more was required of governments than 'getting prices right'.

The negative aspects of the Bangladesh public sector are: (i) a state apparatus which extends beyond the core functions of the state. A large part of the Government of Bangladesh (GOB) is engaged in activities it should not be, and direct public sector interventions has created market distortions and crowded out private sector productive activity; (ii) a disabled economic environment with an intricate web of discretionary and disruptive regulations; (iii) a non-transparent system which is replete with unpredictable and surreptitious decision-making on policy and operational aspects, and weak accountability; (iv) an oversized, complex and nearly unmanageable bureaucracy and institutional apparatus; (v) demotivated and underpaid public employees at the senior and mid-management levels; (vi) an adversarial relationship between the public and private sector growth, and (vii) overmanned SOEs with powerful public sector labour unions which have stymied efforts to reduce the massive losses by public enterprises, improve the efficiency of their operations, or privatizing them.

Three inter-related arguments can be furnished in favour of privatization in Bangladesh: (a) improvement of government's fiscal situation; (b) efficiency improvement following privatization; (c) promotion of private sector development.

In the presence of market failures and market imperfections in Bangladesh, privatization alone however, will not necessarily improve efficiency and promote competition. Regulatory mechanisms must be put in place to prevent privatized entities from exacting monopoly rents in cases where they are the only producer or are amongst a few suppliers.

Governance and Corruption

Corruption is one of the worst forms of misgovernance and it has far-reaching deleterious effect on the development process. The worst kind of corruption is that involved in an ordinary citizen's attempt to acquire public goods.

Corruption has been defined as the misuse of power for private gain. It is not confirmed to bribery, but can assume a number of other forms like nepotism, patronage etc. It straddles both public and private sectors. A private sector company or corporation enjoying a monopoly or near monopoly, can sometimes ration the supply of a scarce good instead of using the price mechanism to clear the market. In that event, it will get illegitimate revenues from the market. Corruption can be practiced independently by politicians and bureaucrats as well as through a nexus between the two. This nexus can extend further and include criminals and drug traffickers.

The fundamental cause of corruption is power. Advantage can be taken of any position of power to indulge in corruption. There is "wholesale corruption" as in the case of huge cuts from big deals, and "retail corruption" which takes the form of small bribes or cuts in the process of innumerable transactions for the provision of public goods. There is "centralized corruption" when it is indulged in mainly by a small coterie of politicians and senior bureaucrats at the centre, and "decentralized corruption" when it operates in many sectors and also at the state and local levels (Dubey, 1998).

Economic Costs of Corruption

There is substantial empirical evidence on the economic costs of corruption. This evidence contradicts earlier and more benign views of corruption that explain it as mainly "speed money", an expeditious way to circumvent red tape and avoid bureaucratic delays. Under this view bribes are seen as a way to reduce transaction costs and facilitate investment, but this simplistic view ignored the major costs of corruption. First, it is difficult to limit corruption to areas where it could be economically desirable. As corruption becomes widespread, it creates incentives for talented people to move into rent seeking activities and away from areas that are more productive from a social standpoint. But corruption also lowers the incentives to innovation and thwarts competition. Existing firms' contracts with corrupt officials gives them a head start to obtain licenses and financial resources. Innovation and competition will suffer because potential entrants will have a difficult time penetrating these established networks (The World Bank, 1998).

Corruption tends to increase the share of public investment in total spending, essentially by encouraging the adoption of large projects where there is more scope for corruption. At the same time, corruption tends to reduce the share of operation and management spending and to lower the productivity of the capital stock. There is also some evidence that corruption affects the composition of expenditure. For a large sample of countries, governmental spending on education as a share of GDP is negatively correlated with the degree of corruption.

Corruption also lowers Foreign Direct Investment (FDI) because from the firms' standpoint it is equivalent to an extra tax. The empirical evidence suggests that the impact of corruption on FDI is larger than the actual amount of bribes compared to taxes because of the inherent arbitrariness and uncertainty that is associated with corruption.

Combating Corruption in Bangladesh

In order to curb corruption and increase transparency in Bangladesh, the following measures can be taken: (a) announce a public policy on transparency and establish a task force, made up of civil society members drawn from various professional and occupational groups; (b) overhaul the Anti-Corruption Bureau, establishing an independent Board along the lines of the Singapore's Anti-Corruption Bureau; (c) strengthen the system of Parliamentary Standing Committees, with first priority on the Public Accounts Committee, and review existing rules of Parliamentary Procedures to repeal sections which prevent public hearings within committees; (d) create an Ombudsman's Office, as sanctioned by the Constitution as a check on the functioning of executive agencies and to adjudicate disputes and grievances from the public, in a timely and cost effective manner; (e) repeal the official Secrets Act 1939 and replace it with a Freedom of Information Act; (f) set clear performance standards for the public sector service providers and publish standards in a Citizens Charter, and hold officials accountable to these standards; (g) establish special anti-corruption courts to ensure speedy trials thereby creating an impact on the anti-corruption drive (The World Bank, 1998).

A Historical Perspective on Governance Crisis in Bangladesh

In 1975 there occurred a significant shift in the development vision of Bangladesh following the violent overthrow of the Government. A state driven economy with a dominant role of the public sector, somewhat loosely categorized as socialism was rejected in favour of a market driven economic system with a dominant role for the private sector. Since then successive regimes have tried hard to reduce the involvement of the state in trade and industry and encouraged the nascent private sector to fill that gap. Foreign aid supplying countries and the multilateral donor agencies played a significant role in formulating the post-1975 economic policies in order to realize this redirection of the developmental vision (Akash, 1998).

Over the last two decades Bangladesh has witnessed a progressive loss of ownership over its developmental vision. This process has been driven by an increasing dependence on foreign aid to underwrite Bangladesh development process. Aid dependence has provided leverage to the aid donors to influence the direction of Bangladesh's policy agendas. This influence of the donors over policy direction in Bangladesh has persisted even after the degree of aid dependence has declined in the 1990s. In the absence of any domestically designed developmental vision Bangladesh's development programme over successive five years plans has derived from an aggregation of numerous projects, a considerable number of which are in fact carried over from the past plan period. Whatever autonomous vision informs the thinking of the government of Bangladesh (GOB), this has to be adjusted with the available programme of Aid. The GOB thus depends on the coincidence between the long term vision of the GOB's five year plans and the short term ad-hoc goals of the various aided projects of the ADP, to give substance to its vision. Within this pattern of relationships between the GOB and its donors, GOB functionaries remains interested in negotiating as many projects as possible within their respective ministries, irrespective of their conformity with the long run plans of the government. Thus heavy aid dependence has logically led the GOB to not only lose control over its policy agendas but also over its functionaries where project fetishism has contributed to a loss of domestic ownership over the GOB's development vision (Akash, 1998).

The particular sequence of events through which the donors formally took over the control of the development vision of Bangladesh was described most elaborately by a former finance minister (Syeduzzaman, 1991). According to him in March, 1986, IMF approved a general scheme for a structural adjustment facility loan known as SAF, for all low income countries of the world suffering from severe resource imbalances. Bangladesh negotiated two loan arrangements under SAF, one for the FY 1986-87, and the other for the FY 1987-88. A policy framework paper (PFP) was prepared as the basis of cooperation between the WB, IMF and the then Government. Under the PFP detailed quantitative macro economic targets were set for the next three successive years from 1986 to 1989. The targets were: (a) to have an average GDP growth rate of 5 per cent per year; (b) to moderate the rate of inflation to 7 per cent by the year 1989; (c) to contain the current account deficit and budget deficit to no more than 7 per cent of the GDP; (d) to raise the revenue GDP ratio from 9.5 per cent of GDP to 10.5 per cent in the third year.

Many of these targets were in consonance with the Third Five Year Plan targets and therefore one may argue that in one sense we had at that time a consensus on major macro economic goals between the military regime and the Bretton Woods Institutions (BWI), the World Bank and the IMF.

In spite of the consensus which prevailed between the donors and the military regime on the reform of Bangladesh's macro economic policies, the actual performance of the economy did not register any noticeable improvement. GDP growth rate could not reach the target of 5 per cent set in the reform model, rather in 1987-88 it came down to the level of only 2 per cent due to a devastating flood in that year. The tax-GDP ratio, the overall deficit of the Government and net credit absorbed by the Government, all mutually agreed macro targets, remained unfulfilled. In fact, in 1989-90, external resources financed 37 per cent of the TGE (Total Government Expenditure) and 103 per cent of the development budget. The latter rate implies that by 1989 Bangladesh was already running a huge deficit on the revenue budget and therefore external aid became not only the sole source of development finance but also underwrote a part of the current deficit. Donors were increasingly dissatisfied with this economic performance and a new Policy Framework Paper (PFP) was negotiated between the GOB and the World Bank and IMF in Washington DC in August, 1990 and endorsed at an aid consortium meeting in Dhaka in November, 1990 by the GOB and the donors. This PFP of 1990 has remained the master document guiding policy reforms in Bangladesh in spite of the fall of the Ershad regime in December, 1990 and has been embraced by the BNP regime in office from 1991-96 and the present Awami League regime in office since 1996. Currently a new PFP is under negotiation.

In general the donor driven/mutually agreed vision of the 1980's has proved inadequate to transform the Bangladesh economy. During 1973-81, the average GDP growth rate was 5.8 per cent, but in the 80's this fell to 3.5-4 per cent, at a time when Bangladesh had an intimate ongoing relationship with the BWI.

From 1990 to 1994 the macro resource balance improved but only at the cost of a stagnant growth rate and weak development investment. From 1994 to 1997 the resource balance marginally deteriorated while the growth rate of GDP picked up slightly only in the last year. But this stimulus in growth was driven largely by agricultural growth.

The donors, particularly the WB institutions, do not associate Bangladesh's weak economic performance with the policy agendas under implementation over the last 15 years, since they do not recognize any fundamental flaw or inconsistency in their basic vision or strategies. The donors diagnosis of Bangladesh's poor performance is thus focused on the various implementation failures which are collectively termed as governance failures. The key areas of governance failures pertaining to the macro economic performances of Bangladesh are identified as follows: (a) Fiscal Management; (b) Quality of Public Spending; (c) Reforming the Financial Sector; (d) Creating an Enabling Environment for the Private Sector; (e) Appropriate Pricing of Tradable Commodities, etc.

In contrast to the donor's perception of causality in Bangladesh, domestic policymakers as well as managers of the economy usually complain against the harshness of the donor's reform proposals and suggest that because of political constraints as well as lack of effective institutional capacities the pace and outcome of reform has been weaker than actually committed to the donors.

A possible argument for the weak outcome from the donor driven reform agenda in place in Bangladesh over the last decade is presented below. First, some conditionalities of the donors were acceptable to the Government but not to the people. Here the GOB made no serious effort to mobilize either political support in Parliament nor popular support within civil society or even amongst beneficiaries behind the conditional reform package. The reforms thus required assured a donor driven character where the commitment and capacity of the GOB to implement the reform remained weak. Second, if the pace of adjustments is too rapid then it causes much pain to affected social groups. Depending on the strength of such groups some policies become politically infeasible e.g. a sharp elimination of agricultural subsidies in one or two years may lead to a severe shock to some farm groups who may resist such reform by putting pressure on their elected representatives as well as on the local machinery of government (Akash, 1998).

A too rapid reduction of tariff has a revenue reducing effect which needs to be seriously considered before tax reforms are put in place. The government may not have the capacity to implement a compensatory move to increase collections from direct taxes. Furthermore, such tariff reforms impact on local industries faced with an influx of imports. The capacity of affected industrialists to resist such reforms depend on their sectoral strength and political influence. Elimination of the differential between two exchange rates within a short time frame may serve as a disincentive to the workers who send remittances encouraging them to slow down remittances which may cause problem for the balance of payment situation (Syeduzzaman, 1991).

Governance of the Fiscal Sector Economy

Hassan (1997) has estimated the size of underground economy (UE) for Bangladesh, and analysed its impact on government fiscal position and the allocation of economic resources in the aggregate economy. This study estimates the size of such UE by using a variant of Tanzi currency demand model (1980). The key assumptions of this model are: UE activities are carried out mainly through the use of currency and the underground income velocity of money is the same as the observed velocity. Unlike prior studies, this study does not only estimate the underground GDP but also its three components (domestic, import and export sectors), thus providing insights into the dynamics of the UE. For Bangladesh, the UE averaged about 22 per cent of formal GDP during the 1972-95 period.

The IRBD, 97 highlighted the problems faced by the fiscal sector and the role of governance in addressing these problems (Chowdhury, 1998).

i. **The Tax Structure:** Fiscal management is interlinked with macro-economic performance both as a cause as well as an effect. The challenge in the area of improving the quality of governance in this sector of the Bangladesh economy is accentuated by the fact that 80% of total public revenue in the country is generated through taxes, of which 80% in turn is generated from indirect taxes. In recent years the share of direct taxes has come down from 22.3% in FY 1991 to 19.7% in FY 1997. This has also been the case with indirect taxes from domestic sources when compared to taxes on foreign trade where taxes on domestic goods have come down from 26.1% to 23.3%, whilst the matched share of taxes on international trade has gone up from 49.9% to 55.0%. To compensate for the stagnation in VAT collection (averaging 30% of total taxes for the last 4 years) the share of supplementary taxes has gone up substantially: it has shot up from 1.7% (in FY 1992 when VAT was introduced) to 15% in FY 1997. The coverage and depth of the tax net continues to remain narrow and shallow.

ii. **Presumptive Tax:** 80% of the direct tax is in fact presumptive. As a result National Board of Revenue (NBR) is involved in the collection of only 20% of the direct taxes.

iii. **VAT:** Too many exemptions along with lack of transparency of accounts at the retail stage has led to stagnation of VAT collections following the initial upsurge. VAT imposed on imports is very effective, but its efficacy declines when imposed at the domestic retail stage.

iv. The rate of duties shown in the budget statement are usually lower than what is approved by parliament at the time of passing of the budget. These rates are enhanced through Statutory Revenue Orders (SRO) which also demonstrates a lack of transparency.

v. Previously, tariff valuation disputes or authority to collect taxes were left to the executive branch where appeals were made to a tribunal. In recent years such assessments are increasingly being challenged by assesses in the law courts. The resultant issue of stay orders by the courts delays revenue collection which because of the slow functioning of our courts has led to a deceleration in revenue collections.

vi. Lack of any systematic data on updated lists of tariff values has led to confusion and scope for discretionary exercise of state power and rent-seeking.

vii. Preshipment Inspection (PSI) has not proved a successful experiment for Bangladesh. Most PSI firms involved in Bangladesh tend to be open to malfeasant conduct. PSI agencies, unless firms of impeccable international integrity are to be drawn in, have thus failed to substitute customs officials as a basis for both promoting integrity and expediting customs revenue collections in Bangladesh.

viii. Under the ongoing system of import policy reforms, virtually all quantitative restrictions (QRs) have been removed and customs classification of goods have been simplified; dispersion of rates have also been lowered. All such developments should have substantially reduced the scope for corruption. However, there is little evidence that malfeasance in the collection of customs revenue has been reduced.

ix. Imports have gone up, but the physical expansion of the Customs Houses is yet to accommodate this increase. Thus the burden on revenue officials has also increased, which has further contributed to delays in the clearance process.

x. **Direct Taxation:** The tax base continues to remain narrow despite the decision in the 1997/98 budget to make it mandatory for car, house owners and Stock Exchange (SE) members to submit tax returns. Tax intelligence is very weak and the taxation department lacks ability to conduct internal and external surveys. Assesses provide strong resistance to tax officials; on the other hand some tax officials connive with assesses and help them to avoid taxation.

xi. **Establishing Accountability:** Any attempt to improve the governance of the fiscal system must focus on restoring a chain of accountability from the Parliament, through the Finance Minister, to the chairman, NBR down to the lowest echelons of the revenue department where each individual must have an assigned fiscal responsibility and be held accountable to a person in authority above them.

xii. **State and Society:** Weakness in the revenue collection process and the capacity for rent-seeking are driven by a culture of tax avoidance which has become part of the social fabric of Bangladesh society over many years. This reluctance to meet our fiscal obligations encourages collusive behaviour between the state and individuals in civil society to share the spoils of tax avoidance at the expense of the exchequer.

Governance of the Financial Sector Economy

A. Overview of the Banking Sector

Three pillars of good banking — an effective legal system, good management, and a strong and effective regulatory/supervisory system — need to be rebuilt to establish a robust and a competitive banking system. Since the late 1980s, the banking system has been operating in a reasonably stable macro-economic environment. Overall, the macro-economic situation has been neutral to positive for the financial sector (The World Bank, 1998).

Financial depth has increased from 25% of GDP in the late 1980s to 36% in 1997. Real interest rates have been positive. Overall credit-to-GDP ratio has increased while credit flow to government has declined with concomitant increase in the share of private sector credit in total credit. However, the growth in credit is not matched by growth in base money and M2, hence drawing down of reserves and foreign assets. Credit growth in the face of contracting base money and M2 is also putting pressure on the banks to draw down on their liquid assets.

Over 94% of the commercial banking system is insolvent and badly managed. According to the Bangladesh Bank (BB's) current lax guidelines, the non-performing loans are 32% for Nationalised Commercial Banks (NCB) and 39% for Private Sector Banks (PCB) and capital inadequacy is about $0.8 billion. If generally accepted international criteria are used for loan classification and provisions, around 50% of the total portfolio of the NCBs and PCBs is non-performing; on this basis, capital inadequacy is estimated at around $2.3 billion (7.5% of 1997 GDP) for these banks, assuming no recovery of collateral. Unlike the situation in most other countries, the portfolio quality of private banks in Bangladesh is as bad as (slightly worse than) that of the NCBs. There are virtually no good banks, except for the foreign banks which are only 6% of the system (The World Bank, 1998).

The soundness of most PCBs has been severely undermined by insider lending, fraud and negligence. Weak supervision and inadequate enforcement have led to the present predicament. Seven of the worst PCBs, which are under MOU arrangements with the BB, hold 17% of total deposits and 60% of deposits of the private domestic banks.

B. IRBD '97 View on Financial Sector

Bhattacharya (1998) recommends the following policy agenda to improve governance in the banking sector.

i. **Ownership of Agenda:** Reforms need to be debated in the parliament; the locus standi of the Banking Reforms Committee (BRC) should be specified and it should be empowered to act expeditiously to carry through its reform recommendations.

ii. **Approach to Reforms Process:** The Commercial Bank Reform Project (CBRP) has a narrower focus than the original Financial Sector Reform Project (FSRP). However, the CBRP, in spite of being a Commercial Bank Reform Project does not include any significant action as regards private commercial banks. The DFIs are also outside the purview of this project. The CBRP's scope should be reviewed and derived from the recommendations of the BRC.

iii. **Autonomy of BB:** The charter of Bangladesh Bank (BB) needs change. It should be allowed to work independently within the policy parameters spelt out by the Government of Bangladesh (GOB). It should be kept politically insulated through a consensus between the GOB and opposition parties to preserve the independence of the BB.

iv. **Role of Banking Division:** The Banking Division is used by the government to impose its financial priorities on the NCBs.

This task should be addressed by the Ministry of Finance which should be vested with the responsibility of formulating Financial and Monetary Policy. Policy directives should be exclusively implemented by the Bangladesh Bank which should operate with complete authority within a given policy mandate.

v. **Corporate Governance of Banks:** Politicians and defaulters should be barred from board membership; the chairmen of the NCBs should be appointed through a process of public hearing in the Parliament Standing Committees.

vi. **Loan Recovery:** Currently good borrowers are penalized. The Financial Loan Court Act is a welcome development but the lack of trained judges are a constraint to make this work. The maximum period of 3 years for settling default loans should be strictly followed.

vii. **Debt Recovery:** A debt collecting institution should be set up exclusively designed for this task.

viii. **Loans to SOEs:** SOEs as clients should be treated at par with other clients. Special provision for SOEs, if called for in the public interest, should be made through the national budget.

ix. **Loan Amnesty:** Financial discipline is negated by loan amnesties. If need be banks should be reimbursed for amnestied loans through budgetary allocations administered in a transparent way. To use public funds to bail out private banks defaulting due to insider lending should be avoided since this is inequitable.

x. **Rural Finance:** New initiatives are needed for financing productive activity in the rural economy which are not covered by the prevailing micro-credit institutions: (a) Agricultural finance to small farmers remains a priority concern. To this end wider use should be made for credit to farmers through Grameen Bank and NGO micro-credit institutions; (b) The rural loan portfolio of the NCBs should be redirected towards financing of non-farm, agro-related activities; (c) Bangladesh Krishi Bank should exclusively target its lending activities to the small and subsistence farmers and should assimilate some of the credit management techniques of the Grameen Bank to readjust its mission.

xi. **Privatization:** Policy and decisions on bank privatization should be made on empirical rather than ideological grounds following completion of the restructuring process of the NCBs.

xii. **New Initiatives for Industrial Financing:**

a. A New Agency dedicated to Loan Recovery (using such instruments as asset swaps, asset conversion, debt sales, liquidator/receivership).

b. A New Investment Finance Company to: (i) mobilize funds for industrial term loan financing, (ii) to actively engage in industrial investment promotion activities.

c. Sources of Funds: NCBs, Local private Banks, Foreign Banks, IFC, GOB, Global Financial Market, FDI, NRB/Migrant Workers, Local Capital Market.

d. Mutual Funds for the Poor: Dedicated to mobilize the savings of the poor and to make them stakeholders in the corporate sector.

e. Securitization of the loan portfolios of the micro-credit providers designed to bring in global sources of funds to support micro-credit.

xiii. **Governance Challenge:** Quality of Governance in the Banking Sector must be improved through the following measures: (a) by means of prudential regulation and supervision, (b) by infusing a high degree of competitiveness in the financial market; (c) the reform process must be isolated and insulated from pressures of vested interests; (d) a political consensus must be built to support the reform in this sector, (e) civil society must be mobilized to support the reform process.

C. Scope of an Autonomous Bangladesh Bank

i. The Conduct of Monetary Policy

Over the past 23 years Bangladesh Bank has essentially had its monetary policy directed by the Ministry of Finance (MOF). Years of such direction has resulted in a very conservative approach by the BB staff which essentially is not prepared to take control of monetary policy even if the MOF wants to relinquish this responsibility to the BB. This history of receiving detailed guidance has greatly reduced the capacity of the BB to act autonomously. The BB needs to train its staff to manage monetary policy. There is also a need for a clear legislative mandate to focus monetary policy on the objective of maintaining a stable inflation rate.

ii. Management of Exchange Rate Policy

The Bangladesh Bank follows a very conservative exchange rate policy with marginal adjustments determined by purchasing parity power principles. The purchasing power parity states that exchange rate depreciates essentially according to the difference between OECD inflation rate and the Bangladesh inflation rate.

The management of exchange rates and the exchange control system is both technical and political. The exchange rate can be managed by the BB according to an objective legislated by the National Assembly. With such an objective, the BB can manage the exchange rate following any number of technical schemes.

iii. Bank Supervision and Examination

First, the Bangladesh Bank should be given autonomy to supervise banks and the authority to close them if necessary. The BB can examine the bank capital adequacy by strictly applying the rules. Second, the BB should be allowed to take appropriate action against any bank, including the NCBs, for failing to maintain adequate capital or failure to make adequate loan loss provisions. Third, the BB should be allowed to force banks to limit large loans, including such loans to public sector companies. Finally, the BB should adopt a life boat operations to take over banks and restructure them whenever necessary.

iv. Building of an Efficient Financial Market

Apart from the details of monetary policy, exchange rate policy, and bank supervision, there is the overall responsibility of the central bank to support the development of a healthy growing financial sector that can contribute to the development process. The central bank can and should act as an advisor to the Ministry of Finance on what needs to be done to build the financial sector. Ultimately, the legislation for the financial sector must rest with the Ministry and the central bank can only provide its advice. However, if the central bank works through its research wing on these critical issues it can provide a very important input on these matters.

Governance of the International Economy

The IRBD '97 discusses the following governance issues of the international economy of Bangladesh (Rashid and Rahman, 1998).

I. Import Policy

a. Import policy in the 1990s continued to be driven by donor perceptions on policy reform and donor conditionalities to implement these reforms. Lack of vision as well as ownership to direct a reform agenda has tended to undermine the liberalization policy of the GOB which is facing increasing resistance from the local industrialists who are finding themselves unable to cope with the resultant competition from imports, particularly from India.

b. Insufficient attention was given to the speed, phasing and sequencing of liberalization. The donors remain interested in the speed of reforms rather than the removal of supply side constraints which provided an uneven playing field for local industry in competing with a ready supply of imports.

c. The GOB needs to put in place an incentive regime whereby investment activities and not indenting or trading activities would be the most profitable business undertaking.

II. Tariff Policy

a. Determination of Tariff Policy: The Tariff Commission's (TC) role in determining tariff policy (according to Allocation of Business Among Different Ministries and Divisions and Rules of Business) remains largely advisory and limited to making recommendations to the NBR. This has constrained the effectiveness of the TC — in general, only 25-50% of its recommendations are fully implemented.

b. In recent years the participatory process through the TC's Consultative Committee was adopted to encourage policy makers, business groups, entrepreneurs, chambers, NGOs, consumers to hold dialogues for determining tariff policy. This has yielded good results. But since the chambers do not have any in-house research cells or analytical capacity they often fail to articulate their demands adequately. Analytical capacity inside the GOB is also deficient.

c. There is a prevalence of revenue consideration rather than industrial/investment considerations in the tariff policies.

III. Administering the Import Policy

a. At present three methods are adopted to assess imports for levying customs duties: (i) invoice value, (ii) tariff value and (iii) value certified by PSI. The prevalent system leaves much discretionary power with the customs officials.

b. Changes would need to be made in the Customs Act to ensure GATT compatibility. It is feared that once Bangladesh switches to the WTO valuation system, mis-invoicing by the traders may become more common.

c. The GOB does not have a system of on-going monitoring of the impact of import policies, in spite of the fact that this has such important implications for the viability of the producing sectors of the economy.

IV. Export Management

a. The export sector now accounts for about one-third of capacity in the modern manufacturing sector. Thus, more efficient management of the export sector has become closely interlinked with the industrialization process in Bangladesh.

b. The incentives put in place to promote export cannot be fully realized due to the lack of implementation capacity of such export promoting institutions as the DEDO, EPB and Bangladesh Bank. A survey for IRBD 1997 shows that RMG factories using back-to-back L/C facilities need, on average, 19 person-days over and above the normal time for every export consignment, through delays in customs clearance, banking transactions and interaction with government agencies. This undermines Bangladesh's export competitiveness.

c. Creation of an export-import bank (EXIM) as in India and Pakistan allowing duty drawbacks through dealing banks (instead of DEDO) and removal of discrepancies in the incentives between exports and deemed export should be given due attention by policymakers.

V. *Coping with Globalization*

a. Withdrawal of the MFA quota, GSP conditionalities, sanitary-phytosanitary requirements etc. will have serious implications for Bangladesh's export performance in the near future. Bangladesh must be cautious that market access problems of the type faced in FY 1997 are not repeated. Another failure of governance is that whilst the EU rules of origin for knitwear are possibly inappropriate and unfair, the failure of the GOB to monitor the issue of GSP certificates reflects both lax administration and a tendency for malfeasant behaviour on the part of some business persons.

b. Further value addition in the RMG sector is becoming an essential requirement if Bangladesh is to optimize its foreign exchange. More active effort involving a joint effort by the GOB and RMG exporters is needed to establish Bangladeshi buying houses in North America and Europe which can do business directly with retail houses.

c. The Dispute Settlement Body (DSB) is expected to become very important in the WTO where debates on such issues as anti-dumping duty (ADD), countervailing duty (CVD) etc. would be settled. Bangladesh needs to develop the expertise to carry on complex trade negotiations in SAPTA, WTO, UNCTAD.

d. Information is a critical input for export promotion. Trade related focal points in Bangladesh must be connected to the GTPN introduced by the UNCTAD. Various business chambers in Bangladesh have limited ability to carry out independent research on how to cope with the increasingly complex problems of globalization manifest in the WTO rules. Whilst the chambers are becoming increasingly involved in recent years in the trade policy formulation process, they need to invest in supporting local professional institutions which can accumulate expertise to offer competent professional advise on the implications of globalization.

e. Bangladesh's infrastructure, transport, port facilities are not commensurate with a dynamic export-led growth strategy. The potential of accelerated and enhanced regional cooperation has also remained unrealized because of underdeveloped infrastructure. Whilst many of the problems of improving the infrastructure demand investments in the modernization and expansion of capacity, both the management of surface transport as well as the ports suffer from serious problems of governance which reduces their efficacy.

f. A comprehensive policy of skills development is absent. The vocational school system is delinked to the export sector. Some private entrepreneurs are coming forward to provide training to the manpower going abroad; but training of manpower, skill upgradation etc. for export-oriented industries as well as labour exports has so far remained limited to on-the-job training.

Conclusion

The basic thesis of this paper has been that good governance cannot be realized without the injection of a moral dimension into all individual and collective decisions that directly or indirectly affect the allocation and distribution of resources. In fact, it is not possible even to define efficiency and equity without the help of moral criteria. The secular orientation of the market system may enable it to reduce imbalances and foster higher growth, but it will not make it possible for it to bring about the kind of revolutionary changes that are needed in individual and collective behaviour for realizing development with justice.

However, neo-classical economies continues to assert that the market system can help bring about such a reallocation in spite of its secular approach to the solution of human problems. It assumes that unhindered freedom to serve self-interest and to own and manage private property motivates the individuals to do their best. This maximizes efficiency, which benefits not just the individual concerned but also the society.

While liberalization of the economy to let the individuals serve their self-interest does motivate them to render their best, it serves social interest only where social interest is in harmony with individual self-interest. Liberalization alone will not be able to promote good governance. A number of other measures need to be adopted. First, the filtering effect of market-determined prices needs to be complemented by the moral filter to enable individuals and groups to evaluate their behaviour and their claims on resources from the point of view of their impact on social well-being. Second, individuals and groups need to be motivated appropriately to keep not just their self-interest but also the collective social interest in mind while expressing their preferences in the market place. Third, the economy and financial intermediation need to be restructured in a way that would be conducive to the use of all available resources by the private as well as the public sectors for the realization of development with justice. The government cannot, in this framework, behave as a passive onlooker. It must play a complementary role to guide and facilitate the efficient and equitable use of resources by the private sector.

TABLE 1
Function of the State

Addressing market failure		Improving enquiry	
Providing pure public goods		protecting the poor	
Defense			
Law and order		Antipoverty	
Property rights		programmes	
Macroeconomic management		Disaster relief	
Addressing	Regulation	Overcoming	providing
Externalities:	Monopoly:	Imperfect	Social
		information:	insurance:
Basic	Utility	Consumer protection	
education	regulation	Financial regulation	Pension scheme
Environmental	Antitrust policy		Family allowance
Protection			Unemployment
			insurance
Coordinating private activity:			Redistribution:

Source : World Development Report 1997, World Bank.

References

Akash, M.M. "Governance and Development", in *Crisis in Governance: A Review of Bangladesh's Development 1997.* Centre for Policy Dialogue; University Press Limited, 1998.

Bardhan, Pranab (1997). "Corruption and Development: A Review of Issues," *Journal of Economic Literature.*

Bhattacharya, Debapriya. "The State of Governance in Bangladesh's Banking Sector: Perspectives on the Reform Measures," in *Crisis in Governance: A Review of Bangladesh's Development 1997*; Centre for Policy Dialogue; University Press Limited, 1998.

Chowdhury, Omar Haider. "Fiscal Management and Macroeconomic Performance." in *Crisis in Governance: A Review of Bangladesh's Development 1997.* Centre for Policy Dialogue; University Press Limited, 1998.

Dubey, Muchkund (1998). "Good Governance and Economic Development" Paper Presented at a seminar on "Bangladesh Beyond 2000" organized by the American Chamber of Commerce in Bangladesh.

Evans, Peter (1995). *Embedded Autonomy: States and Industrial Transformation.* Princeton University Press, Princeton.

Hassan, M. Kabir. "Regional Cooperation in Trade, Finance and Investment Among SAARC Countries: The Bangladesh Perspective," Paper Presented at a Seminar Organized by Centre for Development Research on June 20, 1998.

Hassan, M. Kabir. "The Performance of the Financial Sector Reform" in *Growth or Stagnation?: A Review of Bangladesh's Development 1996*. Centre for Policy Dialogue; University Press Limited, 1997.

Hassan, M. Kabir. "The Crisis of Governance in the Banking Sector," *Thoughts on Economics*, 1998.

Hassan, M. Kabir and David Tufte. "Exchange Rate Volatility and Aggregate Export Growth in Bangladesh," Applied Economics, December 1997.

Hirst, Paul and Grahame Thompson. *Globalization in Question: The International Economy and the Possibilities of Governance*. Polity Press, 1996.

Huntington, Samuel (1968). *Political Order in Changing Societies*. New Haven; Yale University Press.

Lal, Deepak (1985). *The Poverty of Development Economics*. Harvard University Press, Cambridge, Massachusetts.

Megginson, Nash and Radenbrog (1992). *Efficiency Gains from Privatization*. World Bank Study.

Rashid, M. Ali and Mustafizur Rahman. "Management of Import Liberalization and Export Promotion Strategies in Bangladesh," in *Crisis in Governance: A Review of Bangladesh's Development 1997*. Centre for Policy Dialogue; University Press Limited, 1998.

Rodrik, Dani. *Has Globalization Gone Too Far*. Institute for International Economics, March 1997.

Sattar, Zaidi (1997). "Macroeconomic Impacts of Privatization Programme in Bangladesh," Paper Presented at the Final Workshop on Institutional Support to the Ministry of Finance and Asian Development Bank.

Sobhan, Rehman (1993). *Rethinking the Role of the State in Development: Asian Perspectives*. University Press Limited, Dhaka.

Syeduzzaman, M. (1991). "Bangladesh's Experience with Adjustment Policies" in Sobhan, R. (ed.) *Structural Adjustment Policies in the Third World: Design and Experience*, a BIDS and WIDER Seminar Report, University Press Limited, Dhaka.

World Bank (1996). *Government that Works: Reforming the Public Sector*.

World Bank (1997). *Bangladesh: Trade Policy Reform for Improving the Incentive Regime*.

World Bank (1997). World Development Report, 1997. *The State in a Changing World*. Oxford University Press, Oxford.

World Bank (1998). *Strategy for Establishing a Sound and Competitive Banking Sector*.

CIVIL SOCIETY AND GOVERNANCE

Atiur Rahman
Syed Naimul Wadood
Mohammed Abu Eusuf

Introduction

The issue of the relationship between governance and civil society has been gaining importance among various stakeholders involved in development. The post-Soviet enthusiasm in pluralism and a sad commentary on the visible failure of 'aided' development programmes in many of the aid recipient countries may have encouraged the development of a perception which tries to locate the issue of governance in the context of enhanced civic engagement. Putnam's (1993) seminal work on social capital has also contributed significantly in zooming the intellectual mind on this interlinkage. This is still an emerging area of debate.

Governance and Its Operational Framework

The concept of Governance has been squarely placed in its right context here in Bangladesh in the latest Independent Review of Bangladesh Development (IRDB) report by the Centre for Policy Dialogue (CPD), "Crisis in Governance: A Review of Bangladesh's Development 1997". The concept of Governance, as it has been discussed there (Akash, 1998) and elsewhere, is a key term that lacks a clear-cut definition, and therefore, is a source of much confusion. According to Akash (1998), this term has been used rather loosely and for that instance, has turned into an "umbrella concept" enabling it to incorporate a variety of social, political and cultural variables within its discourse. This concept of Governance has, as he puts it, by and large included a large number of actions by both state and government.

Different institutions have defined the term 'Governance' in different ways. This discussion will follow the findings of the secondary literature outlined by Guhathakurta and Karim (1998). Here are the brief outlines of the findings in a Tabular form that they have presented in their article.

SIMILARITIES AND DISSIMILARITIES IN DONOR PERCEPTION

Key Indicators	Donors			
	ODA	USAID	UNDP	World Bank
View of State	political decision-making and executive branch	upper bureaucracy and political parties with civil society groupings	market-based (E. Europe) contingency -based (Asia)	market efficiency correcting market failure
Concept of Civil Society	civil society to include business interest	non-business and non-partisan	freedom of association & participation	freedom of association expression of opinion
Views of Politics and Administration	checks and balances to work inside bureaucracy	checks and balances to work outside bureaucracy	participatory institutions to work with govt.	political commitment of govt. or dialogue
Interest of Donors	employment investment economic objectives	political influence and strategic objectives	human development	structural adjustment
Political Recipients	direct to political parties but not for partisan politics	distrust of political parties but prefers NGOs	mainly through govt. with NGOs complementing	mainly govt. NGOs too
Local Govt.	2 tier system reaching upto centres	reaching upto govt.	–	–
Perception of HLs of the System*	cultural and historical contexts	no cultural distinctions	cultural variations only in Asia	no cultural distinction

Source : Guhathakurta, M. and Karim, S. (1998) in Sobhan, R. (ed,), "Towards a Theory of Governance and Development Learning From East Asia", Table 4.1, p.91. UPL, Dhaka, 1998.

* HL = Higher Level.

Given such a diversity of perceptions among donors who are indeed key players in the development discourse of Bangladesh, IRBD (Akash IRBD, 1997) has come forward with a simple model of governance that aims at explaining the role of government in the process of economic development. Here we can proceed with the discussion in line with the operational model developed by Akash (1998). A brief description of the model runs as follows:

> The key variables which have been identified in that model are: (a) vision, (b) commitment and (c) capacity. Governance is here treated as a complex of process — it is treated as a process of formation and realization of a vision of the political authority of a country given the two constraints of capacity and commitment. This model is in reality a dynamic model as all the three variables are continuously changing over time.
>
> Firstly, the point of departure is formation of vision. The inputs for vision can come from many diverse sources such as, political leadership, bureaucracy, private sector, donors, NGOs, pressure groups, mass organizations and other members of the society. This vision gains some sort of legitimacy by accumulating a minimum level of support within society and through this process it becomes a national vision rather than an individual's isolated vision. Then a more serious vision is formed through a formal and informal process of discussions/negotiations with various classes and social groups. Through a process of interactions with many groups — more serious visions are formed when the question of ownership of vision plays a crucial part in it. Ownership of vision can be endogenous or non-endogenous in nature. If the vision is endogenous, it can be expected to have greater support among the local stakeholders and more concrete/realistic pattern. If, on the other hand, the ownership of the vision lies within non-endogenous sources, its support is likely to be weak among the local stakeholders and have less level of commitments toward it.
>
> Secondly, the necessity of concretization of vision arises. The government has to set up long term goals, short term goals, programmes and projects to implement the vision.
>
> Thirdly, the primary commitments need to be translated into a concrete one and these need to be owned endogenously for higher level of commitments towards it. Higher level of commitments require the government to take some hard decisions and show sincerity for implementing it. This successful completion of this step on the part of the government depends on some mobilization works, i.e. to create a supportive state machine, to create a sound institution basis, to mobilize support from the civil society, to mobilize adequate resources and to mobilize private sector supports.

Fourthly, the question arises over the capacity of the government to implement the vision. This capacity depends on five factors, i.e., (a) support from the civil society, (b) support from the private sector, (c) supportive institutions, (d) support from the state machine, and finally (e) adequate resource base.

The three variables, vision, commitment and capacity — highlights the importance of civil society in the context of governance. Without the aid of civil society in the steps of gathering inputs for vision, mobilizing support for hard decisions and implementing the vision — good governance is not an easy task. This model of Akash (1998) clearly indicates that one of the crucial components of good governance is civil society — strengthening of governance depends, among others, civil society as a variable.

Civil Society

Definition of Civil Society

The concept of 'Civil Society' has been a much debated one — as this has always been subjected to widespread disagreements over definition, scope and policy formulation. As one goes through the volume of literature on this topic — one finds that it is one of the most hazy terms in development discourse.

Civil society, according to Harry Blair (1993), comprises the collective of those social organizations that enjoy autonomy from the state, and have as one important goal, among others, to influence the state on behalf of their members. A strong civil society directly supports democratic participation, assure the right and probity of the citizenry and contributes towards a deepening of policy accountability.

According to North-South Institute (1998), the definition of civil society depends on the "philosophical vantage points". It argues, "It may be defined with regards to the way it has to be looked at: it may be seen as particular types of activities or roles, or particular types of organization or particular location within society or the polity. Again, is civil society a mechanism to fight capitalism? Then, the definition can not include the market, but must go in direct confrontation with it, explicitly or implicitly. On the other hand, if civil society is defined as mechanisms which battle the excesses of state — then it would not include local government. Furthermore, pluralist approaches would lead to counting and classifying organizations; institutionalist approaches lead to examination of networks and relationships; behavioural approaches would be questioning of intra-institutional dynamics."

Blaney and Pasha (1992), however, pointed a workable solution to the problem of defining civil society — they argue that civil society must be understood from a variety of angles: both as structure (of organizations, social and political 'space' and relationships) and as process (the ways in which the elements of the structure come into being). The three approaches may be briefly discussed under the headings of: structure, relationships and activity and environment. Here the discussion follows the structure outlined by North-South Institute (Blaney and Pasha, 1992).

Civil Society as Structure

One can define civil society as a structure — the constituent parts of it are organized groups. Most often, one describes these groups by excluding those that belong to the private sector and the state (although, there is controversy over the exclusion of the private sector and lower orders of government) and they are accorded with a positive moral mandate. According to Shethi, civil societies are the locus of action by actors bent on change, whether these are foreign or domestic development groups, charities for relief, action groups devoted to consciousness-raising and mobilization of the oppressed, protest groups, political groups, pre-party political formations and support groups (Shethi, 1993). Some others would further underscore their opinion that these groups are not themselves interested in acquiring political power, so the political parties remain outside the civil society. UNDP tends to define civil society more or less in this fashion (UNDP, 1993).

Civil Society as Relationships and Activity

Civil society, by some others, has been defined as a pattern of relationships with each other. The questions that arise are: in what ways are those organizations linked with each other? Are they separate and discreet entities or are they tightly linked with each other? What is their combined interest or is there any combined interest? Whose interest they serve, whose interest they protect? Who are the opponents of civil society? How public opinion is formed about their issues or how their opponents shape public policy?

Again, relationships need to be identified with actual activities. Some academicians define civil society by what it does — by their activities in opposition to the state. White argues, the use of civil society "implies a certain power relationship between state and society such that there are limitations on the state's capacity to pervade and control society to insulate themselves from, and exert influence upon, the state" (White, 1993),

Civil Society as Enabling Environment

Other academicians view civil society as enabling environment. Blaney and Pasha (1992) argue that the starting point is "the stabilization of a system of rights, constituting human beings as individuals, both as citizens in relation to the state and as legal persons in the economy and the sphere of free association". Civil society can exist only if these ideas and rights are firmly established a priori and is expected to work to put and maintain their existence. A short list of ideas and rights to be protected and further enhanced by civil society are: rights needed to participate in organized groups, a democratic political system of some sort, a culture of association that allows the organization of groups for moral ends and a middle class with disposable income and time to support organizations.

Civil Society: A Western Notion?

Civil society, viewed in this context of structure, relationships and activities and enabling environment — immediately leads to the question whether this concept is simply and purely a Western notion or not. It is not necessary that every society may except this concept — for most of the societies outside the Western ones it may as well be termed as non-endogenous notion, given each society's specific cultural preconditions.

Hutchful (1995-96) argues that changing the notion of civil society to fit the African case may have substantial repercussions for the theory itself. This notion is associated with fundamental transformations in Western society and economy which do not necessarily apply to the African condition (capitalist modernization, urbanization, the 'communication revolution' and growth of literacy, the dissolution of traditional bonds and the decline of religious consciousness) (Hatchful, 1995). African 'associational life' (Bratton, 1994) is often made up of ascriptive groupings rather than voluntary ones, may be entwined with the state, may be ravaged by forces outside the state altogether (ethnicity, sectarianism). Arguing for some sort of cultural specificity, Blaney and Pasha opines that "the complex of relations of modern state capitalist economy, rights-bearing individuals and a particular form of associational life" cannot be assumed to exist in other countries a priori. They argue that civil society exists because of a capitalist system — one which depends on the division of labour, on inequality, on the perceived division between the political and the economic.

Therefore, for most of the non-western states, which lack the required level of development of capitalist system, and so to say, the specific socio-cultural preconditions for existence of a "civil society" per se — the notion of "civil society" may be perceived as another "package" handed over by the Aid Agencies and to be "implemented" as aid conditionality. This debate over definition and political economy of the term itself needs to be addressed to have a better organization of the "Civil Society".

Idea of Civil Society: A Journey through History

Wood (1990) points out that the idea of 'civil society' and the conceptual opposition of 'state' and 'civil society' has been associated with the development of capitalism. "There has always been a long intellectual tradition in the West", even reaching back to classical antiquity — which has delineated a terrain of human association, some notion of 'society', distinct from the body politic and with moral claim independent of, and sometimes opposed to the state's authority. Whatever other factors have been at work in producing such concepts, their evolution has been from the beginning bound up with the development of private property as a distinct and autonomous locus of social power.

The modern conception of 'civil society'—a conception which appeared systematically for the first time in the eighteenth century — is clearly distinct from the earlier versions: now 'civil society' represents a distinct sphere of human relations and activity; distinguished from the state — it is neither public nor private — but perhaps both at once. "A necessary but not sufficient precondition for this conception of civil society was the modern idea of the state as an abstract entity with its own corporate identity, which evolved with the rise of European absolutism; but the full conceptual differentiation of 'civil society' required the emergence of an autonomous 'economy', separated out from the unity of the 'political' and 'economic' which still characterized the absolutist state" (Wood, 1990).

Hobbes and Locke: Early Thinkers

Hobbes, without using the term directly, defines civil society as the area "wherein the liberty of a subject lieth ... only in those things which in regulating their actions, the sovereign hath preterited: such as is the liberty to nuy, and sell, and otherwise contract with one another; to choose their own abode, their own diet, their own trade of life; and institute their children as they themselves think fit; and the like," without, however, limiting the "sovereign power of life and death".

In Locke's conception, civil society has two dimensions. It provides redress and security against anarchy and arbitrariness of the 'state of nature', and on the other, through the devolution of legislative powers "in collective bodies of men, call them senate, parliament or call what you please", gives them (the population) security against the arbitrariness of the governemnt.

Hegel: Next Philosopher

Hegel's concept of civil society embraces the realm of economic interests, labour, private property and class distinctions. Civil society in Hegel's terminology simply refers to the totality of the material conditions of life. While conceding the duality of political society (the state) and civil society (material conditions of life), Hegel lays down that concrete freedom consists in three identities:

> "In contrast with the family and civil society, the spheres of private rights and private welfare, the state is from one point of view on 'external necessity' and their higher authority: its nature is such that their laws and interests are subordinate to it and dependent on it. On the other hand, however, the state is their 'immanent' aim: its strength lies in the unity of its universal end and aim with the particular interest of individuals." (Easton and Guddat, 1967)

Marx and Engels: New Light

Marx and Engels, as opposed to their predecessors, give an independent identity to civil society, that is, they refuse to concede the fundamental identity of the state and civil society. As they say in German Ideology (as quoted in Roy, 1995):

> "Civil Society comprises the entire material interaction among individuals at a particular evolutionary stage of the productive forces. It comprises the entire commercial; and industrial life of a stage hence transcends the state and nation even though that life, on the other hand, is manifested in foreign affairs as nationality and organized within a state. The term civil society emerged in the 18th century when property relations had already evolved from the community of antiquity and medieval times. Civil society as such only develops with the bourgeoisie. The social organizations, however, which evolves directly from production and commerce, which in all ages forms the basis of the state and the rest of the idealistic superstructure, has always been designated by the same name" (Marx and Engels, The German Ideology, Moscow, 1964).

Marx makes a fundamental distinction between the old civil society and the new, while underlying the historical continuity of civil society. Under Feudalism, Marx writes:

> "The old civil society and a directly political character, that is, elements of civil life such as property, the family, the mode and manner of work, for example, were raised into elements of political life in the form of landlordism, estates and corporations. In this form they determined the relation of a particular individual to the state as a whole, that is, his political relation, his separation and exclusion

> from other parts of society. For the feudal organization of national life did not elevate property or labour to the level of social elements but rather completed their separation from the state as a whole and established them as separate societies within society. Thus the vital functions and conditions of civil society always remained political, but political in the feudal sense. That is, they excluded the individual from the state as a whole and transformed the special relation between his corporation and the state into his own general relation to the national life, just as they transformed his specific civil activity and situation into a general activity and situation. ...
>
> The political revolution, which overthrew this domination, turned the state into the people's business and made the political state the business of all .... this revolution inevitably destroyed all estates, corporations, guilds and privileges variously expressing the separation of the people from their community. The political revolution thereby abolished the political character of civil society. It shattered civil society into its constituent elements — on the one hand individuals and on the other the material and spiritual elements constituting the vital content and civil situation of these individuals. It released the political spirit, which had been broken, fragmented, and lost, as it were in the various cul-de-sacs of feudal society. It gathered up this scattered spirit, liberated it from its entanglement with civil life and turned it into the sphere of the community, and the general concern of the people ideally independent of those particular elements of civil life."
>
> — (Writings of Young Marx, cited in Roy, 1995, p.2008.)

Marx demands the abolition of the antithesis between political society (state) and civil society through the abolition of both. This can be achieved by the introduction of unrestricted voting as a means to the fullest extension of democracy, which he broadly equates with the transition to socialism.

Gramsci: Issue Revived

Gramsci, the most important thinker on this topic in the present century, described civil society as the sphere which battles capitalist logic. Civil society, according to him, takes on the notion of 'terrain', a place where the state, the people, the market interact and where the people wage war against the hegemony of the market and the state. What actual institutions belong to 'the people' therefore change depending on their activity on that terrain: the church, as for example, may be identified with the state while the lower clergy may be associated with the people (Hutchful, 1995).

The writing of Gramsci have revitalized the issue of civil society and its potentialities in contemporary socio-political life. Gramsci's contributions to this issue have two distinct aspects, not to be found in early writers. These are: (i) interpenetration of political society and economic society, or the state and civil society; and (ii) a recognizable autonomy of civil society which gives it a distinct space for operation and development. According to Gramsci, there are two major superstructural 'levels: the one that can be called 'civil society', that is the conglomerations of organisms commonly called 'private' and that of political society or 'the state' (Roy, 1995).

Putnam: Concept of Social Capital

Robert Putnam's (Putnam, 1993) 'Social Capital' has reintroduced the age-old issue of civil society to the forefront of development discourse. Putnam attacks the social science tradition that views "the actors of the state and society locked in a zero-sum game and argues that highly active civic associations are strongly associated with effective public institutions. Norms and networks of civil engagement have actually promoted economic growth instead of inhibiting it" (Sobhan, 1998).

The concept of social capital refers to the capacity of states or societies to establish a sense of community which leads a significant proportion of the society in voicing their concern and seeking active involvement in the affairs of the community, and in sharing in the benefits of community action. Putnam uses this model to show different levels of performance of different regional governments and regions of Italy (Sobhan, 1998).

Civil Society: Current Debate

State and Civil Society

Civil society, has by now been constructed in contrast to the state, the law, nature and capitalism — food good or ill. These elements of opposition and moral authority are the two main themes in the current understanding of the term — though the object of opposition has not always been the same. Now the prevalent concept is that civil society is the home of culture, of freedom, of independence (all good notions) which enables others to rein in the state (which can do others harm if permitted) (North-South Institute, web page).

The relationship between "civil society" and "democratic governance" is still an elusive one. Two broad versions are presented about writing of this relationship. The first version is in the writing of Alexis de Tocqueville (Democracy in America) with antecedents in the work of the eighteenth century "Scottish moralists" including Adam Smith, Adam Ferguson and Francis Hutcheson. This approach puts special emphasis on the ability of associational life in general and the habits of association in particular to foster patterns of civility in the actions of citizens in a democratic polity. The second version, articulated mostly by Jacek Kuron, Adam Michnik and their associates in formulating a strategy for resistance to Poland's communist regime in the 1980s. This second argument lays special emphasis on civil society as a sphere of action that is independent of the state and that is capable of energizing resistance to a tyrannical regime. The contradiction between the two arguments is that while the former postulates the positive effects of association of governance (especially democratic governance), the latter emphasises the importance of civil association as a counterweight to the state (Foley and Edwards, 1998).

Civil Society: An Operational Definition

An operational definition of civil society is also much debated. Here one can agree with the operational definition as put forward by Hye (1998). The relevant discussion, in line with Hye (1998), can proceed as follows,

> 'On the one hand, it (civil society) is being contrasted with non-civilian (military society) and on the other, it is being defined to include all institutions other than the formal organs of state. These two extreme positions leave much scope for confusion. For this seminar, the proposed definition of the civil society includes the private sector, voluntary organizations (NGOs), social welfare organizations, professional bodies, trade unions, community based organizations. Special interest groups, research organization,

"advocacy group" and media. This definition excludes the legislature, the judiciary, the governemnt, the local government institutions and the private sector trading and manufacturing units. Civil society covers multifarious activities from provision of limited public goods (micro-credit, primary health-care, etc.), to advocacy for social reform (gender equality, human rights for disadvantaged groups, etc.). The following Table contains the various types of institutions within civil society and their usual functions/activities' (Hye, 1998).

TABLE

Components of Civil Society and Their Function/Activities

Sl. No.	Type	Activities
01.	Media (Press, Radio, TV)	Public opinion forming, information dissemination, entertainment, etc.
02.	Trade Unions	Collective bargaining, awareness creation among members about their rights and public policies relating to them.
03.	Professional Bodies	Maintaining high standard of the profession, protecting the rights of the members, promotion of interests.
04.	Private Voluntary Organization	Advocacy of social change in particular areas, provision of limited public goods to their clientele (credit, primary health, adult literacy, etc.) manufacture and distribution of consumer goods to members of the public (milk processing, fisheries, textiles, etc.), protection of the rights of disadvantaged groups (e.g. minorities, tribal people, destitute women, street children, etc.).
05.	Sports and Cultural Bodies	Promotion of sports and culture through the activities of their members.
06.	Social Welfare Organizations	Promotion of social welfare of members or limited clientele in particular areas through voluntary services of various types.

Source : Hye, Hasnat Abdul (1998).

Components in Details

NGOs

Although NGOs have only recently emerged into the limelight of development initiatives, they are not a recent phenomenon. If one can accept that all non-governmental, non-profit organizations are properly classified as NGOs, one can safely argue that they are the earliest form of human organization. Long before there were governments, people organized themselves into groups for mutual protection and self-help (World Bank, 1991).

Robert Unger (1987) discussess the important role of farmer's organizations in maintaining the vitality of early agrarian-bureaucratic empires. Following the Meiji Restoration in Japan in 1868, farmer's organizations, especially seed-exchange societies, played a vital part in agricultural improvement. In 1937, 25 million farmers in Europe belonged to 25,000 rural cooperatives (Esman and Uphoff, 1984). In the Western democracies, NGOs helped, served as a counterweight to the excessive power by the state, and developed many services essential to community well-being and economic growth (Bratton, 1989 and Hall, 1987).

Trade Unions

Trade unions are an integral part of civil society now-a-days. Not long ago it was not accepted as well; Trade unionism had its origin in the critically low standard of living of the average nineteenth century worker and his family. This low level of wages were in part accounted for by the low level of national incomes and in part by the absence of collective bargaining on the part of the labourers.

The harsh conditions of life led the workers to the socio-political consciousness ranging from political movements, revolutionary socialism, which is today Marxism or Communism to Fabian Socialism, which tried to change the existing order gradually through existing political systems. Other outcomes of this long suffering of the workers are the unions which was to some extent a club providing some protection for these workers who were unemployed, disabled or retired and to some extent a bargaining agent.

Media

Around 20000 years B.C., cave painting, the earliest form of written communication was done and the inception of the history of communication began. The Early Civilizations, i.e., Sumerians, Assyrians, Babylonians and Persians and later the Chinese, Indians, Greeks, Romans — each of them advanced the cause of the advancement of communications. But it was in 1450, Johan

Gutenberg of Mainz, Germany introduced metal movable to Europe. Six years later he printed the famous Gutenberg Bible, ushering in the European age of printing. This introduction of the print media revolutionalized the whole concept of mass communication. This century has seen so many revolutionary changes in mass communication, i.e., intention of radio, television, expansion of the newspaper industry — that some would say that we live in an age of the media. It is now shaping the public opinion on every single issue of our existence — national as well as international.

Civil Society and Governance-Interlinkages

Role and Functions of Civil Society: Global Context

A strong civil society is considered one of the prerequisites for democracy. Diamond identifies at least six functions of civil society in shaping democracy:

a. Civil society is a reservoir of political, economic, cultural and moral resources to check the process of the state.

b. The diversity of civil society will ensure that the state is not held captive by a few groups.

c. The growth of associational life will supplement the work of political parties in stimulating political participation.

b. Civil Society will eventually stabilize the state because citizens will have a deeper stake in social order. Further, while civil society may multiply the demands of the state, it may also multiply the capacity of groups to improve their own welfare.

e. Civil society is a locus for recruiting new political leadership.

f. Civil society resists authoritarianism (Diamond, 1991).

Kumar (1993) mentions the role of the civil society in terms of a world context of rapidly shifting context of ideologies, where socialism is losing its ground and radicalism requires a deep rethinking.

> "the terms of civil society, its attractive combination of democratic pluralism with a continuing role for state regulation and guidance, make it appear hopeful to societies seeking to recover from the excesses of state socialism: at the same time it seems to offer help in

the refashioning of radical politics in those societies where socialism has lost whatever appeal it once possessed."

Globalization

As Roy (1995) puts it, "Globalization, which has now become the all pervasive catchword of the high priests of capitalism the world over, is, however, not really a new development. It is inherent in the organic logic of capitalism. All of its principal elements were succinctly enumerated a century and a half ago."

Besides, one can proceed with the observation that civil society, which has gained particular attention among the academicians and policy-makers during the last two decades in a specific global context, can play some pivotal roles which are particularly related to governance issues. The main ideas related to this issue can be proceeded as follows:

Dismantling of the Welfare State

The World of the '90s has clearly found that the state as provider of basic social services has tried to shrink as much as possible. The notion of small government has sent the signal to everyone that the state will not want to overcommit itself in welfare concerns. This shrinking of the government as well as all-too-familiar indifference of the market-driven private sector has led people to put their expectations in the Third Sector of the Civil Society that it will provide those services instead, and will, moreover, provide them more efficiently.

Decline of the Social Capital

A reasonable fear that runs across all the conscious citizens of the world is that the harsh conditions of impersonal market economy is breaking up of the bonds that have tied together a group of the people to each other, i.e. nationalism, religious bonds, common norms and discipline, throughout the last couple of centuries. The point is that there may not be much social capital left for keeping the nations intact. Here arises the need for the civil society to play its constructive part and allay the fear of decline of the much-needed social capital.

Globalization of Democracy

The Fall of the Berlin Wall — the Fall of Communism as a State Concept — heralded, as Sartori argues, an exaggerated euphoria of '*end ideology*' — and it has been linked to number of causes (Sartori, 1991). This description of the world accords a powerful causative role to civil society and to foreign policy-makers. It issues a clear set of prescriptions also. This change in the global context has led some Aid donors to think over the prospect of using the civil society components of the developing world to their own advantage. This has raised the value of the concept of civil society for them.

Collapse of Sovereignty

Civil society, some argue, reflects the change in the global aspect more than any other component of the society. One particular point about the civil society is that, extending it to its last logical conclusion, it turns into global civil society which by its definition doesn't bother about nation states. Some would argue that the rise of the civil society as well as the global civil society is the harbinger of destruction of the sovereignty of the state. Lipschutz argues that we are seeing a rise in global civil society because of a leaking away of sovereignty (Lipschutz, 1992).

Failure of Aid

An important factor in the promotion of civil society is the world-wide agreement that aid has failed, partly, because of the failure of states to which aid has been given; partly because of the failure of aid bureaucracies; and partly because of an over dependence on the free market theory which has failed miserably to deliver the goods. Thus civil society is getting hold of one of the strongholds of the traditional state: it is now funnelling off aid that was once the sole agency of the state.

Role of the NGOs

Though the NGOs are not historically a new phenomenon, it has become the most vibrant section of the civil society in recent decades. They have completed some excellent tasks especially in the developing countries where they have showed the path for innovations in poverty-reduction strategies, micro-finance initiatives, environmental protection, empowerment of women, and empowering the people who were thought to be politically and socially voiceless. As World Bank (1991) puts it, "The emergence of NGOs in the economy has been an important phenomenon of the 1980s. NGOs have been heralded as new agents with the capacity and commitment to make up for the shortcomings of the state and the market in reducing poverty. This trend has been reinforced by cumulative evidence from the developing world on positive contributions of NGO interventions and other grass-roots initiatives to poverty reduction. Donors of different sectors have thus begun to pay greater attention to the role, potential and limits of NGOs in the development process."

Examination of NGO potentials to assume more central roles in shaping national development agendas has led to the formulation of a simple scheme for classifying NGO strategies. It distinguishes between three generations of NGO strategies (Korten, 1988).

Generation one NGOs have been known for their roles in the delivery of welfare services. Second generation strategies aimed at strengthening local self-reliance. Through a third generation strategy, the NGOs seeks to achieve changes in the institutional and policy context consistent with greater local control and initiative. Third generation strategies require strategic management where the role of the existing institutions needs to be assessed in a dynamic context and optimum actions are to be planned with a long run view. The third generation strategies emphasised the participation of people in governance by its stress on changes in institutional and policy context consistent with a greater local control and initiative.

Role of the Mass Media

The central objective of the operations of the modern mass media mechanisms is to energise civil society. As C. Wright Mills pointed out years go, under the new dispensation the essence of the role of the media can be described as:

> "... there is a movement from widely scattered little powers and laissez-faire to concentrated powers and attempts at monopoly

control from powerful centres. And, in both centres, economic and opinion, power is partially hidden; they are centres of manipulation as well as of authority. ....

In the simple democratic society of primary politics, competition of opinions and ideas goes on between people holding various views which service their special interest and their reasoning. But in the mass society of media markets, competition goes on between the crowds of manipulators with the mass media on the one hand, and the people receiving their communication on the other. Answering back by the people is systematically unavailable" (Roy, 1995).

Civil Society and Governance: Bangladesh Context

Dilemma of Definition of State

The three basic features of good governance, namely accountability, ensuring law and order and transparency have not been ideally present in the activities of the post liberation governments. People's participation in governance has also been ignored. Bangladesh had been under military rule for a long period and constitution was suspended and parliament dissolved during the periods. Even during civil rules, the activities of the governments and the parliament left a lot to be desired (Rahman and Mustafa, 1995).

The basic problem of governance in our country has been due to the absence of certain crucial institutions. The most important of those was till recently the practice of smooth transfer of power Much of the political history of the country has been shaped around it and more often than not power transfer has been associated with violent political crises. The politicians were of course, much concerned with this issue and some progress has been made in ensuring fair election after introduction of the concept of care taker government and strengthening of the Election Commission. The concept of democracy among the political leaders remain confined to 'fair elections' only. Good governance is not yet a notable concern among them. Had this been the major concern of them, the quality of political culture would have been much more improved. The lack of respect for the opponents, the myopic vision for scoring points over others on petty issues and absence of effective consensus on issues related to economic and other reforms can explain to a great extent for the poor quality of governance in Bangladesh.

The definition of the state itself has gone through some drastic changes in the recent decades. One may have a fair account of this redefinition of the state in a recent Paper (Hye, 1998). One can follow this line of arguments as follows,

> Traditionally State has been defined as composed of only three official components such as Parliament, Judiciary and Executive Government whereas the local government bodies, private sector and the civil society have been considered as the external components of the state mechanism. Local bodies, Private Sector and Civil society, on their part, either existed in their inchoate conditions or were considered to be simply non-existent at that stage. The local governemnt bodies were used as mere peripheral subsidiaries of the government branch lacking any sort of self-control. Despite some progress in revamping local government bodies, there is still enough room to be dissatisfied with the pace and sequencing of the reforms in this sub-sector which remain far off the desired mark. But the point is that the relative position of the different organs of the state changes with the passage of time and as a dependent variable of different crosscutting factors, the development of the 'informal' organs of the state gains impetus when the state through its formal organs — Parliament, Judiciary and Executive Government encourages the private sector and the civil society to participate in governance. This process gives rise to new 'organs' of the state in terms of their social acceptance, autonomy and the resources which calls for a redefinition of the state itself. So a redefined governance arises in place of the traditional governance either because of deliberate politics pursued by the state in an evolutionary way or through an increasingly vibrant private sector and an expanding civil society including NGOs and other agencies as well (Hye, 1998).

The State is not now-a-days a *State* in the traditional definition of the term — it is increasingly going to be considered to be a part of the global village. Therefore, the traditional States have had to concede some of its power to the extra-state or subsidiary-state components as a compromise in order to keep the ever-growing civil society content. Again, some specific local events or flow of events or particular strengths of some of the components of the civil society may take some of the power or authority away from the traditional state. As, for instance, the spectacular success of the NGOs in Bangladesh in addressing poverty issue of the Bangladeshi rural community has compelled the successive governments of the recent past to negotiate with them and accept them as legitimate development partners.

Given the history of the governments, their composition, the important pressure groups and the overall backwardness of the country, it is evident that a top-down approach for favourable changes towards good governance may not be initiated by the government or the major political parties in the foreseeable future. The task, therefore, falls on the people again.

Role of NGOs

Currently, NGOs play marginal roles in policy formulation and only very recently they have become more active in advocating special needs of the disadvantaged. Their emphasis on empowerment of women is quite well taken. However, they have not yet been able to make this a central element of their advocacy efforts. The civil society, though gradually forging links with the NGOs, is still either suspicious or indifferent to the NGO initiatives on empowerment of women, or for that matter the very poor (Rahman, 1995).

The success of a strategy on good governance is dependent on how best or how fast the NGOs can remove this gap in mutual trust and create a stronger socio-cultural base for a more integrated community action.

NGOs concentrated their activities over the last two decades in the following areas: (i) Establishment of effective democratic process at the grassroots; (ii) Poverty alleviation; (iii) Women's rights; (iv) Education; (v) Health and family planning; (vi) Environment (Task Force Report, 1991).

Role of Trade Unions

In the urban areas, an important pressure group was the trade unions. They exerted significantly more influence than their numbers suggested. Concentration of workers at urban centres allowed them this power. Perhaps the only attempt to encourage participation under the Fourth Five Year Plan (FFYP) was foiled ironically by the participants themselves. Trade Unions were asked to take part in management in the public sector enterprises. This necessitated the determination of the structure and the level of wages through negotiations between the workers representatives, state enterprises and the government at the national level. This ruled out collective bargaining as the norm of negotiations and trade union membership outside labour leaders. The actual workers did not like this plan and had no ways to express their grievances adequately (Rahman, 1995). In subsequent years the management of public sector enterprises faltered and despite strong trade union movement the fate of the ordinary labourers has been perhaps sealed for ever. The move for speedy privatization with 'golden handshakes' has not seen much success and this particular governance failure may lead to many other fallouts in subsequent years.

Role of Media

The media is playing an important role in the Bangladesh context as related to public opinion formation and information dissemination though its role has been seriously restricted by the constraints of low literacy and low purchasing powers of the common people. The legal environment for free press is quite sound and the barrier imposed by earlier governments on it has been removed. In the new context, some newspapers have been regularly taking up governance issues with the policy makers. In fact, some have gone further and organized members of civil society to sit in round tables to discuss diverse policy issues including those which mean a lot in terms of improving the quality of life for the citizens. A sample newspaper scanning will illuminate that most of the news items published are linked directly or indirectly with the governance agenda. For bad or worse, it is not possible for anyone concerned with governance to ignore the press and undermine its role in governance.

The Radio and the National Television are heavily government controlled and for that reason they can not play their respective roles in good governance. However, some innovations have been attempted in terms of programmes like *Obhimat* ('opinions'), and development dialogue in furthering the cause of good governance.

Role of Cultural Organizations

Different cultural organizations have played a major part in forming public opinions about governance issues. The cultural organizations, though their commitment is perceived to be towards art or entertainment, are highly conscious of the management of the state issue, i.e. governance issue, through their awareness of and advocacy for redressing the issues of social ills and mismanagement in the state organs.

Role of Other Bodies of Civil Society

Different professional bodies, though primarily concerned with their own professional requirements and efficiency, have contributed to the cause of civil society enormously. The Lawyers' organizations, the Journalists associations, the doctors associations and many other professional groups have contributed to the cause of civil society as an good governance issue. The Human Rights Associations, the Women's Organizations have all played their respective parts in the development of civil society and promotion of good governance.

Conclusion

The above review brings into focus diverse perceptions of different stakeholders who actually matter about governance and civil society. However, the perception of the ordinary people, the primary stakeholders in good governance is missing here. The concepts are still emerging and it is too early to arrive at a conclusive statement on both of these terms. But the examination clearly reveals that good governance as the ultimate objective can only be ensured in a healthy civil society composed of many elements practicing democratic norms. A positive political culture with sincere respect for the opponents can be a great boon in arriving at national and local consensus on major developmental issues including good governance. Despite a well written constitution, an old democratic political legacy, myriads of organized groups, pluralistic attitude among citizens, desirable political culture is still missing in Bangladesh. This single limitation can explain to a great extent the lack of emergence of good governance in Bangladesh despite the presence of a number of necessary factors which have been helping in the gradual strengthening of civil society. The picture is, of course, not all that bleak. Bangladesh has already come out of the famine syndrome; per capita income has doubled over the two decades or so, food security is round the corner, millions of women are now part of organized groups enjoying micro-credit and social development services and elections are held regularly without much rigging here. These are indeed brighter aspects of Bangladesh. Hopefully, they will soon overwhelm the darker ones and a fuller canvass of good governance will then become visible to most of us.

References

Akash, M.M. "Governance and Development", Chapter 2, in Sobhan, R., ed., "Crisis in Governance A Review of Bangladesh's Development 1997", University Press Limited, Dhaka, 1998.

Blaney, David L. and Pasha, Mustapha Kamal. "Civil Society and Democracy in the Third World: Ambiguities and Historical Possibilities," in *Studies in Comparative International Development*. Volume 28, Number 1 (Spring 1998), pp.3-24.

Bratton, Michael, 1998. "Poverty, Organization and Policy: Towards a Voice for Africa's Rural Poor", Paper prepared for a colloquium on the Changing Nature of Third World Poverty: A Policy Perspective, sponsored by the Centre for the Advanced Study of International Development, Michigan State University, Lansing, March 13-15.

Bratton, Michael. "Civil Society and Political Transitions in Africa," in J.W. Harbeson et al. (editors). *Civil Society and the State in Africa*. Boulder and London: Lynne Rienner. 1994, pp.51-81.

Diamond, Larry (editor). *The Democratic Revolution: Struggles for Freedom and Pluralism in the Developing World*. Perspectives on Freedom No.12, Freedom House, 1991.

Easton, D. and Guddat, Kurt H. (ed.). "Quoted by Marx, Writings of the Young Marx and Philosophy and Society," Anchor Book, New York, 1967, p.152, emphasis in the original.

Esman, Milton J. and Uphoff, Norman T. *Local Organizations: Intermediaries in Rural Development*. Ithaca, Cornell University Press. 1984.

Foley, Michael W. and Edwards Bob. *The Paradox of Civil Society*. Journal of Democracy 7.3 (1996, 38-52, Webpage).

Gellner, Ernest. "Civil Society in Historical Context," *International Social Science Journal*, Volume 43, August 1991, pp.495-510.

Gramsci, Antonio. "Selections from Prison Note Books", edited and translated by Q. Hoare and G.N. Smith, International Publishers, New York, 1973, p.12.

Guhathakurta. M. and Karim, S. "Perceptions of Governance by Bilateral and Multilateral Donors", Chapter 4, in Sobhan, R., ed., "Crisis in Governance — A Review of Bangladesh's Development 1997", University Press Limited, Dhaka, 1998.

Hansen, Gary. *Constituencies for Reform: Strategic Approaches for Donor-Supported Civic Advocacy Programmes*. USAID Programme and Operations Assessment Report No.12, Centre for Development Information and Evaluation, Washington, February 1996.

Hutchful, Eboe. "The Civil Society Debate in Africa," in *International Journal*, Volume 51, Winter 1995-96.

Hye, Hasnat Abdul. "Good Governance" Concept Paper, the International Conference on Good Governance, jointly organized by Local Government Division, Ministry of LGRD and Co-operatives, Government of Bangladesh and United Nations Development Programme, Dhaka, August 4-6, 1998.

Korten, David. *Getting to the 21st Century: Voluntary Action and the Global Agenda*. West Hartford, CT: Kunarian Press, 1990.

Kumar, Krishnan. "Civil Society: an Inquiry into the Usefulness of an Historical Term", in *British Journal of Sociology*, Volume 44, Number 3, September 1993, pp.375-395.

Lipschutz, Ronnie D. "Reconstructuring World Politics: The Emergence of Global Civil Society", in *Millennium*, Volume 21, Number 3, 1992, pp.389-420.

Lipsey, Richard G. *An introduction of Positive Economics*. English Language Book Society and Weidenfeld and Nicolson, 1974.

Mills, C. Wright. *Power, Politics and People*. Ballantine Books, New York, p.581, quoted in Roy, Ajit (1995).

Moore, Richard J. *Governance and Development: A Progress Report for the LAC Region*. LATPS Occasional Paper Series, 1993.

Moore, Mick (1993). "Declining to Learn from the East? The World Bank on 'Governance and Development'". *The Journal of the Institute of Development Studies*. Vol.24, No.1. January 1993.

Progress Publishers. "The German Ideology". This is a particular version, see also Marx and Engles. Moscow. 1964. p.48.

Putnam, D, Robert (1993). *Making Democracy Work*, Princeton University Press, Princeton, New Jersey.

Putnam, Robert with Robert Leonardi and Rafaella Y. Nanetti. *Making Democracy Work: Civic Traditions in Modern Italy*. Princeton: Princeton UP, 1993.

Rahman, Atiur and Mustafa, Shoumi. *Governance and Participation: The NGO Experience in Bangladesh*. Shamunnay Working Paper # 9, January 1995.

Roy, Ajit. *Civil Society and Nation State in Contest of Globalization*. Economic and Political Weekly, Vol.XXX, No.31 and 32, August 5-12, 1995.

Sandman, Peter M.; Rubin, David M. and Sachsman, David B. *Media, an Introductory Analysis of American Mass Communication*. Prentice Hall Inc. Englewood Chiffs, N.P. 1972.

Sartori, Giovanni. "Rethinking Democracy: Bad Polity and Bad Politics", an *International Social Science Journal*, Volume 43, August 1991, pp.437-450.

Sethi, Harsh, "Action Groups in the New Politics", in Ponna Wignaraja (editor), *New Social Movements in the South: Empowering the People*, London and New Jersey: Zed Books, 1993.

Sobhan, R., edited. Centre for Policy Dialogue, "Crisis in Governance — A Review of Bangladesh's Development 1997", University Press Limited, 1998.

Sobhan, R., edited. Centre for Policy Dialogue, "Towards a Theory of Governance and Development — Learning from East Asia, University Press Limited, 1998.

The North-South Institute — Civil Society Research Project, "Civil Society and the Aid Industry", Draft Working Paper. "Civil Society: The Development Solution?" (Last Modified: April, 1998): Web page, Forthcoming in October 1998 in Book Form by Earthscan (UK).

The Report of Commission on Global Governance. *Our Global Neighbourhood*. 1998, Webpage.

UNDP. *UNDP and Civil Society*. New York: UNDP, 1993.

Unger, R.M. *Plasticity into Power: Comparative-Historical Studies on the Institutional Conductions of Economic and Military Success*. Cambridge: Cambridge University Press, 1987.

Uphoff, Norman (1987). "Drawing a Social Energy in Project Implementation: A learning Process Experience in Sri Lanka", paper presented at the American Society for Public Administration meeting, Boston, March.

White, Gordon. "Civil Society, Democratization and Development (1): Clearing the Analytical Ground", in *Democratization*, Volume 1, Number 3, Autumn 1994, pp.375-390.

Wood, Ellen Meiksins. "The Uses and Abuses of Civil Society", in R. Milliband, L. Panitch and J. Sanille (editors). *The Socialist Register*. London: Merlin Press, 1990, pp.60-84.

World Bank. "Non-governmental Organizations and the World Bank", edited by Samuel Paul and Arturo Isreal, Washington, D.C., 1991.

World Bank. *Government that Works, Reforming the Public Sector: Bangladesh*, University Press Limited, 1996.

Writings of Young Marx, pp.238-39, quoted in Roy (1995).

CIVIL SOCIETY AND GOOD GOVERNANCE: RELEVANCE FOR BANGLADESH

Jeffrey E. Key

This paper broadly addresses the theme "civil society and good governance." The task is threefold: to define civil society, review its historical evolution, and explain its relevance to Bangladesh; to explore the theoretical relationship between civil society and governance; and to analyze the role of civil society in relation to the global transformation of relations between the state, society, and private sector.

Civil Society and Its Prospects in Bangladesh

John A. Hall noted that civil society is complicated because it is both a social value and a set of institutions (Hall, 1995). That distinction is important. While countries rightly seek to promote the growth of civil society, one cannot assume that a civil society exists in some nascent form everywhere. Indeed, the long list of places around the world where upheaval and strife seem intractable suggests that civil society is a scarce commodity in the late-20th century. Civil society should not be taken for granted.

Defining Civil Society

Mahmood Monshipouri's expansive definition provides a useful starting point for discussing civil society:

> In general, civil society is thought to provide a buffer between state and citizens: it counterbalances the power of the state by promoting

> various societal interests *vis-à-vis* the ruling elite. Thus conceived, civil society includes professional associations, guilds, syndicates, labour unions, federations, political parties, and other non-governmental groups. Some scholars even include "informal politics" as a component of civil society, arguing that clans, tribes, and religious groups can be considered part of the definition (Monshipouri, 1997).

Monshipouri's definition is problematic on two levels. It is misguided in posing civil society against the state, thereby establishing it as a threat to be suppressed and precluding the possibility for a positive, dynamic partnership in meeting human needs. It should not be difficult to concur with Hall's admonition that it is necessary to "go beyond the traditional definition of civil society as the self-organization of strong and autonomous groups that balance the state" (Hall, 1995).

Monshipouri's definition is also so broad as to make it impossible to operationalize. Such a broad rendering of the term makes virtually any social collective which is not part of the state an element of civil society. A much narrow construction is needed. Borrowing again from Hall, "membership of autonomous groups needs to be both voluntary and overlapping if society is to become civil." While some religious and ethnic associations may be included within civil society even though they are naturally exclusive, it is problematic whether political parties and economic interests such as labour unions and manufacturers, associations should be included. Such narrowly self-interested groups, while essential elements of a pluralistic democracy and a vibrant economy, may not be voluntary and do not allow for overlapping membership.

Though civil society is distinct from the political system, it is constantly interacting with government on matters both major (e.g. pressurizing officials on policy matters) and mundane (e.g. registration of a society). Civil society promotes fuller participation in public life in two ways. Most importantly, civil society is predicated on the notion that every individual has inherent rights and worth within the larger society. Secondly, it reinforces the principle that individuals can gain power by joining together with like-minded persons. This view combines Hall's normative and institutional dimensions. The notion of civil society to which I subscribe, is thus akin to those "associations" identified by Alexis De Tocqueville in his classic work 'Democracy in America'. Like Tocqueville, I am only concerned here with "those associations in civil life which have no political object" (Mayer, 1988). This deeper meaning of civil society and its relationship to democracy must be understood. According to Tocqueville:

> In democratic countries knowledge of how to combine is the mother of all other forms of knowledge; on its progress depends that of all the others. Among laws controlling human societies there is one more precise and clearer, it seems to me, than all the others. If men are to remain civilized or to become civilized, the art of association must develop and improve among them ... (Mayer, 1988)

Such associations, he argues, prepare people for democracy. "Civil associations," he notes, "pave the way for political ones." Civil society is thus logically prior to democracy; while there can be civil society with no democracy (as in Eastern Europe before 1990), there can be no democracy without civil society. Likewise, Monshipouri observed that while civil society is not singly a sufficient condition for democracy, it is necessary for its durability.

Before discussing the evolution of civil society, a potential criticism of the approach being taken must be addressed. Most glaringly, Tocquville's analysis was based on early 19th century America. This is hardly a suitable model for the rest of the world given that slavery was still practiced in America at that time. However, the later work of quintessential civil society groups, abolitionists in the early to mid-19th century and civil rights organizations in the mid-20th century, helped bring African-Americans into the economic, social, and political mainstream. These groups were motivated by their commitment to building a more inclusive country. Inclusion of marginalized groups is a dominant theme in the civil society literature. Tolerance for difference is a corollary to inclusion. In the context of Bangladesh, for example, the Chittagong Hill Tracts settlement might be considered a triumph of civil society.

Despite the positive picture of civil society being offered, no grand claims are being made herein. Encouraging civil society will not transform Bangladesh or any other country into a model democracy. Beyond a broad commitment to social inclusion and tolerance, there is no predetermined set of values for civil society nor does it require consensus. No single group has a special claim on virtue and honest contention between groups on important issues is to be expected. Accordingly, "Civil society is thus a complex balance of consensus and conflict, the valuation of as much difference as is compatible with the bare minimum of consensus necessary for settled existence" (Hall, 1995).

Evolution of Civil Society

Civil society was originally a European phenomenon. The earliest discernible development of civil society was associated with complex social and economic forces at work in the 18th century as power devolved from monarchs to popular assemblies. The rapid increase in literacy at that time granted greater access to what the German philosopher Jurgen Habermas labelled "the public sphere" (Habermas, 1989). In particular, Habermas saw the rise of fraternal bodies which observed equality among members and practiced regular internal self-governance as a harbinger of the spread of this sphere (Jacob, 1991).

Changing social, economic and political conditions have compelled individuals to form organizations of one sort or another to meet their needs. This evolution of civil society reflects increasing levels of activism and demands on government. Commonly cited examples of civil society organizations include social welfare bodies, community groups, and interest groups.

Social welfare organizations are often the earliest manifestations of civil society. In the West, these sprang up to help alleviate the human suffering associated with industrialization and urbanization before the welfare state came into being. Motivated largely by religious sentiment, such groups made few demands on the state beyond calls to help curb the vices which attracted increasing numbers of the urban poor. The social transformation accompanying more advanced economic development, notably the rapid expansion of the middle class, gave rise to still other forms of civil society organization. Growing demand for government services such as public education in the late-19th and early-20th centuries prompted an expansion of the state downward toward the people. Local government became increasingly important as the primary providers of these services. The civil society analog to this growth of local government was the formation of community organization.* Limited in both size and programme, such groups sought more and improved services for their community. Politically, they could be bothersome but not threatening. Often with a local notable as their patron, community groups were hardly revolutionary. The impact of technological revolution on transportation and communication in the 20th century gave people new-found mobility of body and mind which prompted still further innovation in civil society. No longer bound by time and distance, widely dispersed persons with shared interests in larger issues began to join together. Essentially non-ideological, interest groups pursued narrow agendas and sought to influence policies touching their particular issue. Government was also becoming more open by extending the franchise. Modern interest group politics emerged as politicians began actively soliciting the support of such groups as a means of bolstering their electoral fortunes.

Civil society and NGOs in Bangladesh

In discussing the evolution of civil society in the context of Bangladesh, several realities stand out. Most importantly, in the relatively young countries of the developing world, the evolution of civil society lags behind state building and economic development. Though the lives of citizens are dramatically transformed, there is insufficient time for the relationship between the "new" state and "old" people to mature. Artificial means are employed in an attempt to close this gap. The "non-profit" or "non-governmental" organization (NGO) model borrowed from the advanced industrial countries of the West is an attempt to accelerate the growth of civil society. This approach may not work.

---

* Community is used here to refer to people living in close proximity to one another as in a neighbourhood in a city or a village in a rural area.

Civil society organizations in Bangladesh have increasingly taken the form of NGOs. They have been active in Bangladesh since independence and have grown in size and number in response to new needs and a massive increase in donor funding.[1] The lessons and limits of the multiple relief, community development, and social mobilization approaches became apparent in the 1980s at the same time that donors began searching for an alternative to channelling development assistance through government agencies. This confluence of forces shaped the current stage in NGO development in Bangladesh. With donors now willing to underwrite the direct provision of services to the poor, NGOs in Bangladesh scrambled to develop such programmes. Some NGOs have undergone a startling ideological re-orientation in order to gain access to donor funds.[2]

Today, there are thousands of organizations registered under various statutes governing NGOs. Registration with the NGO Affairs Bureau to receive foreign funds increased dramatically between 1981 and 1985 as donors interest in NGOs grew and an even larger increase occurred after the return to democracy in 1991.[3] Despite the growing numbers, the NGO landscape is dominated by a few very large organizations. Direct donor funding caused this concentration of power and resources as donor representatives looked for NGOs with the "capacity" to absorb ever larger sums.[4] Through 1996, thirty NGOs had received around 80 per cent of all donor aid to NGOs, of which 60 per cent went to only eight (Sobhan). These dominant NGOs, referred to by descriptive names such as the "Big 8" or "G 7" are some of the most powerful institutions in Bangladesh. Their leaders are nationally, even internationally, known figures.[5] They constitute an NGO elite.

The increase in direct donor funding and subsequent expansion of the NGO sector have placed such organizations under increased scrutiny. Their openness and accountability, relations with donors, and the efficacy of their programmes have been questioned. Several realities emerge from this criticism. Most Bangladeshi NGOs are controlled by one person who is not accountable to an independent group of trustees (Shelley). To ensure a steady flow of funds, NGOs initiate new programmes to keep up with changing donor priorities.

The resulting competition for funds has bred cynicism (Choudhury, 1995). Recent signs that partisan political rancor has spread to the NGO community have deepened this skepticism. Though they have done much good and will do more, NGOs can no longer be seen as a panacea for the country's problems.

This leads us to the question of the role of NGOs in civil society. Babar Sobhan's study of NGO financing in Bangladesh raised this issue and concluded that a strong NGO sector is not necessarily synonymous with a strong civil society (Sobhan). I agree with this assessment. To the extent that many NGOs operate primarily as contractors executing donor programmes, their autonomy is reduced and their contribution to civil society is diminished. The explosion of human rights NGOs in the 1990s is an example.[6] It is impossible to determine whether their growth is a by-product of democratization or merely a cynical response to donor initiatives and new funding being made available for such activities. Such troubling questions about the moral foundations of the very organizations which should be guiding civil society clouds its future. Though some argue that there has been a globalization of civil society which mirrors the globalization of economic and social forces, Bangladesh cannot have a civil society composed largely of organizations dependent upon foreign funds and inspiration.

NGO involvement in politics is equally problematic because close affiliation with a party also undercuts their autonomy. NGOs rightly advocate policies within areas of their concern. At times, they may be required to take a costly public stand in order to maintain their moral authority. However, involvement in partisan struggles requires sacrificing the latitude necessary to be an effective advocate in the future. Indeed, democracy assumes periodic turnovers in power which make conspicuous partisanship unwise. Thus, NGOs' inclusion in civil society necessitates that they be circumspect in dealing with donors and politicians alike. Within this ideal framework, NGOs remain free to criticize (or cooperate with) donors and the government of the day in support of their agenda.

To restate the point; Bangladesh needs NGOs now and in the future. Nevertheless, hope for expanding civil society lies elsewhere.

Prospects for Civil Society

Having offered a critique of the current state of civil society in Bangladesh, it is necessary to identify the reasons to be optimistic about the prospects for the expansion of an authentic, indigenous civil society.

The Bangla language movement in Pakistan times laid a foundation for the further development of civil society after independence. In seeking to secure Bengalis their linguistic rights and thus allowing them to be fully included within Pakistan, the movement established the principle that popular sentiments as expressed by and through organizations should be acknowledged by those who govern. This tradition has deeper roots in Bengali history and culture.* The fact that the independence movement drew inspiration from the sacrifices of the language activists reinforces the point made earlier that civil society promotes democracy.

Another dimension to civil society worth mentioning is the mass media.

An independent mass media is critical to civil society because it serves as a mechanism for communication among like-minded person:

> In a democracy an association cannot be powerful unless it is numerous. Those composing it must therefore be spread over a wide area, and each of them is anchored to the place in which he lives by the modesty of his fortune and a crowd of small necessary cares. They need some means of talking every day without seeing one another and of acting together without meeting. So hardly any democratic association can carry on without a newspaper. (Mayer, 1988)

The press plays a dynamic role in the civic affairs of Bangladesh and the citizenry has access to news from multiple sources. In particular, the large number of competing newspapers and magazines bodes well for civil society here. Moreover, though newspapers were the sole form of mass media in Tocqueville's early-19th century America, the point he makes is equally applicable to modern forms such as radio, television, and most recently, the

---

* Limited space herein and the author's inadequate knowledge of Bengali culture and history do not permit this important point to be explored future. It is certainly worthy of a major research project.

internet. If Tocqueville were observing Bangladesh today, he would likely comment on the dramatic impact Grameen Phone is having in the rural areas as well as the cyber cafes around Dhaka.

Civil Society and Governance

A strong, vibrant civil society is essential for good governance. As suggested earlier, participation in civil society helps prepare citizens to fulfil their civic obligations as well as to exercise their rights. It also facilitates two-way communication between the state and the people. Commentators over the centuries have all noted the vital importance of rulers knowing the condition of their subjects.* Meeting with civil society groups is the most efficient way for public officials to gather such information as well as to explain particular government actions. Though such dialogue is often contentious, it builds trust and represents an investment in the relationship between the government and the governed.

Civil society should not be viewed as a "threat" to the state. This perception is a consequence of the popularization of the term during the movements against communist governments in Eastern Europe nearly a decade ago.** At that time, civil society indeed reasserted itself vigorously in order to reclaim its space in the public sphere. This action was not representative of normal relations between civil society and the state. Rather, it was a natural reaction to the unnatural extension of those particular states' control into the associational life of their citizens. Virtually all private groups in the former Eastern Bloc were either formally affiliated with ruling communist parties or needed party approval to operate. Tocqueville warned of the consequences of such a policy:

> A government, by itself, is equally incapable of refreshing the circulation of feelings among a great people, as it is of controlling

---

* For example, medieval Islamic writers like Nizam ul-Mulk Tusi and Kai Ka'us Iskander stressed the importance of such information.

** Other examples from around the world can be found but the dynamics rarely capture the role of civil society so clearly. The fall of Marcos is the Philippines is one such case. Though the importance of "people power" was indisputable, the events were more akin to a mass movement than an organized mobilization of forces by various groups.

> every industrial undertaking. Once it leaves the sphere of politics to launch out on this new track, it will, without intending this, exercise an intolerable tyranny. For a government can only dictate precise rules. It imposes the sentiments and ideas which it favours, and it is never easy to tell the difference between its advice and its commands. (Mayer, 1988)

Rebellion spread from a few organizations that the state did not control such as churches, environmental groups and, in Poland, the Solidarity labour union.* The collapse of those regimes was proof of the power of civil society when roused.

Just as civil society is not a perpetual challenge to the state, it can never be a substitute for the state. With the possible exception of a few cases where NGOs and other civil society organizations helped to maintain refugee populations until legitimate civil authority was restored, there are no cases of civil society governance.** It would be naive to view civil society as a surrogate or substitute for the state (Monshipouri, 1995).

If civil society is neither a threat or a potential substitute for the state, what then is the relationship between the two? While allowing for periodic challenges to state authority from elements of civil society, the relationship is best understood as a positive, symbiotic one. Civil society is more likely to prosper within an effective state and weak states can become stronger by allowing "pluralism in associational life" (Monshipouri, 1995). The basis for this mutually beneficial relationship is straightforward; civil society is able to succeed where government cannot in certain crucial matters but there are many tasks which are properly governmental undertakings. Tocqueville wrote eloquently of how only civil society can improve the character of citizens:

> The morals and intelligence of a democratic people would be in as much danger as its commerce and industry if ever a government wholly usurped the place of private associations. Feelings and ideas are renewed, the heart enlarged, and the understanding developed

---

* Some were thought to be sufficiently infiltrated by state agents to be controlled while others were simply thought to be non-threatening.

** The millions of Afghan refugees during the Soviet occupation were largely "governed" by non-statal entities.

> only by the reciprocal action of men, one upon another. I have shown how these influences are reduced almost to nothing in democratic countries; they must therefore be artificially created, and only associations can do that. (Mayer, 1988)

On the other hand, only the state can enact and enforce laws to preserve general order, support a currency, provide for national defense, or build and maintain a country's infrastructure.

The relationship between civil society and the state is always in delicate balance. To secure the benefits of a strong civil society, those who govern must be careful not to regulate private associations too closely. In particular, policies designed to shape civil society to fit the wishes of the state will stifle the formation of associations generally and cause the public to be suspicious of those which do form. Specifically, banning or harassing groups concerned with important matters such as human rights has an especially negative impact on civil society.

Borrowing again from Tocqueville:

> When citizens had the faculty and habit of associating for everything, they will freely associate for little purposes as well as great. But if they are only allowed to associate for trivial purposes, they will have neither the will not the power to do so. (Mayer, 1988)

Authoritarian politics are especially detrimental to civil society. Where political associations are forbidden, civil society groups will be "few, feebly conceived, and unskilfully managed."

Several observations about the special place of mass media and human rights in the civil society-governance also merit mention. The importance of the mass media in supporting civil society was stressed earlier in this paper. The communications revolution made possible by technology raises important regulatory issues for governments. Care must be taken in formulating communications policy to avoid choking off the broad exchange of ideas essential to a vibrant civil society. With the exception of pornography and other socially harmful materials, attempts to regulate media content deserve special scrutiny by the guardians of civil society. Censorship invariably leads to more stifling self-censorship and civil society is done irreparable harm in the process. However, there are different models for a free press within a democracy. The British press is somewhat more restricted while in the US it is unfettered.*

Finally, the expansion of civil society is a key component of political liberalization which promotes such civil rights as freedom from arbitrary arrest, torture, degrading punishment; freedom of opinion, speech, faith, and assembly; and the right to life, security, and the ownership of property (Monshipouri, 1995). Enshrining these fundamentals rights in law and safeguarding them in the higher and lower courts, places of detention, and most importantly, where people live their daily lives, will nurture civil society.

Civil Society and Political, Economic and Social Change

Around the world, state interest and sovereign authority are being limited on normative and moral grounds while civil society expands simultaneously. Countries are moving toward a more positive sovereignty, in which the state's role is tied to its legitimacy and capacity to provide security, collective good, and social justice. Legitimacy is especially important to what Robert Jackman labelled "national political capacity" (Jackman, 1993). Within this model, the exercise of force represents a failure of state power. The focus on legitimacy is understandable given that many recently formed states suffer form what Max Weber labelled the "liability of newness." In young countries, governmental and political processes are much less routinized and there is correspondingly greater temptation to resort to force rather than to resolve conflicts peacefully. Well founded states strive to avoid conflicts altogether by working with and through civil society organizations. This new thinking should not be seen as a shift in power from the state to civil society but rather as the natural evolution of the relationship between those who govern and those who are governed. Couched in positive terms, governments are learning to govern better through heeding the popular voice and citizens are learning to be better citizens through exposure to the regular rules and disciplined practices of associations of civil society.

---

* Interestingly, British democracy has not suffered from these limitations but there has been considerable reflection recently in the US about the negative effects of journalistic excess there.

Beyond advancing the civic maturity of the citizenry, the expansion of civil society benefits governments in other important ways. Over time, even the state's security situation would be improved. Domestic considerations are increasingly replacing foreign threats as the primary concern of governments, creating what has been labelled the "Third World security predicament (Ayoob, 1995). One valuable lesson learned in the last decade is that suppression of civil society broadens the appeal of populist and extremist groups (Monshipouri, 1995). A more benign posture toward civil society diminishes the appeal of violent fringe groups.

The private sector has a large stake in the expansion of civil society because civil order fosters economic growth. Stated in simple business terms, fewer hartals mean fewer disruptions in production and delivery schedules and fewer lost contracts. Less unrest also translates into increased foreign investment. The philosopher Francis Fukuyama made this connection between a healthy civil society and prosperity (Fukuyama, 1995). He argued that spread of groups based on trust and obligation rather than kinship or legal contracts promote prosperity.

The synergies arising out of the emerging relations between the state, private sector, and civil society must be put to practical use. Creative solutions must be found.

Upward redistribution of the benefits of economic liberalization and downward distribution of the costs of structural adjustment further alienate those on the bottom of the socio-economic pyramid. This alienation leads to unrest which makes economic expansion unsustainable. Pakistan is arguably a relevant case. Though increasingly political openness and an expanding civil society slow such reforms, as has occurred in Russia, they also help to absorb the social and political backlash. The practical implications for governments are apparent," ... providing effective protection for the lower classes — that is, constructing social welfare systems — is an appropriate function of government" (Monshipouri, 1995). Since provision of social services is an Olympian undertaking in Bangladesh, the state must mobilize civil society to the task. NGOs will certainly continue to be helpful partners as in the past but their limited efforts do not nearly cover the state's shortfall. Tapping still more powerful reserves will be critical. Religious groups and the business community deserve special consideration.

Islam and Civil Society

Islam has important implications for civil society. Contrary to the views of its detractors, Islam is an inclusive faith which prescribes almsgiving and reinforces community.* Moreover, there is great diversity of opinion among Islamists and there is no reason to assume that their views are collectively inimical to civil society. Such groups have an active role to play in civil society because religious values are often most clearly at odds with those espoused by states. In the United States and elsewhere, there is growing reflection on the excessive secularization of public life in the modern world. The systematic exclusion of religious values from public discourse in the name of secularism has created a spiritual vacuum which is contributing to a host of social ills. Religious activists, scholars, and public officials alike are struggling to find active ways to accommodate religious sentiments in public life. Notably, the contributions of social programmes operated by religious groups are now being lauded for being cheaper, more effective alternatives to government programmes.** Of these, faith-based education, drug treatment, and job training schemes are frequently cited as being demonstrably more effective than similar government efforts. Marvin Olasky is the best known scholarly proponent of government support for welfare programmes run by religious groups (Olasky, 1992). Olasky argues that they succeed because they are run by people who have "a warm heart and a hard head." This growing awareness of the power of religious conviction to transform social conditions is a phenomenon which exists across cultures.***

---

*For example, the constitution of Medina expressly included Christian and Jews.

**This argument provided the justification for the inclusion of the Charitable Choice Provision in the Welfare Reform Act, 1996 in the US. This provision permitted government funding for private sectarian institutions to provide various social services.

***For example, Sri Mulyati of McGill University cites the success of Islamist education and drug treatment in Indonesia in "Sufism in Indonesia: The Qadirriyah wa Naqshbandiyyah" a paper presented at the Southwest. Conference of Asian Studies, San Antonio, Texas,

Not surprisingly, Robert Wuthnow afforded religion "special significance" in his pioneering study, Between States and Markets: The Voluntary Sector in Comparative Perspective (Wuthnow, 1995). The mosque-based micro-credit and primary education programmes initiated by the Government of Bangladesh earlier this year should be studied closely.

Private Sector's Role

The private sector has an important contribution to make as well. If businesses are to be the primary beneficiaries of the economic liberalization accompanying structural adjustment, they should be expected to underwrite some portion of the costs of the programmes which will be necessary to ease the accompanying suffering inflicted upon the lower classes. This will require companies to rethink their ways of doing business and to incorporate "socially conscious" practices into their strategic plans. Examples of socially conscious business practise include making literacy and other life skills training available to unskilled workers, donating goods and services or selling them at cost to NGOs, and encouraging voluntarism by management. Though these ideas initially seem wildly idealistic and wholly unsuited to this context, there is no logical reason why this should be so. Many companies around the world are finding such schemes "profitable." While admitting that much of the literature is as yet anecdotal, socially conscious business practices have been found to produce higher morale and productivity among workers and management and generated positive publicity which augments advertising efforts.

The business community must do more than token acts. Corporate philanthropy is the next step. Fortunately, the past legacy of such civic-mindedness is quite right in South Asia. The revival of the Bengal Initiative in Calcutta three years ago stands as a challenge to the captains of industry in Dhaka to commit to a comparable project (Biswas, 1995).

October 17-18, 1997. Hindu *Seva* (service) programmes in India and Buddhist ones in Sri Lanka are also notable.

Recommendations

Civil society cannot simply be expanded by design because it is so vast and is an organic entity at once within and distinct from the larger society. Even so, several practical suggestions come to mind immediately in response to the question. "What can be done to strengthen civil society in Bangladesh?"

- Strengthen human rights safeguards and open a national dialogue on human rights among politicians, activists, journalists, and victims.
- Strengthen existing laws and administrative procedures affecting NGOs in the light of their evolution into business-like entities but remove barriers to new, truly voluntary, non-profit groups. Create an independent institution separate from both government and NGO control to evaluate NGO performance.
- Strengthen local government politically and administratively because it is the level of government closest to the people and the incubator for civil society.*
- Strengthen existing joint training programmes for NGO workers and civil servants and expand them to include business executives.**

Notes

1. By the mid-1990s, 17 per cent of foreign aid to the country was directed to NGOs. Babar Sobhan, Occasional Paper Series Number 14, "Partners or Contractors? The Relationship between Official Agencies and NGOs: Bangladesh," INTRAC (Oxford, England: March 1997).
2. A clear example of such a re-orientation is that of the Association for Social Advancement (ASA).
3. The total increase for the period was twenty-fold, from 45-848. Sobhan, "Partners or Contractors?" pp.4-5.

---

* The Union Parishads (UPs) should be the focus of these efforts.

** ADAB sponsors a secondment programs to expose civil servants to NGO work and the PRIP Trust runs a GO/NGO course.

4. "Capacity" is a euphemism used by donors to mean that an organization is sophisticated enough to receive large sums of money and appear to use it productively.
5. When the author commented about the difficulty of getting appointments with the heads of Bangladesh's largest NGOs, a NGO staff member remarked, "It would be easier for you to get an appointment with the Prime Minister."
6. Over half (77) of the 145 members and observers of the Coordinating Council for Human Rights in Bangladesh (CCHRB) began their human rights activities after 1990. Source. Co-ordinating Council for Human Rights in Bangladesh, Directory of Human Rights Organizations (Dhaka: CCHRB, 1997).

References

Ayoob, Mohammed, *The Third World Security Predicament: State Making Regional Conflict and the International System* (Boulder: Lynne Reinner Press, 1995).

Bendix, Reinhard, *Kings or People: Power and the Mandate to Rule* (Berkeley: University of California Press, 1978).

Biswas, S., "Calcutta's Willing Spirits," *India Today* (30 April 1995), p.19.

Chowdhury, Nina, "NGOs III — Welcome to the Rat Race," *The Daily Star*, 1 May 1995.

Fukuyama, Francis, *The Social Virtues and the Creation of Prosperity* (New York: Free Press, 1995).

Habernas, Jurgen, *The Structural Transformation of the Public Sphere, An Inquiry into a Category of Bourgeois Society* (Cambridge: MIT Press, 1989).

Hall, John A. ed., *Civil Society: Theory, History, Comparison* (Oxford: Polity Press, 1995): 2.

Hall, J.A., *Civil Society, op. cit.,* p.15.

Hall, J.A., *Civil Society*, p.6.

Jackman, Robert W., *Power Without Force, The Political Capacity of Nation-States* (Ann Arbor: University of Michigan Press, 1993).

Jacob, Margaret C., *Living the Enlightenment, Freemasonry and Politics in Eighteenth-Century Europe* (New York. Oxford University Press, 1991): 20.

Mayer, J.P. ed., *Democracy in America* (New York: Harper Perennial, 1988): 513.

Mayer, *Democracy in America*, p.518.

Mayer, *Democracy in America*, p.516.

Mayer, *Democracy in America*, pp.515-16.

Monshipouri, Mahmood, "State Prerogatives, Civil Society, and Liberalization: The Paradoxes of the Late Twentieth-Century in the Third World," *Ethics and International Affairs*, 11 (1997): 247.

Monshipouri, "State Prerogatives, Civil Society, and Liberalization," p.247. Augustus Richard Norton, ed., *Civil Society in the Middle East*, Vol.1 (New York: E.J. Brill, 1995), 1-25.

Monshipouri, "State Prerogatives," p.249.

Monshipouri, "State Prerogatives," p.237.

Monshipouri, "State Prerogatives," p.247.

Monshipouri, "State Prerogatives," pp.241-2.

Olasky, Marvin, *The Tragedy of American Compassion* (Wheaton, IL: Crossway Books, 1992).

Shelley, Mizanur Rahman, "NGO Movement in Bangladesh," Centre for Development Research Bangladesh, undated paper, p.10.

Sobhan, Babar, "Partners or Contractors?", p.14.

Sobhan, Babar, "Partners or Contractors?", p.23.

When the author commented about the difficulty of getting appointments with the heads of Bangladesh's largest NGOs, a NGO staff member remarked, "It would be easier for you to get an appointment with the Prime Minister."

Wuthnow, Robert, ed., *Between States and Markets: The Voluntary Sector in Comparative Perspective* (Princeton, NJ: Princeton University Press, 1991): 19-22.

GOVERNANCE AND INTERNATIONAL DEVELOPMENT COMMUNITY

Abul Maal A Muhith

At the outset it should be clarified that we are dealing with governance in a country. This clarification is necessary because governance of the international public sector is an equally engaging issue in the post-cold war world, and international development community is seized of that issue as well. Reform of the UN system, different from periodic reorganization, is an agenda that is now a decade old. In 1995 a high-powered Commission issued a report on Global Governance [OUP, 1995]. The interest of the international development community in governance came to the forefront in the decade of 1980s even before the collapse of the iron curtain. But it would be wrong to assume that the subject of governance was not a concern of the international development community even in the halcyon days of development cooperation. It was only phrased in different terms like "development administration" or "institution building".

The World Bank has broadly defined governance as "the exercise of authority, control, management, power of government." For their purpose they are interested in "the manner in which power is exercised in the management of a country's economic and social resources." [World Bank, 1992]. This limitation has been imposed ostensibly to keep away from interference in domestic political affairs. The Bank considers that it can delve into four sets of governance issues; namely, public sector management, accountability, the legal framework for development and information and transparency. UNDP accepts the same broad definition but states it in a somewhat different language "as the exercise of political, economic and administrative authority to manage a nation's affairs." It is acknowledged that the main focus of attention are three domains of governance: the state, the private sector and the civil society [UNDP, 1997]. Good governance by definition must enshrine participation because it is "the act or manner of governing, of exercising control or authority over the actions of subjects" [Oxford Dictionary].

At the end of the ideological divide marked by the cold war, a kind of consensus emerged on the elements of good governance. To list them briefly may be useful in examining the role and involvement of the international development community in governance. First, there should be political pluralism — periodic fair elections, peaceful transfer of power and freedom for dissent. Second, there should be the rule of law and protection of human rights — a system of laws and regulations, clear property and civic rights, a fair judicial system, upright enforcement apparatus, and freedom of expression, movement and association. Third, the government should essentially be involved in managing an enabling environment that permits the full realization of the creative energies of individuals without any let or hindrance. This means a greater reliance on private initiative, open economy, limited government and control of corruption. Fourth, there should be a participatory process for decision-making and implementation of action plans or projects; the private sector should be consulted and the civil society should be involved. Fifth, there should be open accountability for actions in the public domain whether the actor is government or a private corporation or an NGO. Sixth, there should be transparency in operations of the public sector and also in specific areas of private sector operations hinging on public concern. This can be best ensured by a system upholding and enforcing the freedom of information. Finally, there should be maximum devolution of powers to local community levels and decentralization of planning and implementation in national activities. This will ensure people's participation, transparency of operations, accountability and mitigation of corruption. Corruption and associated secrecy are the antithesis of good governance and mitigation and control of corruption require political pluralism, rule of law, people's participation, limited government, devolution and decentralization, and accountability and transparency.

Issues of Governance

In development theology the interest in governance has always been there although the focus has changed with time and experience. In the immediate post-war period the emphasis was on assistance in setting up governmental structure and training personnel for public administration. President Truman's Point Four programme initiated action in this area and it was soon taken up by the UN Expanded Technical Assistance programme, begun in 1949. One may recall the work in the decade of 1950s of Paul Appleby in India or Bernard Gladieux or Rowland Egger in Pakistan in reorganizing the government structure. In many under-developed countries UN as well as bilateral experts went not only to provide technical cooperation but also to perform operational duties on a temporary basis. Training programmes covered both civil servants and military personnel but seldom any judicial, legislative or political functionaries. Perhaps because of the sensitive concept of state sovereignty the interventions were in reorganizing public administration and not political organs. But, of course, the line of demarcation was always thin. Egger in 1953 recommended restructuring of ministries with political appointees. Gladieux recommended restructuring of district administration in 1955. And Appleby in his second assignment in India wrote on democratic decentralizaiton in 1962. These were all substantive recommendations on political reorganization. In perhaps the earliest report of its kind "Measures for the Economic Development of the Under-developed Countries" produced in 1951 by the UN, great emphasis was placed on good governance as a precondition for development. However, in order to keep out of politics the primary attention was focused on administrative arrangements and training of personnel and experts. Governance thus was made a narrow concern limited to organizing bureaucratic structures and project management. Economic policy issues did feature, notably in the case of India's agricultural programme in the 1960s, which is touted by the early Bank historians, Edward Mason and Robert Asher, as a classic case of aid and influence [Brookings, 1973]. But issues that are now identified as more fundamental to good governance belonged to the forbidden area. Bilateral donors and the UN development system invested heavily in training and fellowship, which certainly had its sunny side. But lack of simultaneous healthy political development wasted a great deal of the trained manpower or put round pegs in square holes.

The rapid growth of parastatals or public corporations is also a gift of the interest of the international development community. There were, of course, the early precedents in Railway Board of India set up in 1892 and Tennessee Valley Authority of USA set up in 1933. Finding it too complicated to restructure existing establishment and reform civil service rules and regulations, many development partners took the easy option of insisting on new structures for specific objectives. Considerable attention was paid to setting up public corporations or autonomous bodies to undertake various jobs such as implementing projects, undertaking businesses, establishing and operating industrial enterprises, or providing social or economic services. These bodies were invariably devoted to achieving some discrete and identifiable goals. They were not restricted by personnel regulations of civil services and enjoyed financial autonomy. In particular, they had a free hand in fixing emoluments of public servants and recruiting, promoting and disciplining them; they also enjoyed latitude in contracting procurement and sales. Agricultural Development Corporation (ADC) or Water and Power Development Authority (WAPDA) were products of USAID initiatives or Inland Water Transport Authority (IWTA) was set up at the initiative of the World Bank. These initiatives ultimately proved ineffective and costly. The corporations in course of time imbibed the culture of the mainstream bureaucracy and became more inefficient and virtually unaccountable. They contributed to the mushroom growth of the public sector and bloated bureaucracy; in fact, they grew with the support of the development partners. At the time it looked that telescoping the process of growth required wide public intervention. At an earlier point of time export pessimism was the ruling doctrine of international development theology and import substitution was universally promoted. But when adjustment was called for, inertia prevented reorientation.

The World Bank popularized the exercise of medium term development planning and supported planning structures in many countries. The Planning Commission in Pakistan, for example, was supported by the Harvard Group financed first by USICA (forerunner of USAID) and then by the Bank. The Bank prepared an economic report on India in 1949 before undertaking lending operations to the country and in 1952 it prepared an evaluation of India's First Five-Year Plan. To obtain Bank's assistance it appeared that some kind of a national plan must be put together by a country. The Bank dispatched a mission in 1950 to look at Columbia's request for project assistance and they helped the country in drawing up a virtual national plan. Warren Baum and Stokes Tolbert rightly claim that the Bank introduced the concept of project lending; the offer of two loans to Chile in 1948 marked the beginning [W. Bank, 1985]. Again according to the early historians of the Bank, the Bank also devised and popularized the national development finance companies (DFC). Initially support to pure public sector investment bank as in Ethiopia or Turkey was provided and later joint ventures like Industrial Credit and Investment corporation of India (ICICI) and PICIC were promoted [Brookings, 1973]. BSB and BSRS of Bangladesh (originating from Industrial Development Bank of Pakistan and Pakistan Industrial Credit and Investment Corporation) were essentially set up at Bank initiative. The standard Bank lending was for projects within the framework of a national plan or investment programme and to the private sector through the intermediation of national DFCs. Appraisal of projects thus became the most important preoccupation of the Bank.

Development specialists and development partners, at times perhaps unwittingly, preached the virtue of authoritarian regimes capable of "delivering development" and thereby created another problem. "The man on horseback" was considered a worthy modernizer capable of moving forward, unfettered by "inefficient, indecisive and querulous peoples' representatives." Very soon, however, the costs of legitimization of military regimes, the problems associated with their succession, misallocation of scarce public resources for security and the specter of coercion and corruption on which they flourished brought about disillusionment. The patronage of authoritarian egimes entailed compromising accountability and transparency and forsaking countervailing forces. This brought home the message of the impossibility of sustainable economic development without a parallel and complementary process of political development. The distortions and disequilibria that came to light in the wake of payments crisis of the 1970s highlighted the baneful impact of neglect of the real issues of governance. For a while the development partners skirted the fundamental issues and concentrated on technical palliatives represented by stabilization policies, public expenditure controls, restructuring and/or closure of the parastatals and civil service reforms.

Current Activitism on Governance

Many of the burning issues of governance today are direct results of development cooperation experiments of the first quarter century of post-war period. They must now be overcome so that the global economy can reach a new plateau of development. And surely the signs are propitious. The world is inexorably moving towards economic integration; the movement towards free trade is much faster now; resource allocation is more efficient; and capital movement, despite the Asian setback, is considerably freer. There are warning signals, no doubt, about marginalization of many economies, unequal and inequitable benefit streams for more advanced economies and need for special measures for vulnerable and underdeveloped economies. The information revolution instead of opening every door to progress is making a number of countries laggards mainly because of weakness of basic communication infrastructure in these countries and partly because of weakness in governance as in Bangladesh (in this case breaking the monopoly of Bangladesh Telegraph & Telephone Board (BTTB).

Actual attention to the real governance issues both in the countries concerned and the international development community had to await the end of the cold war. The waste of resources due to unneeded security concerns, engendered by cold war politics, can now be dispassionately reviewed. The suppression of dissent, the denial of human rights and hindrance to free exercise of franchise right, tolerated by cold war considerations, can now be seriously questioned and resisted. The inefficient and corrupt methods of disposal of state business, acquiesced in under cold war conditions, need not be tolerated any more. Thus constraints to serious consideration of the issues of governance no longer remains. In the changed circumstances of globalization of production function, open global trade, rapid integration of the world economy and the march of information revolution, the concept of national sovereignty is no longer considered that sacrosanct. This is the context in which the role and involvement of the international development community in issues of governance should be considered.

Issues of governance are to a significant extent non-economic in nature. Free and fair elections; freedom of expression, movement and association; parliamentary overview of executive actions; reliable, independent and effective judicial process; establishment of the rule of law; regulation of the exercise of discretion by the executive; and effective and responsive process of legislation are obviously in the domain of political process. Legal framework for property rights and business contracts; macro-economic framework for pricing, investment, exchange and trade regime; regulation of infrastructure facilities and services; and management of the financial sector and labour market are clearly in the economic realm. The execution of policies in these matters, conducive to a favourable environment, demands technical and administrative measures. Administrative measures are, indeed, in the twilight zone — they cannot entirely be based on economic and technical considerations and must be considered in a proper political context. In articulating the right policies and undertaking the necessary measures four parties i.e. the state, the citizens, the private sector and the civil society have to play their roles diligently and adequately. Securing citizens' participation is the most difficult because unless deliberately organized they are an amorphous lot. In devising policies and adopting measures with participation of all the parties, the experience and wisdom of the international development community can be both helpful and influential. First, global mandates invariably have an advantage as they can be promoted, perhaps in a graduated manner, even if there is opposition in a country. A case in point is the CEDAW provisions.* Second,

* Convention for Elimination of Discrimination against Women.

policy dialogue and technical cooperation can contribute substantially to the process of improvement in governance. For meaningful and healthy dialogue a move away from project addiction to policy consideration is a must. Again, such policy dialogue should better be under the aegis of a multilateral or Aid group umbrella so that individual bilateral pressures are held in check.

The catch is in the partnership role, it cannot be patron-client relationship as prevails between donors and recipients of aid. There is no standard model here that the World Bank, IMF, WTO or a UN Specialized Agency, not to speak of a bilateral development partner, can transfer or implant in a country. Governance issues must seek indigenous solutions in which exogenous experiences can only provide some tentative guidelines. The integrity of the electoral process can be ensured only according to feasible practices in a country. International action may consist of election watch and lessons on voter registration and identification and such other relevant practices. To ensure the neutrality of the electoral process the constitutional provision for a caretaker government made by Bangladesh may not be acceptable to other democracies, but this was what the nation wanted and this has served the nation well. Ineligibility of bank loan defaulters in seeking election, banning of the use of scooters on election day, or holding of state-organized projection meetings for the contesting candidates may be relevant only for Bangladesh. The involvement of UNDP in this matter is certainly welcome as long as the parameters are clearly understood. The matter of devolution of powers and decentralization of planning and implementation of projects surely depends a great deal on traditional social formations and power relations in a country. But experiences of more developed economies can fine-tune the system of local government and especially their financial standing in a big way. It is good that UNDP has accepted the role of supporting the government in its search for an appropriate system of local government for the country.

The ultimate decision is political and it has to be taken by the national government. Strengthening of parliamentary practices and traditions certainly needs a study of the system in vogue in other democracies but it must ultimately be shaped by the nation itself.

The parliamentarians, academicians and the civil society of Bangladesh in the final analysis have to articulate the policies, practices and the instruments. The assistance that the UNDP is providing is in the right areas; it is exposing the parliamentarians to relevant experience; helping scholars, jurists and politicians to come forward with recommendations on reforms and practices and providing help for institution building. The reform of the judicial process has to be indigenous, even though many legal rules and procedures can be easily transplanted from experiences in other countries. Transfer of magistracy to the judiciary and placement of the control of judiciary under the Supreme Court in Bangladesh can easily accomplish independence of judiciary from the executive in a substantial manner; and this is a matter for national political decision where no input from outside is necessary. The World Bank can, of course, assist with exposure to relevant experience and training of manpower as long as it is understood that many fundamental issues are purely matters of national decision. What it boils down to is recasting of conditionality to which the international development community is used under the programmes of the Bretton Woods institutions. In all the cases mentioned here only a range of the types of interventions can be listed but what actually will be required and when cannot be predicted with certainty; scheduling of measures also cannot be definitive and even their sequencing may undergo change.

In certain areas, more so in administrative and economic management, the international development community can be more helpful. In establishing an effective legal framework for regulation of banks and financial institutions and healthy and prudent practices in the financial sector, for example, surely the experiences of USA, UK or Switzerland will be useful but they will have to be tailored to the needs and ethos of Bangladesh. International standards certainly would have to be honoured but the systems and procedures must cater for local circumstances. The involvement of the World Bank, Asian Development Bank and USAID is very appropriate in this respect. As for macro-economic management, the Bretton Woods institutions can provide usefuls models but wholesale transplantation presents serious problems. The addiction to models in the international public sector, induced partly by the arrogance of competence and partly by lack of field experience, is a serious drawback that cannot be remedied by immersion exercises. The devolution experiment that is being tried by the Bank holds much better promise. Flexibility in the application of models and scope for innovative interventions must be institutionalized in macro-economic management techniques. Civil service reforms in respect of recruitment, training and career development or audit function can easily follow developed standards and practices borrowed from abroad. But downsizing, restructuring or grading are matters for national political consensus. A number of development partners are active in this sector notably World Bank, UK, USA, UNDP and ADB. The progress has been very slow and achievement minimal or none. The deficiency is lack of political decision in complementary and parallel issues. The international development community can act or support only when the internal dynamics reach a conclusion and in the meantime it can act only as a pressure group. Establishment of district government services, elimination of secretariat directorate dichotomy, setting up of ministerial policy cells, unbundling of various public services, abolition of cadres, and provision of lateral entry into bureaucracy are matters in which development partners cannot play any role except to plead for reforms. I have deliberately listed these reforms because they are fundamental to improvement in governance and to ensuring accountability and transparency in government operations. They are also essential for improving delivery of public services, controlling the caprices of executive actions and securing drastic reduction in consumption expenditure by the public sector. These measures will also substantially mitigate corruption in public service.

The development partners also can contribute to efficiency in public expenditure. The work that the World Bank, for example, has been doing in the area of divestiture from public undertakings (e.g. Railways in Cote D'Ivore and Burkina Faso), strengthening of safety nets (e.g. East Europe) and restructuring of the financial sector (e.g. Venezuela) is, indeed, laudable [W. Bank, 1997]. The involvement of the Bank in rationalization of security expenditure in Argentina and development of infrastructure by private enterprise in Bangladesh are also examples of good intervention. The serious attention that the World Bank is paying to corruption mitigation is a step in the right direction in as much as it recognizes corruption as an impediment to development. The advocacy role that this attention is playing is, in my view, more important than what the proposed measures can accomplish. Here also the main curative is widespread national sensitivity. A freedom of information law patterned in the model of USA or Sweden can do a lot in arresting corruption. Of course, privatization of many a government operation can strike at the root of corruption.

One of the primary issues of governance is sustainable development, which means protection of the quality of life for the present generation without impairing the prospects of future generations. An area eminently suitable for intervention by the development partners is environment protection programme that many countries are undertaking, sometimes willingly and at times under pressure. Both in the designing of measures and in the introduction of pollution abatement or environment friendly technologies, support of the development partners is essential. This is an area that cannot be left simply to the wishes of national governments because the global commons — the air, the water, the temperature, the climate — or in one word the existence of mankind, cannot be allowed to be threatened by national actions or lack of actions. The concept of state sovereignty in this case has to be sacrificed at the altar of greater good of the human kind. UNDP, ADB and World Bank are all rightfully involved in this sector.

New Aid Partnership

The paper is concluded with a comment on the future of aid, the relationship that was formally entitled and ennobled as development partnership by the great visionary Lester Pearson in 1969. It was the success of Marshall Plan that induced USA to take up the challenge of development of the under-developed economies that were emerging as post-colonial independent states. The urgent but unheeded plea for concessional development aid that the UN was making since its birth was then taken out of its jurisdiction and USA intensified its development assistance programmes beginning in

1954 and soon afterwards in 1960 IDA was established as an affiliate of the World Bank. Meanwhile, the clarion call for burden sharing that US started making in mid-1950s resulted in growth of bilateral aid programmes in the OECD countries. The results of aid flow were not that spectacular despite formation of many Aid Groups and growth of large aid bureaucracy. When a kind of aid fatigue developed another visionary, Willy Brandt gave a call for Marshall Plan for the developing countries in 1979. However, the time then was out of joint — stagflation ruled the developed world and debt crisis stared the developing world in the face. The distortions and disequilibria, which in a changing world are only normal, suddenly came to the centre-stage. The decade of 1980s began with experiments in structural adjustments and economic reforms, finally zeroing on issues of governance at the end of the cold war.

The world of 1990s is very different. ODA is a very small element in resource transfer while DFI has moved to the forefront. In 1996 out of a net flow of $304 million ODA was $58 million (19%) and DFI was $234 million (77%). In 1990 the comparative ratios were 43% and 39% [DAC Report, 1997]. The momentum for integration of the global economy has left behind centre-periphery debates. Globalization of production process is a reality and complaints of exploitation by multi-nationals do not surface that much now. Above all, information revolution has obliterated time and space elements providing opportunities as well as pitfalls.

In the world of the new millennium, current aid relationship will in all probability give way very soon to a regime of new partnership. It is rumoured that after about a half century of operation IDA will cease to raise new funds; sixteenth will be the last replenishment for IDA. In probably twenty-five years from, now aid will be available only for poverty eradication and environment protection programmes. Further, this will be available only to a limited number of vulnerable and debt-ridden economies that will most likely have been bypassed by the current process of rapid integration of the global economy. Partnership for intellectual and technology exchange, without which economies will degenerate and get stale, will be the only form of universal development cooperation in the public sector. Naturally the cost of this exchange will be borne more by the well-to-do partners. At last Lester Pearson's development partnership will be a reality!

References

Report on Global Governance, Oxford University Press, 1995.

UNDP, *Governence and Sustainable Development*, New York, 1995.

World Bank, *The State in a Changing World*, World Development Report, 1997.

World Bank, *Governence and Development*, The World Bank Task Force, Washington DC, 1992.

GOVERNANCE AND IDC: BANGLADESH EXPERIENCE

Imtiaz Ahmed

Few will deny the intricate relationship between the current compulsion for 'good governance' in developing countries, particularly in Bangladesh, and the policy initiatives of the international development community (IDC).[1] Contrary to the general assumption, neither the 'government' no the IDC is wholly responsible for the state of misgovernance in this country. Rather, misgovernance in Bangladesh is a product of historically constructed structures which the government, somewhat structurally, if not for the lack of imagination and political interventions, keeps reproducing. And secondly, at the present historical conjuncture, politically, economically as well as culturally, 'good governance' in Bangladesh can neither be thought nor practised without taking the IDC into consideration.

The first section of the paper will examine the organization of the 'government' as well as the organization of the IDC-centered 'globalization' focusing particularly on the transformative nature of the two and the concurrent reproduction of *governmentality* (that is, the 'mentality' of relying on the government to reproduce things)[2] and the state of misgovernance in Bangladesh. The second section will focus on the relationship between governance and the power of non-governmentality, focusing particularly on the specific nature of Bangladesh's civil society and the limitation of non-governmental organizations in overcoming the state of misgovernance. The concluding section will then reflect on the question, *what is to be done*?

Government, Globalization and Governmentality

'Government' was never an all-encompassing entity in this part of the world. During the 500-years of the Mughal rule and even before, the 'government', as it was understood then, busied itself in collecting revenues and all the 'good things' in the society mainly for the consumption and enrichment of the sovereign and his/her close associates. The relationship between the sovereign and the people was mostly linear with the latter providing all the 'wealth' and, at times, also 'wisdom' to the sovereign.

Colonialism in South Asia went through two phases. In the first phase (running from 1757 to the end of the 18th century), the colonial power, given its youthful position, settled for a conciliatory gesture towards the traditional elite. During this phase, the colonial power even promoted indigenous education, and there was an element of genuine interest among some British officials in propagating India's culture and languages. But the policy itself was no less related to the colonialist need for a class of native officials well versed in Persian, Arabic or Sanskrit so that the latter could assist them in governing the country.[3]

The second phase of colonialism, understood more as 'colonialism proper' (a synonym for intellectual dependency of the South Asians on the West), began in 1835, with the introduction of English as a medium of instruction. Thomas Macaulay and his education policy were instrumental in organizing and reproducing this phase. Consequently, in less than a hundred years or so, the task of the government, including the nature of governance, was radically transformed, with critical long-term consequences.

In fact, as early as 1926, Nirad C. Chaudhuri, with his usual flare of sarcasm, gives us an unique account of what 'colonialism proper' had done to the Bengali mind, notwithstanding the fact that such colonized mind has otherwise been active in the nationalist struggle against the British:

> [In] Bengal, the intellectual classes who are the backbone of the political opposition (to the British) show no fanatical zeal to ban European ideas. It would be hardly an exaggeration to say that they show, on the contrary, unconsciously rather than out of a deliberately

> adopted principle, a cosmopolitan readiness to assimilate European ideas and institutions which is in surprising contrast to the prevailing racial and political bitterness ... [The] real cultural role of the Bangalis ... is to assimilate, by slow degrees, the ways of Europe, till at last, civilization in India becomes the provincial edition of the civilization of Europe, palely reflecting like the moon, its borrowed light from the great sun beyond ... (Choudhury, 1996)

In the wake of 'colonialism proper' with the government ***surveilling*** and ***controlling*** the task of knowledge production and diffusion, the relationship between the government and the people got transformed from one of linearized state of resignation to something that can best be referred to as menacingly 'governmental.'

The Pakistani phase of semi-colonialism further governmentalized things and ideas in Bangladesh, indeed, to a point where guarding the national flag, building a highway, making curriculum for the school, even collecting household garbage, all became the responsibilities of the government. Indeed, governmental policy, whatever may have been its target and field of operation, increasingly came to be viewed as ways and means of policing the people. Resistance at that time was built on the belief that if the semi-colonial (Pakistani) government were removed the government of free Bangladesh would be able to deliver things. In the process, however, neither the practice of rendering governmental policy (the cause of the contention) nor the culture of policing the people (the cause of the action) got removed. Bangladesh, for that matter, remained highly governmentalized since its very inception in 1971.

It is in a milieu like this that the IDC, or more appropriately, the pacesetter and real gainer of global capitalism or ***globalization*** as it is often called, came to play its part in Bangladesh. As will be argued below, the attraction for things central to globalization never ceased to awe Bangladeshis, even when alternative economic practices in the like of 'socialism' or state control development were pursued.

There are two distinct ways of conceptualizing globalization. The first one, and the most commonly used one, has come in the wake of an OECD publication which, while crediting the term to Theodore Levitt, who first used it in 1985 in his book, The

Globalization of Markets, sees globalization as 'a seamless or borderless, global economy' (Frontier, 1997).

There exists a subtle difference between the 'internationalization of economy' and 'globalization' according to this perspective. While the former primally refers to the internationalization of trade and later on, the internationalization of finance and investment, each coming in the wake of precise historical moments of capitalism, (Maitra, 1997) globalization refers to the complex combination of all this but more importantly one that is inclusive of a thoroughly transformed production structure. The latter can be best described as the organization and development of a denationalized form of production.

That is, multi-national or rather transnational companies now collect resources in several countries, process them in another several countries and finally, export the finished products to the rest of the world (Frontier, 1997). A fully finished product, therefore, no longer has one single birthmark; it has multiple birthmarks since several countries have gone to produce it. Put differently, unlike the previous internationalization of things, in the globalization phase of capitalism the thing itself is the product of the international or global market. IDC's policy initiatives in Bangladesh are often a response to this precise nature of globalization. But again, this is only one way of conceptualizing globalization.

The second way of conceptualizing globalization is very much intrinsic to the developing country or Bangladesh's craze for modernity, that is, the organization of the (post-colonial) nation state in the image of the modern 'Western' state. In fact, Chaudhuri's observation that "the real cultural role of the Bangalis is to assimilate the ways of Europe" (Chaudhuri, 1996) is indeed a subtle way of viewing globalization from the standpoint of those who are at the receiving end and are not the pace-setters and real gainers of the global economy. The meaning here is as cultural and intellectual, as it is economic, with the global economy remaining intrinsically related to globalization. Put differently, if OECD's definition could be referred to as globalization from the top, the modernist aspirations of the Bangladeshis could be referred to as globalization from the bottom. An example will make this clear.

In 1972 Bangladesh approved a Constitution with four Fundamental Principles of State Policy, namely, nationalism, democracy, secularism and socialism. In so far as the last principle was concerned, it remained more of a rhetoric since the development of the nascent state was sought more by playing with the core actors of the global economy than nurturing things central to socialism, like equitable distribution of wealth, self-reliance, egalitarian consumption standards, etc.

In this context, Nurul Islam, once the Chairman of the Planning Commission of Bangladesh, noted:

> The most politically delicate choice was the relative dependence of the Plan on foreign aid; with the oft-repeated emphasis on self-reliance and socialism, heavy dependence on foreign aid, particularly that from the non-socialist countries, especially the big powers, created a political dilemma for Bangladesh. There was the choice, on the one hand, of severe austerity, the brunt of such austerity would have fallen on the already impoverished masses and this could have been made partially politically palatable, by a universally accepted regime of egalitarian consumption standards; this in turn would have required a degree of ideological motivation, not discernable in post-independence Bangladesh. On the other hand, there was the option of seeking a large inflow of foreign aid from the rich, powerful nations, which brought with it *certain restriction on the freedom of action in political and economic decision-making.* Bangladesh opted for larger foreign aid (emphasis mine) (Islam, 1977).

In the backdrop of 'socialism,' therefore, the government of the time was busy making Bangladesh a (dependent) partner of the global economy. In this sense, globalization was no less a goal of the Bangladesh government as it was for the global capitalist forces or the IDC. In the process, however, as Islam somewhat unintentionally suggested when referring to the 'restriction' foreign aid invited, Bangladesh economy lost its 'national' character.

Indeed, in so far as Bangladesh's interaction with the IDC is an offshoot of governmental policy, the nature of the interaction, including the very process, became highly governmentalized. In this context, any measurement of dependence based on the flow of foreign aid, for instance, must remain flawed since the flow of foreign aid is not the cause of dependence but rather its consequence. And when foreign aid is the result of dependence, there grows both with the government and the IDC structures to organize and reproduce the aid flow. The former will not survive without it; the latter will cease to be 'IDC' without it. In such a situation neither the IDC nor the government can escape corruption or resist corrupt practices.

According to Rehman Sobhan:

> Bangladesh's external dependence originated in the 1960's. The acceleration of development activity in the then East Pakistan, contributed to the transformation of the economy from a net exporter of capital to West Pakistan to a net importer of capital through the medium of foreign aid receipts. What is more notable is the growth and persistence of Bangladesh's external dependence for nearly 30 years (Sobhan, 1993).

The state of dependence is then validated by measuring the total foreign aid flow, its percentage in public expenditure programmes, its gradual creeping in into the revenue budget, and so on.

Sobhan's case of dependence otherwise rests on two critical points. Firstly, the fault lies with Pakistan of the 1960's and 'our failure' to rectify that situation. Secondly, foreign aid and correspondingly the donors are responsible for Bangladesh's state of dependence. The way out, as the logic of this position would dictate and as Sobhan had suggested, is to "assert our own authority in our relations with donors." (Sobhan, 1993)

On the surface, Sobhan's line of argument and policy prescription sounds reasonable. But then, is it really so? More precisely, is it true that if "we really can assert our own authority" we can overcome Bangladesh's state of dependence? And then, who is this 'we'? If it is the Government of Bangladesh (GOB), what is stopping it? I suspect the answer would be 'donors'. If so, how can the GOB that is already the supreme authority of the country demand more 'authority' in dealing with donors? Where will this fresh and newly desired 'authority' come from? On the other hand, if 'we' means non-GOB forces, the question will be, how will they be able to 'assert their authority' *vis-à-vis* the donors?

Although there is substantial merit in Sobhan's critique of donor's role in Bangladesh, his position seems to be flawed on two accounts.

Firstly, it is beset with a contradiction between the line of argument and policy prescription. That is, if we are already dependent (Sobhan's contention), how can we have 'our own authority' (Sobhan's policy prescription)? Or, to put it in a different way, if we are already dependent then where will 'our own authority' come from? Is it not the case that a dependent being is already bereft of authority?

Secondly, it expounds a partial and as such a limited view of globalization. While problems relating to the issue of globalization from the top have been well addressed, the critique is silent (or, should I say, remains unaware) of the issue of globalization from the bottom. If we take that the solution lies in having 'our own authority' then the question remains, what will 'our own authority' do? If it is 'the ways of Europe' (as Nirad Chaudhuri had said), and in a situation where alternative development scenario is pathetically lacking, will it not land us to the very place that we wish to replace? Put differently, globalization from the top or the power of the IDC cannot be contained or replaced by developmental efforts arising from the modernist goal of globalization from the bottom. The latter, in fact, is the mirror image of the former.

In relation to the issue of foreign aid and dependence, particularly the role of the IDC and the government, the argument can be summed up as follows:

- — So long there is dependence there can be no substantial (government) authority *vis-à-vis* the donors;
- — (Government) authority *vis-à-vis* the donors can be attained only by way of reducing dependence;
- — Government is conditioned to reproduce itself by remaining dependent on the flow of foreign aid;
- — Government has attained its (dependent) position by way of organizing and reproducing a governmentality, which seeks a role for the government in every sphere of life, be it economic, political or social; and
- — More the government seeks a greater role for itself, the more it becomes dependent.

The resolution of dependence and misgovernance, therefore, is far more complex than is evident in any discussion of foreign aid and dependence.

Privatization

In battling against BWI (Bretton Woods Institutions — the World Bank and the International Monetary Fund) agenda for privatizing State Owned Enterprises (SOEs), particularly against claims made on their behalf that privatization is better than state ownership, (Shirley, 1998) M.M. Akash has made a pertinent observation:

> [The] Chinese and Korean success stories in the field of SOE reform merely shows that *real development can occur under the dominance of both the state sector and the private sector*. The crucial issue is whether the concerned country leaders are able to establish an efficiency oriented set of rules of the game and enforce them effectively over a long term, *for every economic agent*, be it private, collective or state (emphasis mine). (Akash, 1998)

In placing the critique, however, Akash has fallen into the trap of Bretton Woods Institutions (BWI) or donor discourse. Akash's position is no more a case of either/or; that is, one need not make a choice between having either 'the state sector' *or* 'the private sector'. This I am sure is a great relief for the donors, particularly for the World Bank! In fact, if we take the World Bank's policy statement on 'good governance' — *World Bank* (1992), this is precisely what it is advocating. To cite:

> Much of the Bank's current policy and research work in public sector *management* bears on issues of 'governance'. For example, studies under way are examining how to *introduce greater* public accountability into public finance and civil service management ... (emphasis mine). (World Bank, 1992)

Do we really need the World Bank or someone favouring the private sector to come and say that there is some problem in our SOEs and that we need to do away with them? And then, where will you get an entrepreneur of this kind in this world who feels 'happy' after losing Taka 95 million* and that again in one year simply because the loss was less than the previous years?

Three critical things need to be pointed out here. Firstly, in refuting the choice between the state sector and the private sector and agreeing that both could play a part in the development of the state, Akash somewhat unmindfully limits the possibilities of development within a paradigm harbouring dichotomous choices! That the 'state' and the 'private' have undergone immense changes, both quantitative and qualitative, and are no longer found in their puerile (classical) form (if there was ever!) is one point that is never taken up seriously. That there can be things of the 'private' in the 'state' (e.g. sexuality) and things of the 'state' in the 'private' (e.g. education) is something that is wholly lacking in Akash's position.

Secondly, if the SOEs are incurring loss and are sustained by government money, which in turn is borrowed or received from the donors, is it not natural that the latter would feel disturbed (given the financial loss and the uncertainty of making a profit out of the loan) and press for a solution that they feel comfortable with (for reasons of their own experience and know-how)? Put differently, if donors go on to finance the entire Annual Development Plan and a part of the revenue budget, is it not natural that they would put forward their own 'pride and prejudices'.

Finally, in any discussion of SOEs in Bangladesh it is important to reflect on their genealogy. The state sector in Bangladesh came into being not as a result of an economic marvel but because of governmental policy, pure and simple. The government took the task of not only policing and keeping intact all governmental structures built during the Pakistan rule but also owning (almost out of Hobson's choice) all non-Bengali (including some Bengali) private industries. It was more a policy of 'fill in the blanks' for that matter. And later on, also the policy to denationalize state units was based not on any economic performance (in the good sense of the term) but rather the lack of performance and that again, by a governmental policy, albeit this time under donor pressure.

---

* At the time of writing 1 US dollar was equal to 45 Bangladeshi Taka

In so far as both these policies (nationalizing as well as denationalizing) were highly governmental, it had critical implications with respect to the organization and reproduction of the economy. There is no substantial difference in so far as running these (nationalized and denationalized) enterprises is concerned. If in the nationalized phase, the bureaucrats were given the power to run business, in the denationalized phase the power is mostly given to the nouveau riche or those having dubious connections with governmental and banking authorities. It was therefore not a question of efficiency but the long-drawn structural configuration which did not allow the real, autonomous entrepreneurs to emerge.

Governance, IDC and the Power of Non-Governmentality

When referring to the development of 'colonialism proper', we indicated how South Asia, including Bangladesh, became intellectually dependent on the West. This could be best found in the filtering of one policy prescription after another of the IDC through the minds and activities of the Bangladeshis. One could come up with a list of such policy prescriptions proposed one time or another by the IDC, like 'modernization', 'green revolution', 'sustainable development', 'civil society' 'democratization,' 'governance' and so on.

If blind acceptance of IDC-sponsored policy prescriptions reflects the state of dependence, a greater problem has been the outright rejection of such policy prescriptions by critics by referring to them as either 'imperialist goals' or simply 'fads'. Even if, we take that the IDC has its own 'interests' (whatever it may be and there is no reason why it shouldn't), the outright rejection of the policy prescriptions is bound to put the critics into the not-so-helpful situation of 'throwing the baby with the bathwater'!

Two points need to be understood in this context. Firstly, given the problem at hand, the need for a policy prescription (not necessarily of the IDC's) cannot be denied. For instance, the four key dimensions of governance put forward by the IDC, more specifically by the World Bank — (i) *public sector management;* (ii) *accountability;* (iii) *the legal framework for development;* and (iv) *information and technology* — remain to be addressed by members of both political and civil societies whether we take the World Bank prescription or not.

Secondly, the IDC is able to put forward its policy prescriptions not so much for its own merit as for our (intellectual) dependence or inversely, lack of imagination and creative responses. It must be kept in mind here that concepts like 'civil society', 'sustainability' or 'democratization' were not invented by the World Bank or those who man the offices of the donor community. These are pretty old concepts and long advocated by scholars, activists and dissenters of both East and West.

The IDC bears certain responsibilities for its somewhat naive insistence of carrying out its policy prescriptions. The naivete there is not so much for reasons of them being abstract and unsound or theoretically untenable, or even for them being highly ideological, but more for the reason of them being applied to a precise condition. In this context, we have already referred to the precise nature in the organization of political society or 'government' in Bangladesh and the problem it faces in any interaction with the IDC. The case, indeed, is no different (in fact, somewhat more problematic) when it comes to the organization of the non-governmental sphere, broadly referred to as the civil society, and its interaction with the IDC.

To begin with, not unlike the organization of the 'government', there is a precise colonial legacy in the organization and development of the civil society in Bangladesh.

Two critical things emerged from the encounter with colonialism. First, colonialism gave birth to a polarized political milieu on a countrywide scale. This is best reflected in the struggle between the colonial government and the colonized subalterns. At a particular moment of history, this took the form of a struggle between the 'colonial' and the 'nationalist' forces, the organization of which led to the polarization of things in both 'public' and 'private' spheres of life, like, education, historiography, music, even dress worn by individuals! This polarization, in so far as it restricted political manoeuvres and civil expressions was destined to polarize other areas as well.

Equally critical is the second milieu, which in one sense is both the cause and the symptom of the first. Indeed, in the face of polarization, the colonized subalterns could do little other than resort to violence in the campaign to redress the wrongs done by the colonial power.

In the wake of the struggle against colonialism, the area that is commonly referred to as the civil society also got polarized and violent. Put differently, civil society in colonial South Asia, unlike that of the West, could no longer boast of its civilizing and consenting roles. In fact, colonialism reconstructed civil society to such an extent that the latter soon got into the business of organizing and reproducing violence and intolerance in the like of political society. This reconstruction tainted political parties, voluntary associations, intellectuals, media, schools, sports clubs, even 'think tanks,' all that civil society represented.

Given the polarized nature of the society, one could easily identify a set of areas where a policy prescription in the phase of research, evaluation and implementation must face competition and conflicts. There are, in fact, four such areas, each influencing and distorting and ultimately, impeding the realization of IDC-sponsored policy prescriptions.

The first one is a known one, and often cited to get back at the government or inversely, to caution the rise of the NGOs. This has lately been resolved, incidentally with not so much of creative efforts as by pushing for greater government-NGO cooperation, the other name for successfully *governmentalizing the NGOs!*

The second one is also known but less readily admitted. This refers to the partisan approach to any IDC activity. To give an example, if the Awami League takes over the task of implementing a donor-led policy, it will be opposed by the BNP and vice versa for no other reason than for the sake of opposition. In the process, many a policy, even when well intended, failed to see the light or get materialized simply because the other side, when reaching the position of power, felt the need to downgrade or abandon it lest it be taken as the success story of its rival.

The third one is also known but seldom admitted. This refers to the inter-ministerial and/or inter-NGO, even inter-'thing tank', rivalry and competition over donor funds. In recent times, particularly with the rise of more NGOs and 'research centres', and a world-wide shrinking of funds, it has attained a critical dimension, with NGOs and 'research centres' even ceasing to share information on any IDC project unless the said project is fully completed and published.

The last one is hardly brought into the public discussion but is present everywhere. This refers to the intra-ministerial, intra-NGO, intra-'thing tank', almost boiling down to that of individual rivalry and competition over donor funds. So intense is the competition and rivalry in this area that often group/personal relationship gets dictated by the amount of access or success one group/individual has over another in dealing with the IDC.

Against the backdrop of rivalry and competition in all of these areas, what can we expect from the society-IDC relationship? Mainly two things. First, excessive amount of rivalry and competition, and that again only for funds, tends to paralyze ideas and creativity. Much of the energy, in fact, is wasted in keeping the relationship with the IDC intact or even worst, keeping to oneself an indigenously developed project or abandoning it altogether once donor fund fails to come through. In a situation like this, there is a rapid fallback on the ideas and activities of the IDC, eager to 'research', 'evaluate' and 'implement' them on their behalf.

Secondly, and this is somewhat implied in the first and also referred to in Section I, both the civil society and IDC (particularly in Bangladesh) fall victim to corruption or corrupt practices. Incidentally, the IDC is less attacked for such vices in the post-war reconstruction of Europe and Japan or even in the post-Mao China!

Misgovernance, as the concept readily suggests, tainted the government more than the non-governmental sphere. In fact, if misgovernance has paralyzed the government, particularly its developmental sector, it seems less evident in the non-governmental developmental sector. Indeed, for reasons of sheer extra efforts (which includes even making up for the lost time caused by political disturbances), a better salary and, above all, ingenuity of certain individuals, non-governmental organizations have fared better in developmental activities.

There is some merit in this observation. In fact, one way of getting a sense of the rising trend towards non-governmentality is to see the growing frustration of the donors with the governmental sector and the corresponding rise in their interests in the activities of the non-governmental sector.

There are two things, however, that need to be pointed out with respect to the power of non-governmentality. First, in its present phase, the success of non-governmental organizations is largely measured in terms of the failure of the governmental sector. This point is pertinent because non-governmental organizations have not succeeded in getting rid of the 'mentality' of the government. So long certain 'noble' individuals are at the top and remain the 'mental', things probably would go well for these organizations. But then, in the absence of a proper structure of non-governmentality, there is no guarantee that such an efficient working of things will continue after the retirement or demise of the 'noble' individuals.

Secondly, the power of non-governmentality is yet to be realized nationally and politically. Almost 25% of donor's funds currently go to the non-governmental sector. This has come about very rapidly, an increase of almost 10% in the last decade. (Sen, 1988)[22] If this trend continues, the non-governmental sector is bound to overtake the governmental share of donors' funds, including the volume of developmental activities, in coming decades. This obviously demands some kind of redistribution of power in favour of non-governmental sector.

What is to be done?

How does then one go about transforming the state of misgovernance in Bangladesh, particularly in the context of its relationship with the IDC? There is, of course, no easy answer to this. One meaningful approach would be to seek solutions in all the areas mentioned above.

1. Degovernmentalizing Governmental Power

This essentially refers to the task of disempowering the power of the government, governmentality, and the governmentalization of things. SOEs ought to be creatively degovernmentalized not for IDC's preference but simply because of the loss factor. Keeping itself out of SOEs or the economy can be a first step in that direction.

Another area, albeit a qualitatively different one, where degovernmentalization is a pressing task is to the excessive governmentalization of the organization of national security, one that goes in the name of defence. The World Bank in its Periodic Economic Update, Bangladesh (1998), while reflecting on the increase of the defence budget to Taka 2,900 crore, pointed out:

> The defence budget is almost equivalent to the cost of Primary Education. One per cent cut in the defence budget would be enough to sustain the Female Secondary Stipend Project from the government's own resources.

This presupposes two things. One, the government can readily reallocate its defence expenditure. And two, the government alone is in a position to do so. In fact, the factor that had pushed for a higher allocation of defence expenditure is not the government itself but the very governmentalization of things related to national security. Indeed, in the absence of an alternative defence strategy and an alternative defence structure, it is futile to recommend the reallocation of defence expenditure.

2. *Decentralizing Representative Government/Governmental Representation*

The IDC has been very forceful in its demand for accountability and transparency in all governmental activities. Much of the focus in this context has been limited to the need for reforming government institutions. While this definitely is something that needs to be pursued, this would not be enough in overcoming misgovernance. This is because accountability and transparency has to do more with the issue of representation than the mere ill practice of the government. Let me explain.

In the light of the population growth and the number of voters in Bangladesh, one Member of Parliament (MP) represents on the average a little over 189,000 voting citizens. (Thiagarajah, 1996) Incidentally, adding non-voting citizens (children and minors in particular) would make this figure even higher. Such a representation makes a mockery of democracy for it is impossible for an MP to meet in person and represent those who have voted her or him to power. Consequently, 'intermediaries' (ranging from corrupt officials, hired goons, and the like) end up having the real power as both MPs and the people, albeit for different reasons, become dependent on them. Unless a way is found to correct this situation, governments will always suffer from ***misrepresentation***.

The way out is to have several parliaments, with at least one at the divisional level. There may be a common structure (i.e., a federal parliament), joining all these parliaments, but it will have lesser power compared to the parliaments in question.

In order to begin this task, however, let the one-chamber Parliament be first made into two — Upper and Lower Houses. The present parliament could easily be made into a Lower House. As for the Upper House, the best would be to follow the 'model' of the interim government. 'Neutral persons' would then have a more lasting role and also a little longer than 3 months! With such a thoroughly decentralized, broad based representation, the IDC will have fewer cause to complain.

3. Democratizing Developmentality

There is always an element of tension between the developing countries, including Bangladesh, and the IDC with respect to the very meaning and practice of 'development'. Much of the criticism, as indicated when referring to foreign aid and dependence and IDC's criticism of SOEs, remained directed at IDC's preference for a precise kind of development in Bangladesh. In a way, it suggested two things. First, there is one single meaning of 'development' circulating in the whole of IDC. And secondly, the practice of development in Bangladesh is different from that of IDC's.

Needless to say, both positions are far from being true. Neither there is one meaning of development in the IDC, in fact, not even within the World Bank itself, nor is Bangladesh government's development efforts different from that of IDC's. Any suggestion to the contrary would make life in the IDC absolutely unbearable, while Bangladesh government would be free for all time from the blemish of harbouring 'globalization from the bottom.' And it is this understanding of the situation that leaves a space for effectively democratizing the meaning and practice of development.

This could come in two ways. First, by effectively and creatively making use of the diverse or pluralist understanding and practices of development in the IDC.

Secondly, by providing space to alternative development scenarios practiced in Bangladesh. What is required more importantly, is nurturing them in full. Indeed, in the process, the IDC might also end up benefiting a lot from it.

Time is still there for making 'good governance' a reality in Bangladesh. What we now need is a combination of creative thinking and bold action!.

Notes

1. IDC includes both bilateral and multilateral donors, with an understanding that the hegemonic power of the IDC lies with the 'Western donors'. For an update of the important actors of the IDC in Bangladesh, see *Flow of External Resources into Bangladesh.* (as of June 30, 1997) (Dhaka: Economic Relations Division, Ministry of Finance, 30 April 1998), Table 6.

References

Agrawala. S.K., "The Universities of India", in *The Universities of Commonwealth Countries.* (London 1994), p.799. Also Basu. Aparna. "Policy and Conflict in India: The Reality and Perception of Education." in Altbach, Philip G., and Kelly, Gail P. *Education and Colonialism* (New York: Longman, 1978), p.54.

Ahmed. Imtiaz, *State & Foreign Policy: India's Role in South Asia.* (New Delhi: Vikas Publications. 1993). pp.140-144.

Ahmed. Imtiaz. "Conflict Resolution in Bangladesh: Time for Restructuring Politics." *Liberal Times.* New Delhi. Vol.IV. No.1. 1996. pp.6-7; "Political System and Political Process in Bangladesh: Consensus on Intolerance and Conflict?" *The Journal of Social Studies.* No.78. October 1997; *The Efficacy of the Nation State in South Asia: A Post-nationalist Critique.* (Colombo: International Centre for Ethnic Studies. 1998) (in press).

Akash, M.M., "Bureaucrats in Business: A Review," in reform of state owned Enterprises and Privatization, Pathak Samabesh, Dhaka, 1998.p.79.

Chaudhuri. Nirad. C., *The East is East and The West is West.* (Calcutta: Mitra & Ghosh Publishers, 1996), pp.4-5.

Foucault. Michel. "Governmentality", in Burchell. Graham. et al. *The Foucault Effect: Studies in Governmentality.* (Chicago: The University of Chicago Press, 1991), pp.102-103.

Islam. Nurul. *Development Planning in Bangladesh: A Study in Political Economy.* (London: Hurst Co., 1977), p.8.

Maitra, Priyatosh, "Social and Employment Effects of Globalization", *Frontier*, Vol.30, Nos.9-12, October 4-25, 1997, pp.31-38.

Sen. Binayak, "NGOs in Bangladesh Agriculture: An Exploratory Study", in *Agriculture Sector Review.* Vol. 5, UNDP, 1988.

Shirley, Mary. "Overview of Bureaucrats in Business: the Economics and Politics of Government Ownership", in Rehman Sobhan, M.M. Akash, Tanweer Akram, eds., *Reform of State-Owned Enterprises and Privatization.* (Dhaka: Pathak Shamabesh, 1998).

Sobhan, Rehman, *Bangladesh: Problems of Governance.* (Dhaka: UPL, 1993), p.223.

The Daily Star, 23 July 1998, p.6.

"The Myths of Globalization", *Frontier*, Calcutta. Vol.29. No.51, 26 July 1997, p.7.

The World Bank. *Governance and Development.* The World Bank Task Force, Washington D.C., 1992, p.57.

Thiagarajah, Jeevan. ed., *Governance and the Electoral Process in Bangladesh: Parliamentary Elections 1996.* (Colombo: International Centre for Ethnic Studies, 1996), p.170.

CONTEXTUALIZING GOVERNANCE AND IDC IN BANGLADESH

Meghna Guhathakurta

Governance in Bangladesh

After Bangladesh became independent, it was widely believed that once reconstruction tasks were over, the domestic economy would provide most of the resources needed for development. This view was mistaken because systematic drainage of Bangladesh's resources during the British and Pakistani colonial regimes had left it with a deficit in food-grain availability. Low levels of internal savings and a high proportion of the population living below poverty line led to what in other words could be called a state of chronic external dependence. (Sobhan, 1982)

The political climate which pervaded the post-independence period was both optimistic and uncertain at the same time. The then ruling party (the Awami League) and political leadership in Bangladesh had acquired its pre-eminent role primarily as a nationalist party playing the vanguard role in the emergence of Bengali nationalism in the 1950s and 1960s. Its main claim to popularity and the basis of its mass appeal was the promise of emancipation from the economic exploitation and political domination of Pakistan, giving it a 'socialistic' hue. However, this did not mean that they had a definite plan for initiating any radical programmes for a new political and economic system.

The economic principles of the new constitution was formulated as a result of serious and extensive debates and dialogue among the competing groups and divergent opinions in society. Even the formulation of the Five Year Plan did not become fully operational nor was it treated as a guideline for decision-making in subsequent stages, specifically in the preparation of the Annual Plans. "These general policies were the result of contending radical and conservative forces vying for supremacy within the party. The leadership of the party at the apex stood in the middle, and appeared not to have firm convictions of its own in either direction. It was willing to make advances towards socialistic and egalitarian policies provided they were not seriously challenged by the conservative groups or vested interests." (Islam, 1977). With the political parties in this state, it was often up to the newly formed (1972) Planning Commission to formulate and plan for economic development.

But these strategies failed to stand the test of time. In 1973-74, the world economic crisis combined with the oil crisis, created shocks in the economy which resulted in chronic shortage of foreign exchange and a decline in the balance of payments. Given the appalling state of the economy, heavy rainfall and floods in 1974 aggravated the situation even more and the result was a famine.

After 25 years of independence, Bangladesh remains one of the most overpopulated and poorer countries of the world with a per capita GNP of $160. In all sectors there was a decline in the annual growth rate after 1972, more so in the agricultural sector than in others. A more recent review of the poverty situation however affirms that poverty levels have generally declined from the mid-eighties to the early nineties but the drop in poverty incidence was modest at best, and indeed not sufficient to prevent the rising numbers of the poor. The national head-count index fell at 0.6% per year compounded over the entire period which implies that the total number of the poor in Bangladesh increased at about 1.5 to 2% per year. (Sen, 1995)

It is also a tragic failure for Bangladesh's development that it has not been able to materialize its dreams of self-reliance and has remained an aid-dependent country. On average foreign flows have paid for about two-thirds of total investments, 90% to 100% of public investments, and 55-60% of total imports (UNDP, 1992). Over the years significant changes have taken place in the total aid package. Bilateral aid which was 73.9% in total aid during 1971/76, has decreased to 48.4% in 1996/97. Multilateral aid, on the other hand, has grown from 26.1% to 51.6% over the same period. Among the bilateral donors Japan tops the list in terms of cumulative disbursement followed by USA and Canada. International Development Association (IDA) (the soft lending window of World Bank) is the largest amongst the multilateral development institutions followed by the Asian Development Bank. The share of grants which was 90.5% in 1971/72 declined to 53.2% in 1979/80, 55.4% in 1984/85 and 49.7% in 1996/97. Furthermore, flow of food and commodity aid has declined while project aid has increased sharply from 1.3% to 75.4% over the same period.

Change on Development Policies

Changes occurred in Bangladesh both at the level of development policies and strategies pursued by successive regimes. The shifts in development goals and priorities followed three broad trends: (a) the shift from a self-reliant autarchic goal to integration with the world economy, (b) the shift from public sector to privatization and (c) from a poverty focus to efficiency oriented development. The Plan documents of the country as well as the actual development strategies of successive regimes bears this out.

a. Shift from Self-Reliant Autarchic Goal to Integration with World Economy

The First Five Year plan formulated by the Planning Commission assumed a mixed economy in a state of transition to a fully socialist system. It was widely believed by those within the Commission that aid dependence should be reduced by two methods; first, by delinking the economy from the world capitalist order. This meant that aid and trade ties through which the Pakistani economy had been linked to the western world, had to be diversified so that aid and trade relations could also be established with countries with centrally planned economies and countries which played an important role in the Liberation War, for example India. Second, by emphasizing bilateralism in aid negotiations, aid was to be negotiated on a country to country basis rather than a consortium, thus giving the recipient more flexibility and room for manoeuvre.

The Plan also enunciated the need to limit private ownership of the means of production and ensure the right to work; it required that conditions be created for the emancipation of the toiling masses from all forms of exploitation; that equal opportunity be given to all citizens; that all forms of unearned income be discouraged, and that private ownership of the means of production be limited as prescribed by law.

But world wide recession and local floods created such a havoc in the economy that both planners and the political leadership found it impossible to deal with the situation without external help. In the aftermath of the war, the situation was such that political leadership could have taken some hard decisions if it had wanted to. But deriving their support largely from large landowners and small traders, they could not bring about any effective change. Thus the attempt at initiating land reform measures which limited the ownership of land upto 33 acres per family was retracted as a result of pressures from the landed gentry. Likewise certain key industries were nationalized and their management reorganized in state-run corporations. But they too, in the long run fell prey to the inefficiency and corrupt practices of government officials. (Sobhan and Ahmed, 1979)

The Second Five Year Plan (1980-85) indicated major changes in the development orientation of the government. The Plan was prepared against the background of adjusting to changes in the balance of payments situation following an increase in the oil price in the early seventies. But by the time the Plan was launched, the international trade and aid situation received a significant jolt which affected Bangladesh very adversely.

The main focus of the Plan was on the reduction of poverty through the growth of income and employment by adopting poverty-oriented strategies in the development of the rural sector, especially where the vast majority of the poor live. All other strategies were to be built around this principle. Although it maintained that the cornerstone of rural development was agricultural development, it also maintained that it was not necessary to interfere with the ownership of land. Thus despite its apparently serious concern with rural development, the Plan boiled down to what has been termed as old wine in new bottle i.e. a rehash of the old modernization approach to rural development.

A more significant change in the Government's development orientation was to be seen in its investment policy. It was felt that the initiative, drive and energy of the individual should be given greater opportunity to flourish and contribute to economic development. A policy of encouraging the private sector in a big way was adopted by the Government in December, 1975. The Foreign Investment Promotion and Protection Act was passed in 1980 to institutionalize within a legal framework the Government's commitment to Private Foreign Investment (PFI). This strategy linked itself to the World Bank inspired strategies of export led industrialization and resulted in the creation of export processing zones in Dhaka, and around the ports of Chittagong and Chalna. The continuation of this policy was to be noted in the launching of the New Industrializing Policy in 1982 by the new martial law regime.

The Third Year Plan (1985-1990) marked no major departure from the Second Plane but emphasized a rational sharing of developmental responsibilities between the public and private sector. The private sector was to be entrusted with all enterprises, operations and institutions which could be more efficiently handled by it than the public sector.

The Fourth Five Year Plan had a different approach: participation and decentralization was very much on the agenda. On participation it said decentralized participatory planning would be the most critical input as well as the output of the Fourth Five Year Plan. This was to be accomplished by "integration of decentralized micro-level planning with macro-planning" with the Upazila as the basis,* At a somewhat applied level the Plan proposes "integration of sector-based planning with socio-economic group based planning".

Recently, the Fifth Five Year Plan has just been completed and "its main objective is to ensure provision of basic needs to every citizen promoting new employment opportunities and building proper infrastructure to facilitate production primarily by the private enterprise" (Planning Commission, 1998). In other words, the governments

---

* Upazila is the lowest administrative tier in Bangladesh.

commitment have ranged from welfare needs to privatization along with developing state infrastructure.

It is easy to see that the public policy agenda set out in the above Plan documents have been drafted with attention focused on the donor meetings chaired by the World Bank (Geest, 1996). It is not surprising therefore, that the content and pace of the reform agenda too has been heavily inscribed by World Bank concerns.

b. Shift from Public Sector to Privatization

As spelt out in the First Five Year Plan, development of the industrial sector took the form of nationalization of key industries and financial institutions, guided development of private capital within small and medium industries, and approval of direct investment only in joint ventures with state owned enterprises. New industrial investments were essentially concerned in the state sector giving priorities to import-substituting commodities, particularly capital goods. The proportion of the fixed assets of the industrial sector under government control shot up from 34% in the pre-independence period to 92%. Out of the 725 units that were taken over, 392 were brought into the public sector as state-owned enterprises. The remaining 462, while brought into the public sector, were tentatively earmarked for early or eventual disinvestment (Humphrey, 1992). About 160 of these were released to former owners rather quickly but the remaining 300 small units were turned over to the government appointed management boards. Private investment was limited to the Tk. 15 million with growth allowed upto assets of Tk. 2.5 million or ultimately to Taka 3.5 million through reinvestment of profits. Foreign venture investment was allowed only in joint ventures with the government, with the government holding at least 51% of the shares. Such arrangements led to the virtual strangulation of the private sector so much so that the black market was in reality the major business activity left to the private sector. It was only when the political circumstances changed after the assassination of Sheikh Mujib and the collapse of his regime, that the first phase of privatization was undertaken by the then President General Ziaur Rahman. The change of circumstances was reflected in the amendment of the constitution in 1977 by a Martial Law Proclamation where the word 'socialism' was qualified to mean 'economic and social justice'. This change made the transition to the mixed economy much easier and paved the way for the major privatization drive of 1982. Zia's approach to privatization was based more on caution than conviction. The Revised Investment Policy of December '75 constituted a departure from the previous policy framework but it turned out that most of the enterprises initially identified for divestiture were small units that were losing money under Corporation management. During the six years of the Zia regime (1975-1981) a total of 255 SOEs were divested or privatized in one way or another.

The New Industrial Policy of 1982 and subsequently, the Revised Industrial Policy of 1986 greatly accelerated the scope and scale of the privatization efforts and economic liberalization. The list of industries reserved for the public sector was trimmed to six: arms and ammunition,. atomic energy, air transport, telecommunications, electricity generation and distribution and mechanised forest extraction. During the Ershad regime about 222 industrial firms were privatized. The Industrial Policy announced in 1991 as well as intentions voiced by the incumbent government after the election in June, 1996 embodied the logical culmination of the policy approach set into motion a decade and a half ago.

In the agricultural sector too, there has been a progressive shift towards privatization, deregulation and reduction of input subsidy which began in the mid-1970s and has continued in stages upto the early 1990s. These changes have been advocated by the World Bank and many of the bilateral and multilateral donors. "A significant change in gear began from 1986-87, embodied in a series of policy measures which completed the privatization of the import, distribution and pricing of irrigation equipment and fertilizers by 1991-1992." (Adnan, 1996).

c. From Poverty Focus to Efficiency Oriented Development

From the seventies to eighties and into the nineties, a global shift in development and orientation, can be witnessed from a basic needs and poverty-focused approach to a more efficiency and market-oriented one. Parallel to these patterns of changes, successive, Bangladesh governments revised their development strategies to the extent that recent policies differed radically from the earlier visions of a public-sector dominated economy of the post-liberation period.

Donors have also had their say about this development shift. By the mid-seventies a new direction in aid policies could be noted in the World Bank strategy aimed at small farmers, the New Direction policy of the US Congress of 1973 and the official policy of the Development Assistance Committee of the OECD. These policies emphasized that development aid needed to be made directly accessible to the poor, instead of depending on the trickle-down approach of growth theories or on market mechanisms. This meant providing for (1) internal requirements of the family, such as adequate food, water, shelter, clothing and (2) essential services for the community at large, such as safe drinking water and health care. (Guhathakurta, 1990)

In Bangladesh, the donors enunciated the need to target the poorest in various areas — such as primary education, family planning, urban service delivery and credit provision. They also critiqued the government for the lack of a strategic approach in areas such as agricultural policies, environmental policies and management. By the eighties however, this strategy was coming under assault as well. The questions being asked was: was it at all possible to really reach the poor without revising existing power relationships?

Contributing to the above shift the continuing dependence of Bangladesh on foreign aid has in practice come to mean that the structural adjustment programme has come to permeate virtually every aspect of economic management. From 1986 onwards, Bangladesh has been operating under guidelines set up both by the Structural Adjustment Facility (SAF) by the IMF and the Enhanced Structural Adjustment Facility (ESAF) by the World Bank. In a review of the reform measures since the seventies it was seen that while the attempts to "infuse competitiveness into the economy, particularly through trade liberalization and financial sector reforms continued", institutional reforms, such as increasing the efficiency of public enterprises, improving institutions and the legal framework to support the productive sectors received little attention. (Bhattacharya, 1995)

Governance as an entry point for International Donor Community

From the above account it is clear that problems of governance have been critical in Bangladesh. But the concept of governance which entered the development discourse did not always stem from these realities but from experiences mediated and negotiated through the donor community. This has been spelt out in a previous study (Sobhan, 1998). Some of the key concepts of governance as perceived and understood by selective donors can be mentioned and the nature and direction which aid has taken in Bangladesh can then be analysed with implications of such aid for redefining the nature of the state.

In a previous study of four donor agencies, it was indicated how the specific interests of donors in governance issues affected their perceptions regarding the concept (Guhathakurta and Karim, 1998). UK's colonial legacy for example, placed it in both advantageous as well as disadvantageous positions in the context of ex-colonies: advantageous because of shared institutional organizations, nomenclature and working procedures of governments in post-colonial societies; it has accessibilities in areas where other regencies cannot reach. The reasons for ODA's interest in governance may therefore, be more historical. The USAID's interest is more strategically oriented, more specifically in the context of its construed role in the new world order. "Promoting democracy abroad" has been a strategic and ideological foreign policy imperative for some time. In the post-cold war context, this objective has become more nuanced and elaborate, as indicated by USAID's Democracy Initiative released in December 1990. This meant that pluralistic political reforms are now coupled with free market economic policies, though their relations are not always clear to the donors. Also the agenda has become more elaborate because it includes components such as popular participation in the political process, accountability, human rights, freedom of speech, rule of law etc. The cause of governance therefore, is subsumed under promoting democracy which in turn may be related to development.

World Bank's interest in governance stems from an effective structural adjustment policy, accompanying macro-economic policies (for example financial stabilization). This is evident from the two stages of governance as perceived by the World Bank. They are (1) stabilization immediate devaluation, drastic public expenditure cuts and (2) adjustment — transforming economic structures and institutions through varying doses of deregulation, privatization, reducing subsidies, public expenditures and encouraging realistic prices to stimulate greater efficiency and export-led growth. Because of the WB mandate which limits any Bank activity that verges on the political, the concept of governance which is in essence a political activity has been construed so that it bears administrative and managerial connotations.

UNDP attempts to serve the cause of human development. Elements of governance and governance itself is primarily defined as a form of public/development management, although it is also in the process of integrating processes such as enlarging participation, increasing accountability, augmenting human rights and supporting decentralization that makes it embrace a wider field of notions and activities.

The above examples demonstrate the varied way in which donor agencies look at governance. These different perspective stem from general institutional reviews not oriented to any country in particular. But when it came to translating these perspectives to concrete realities they did not remain so well defined. In the Bangladesh context, development co-operation in governance as of May 1998 takes the following shape: About 74% or more goes towards institutional capacity building of both the judiciary and bureaucracy both centrally and locally, around 15% goes towards building up civil society organizations to develop delivery service in legal aid, civic awareness, human and gender rights, about 10% goes towards reforming electoral and parliamentary processes and a negligible amount to the media and environment. The predominant definition of governance therefore remains in the realm of public management i.e. to develop efficiency in administration. The interfaces between government and private sector or civil society or the media (the primary area of concern for governance issues) has yet to be looked at in a more holistic manner (This will be dealt with in details later). The following table gives a more detailed breakdown by area of governance and donor agencies giving on-going and/or planned support:

Area of Governance	Development
Audit, Taxation, Accounts, Surveys	ADB, UNDP, UK, WB
Electoral process	Asia Foundation, UNDP, Norway, USAID
Freedom of Information	UNDP, Denmark, UK, Sweden, British Council, Switzerland, Norway
Justice and Human Rights	Denmark, Asia Foundation, UNDP, UK, Norway, Australia, Sweden, USAID, WB, UNICEF, British Council.
Institutional Support	Sweden, World Bank, ADB
Land administration	ADB
Local Governance	Asia Foundation, UNDP, ADB, Canada USAID, UNICEF, Switzerland.
NGOs	Asia Foundation, ADB, Sweden Denmark, Canada, USAID, Norway
Parliamentary democracy	Asia Foundation, Australia, UNDP, Canada, USAID, Norway
Public Administration/Civil Service	UNDP, UK, WB, UNICEF, ADB

Source : Current and Planned Development Cooperation in Governance as of May 1998 compiled by UNDP, Bangladesh.

To take a leaf out of the ODA's Departmental Report 1993, the agenda for good governance is generally recognized to be the following:

a. the legitimacy of government, which depends on the existence of participatory processes and the consent of those who are governed;

b. the accountability of both political and official elements of government for their actions. depending on the availability of information, freedom of media, transparency of decision making and the existence of mechanisms to call individuals and institutions to account;

c. the competence of government to formulate appropriate policies, make timely decisions, implement them effectively and deliver services (Glentworth, 1991).

From the nature of aid given to governance issues as outlined above it seems that the second prescription has gained preference over the first. This seems in contradiction to some of the donor studies on governance in the Bangladesh context, more specifically the USAID sponsored study by Harry Blaire on "Analysing and Closing the Bureaucratic Performance Gap in Bangladesh: Three Approaches" (Blaire, 1993). Here Blaire tries to assess the three perspectives for explaining the gap in bureaucratic performance for promoting rural development in Bangladesh: the political economy approach, the institutional approach and the accountability approach. All three offer reasonable analyses of the gap and prescriptions for closing it, but Blaire concludes that only the accountability approach may be tried in Bangladesh with greater success. This approach envisages a role for civil society organizations to create pressure (checks and balances) from within. It is considered the more expeditious of approaches because it can be more incremental than the other two. The political economy school requires a drastic change in the dominant class structure just to get things moving at all. While the public choice approach would not need any upheaval quite that striking, it would require a major break with the past to begin reforming the incentive structure, while accountability, on the other hand, can be introduced in gradual doses. This model however is not being followed by many donors in Bangladesh. This brings us to the question as to who is actually benefiting from governance aid.

Prospects and Implications for Governance Aid

Addressing the question of beneficiaries of aid or development outcomes has traditionally brought us face to face with theories of the state. Thus studies along the lines of the dependency school had time and again reiterated that the domestic beneficiaries of aid in Bangladesh has been indentors, consultants and construction contractors among others; in short, the aid regime (Sobhan and Hashemi, 1990).

But since theories of the state have been undergoing change and modification, specifically in a context where neo-liberal ideology of the minimalist state has attained popularity, it is necessary to see how these theories address the issues of governance discussed above.

The modernist/developmentalist school had differentiated the developmental state run by its praetorian elite committed to modernization from others and this has been the model of development that donors through the fifties and sixties had pursued to achieve in developing countries. Although the model of such developmental efforts has been in countries like South Korea, Singapore and Taiwan, the outcome of such aid in other countries had been to do the opposite resulting in what Myrdal called the 'soft state', where external aid came in to cushion the costs of development (Sobhan, 1998). In such states access and patronage to developmental aid became no less important than land or property in the creation of a new and powerful class.

Recently, two paradigms of economic development have been forwarded in most donor literature on governance: (a) the minimalist state paradigm (b) market-friendly state intervention. In most developing countries like Bangladesh the latter model (the East Asian version) has been preferred. Lately the theory of embedded autonomy by Peter Evans (Evans, 1995) and the communitarian school of Robert Putnam and Ostrom (Ostrom, 1990) has been contributing to the latter effort by rethinking the role of state autonomy. They have therefore, been liberally quoted in the governance literature of the World Bank, ODA etc. The underlying premises of such models have been refuted by Professor Rehman Sobhan in his recent work "Towards a Theory of Governance and Development: Learning from East Asia." What is relevant to note here is that despite the distinct categories mentioned above, the donor community is often not clear or is ambiguous about which category to apply in operationalizing governance support. For want of a more holistic approach to governance this ambiguity often encourages maneuvering for space in a resource constrained situation leading to a generally confused and eclectic agenda.

Finally, since the bulk of aid coming in is project aid, and development cooperation in governance is mostly through project aid, one must not lose sight of the broader policy arena where dynamic changes may be taking place, whether due to globalization politics, environmental degradation or regional issues. Governance support in other words must be broadly construed to help government and civil society equip themselves to handle the problems and issues of the 21st century and not merely limit itself to the curbing or empowering of state power.

References

Adnan, Shapan, "Agrarian Structure and Agricultural Growth Trends in Bangladesh" paper presented at Conference on *Bangladesh 1971-1996: Past Present and Future*. (London: December, 1996): 3-4.

Bhattacharya, Debapriya, "Bangladesh's Experience with the Structural Adjustment and Enhanced Structural Adjustment Facilities," in Roy H. Grieve. Mozammel Huq eds. *Bangladesh: Strategies For Development*. (Dhaka: UPL, 1995): 63-69.

Blair, Harry, *Analysing and Closing the Bureaucratic Performance Gap in Bangladesh: Three Approaches*. (USAID, mimco, 1993).

Evans, Peter, *Embedded Autonomy* (New Jersey: Princeton University Press, 1995).

Geest, Willem van der, "Distribution-Improving Development Policy in Bangladesh: Assessment and Implications fro Future Policy" paper presented at Conference on *Bangladesh 1971-1996: Past, Present and Future*. (London: December, 1996): 7-11.

Glentworth, Garth, *Practical Aid Assistance to Good Government* (ODA mimco, 1991).

Govt. of Bangladesh, ERD. Flow of External Resources into Bangladesh. (Dhaka: GOB, 1998).

Guhathakurta, Meghna, *The Politics of British Aid Policy Formation Towards Bangladesh: An Analytical Model*. (Dhaka, CSS: 1990): 56-58.

Guhathakurta, Meghna and Karim, Shahnaz, *Perceptions of Governance by Bilateral and Multilateral Donors*, in Rehman Sobhan ed. *Towards a Theory of Governance and Development: Learning from East Asia*. (Dhaka: UPL, 1998): 69-98.

Humphrey, Clare E., *Privatization in Bangladesh: Economic Transition in a Poor Country*. (Dhaka: UPL, 1992): 30.

Ibid.

Islam, Nurul, *Development Planning in Bangladesh: A Study in Political Economy*. (London: Hurst and Co. 1977) p.4.

Ostrom, Elinor, *Governing the Commons* (Cambridge, Cambridge University Press, 1990). Robert Putnam. Making Democracy Work: Civil Traditions in Modern Italy (New Jersey: Princeton University Press, 1993).

Planning Commission, Govt. of Bangladesh Fifth Five Year Plan, Dhaka, 1998.

Sen, Binayak, "Recent Trends in Poverty and Its Dynamics" in *Experiences With Economic Reform: A Review of Bangladesh's Development 1995*. (Dhaka: CPD, 1992).

Sobhan, Rehman, *The Crisis of External Dependence: the Political Economy of Foreign Aid to Bangladesh*. (Dhaka: University Press Ltd., 1982): 1-2.

Sobhan, Rehman and Ahmed, Muzaffer, give details of the operation of the corporations in this period in their work entitled. "Public Enterprises in an Intermediate Regime: A Study in the Political Economy of Bangladesh" (Dhaka: BIDS, 1979).

Sobhan, Rehman (ed.), *Towards a Theory of Governance and Development Learning from East Asia*. (Dhaka: UPL, 1998).

Sobhan, Rehman and Hashemi, Syed M., *The Beneficiaries of Foreign Aid* in Rehman Sobhan (ed.). *From Aid Dependence to Self Reliance: Development Options for Bangladesh* (Dhaka UPL/BIDS, 1990): 141-148.

Sobhan, Rehman (ed.), *Towards a Theory of Governance and Development: Learning from East Asia*. op. cit.

UNDP, 1992. Development Cooperation: Bangladesh 1991 Report. (Dhaka: UNDP, 1992).

A GOVERNANCE APPROACH TO DEVELOPMENT: NEW ROLE FOR DEVELOPMENT CO-OPERATION

G. Shabbir Cheema

Governance and the Enabling Environment

The problems of development are complex and the search for solutions is a continuous effort for national governments and the international development community alike. The late 20th century has been a time of accelerated change and of profound transformations in the world's economic, political and social systems, all of which have brought historically unprecedented improvements in human living conditions in both industrial nations and developing countries. At the same time, however, such changes have also brought new uncertainties, complexities and challenges for social and economic development and for the sustainability of progress for future generations. Consequently, much more remains to be done to sustain and ensure that the opportunities of growth and development benefit all people, especially the over one billion individuals that today continue to live in poverty.

The substantial economic and social progress of recent decades has led to a pattern of global interconnection born with the initial expansion of the world economy consolidated into what is now known as the phenomenon of economic globalization. Globalization has not only interlinked markets but has also intensified world-wide social relations, mediated by new information technologies and the increasing proliferation of telecommunications systems. As the world enters the 21st century, successful participation in the global economy is likely to be a key factor affecting the wealth of nations. As a result, national development will depend on improving the capacity of governments and societies to participate effectively in a governance and economic climate that facilitates and expands international competition and cooperation.

The novel predicaments created by the process of globalization have also had a profound impact in the definition of effective development. International conferences have evolved development thinking to what it is today: an approach that recognizes the interdependence of environmental, economic, social, cultural and political issues and puts people at the very centre of the movement towards change that is sustainable. Change is not likely to survive under stressful external and internal circumstances if it does not come from within putting people at the very core of the process and giving them control and ownership of the whole undertaking. To face the new challenges, societies must rethink the ways in which they organize and manage their affairs in order to achieve the goals and aspirations of its people. Few government, if any, are equipped to cope alone with the degrees of change and uncertainty of the present day. More and more, governments need to form partnerships with other actors of society in order to exploit the opportunities and avoid the dangers ahead. The effectiveness of government and its relationship to civil society and the private sector will be key determinants in whether a nation is able to create and sustain equitable opportunities for all its people. To do so, building a country's internal capacity to improve its governance structures, institutions and processes will become a primary means for sustainable social and economic development.

Governance constitutes the overarching process that creates an enabling environment for people-centred development. Social and economic development is inseparably linked to the political, ecological and cultural environment in which it takes place. The path of sustainable development is thus determined by the fundamental interdependence of the conditions prevailing in the different realms of human existence in society. Sustainable development hinges on an "enabling environment" of compatible and mutually consistent conditions in those spheres.

The Meaning and Scope of Governance

Development cooperation promoting an enabling environment must therefore, approach development in a holistic manner which, in turn, requires a comprehensive look at how society functions at the level of individual interactions given its values, traditions and resources. Political, social and economic activity is governed by the structures, rules and norms established within a given society. Generally speaking, this interplay between this institutional framework and individual behaviour is the realm of "governance". While governance in a broad sense encompasses virtually every institution in society, from the family to the state, in the context of development cooperation it is typically associated with the political, legal, financial and economic system of government and its relationship to society at large, including civil society structures. Capacity building is about developing the physical and human assets that institutionally make up and support the process of governance.

Notwithstanding continuing uncertainties about the complex relationship between governance and development, however, a consensus is emerging as to the importance of dealing with development from a governance perspective and of applying development approaches to governance. The new focus on governance is, in part, a response to the failure of achieving sustainable development through a narrow and compartmentalized approach: Traditionally, multilateral development agencies have directed their efforts to build societal capacities virtually exclusively at the public sector thus ignoring important aspects, such as the role of civil society and the centrality of governing institutions. In addition, interventions conveniently adopted a technical, managerial or narrow economic focus with little regard to other conditions including the legitimacy, role and overall efficiency of the state organization. As a result, public sector capacity has been lost to a progressively disabling environment.

By looking at development issues from an enabling environment perspective, hence adopting a "governance approach to development", development assistance should be able to better guard against the pitfalls of unsustainability. To be sure, public sector structures will continue to be at the centre of the development efforts supported by the international development community. While governance captures a very broad spectrum of societal interaction, for the multilateral system it requires above all close attention to existing and potential imbalances and gaps in the way societies organize and run their political and economic affairs. In this sense, governance is the theme giving more coherence and focus to a variety of social, economic, and political development activities which have hitherto been conducted in isolation from one another.

The general definitions of governance chosen from three multilateral donor agencies (see box below) expose a fair amount of convergence. Following the World Bank and UNDP, there are three different, albeit interconnected, spheres of governance: (a) political (b) economic, and (c) administrative. Governance relates to a country or society as a whole (UNESCO, World Bank). It is about processes (UNESCO), as well as institutions and mechanisms (UNDP, World Bank). Governance is the exercise of power and authority (UNDP, World Bank) in pursuit of a society's present and future welfare (UNESCO) and derived from the interests of the citizens (UNDP, UNESCO).

Definitions of Governance: Three Perspectives

UNDP

... "the exercise of economic, political and administrative authority to manage a nation's affairs at all levels. It is the complex mechanisms, processes and institutions through which citizens and groups articulate their interests, exercise their legal rights and obligations, and mediate their differences." (UNDP, 1997)

World Bank

... "the manner in which power is exercised in the management of a country's economic and social resources for development." "Aspects of governance: (i) the form of political regime, (ii) the process by which authority is exercised in the management of a country's economic and social resources for development; and (iii) the capacity of governments to design, formulate and implement policies and discharge functions. The terms usually describe conditions in a country as a whole." (World Bank, 1994)

UNESCO

> ... "a process whereby citizens' needs and interests are articulated for the positive social and economic development of the entire society and in the light of a perceived common good. Governance means more than government: it refers to a political process that encompasses the whole society and contributes to the making of citizens, active contributors to the social contract that binds them together. Their sense of political efficacy is one of the indicators of democratic governance." (UNESCO, 1997)

Governance thus encompasses a wide range of issues from concerns about efficient government, including accountability and transparency, to concerns about human rights, social cohesion, equity (gender, poor), democracy, participation, corruption, military expenditures, countries in crisis, and, last but not least, political thought, culture and discourse. The number of organizational capacities that have an impact upon or are else associated with governance is equally broad extending from the public sector (government organization-civil service-public economic/financial management-local government-public enterprises), the legal framework, governing institutions (legislature and judiciary), to the democratic process (elections), civil society organizations (NGOs, political parties, labour unions, social movements, ...), and the private sector (for-profit organizations and business associations).

Emergence of Governance in Development Cooperation

Recognizing that the forces currently shaping the world are not necessarily restricted to the traditional apparatus of the state, but encompass organizations, institutions, structures and groups outside it, current debates on development questions are increasingly focused on governance dimensions. Thus the development discourse is moving far beyond the narrow economic and state centered parameters of the past.

Development practitioners have begun to elaborate a new paradigm, which has redefined development in terms of people's needs rather than economic forces and which promotes good governance as an important component of a people-centred approach to economic, political, and social organization. Governance as a framework for development has emerged from numerous influences over the past 50 years reflecting the theories and ideas which have configured the modern world.

Historical Roots

Modern concepts of technical cooperation for development had their genesis in the aftermath of the Second World War, specifically in the efforts to rebuild Europe and to support countries in the developing world as they gained independence. The immediate post-war period was also one of optimism in new approaches for global governance, peace and security, and development in general. The era established general principles of human development with the adoption of The Universal Declaration of Human Rights and in a series of UN conventions on the minimum objectives and standards of human well-being.

The programmes designed to facilitate the rebuilding of Europe, in particular the Marshall Plan, laid the foundations for the development cooperation approaches of the 1950's. Led by the Bretton Woods institutions, development focused on rehabilitation and investment in large-scale infrastructure projects. These approaches were driven by western economic theories, which viewed development as essentially an economic problem. Development in this context was therefore variously motivated by political expedients related to the Cold War, by social interests for modernization of former colonies, and by economic pressures for optimal growth.

Development cooperation was viewed as a technical process to increase economic potential through the transfer of aid, technology, and political and economic processes. The vehicle for development within this world order was the state, and in the post-war era generally, the state was seen as the organizer and provider of economic and social development. As a consequence the role and size of the state increased to match the rising demands placed upon it.

Economic Growth Models

Development thinking in the late 1950's and early 1960's shifted with the realization that not all economies were the same.

Development approaches were largely based on the supposition that there were clearly defined stages of economic growth common to all countries. Development mechanisms were oriented to the creation of the conditions for 'take-off' economic growth, prosperity and modernization (Rostow, 1960), and in turn the narrowing of the gap between rich and poor nations.

By the 1960's, technical cooperation focused on building urban industries and infrastructure which would provide the foundations for economic growth. A certain attachment to the ideologies of central planning contributed to the predominant belief that the rate of economic development could be accelerated by large, capital-intensive industries. It was thought that governments could engineer growth by favouring investment in 'leading' economic sectors. Industrialization in the form of large-scale manufacturing projects was seen as the obvious way of achieving a more equal distribution of income between developed and developing nations, and it would sustain economic growth and development of other sectors in its wake. Democracy itself was believed to follow the waves of social modernization which resulted from this growth. These development approaches thus assumed a heavy state role in intervening and managing economic development and had a strong capital accumulation and urban bias.

Despite the urban bias of the economic growth models, significant assistance was directed to rural areas by international aid agencies, largely with the aim of increasing food resources and agricultural productivity. The period of the 'Green Revolution', where donor agencies provided support for agricultural inputs and improved technology and were rewarded with a dramatic rise in the production of mainly rice and wheat. While the Green Revolution increased food production in many countries, the results were generally of primary benefit to large and medium-sized landowners, who had the resources to sustain the technological investment.

Human Needs and Social Justice Approaches

Beginning in the late 1960's and early 1970's, empirical evidence from developing countries demonstrated flaws in the economic growth theories and it became increasingly evident that modernization efforts had failed to tackle the roots of poverty. Income disparities were widening between the developed and developing worlds and within developing countries themselves. The urban bias of technical cooperation had resulted in an overall decline in rural productivity (although this was mitigated by the Green Revolution in some countries) and in the conspicuous realities of high unemployment, urban poor, and social injustice.

The global political economy was also changing. Oil shocks, the liberation of finance from industrial capital, and the spread of the Cold War into the surrogate theatres of Central America, South-East Asia and Africa all contributed to a new development perspective. Obstacles to development were viewed not as a lack of capital or entrepreneurial skills but the dependence of developing countries necessary to maintain the hegemony of the developed world. Challenges to the prevailing economic and development paradigms were mounted by developing countries themselves (see, for example, the centre/periphery concepts of Raul Prebisch in The Economic Development of Latin America and its Principal's Problems, 1950), some of whom proclaimed their desire to disassociate from world markets and to strive for self-reliance.

Changes in social and economic structures to help the poor and disadvantaged were posed as alternative development strategies, and the emphasis of development cooperation shifted towards facilitating the conditions for job-creation and the improvement of basic services in health, nutrition, and education. Improving the distribution of income was also relevant to many countries where growth had not produced a rise in employment as had been hoped. The new thinking was popularized by the International Labour Organization (ILO) in its Basic Needs Approach (ILO, 1976).

Development cooperation under the Basic Needs Approach centred on eliminating poverty and on improving the ability of governments to increase the impact of development aid on target groups, especially women and the rural poor. There was an emphasis on grassroots institution-building, with particular stress on popular participation. The Basic Needs Approach engendered a return to a more people-centred view of development, with a heavy emphasis on participatory methodologies and integrated rural development projects intended to reduce poverty and generate income and employment. Even the international financial institutions adopted the approach and began orienting their programmes towards economic growth with equity.

Structural Adjustment, Liberalization, and Globalization

In the late 1970's and early 1980's, slower global growth, the debt crises (of Latin America and Africa in particular), worsening terms of trade, natural disasters, and political instability all combined to make for poor economic performance in many developing countries. Unsurprisingly, the old strategies of import-substitution and industrialization and the newer ones of self-reliance were subjected to intense scrutiny. The role of the state itself was placed in doubt by the influential voices of 'Reaganism' and 'Thatcherism'. Governments were thought to be pursuing economic policies which were too interventionist. Distortions in markets created disincentives for the productive application of private and public resources, and economic stagnation was the inevitable result. Programmes of stabilization and later structural adjustment as promoted by the World Bank and International Monetary Fund took centre stage.

The objective of the international financial institutions was to help developing countries respond to the external economic shocks of the time, including fluctuating oil prices, declining growth in industrial countries, increasing interest rates, and reductions in capital inflows. The stabilization measures were aimed at reducing both budget and trade deficits, with accompanying cuts in wages and public spending. By the late 1980's, policy prescriptions to improve economic performance emphasized the need to reduce government intervention in the marketplace. Countries in various political circumstances were pressured to undertake structural adjustment programmes targeted at deregulation of the marketplace and more efficient and effective state apparatus.

In parallel with the economic developments of the decade, social and political systems throughout the world experienced significant upheaval. The collapse of the Soviet bloc, the emergence of democratic political regimes in former authoritarian states, the rapid proliferation and accessibility of new technologies, increased interaction among states resulting from improved telecommunications systems, and the continued integration of the world economy all generated new conditions for development. All of these factors generated new conditions for development and both complicated and constrained traditional development approaches by introducing significant changes to the economic, political, and transnational relations within and among states.

The reorientation towards market economics against the backdrop of political and social change has increased the role of the private sector and placed greater emphasis on the fiscal responsibility and responsiveness of the state. This has led to calls for widespread administrative and economic reforms aimed at reorienting the role of governments. Emphasis in development cooperation took a dramatic turn in the late 1980's towards programmes, which supported long-term adjustment and the fundamental realignment of developing country economies away from interventionism. This involved reducing the role of the state, removing subsidies, privatizing state businesses, liberalizing prices, and opening borders to the flows of international trade and finance. The state was no longer regarded as the provider of economic and social development, but rather as a partner, catalyst, and facilitator.

The free-market reforms and structural adjustment strategies advocated during the late 1980's and early 1990's largely underestimated the negative impact on developing country populations. The distress often involved caused some donor agencies to reconsider human-centred development approaches. Conventional development models were dominated by quantitative economics and were heavily weighted towards both economic causes and solutions to underdevelopment. International aid agencies began to search for development alternatives to redefine development strategies concentrating on the basic needs of people.

Rethinking Technical Cooperation

In addition to the political and economic forces which shaped development thinking in the post-war era, the design and implementation of technical cooperation methods came under careful examination in the 1980's. Despite significant technical assistance and training, national institutions in many developing countries remained weak. Criticism of technical cooperation was levelled at Africa in particular, the region that received the highest concentration of international donor aid. Questions were being raised about the use of the aid provided over the previous 40 years and about the nature of the aid in itself (UNDP, 1993).

The criticisms and analysis forced several conclusions. There was a general recognition that the effectiveness of technical cooperation varies across sectors, across regions, across types of operations, and according to the objectives sought. Four major groups of factors have been identified which are believed to limit the impact of technical cooperation.

First, poor project design and implementation, and inadequate monitoring and evaluation systems often constrain effective delivery of technical cooperation. These failures are often caused by inappropriate objectives resulting from a lack of local involvement, misdiagnosed priorities, restricted preparation time and resources, inappropriate technologies, limited local human resources and insufficient and ineffective evaluation indicators.

Second, nearly all technical cooperation relies heavily on long-term expatriate expertise. The inability to achieve a transfer of knowledge and to build national capacity frequently results from a lack of sufficiently trained national counterparts. In some cases skilled expatriates are either unwilling or unable to train local counterparts. Recipient governments are often unable to financially sustain the project's objectives after its completion.

Third, public sector salary structures and working conditions in many countries result in a high turnover of personnel. Disparities between expatriate salaries and those of their counterparts, as well as the minimal skill levels in many public services, makes the transfer of knowledge extremely difficult.

Fourth, technical cooperation is widely seen to be donor-driven. Projects frequently originate with donors and are prepared by donor agencies with insufficient involvement of recipient governments. Implementation and evaluation of projects are also predominantly controlled by donor agencies, and are perceived to meet interests other than the needs of recipients and beneficiaries.

Enhancing technical cooperation clearly requires greater national participation in the design, implementation, monitoring, and evaluation of development programmes. Such participation should include local-level management and oversight of development programmes, including greater use of national resources such as non-governmental organizations (NGO's), the private sector, and civil society organizations. Innovative incentive systems to overcome disparities in remuneration are also required.

It is also implied that a greater emphasis should be placed on the policy environment in which technical cooperation is taking place. Stronger partner institutions beyond simply public sector agencies are required if technical cooperation is to work. The critiques of technical cooperation and the solutions proposed pointed to a number of factors that had not been traditionally part of the development framework. Indeed, the World Bank 1989 report on the increasing poverty and underdevelopment in Sub-Saharan Africa pinpointed a crisis in governance as the key factor in the failure of technical cooperation in Africa. For the first time, donor agencies began to evaluate issues of legitimacy, pluralism, participation, consensus, and human rights as significant precursors to people-centred development.

UNDP Priority Areas in Support of Good Governance

Governance: A Basic Pre-Condition for Sustainable Human Development

Against the backdrop of the above changes and successive stages of transformation, UNDP found itself at a crossroads in the early 1990s. With the publication of the first annual Human Development Report, launched in 1990, UNDP was able to build a comprehensive case to change the development debate from one concerned exclusively with economic growth to one concerned with the impact of economic development on people and with people's role in the development process. The impact of the UNDP Human Development Report showed that the world was ready for such a message.

Thus in the 1990s, the terms human development and sustainable development herald a major shift in the substance and approach to understanding development. The series of global UN conferences in the mid-1990s, most notably the 1992 UN Conference on Environment and Development (the Earth Summit) and the 1995 World Summit for Social Development, clearly established the view of all nations that development was about people and about the interdependence of environmental, economic, social, cultural and political issues. Development, therefore, was no longer understood by focusing or highlighting a neglected dimension of development, but rather as a new framework that places people at the centre and recognizes the importance of linking social, economic, and environmental considerations as the foundations of sustainability.

The cumulative effects of UNDP leadership role in refocusing development cooperation towards human development and developing better techniques for the delivery of technical cooperation, led to a new understanding of the parameters of development cooperation within the organization. The concept of sustainable human development (SHD) took center stage as UNDP's mission, and the links between governance and development were given due importance. Sustainable human development is defined by UNDP as the process by which the range of opportunities and choices for people can increase and be expanded, while protecting those same opportunities and choices for future generations as well as the natural systems upon which all life depend. The expansion of choices and opportunities today and for the future implies that people feel secure, that they are empowered, and that there is equity in the range of opportunities available to them. The protection of those opportunities and the natural environment that supports them suggests that sustainability is a critical factor.

The expansion of peoples' choices is empowering when it increases their abilities to participate in the political, social, and economic forces of the society free from hunger, want and deprivation. This view of participation also infers that there is cooperation, people work and interact to collaborate for development. That same expansion of choices and opportunities can also promote equity, including equity of access to services, goods, employment, income and technology. Sustainability is seen to be more than environmental or ecological. The needs of this generation must be met without compromising the right of future generations to realize their potential and enhance their capabilities free from poverty and deprivation.

For people to realize their potential and enlarge the scope of their choices, the social, economic, and political environments must reflect notions of security, participation, cooperation, equity, and sustainability. The term governance is commonly used to describe the processes that generate these conditions. In this way, governance and sustainable human development can be seen to be indivisible. Governance in the economic setting includes the processes that affect a country's economic activities and the relationships with the economies of other states. It clearly has major implications for equity, poverty, and quality of life. Governance in the political setting is the process of decision-making to formulate policy and laws, which in turn has ramifications for security, equity, participation, and cooperation. Administrative governance, carried out through an independent and accountable public sector, is the system of policy implementation and has resulting consequences for the social setting. Encompassing all three, systemic governance relates to the processes and structures that guide political and social-economic relationships.

UNDP's Governance Policy

Based on its mandate for sustainable human development and its mission to build capacity for good governance, UNDP has devised a policy on governance to guide its work in support of sustainable human development in the domains in which UNDP can make substantial contributions, recognizing the emphasis to be placed on strengthening the institutions and capacities of the state, the private sector and civil society organizations. UNDP strongly stresses the need for a holistic approach in capacity-building for governance with full recognition of the links which exist between institutions, levels and systems.

Five focus areas have been identified to facilitate UNDP's provision of comprehensive programme assistance to governance efforts in programme countries. These areas are as follows: governing institutions, which encompass the key political institutions of the state, including legislatures, legal and judicial systems, and electoral and human rights bodies; public and private sector management, which focuses on institutions responsible for the management of economic transactions and social resources; decentralization, referring to the distribution of the financial and administrative processes of decision-making and management of public programmes among central, regional, and local levels; civil society organizations, incorporating the numerous groups and individuals which can actively contribute to the public policy-making process and participate in the political, economic, and social affairs of the state; and governance in special circumstances, addressing the particular needs of countries experiencing severe political, economic, or social crises and those countries undergoing transitions from centrally-planned to market-based economies.

In seeking to promote good governance within its programmes countries, UNDP is drawing on its extensive development experience, backed by a clear mandate and Sustainable Human Development (SHD) mission. At the same time, however, the organization recognizes that the pursuit of programmes supporting good governance in dynamic, unpredictable environments is a complex process that carries risks. Different environments will require different programmes, and different entry points and types of programmes. The challenge for UNDP is to take a systemic and strategic approach to governance that meets each country's national priorities.

Governing Institutions: Legislature, Judiciary and Electoral Bodies

UNDP support can, in principle, be directed to all the governing institutions responsible for the management of a country — executive, legislative and judiciary — and the processes for their establishment and operation. Soundly functioning national and local legislatures and judiciaries are particularly critical to the creation and maintenance of enabling environments for poverty eradication. Legislatures are forums in which differing interests are mediated and policies, laws and resource priorities directly affecting people-centred development are debated and enacted or established. Electoral bodies and processes ensure independent and transparent elections for the legislatures. Judiciaries uphold the rule of law, bringing security and predictability to social, political and economic relations. Human rights bodies help ensure that governing institutions uphold national laws and internationally recognized conventions.

UNDP involvement with legislative and judicial systems is relatively recent and the development of its capacities in these areas will require special attention. However, even in the early stages of UNDP support for these areas, demand for UNDP assistance has been high in all regions. Because of its impartiality and the trust it engenders, UNDP has a considerable comparative advantage over other organizations in these areas. It can also play a valuable role in helping to coordinate external resources.

Given its limited resources, its often close relationship to government and the importance of these areas in influencing issues of equity and poverty related priorities, UNDP's prime task is to support the development of a country's capacity to strengthen its own governance structures. UNDP therefore, takes a systemic approach, first facilitating government creation of a framework and strategy for institutional reform. This approach, moreover, encompasses the relationship between these state institutions and the private sector and civil society.

Institutional development support to legislatures may include help in establishing effective parliamentary or similar national and local structures, systems, processes and procedures; and support for training of parliamentarians in their roles and in legislative procedures. Support for electoral commissions, legislatures also includes assistance in strenghtening electoral processes, including support for electoral legislation, voter registration systems, and maintaining electoral registers. UNDP offices have played an important and expanding role in electoral processes, which in some instances has been complemented with institutional strengthening. In Africa alone, UNDP has helped 35 countries coordinate their electoral processes in the past three years.

Establishment of systems of justice and laws, ombudsmen and human rights oversight bodies, and effective security systems are some of the areas in which capacity development of judiciaries is supported. Judicial and legal reform activities, which may be supported by UNDP, include improving the structure, organization, and administration of court systems; training judges, magistrates, lawyers and support personnel; improving access to justice by improving subordinate court systems; removing legal barriers to full participation of women, minorities and civil society institutions; and providing specialized assistance in legal education related to constitutional law, electoral law and laws related to human rights. In Vietnam, for example, UNDP has been supporting the rationalization and strengthening of a legal framework and judicial system appropriate to the country's transition towards a market-based economy.

Public and Private Sector Management

Historically, the strength of UNDP has been management development, particularly in developing national capacities. UNDP has learned from its vast experience in this area that there are three requisites for effecting constructive change: a clear vision of goals and of how to reach those goals: the identification and nurturing of people who can take the lead and make progress in reaching those goals; and strong, effective and accountable managerial capacities and institutional structures to implement changes.

Leadership, Policy Development and Management of Change

Support for leadership development and management of change cuts across UNDP governance efforts. Effective leadership is essential to the successful implementation of good governance programmes. It is particularly important in complex systemic change involving civil society and private-sector actors. Effective leadership entails developing the capacities of key national actors and coalitions to increase political commitment to change for Sustainable Human Development (SHD), the ability to bring public and private actors together to define development goals and strategies for the country that are people-centred and sustainable, and the capacity to manage systemic change in often unpredictable situations.

Broadly, UNDP seeks to develop national capacities to articulate national goals, policies and strategies, especially those that are long term and support good governance, with an emphasis on the development of processes that elicit broad national support and consensus. To this end, UNDP supports national institutions and approaches that develop the skills of leaders in initiating and managing change processes that are systemic and complex and that involve stakeholders and beneficiaries from government, the private sector and civil society. This will include assistance for training in participatory planning and implementation techniques, building national competencies and in developing approaches to public-private partnerships and managing globalization and reform. In Uruguay, UNDP's support to the National Debureaucratization Programmes helped the government save US$ 28 million in public services and around the same amount in other areas. The President of Uruguay called this programme "one of the most important landmarks to be left in our country by international cooperation ..., a success saving millions of dollars which has facilitated the life of citizens and leaders".

Additionally, UNDP has concentrated on strengthening management in two areas that are, in its experience, vital to SHD — reform of the civil service, and economic and financial management. This emphasis continues with particular focus on good governance for the eradication of poverty.

Civil Service Reform

The reform of state institutions so that they become more efficient, accountable and transparent is a cornerstone of good governance. Effective reform requires, first and foremost, strong political determination, which should include the support of private and civil society concerns. As indicated above, UNDP has extensive experience and technical knowledge in the fields of public administration reform and management of development. This has ranged from the pioneering work done through national technical cooperation assessments and programmes to supporting comprehensive civil reform processes in all regions. In many countries, UNDP has taken a strategic approach, seeking key partners and coalitions that are politically strong, finding suitable entry points, initiating a policy dialogue that brings stakeholders and beneficiaries together, and introducing reform in a phased, systemic manner.

A wide range of needs can be addressed, including: formulation of strategies; assessment of capacities; reform of governance rules and procedures, including those for the market and the most vulnerable; review and restructuring of functions and networks; improvement of systems, particularly those concerned with planning, management, information and new technologies, budgeting and expenditures, statistics, reporting and accountability; reform of wage and incentive structures; private-public partnerships; and the decentralization of tasks and resources. The central issues of sustainability — ownership, fiscal discipline, incentives, political support and external aid — are equally addressed. UNDP's support to the Government of Eritrea with developing a "home grown" strategy for streamlining the civil service resulted in a reduction of 10,000 staff from a total of about 25,000. The strategy's aim, based on government task forces, was to create a public service characterized by customer orientation, courtesy, responsiveness, and flexibility in an absence of red tape.

Economic and Financial Management

Good governance has both procedural and substantive aspects. This applies to the management of economic and financial matters. In procedural terms, countries need to establish relationships among the state, private sector and civil society and cooperatively develop frameworks that provide incentives for broad-based, sustainable growth. Substantively, several points of intervention are crucial for SHD: macro-economic policies; the management of the external sector, particularly trade, aid, investment and debt; the regulatory market framework and privatization; social safety nets; and resource management. Taken together, sound policies and practices in economic and financial management will contribute significantly to the creation of an enabling environment for SHD.

While the Bretton Woods institutions and several bilateral donors have greater resources and capacity at their disposal to assist developing countries in this area, UNDP plays an important, albeit different, role. Its niche is threefold: (a) UNDP can and brings issues of SHD and poverty into the centre of policy discussions, makes more transparent macro economic decision-making and influences resource allocations to SHD ends; (b) because of its impartiality and the trust it engenders, UNDP can be called upon to help develop national capacities to negotiate with external partners and mobilize resources in line with national priorities; and (c) UNDP simultaneously draws upon its comparative advantages to support national capacities to improve efficiency, accountability, transparency and cooperative relationships among all sectors.

In general, UNDP can help countries to develop processes to involve civil society and the private sector in policy development and the management of development resources, and to enhance the transparency and accountability of economic and financial management processes. A second important role is to help bring business, government and civil society together to address issues and find joint areas for action in areas of poverty, gender, sustainable livelihoods and environment. The creation of an enabling environment to attract private-sector investments and nurture smaller enterprises, through appropriate laws, fiscal and monetary policies, and stable long-term development strategies, is a key priority.

More specifically, UNDP can provide support to build capacity in economic policy analysis, formulation and management, budgeting, "economic administrations" (customs, debt management, etc.), regulatory frameworks and national accounting. Support to public expenditures — and its influence on poverty — is a key entry point to improving the integration of people-centred concerns into budget priorities. The development of capacities to coordinate and manage aid and debt are also important as part of the overall management of development resources. UNDP can also support capacities to manage the integration of countries into global and regional economic/trade structures and systems, and to take advantage of the information and knowledge revolution. Not least, UNDP helps governments introduce, through all the means of support listed above, economic and financial policies that empower and benefit the poor, women and others who may be marginalized by market forces, and that protect the natural resource base.

At the global level, UNDP sponsors the Programmes for Accountability and Transparency (PACT), an initiative that supports the establishment and improvement of financial accountability and management systems. PACT is specifically involved in the areas of financial planning, cost control, accounting, reporting, and auditing in the public sector. PACT also offers assistance in the area of the improved integrity in governance (formerly anti-corruption), debt management, and aid coordination.

Urban Management

Over the past four decades, urban populations in developing countries have increased rapidly. This relentless growth is now seen as irreversible. The effective functioning of cities and towns is essential for equitable, sustainable growth. Urban management involves a multisectoral set of activities that cut across UNDP's focus areas of poverty alleviation, environmental improvement, gender equity and sustainable livelihoods.

UNDP's Urban Management Programmes (UMP), developed and managed in partnership with the United Nations Centre for Human Settlements, is the largest multi-donor technical cooperation programmes in urban development. Urban management issues addressed through this programme include: environment and land management, municipal finance, maintenance of urban infrastructure, regulatory frameworks for the urban informal sector, urban shelter and services, and of course, poverty alleviation.

Decentralization and Support to Local Governance

Decentralizing key authorities and functions of government, from the national level to regions, districts, towns, municipalities, rural areas, settlements and communities enables people to participate more directly in governance processes and can help to empower those previously excluded from decision-making, particularly the poor and women. It is, therefore, a major determinant of whether a nation is able to create and sustain equitable opportunities for all of its people. Closer contact between government officials and local communities and organizations also facilitates exchanges of information that can be used to formulate development programmes that are both tailored to local needs and priorities and realistic, and thus more effective and sustainable.

UNDP and other UN agencies have engaged in extensive efforts to promote the concept and practice of decentralization, accumulating extensive experience in this area as a result. UNDP, in particular, has provided support to many public management reform programmes focused on decentralization and the strengthening of local authorities. A leading example is the Local Initiative Facility for Urban Environment (LIFE) programme which is designed to promote "local-local" dialogue among municipalities, non-governmental organizations (NGOs) and community-based organizations to improve the quality of the urban environment in low-income settlements.

UNDP offers many services at the country, regional and global level to help countries build capacities for decentralized governance. These include systemic institutional analysis and generation of decentralization policy; strengthening local authorities; direct support to civil society organizations concerned with local governance issues; support to rural institutions and management processes; implementation of local pilot projects; and evaluation, documentation and dissemination of decentralization experiences. Finally, decentralization requires active support from the national level. Encouragement of interaction between the national and local levels of government is therefore, crucial to successful decentralization programmes. At the global level, UNDP's decentralized Governance Programme supports research, and the application and strengthening of effective mechanisms, processes and procedures for decentralized governance at all appropriate levels — national, provincial, municipal, district and local.

Civil Society Organizations

Civil society is the well-spring of social capital — the ability of people to work together for common purposes — that in turn is integral to good governance. In more immediate terms, civil society organizations (CSOs) can play an important role in filling the vacuum left by the downsized state, and in advocating and monitoring reforms in ways that foster SHD.

CSOs should be seen as a complement to, rather than a replacement for, the state. UNDP considers collaboration with CSOs an important asset, in view of their responsiveness, ability to innovate, direct relationship to the poor, capacity to stimulate participation and articulate local views, cost effectiveness, local accountability and independent assessment of issues and problems. However, development-related CSOs in many developing countries are weak. They lack capacities in issues analysis, advocacy and outreach, networking, management and revenue-raising. Often, they, too, need to be more accountable and responsive to their stakeholders and more inclusive. They may also operate within constraining legal and regulatory environments.

The traditional partner of UNDP has been government; its ability to work directly with civil society actors is only now being developed. UNDP's ability to work with government remains a comparative advantage, however. In many programme countries, UNDP can capitalize on government trust of UNDP to encourage interaction and cooperation with civil society and private-sector actors, even — or particularly — when such interaction is a sensitive issue.

The first task of UNDP has been to bring government into dialogue with civil society on policies and programmes and to help create a safe and impartial space where all actors can interact and build trust and relationships, seeking ultimately to increase public space. In Panama, following the political crisis in the aftermath of the US invasion and the removal of the Panamanian president, UNDP helped to sponsor a national consultation process which included the spectrum of political, private sector and civil society organizations, ultimately resulting in political consensus and a Pact for Development to strengthen democracy and independence. In fact, UNDP attempts, in all the priority areas of programming discussed in this section, to encourage partnerships with CSOs to support national efforts and to plan and implement UNDP-supported programmes. UNDP may then support national efforts to improve legislation as well as administrative and tax frameworks for CSOs and assist in improving government's relationship with them.

UNDP also considers supporting CSOs to develop their capacities to plan, manage, and implement activities effectively and accountably; research, advocate and monitor SHD issues, including poverty and gender-specific issues, in ways that build on their experience in reaching poor, marginalized, and disadvantaged groups; network, cooperate and share information among themselves for social and development purposes; and participate in aid coordination and management. UNDP also has a role in what may be termed "civic education": helping national actors to define and implement country-specific programmers that build social cohesion, assist in conflict resolution, increase people's awareness of their rights and responsibilities, and nurture participation in development and governance. Assistance to media — to collect and disseminate relevant information on SHD and governance issues in an impartial manner — is crucial.

Governance in Special Circumstances

There are two categories of countries: crisis countries and transition countries. Social and political stability associated with good governance is fundamental to SHD. In crises, systems and institutions that protect the most vulnerable are the first to be destroyed and must be restored. During extended crises, the maintenance of some core of governance institutions and processes may help lessen the scope and duration of the emergency. Furthermore, good governance is by nature preventive: by valuing development assets and building social cohesion and consensus, it can help reduce vulnerability to disasters and conflicts.

UNDP's comparative advantage lies not in humanitarian response and relief but in its long-term development presence and its ability to respond to complex and multi faceted development challenges. In crises where a rapid and coordinated response is required, UNDP will need to work closely with UN and donor partners with greater experience in emergency situations and greater resources. However, UNDP can play a role in planning for development needs while other bodies concentrate on immediate needs. Furthermore, in pre-crisis and crisis situations, the ability of UNDP to work with and bring together government, civil society and private-sector actors in an impartial manner can be valuable.

There is no universal approach to responding to deteriorating and crisis situations. UNDP concentrates on identifying the most suitable entry points and responding quickly in a flexible manner to dynamic situations. A prime example of the role UNDP has performed during crises was the preparation of a responsive strategy for Zaire in mid-1997 to support the work of the Regional Humanitarian Coordinat. The strategy identified zones for sheltering displaced persons and proposed humanitarian assistance programmes. It outlined requirements for coordination and resource mobilization, and it provided assistance to the government for the development of a political strategy for the management of the crisis with strict emphasis on human rights.

While effective governance programmes generally can reduce the risk of crisis, there are specific efforts that UNDP can support before, during and after crises:

Impending Crisis: UNDP can initiate reconciliation and consensus-building processes and build national capacities to avoid, manage and mitigate crises. It can also regularly gather information on indicators that can signal a pending crisis. National human development reports represent an important tool for gauging potential social dislocations and crises. UNDP also fosters a wide network of people and institutions from which it can obtain development information and with which it can cooperate in times of crisis.

During a Crisis: UNDP can support both macro and local planning initiatives and reconciliation processes. In cases of the collapse of the state, UNDP may initiate participatory programme planning and development for specific needs, such as area, city, regional and food-security planning. It can also aim to develop basic governance, management and coordination capacities. During a crisis, partnerships with CSOs — both formal and informal — can prove to be invaluable assets. CSOs can serve as important intermediaries, support participatory planning and reconciliation processes, and implement small-scale development initiatives.

Post-Crisis: UNDP can assess governance-related requirements, give priority to rebuilding those capacities that are the most strategic and high in impact, and help develop programmes for resource mobilization. These can include assistance to rebuild such core institutions as the executive, legislature and judiciary.

Key Issues in Implementation of Governance Programmes

As noted earlier, the manner in which governance programmes and projects are designed and implemented will greatly determine their success. UNDP believes its implementation strategy is both sound and unique. The underlying principles of this strategy are: finding suitable entry points and partners for policy dialogue; responding speedily to national needs while retaining a long-term view; creating opportunities for government-private sector-civil society interaction to develop policy and programme consensus; implementing in ways that are nationally led, sustainable and that develop strategic capacities; and effectively coordinating development and UN-system resources.

Process Consultancy — A Participatory Programming Process

Experience indicates that without the full involvement of major stakeholders and beneficiaries throughout the design and implementation process, programmes are not sustainable. The UNDP Management Development and Governance Division has therefore helped to further develop and test a methodology, called process consultancy, for developing programmes in a participatory manner and developing social capital in the process. The outside expert's role is to support and facilitate consensus-building. The methodology assists UNDP country offices and experts to initiate a process of consensus building, build awareness of the importance of governance, identify key agents of change in all three domains (public sector, private sector, and civil society), develop goals and strategies, and organize capacities for the change process. Process consultancy, combined with the programme approach and national execution modalities (two instruments that support development of national capacities to meet national goals), can serve as a powerful tool for developing the capacities of systems and actors to reach collective targets. This is one proven instrument for which UNDP now provides training and which it uses to develop all management development and governance programming.

Identify Entry points

During the initial programming process, UNDP should identify and consult key government, civil society and private-sector actors who will be involved in governance programmes to assess national needs and identify areas for UNDP support. The dialogue itself should be an impartial process that helps bring national stakeholders together to reach consensus, develop political will for change and understand the importance of good governance. Documents and studies, such as national human development reports and regional strategies are used to provide analysis, options and methodologies and serve as a means of stimulating dialogue. In this dialogue, UNDP advocates its approach to governance within the national context. Synergies and linkages are sought between governance, poverty, sustainable livelihoods, gender and the environment.

Experience shows that UNDP is most effective when it is able to respond quickly and flexibly to unfolding needs and opportunities, while retaining a long-term view on sustainability. At times UNDP must be willing to take risks to take advantage of fast-evolving opportunities, some of which may be directly related to governance — for example, national elections, changes in government bodies, annual planning and budgetary discussions, national campaigns and conferences on specific themes. Some of the most effective governance programmes, however, have been initiated through other entry points — such as poverty, gender, the environment and integrated rural and urban programmes.

Developing Strategic Capacities

UNDP's approach to capacity development is based on two important principles. First, it asks, "capacity development for what?" and advocates that the answer is closely related to people-centred sustainable development. Second, it claims that how capacities are developed influence the 'what' as well. UNDP advocates that capacity development design take into consideration the key characteristics of good governance — participatory, transparent, equitable, accountable, and strategic vision.

The success of good governance programmes depends on developing capacities to articulate goals and manage change. The UNDP approach to capacity development emphasizes, first, the importance of sustaining and expanding existing capacities, and second, targeting high-impact capacities for assistance. Criteria for strategic interventions include: the degree of impact on policies, development resources, and the enabling environment, particularly to eradicate poverty; whether key leadership and managerial capacities will be strengthened; and whether support will broaden participation. Because most governance programmes involve, for example, judicial systems, financial management systems, parliamentary systems, and decentralized governance systems, a systems approach to capacity development — which places institutions and actors within processes that perform specific tasks — is most appropriate. Earlier this year, UNDP released a technical advisory paper on Capacity Assessment and development which expands the understanding of the concept in both a systems and strategic management context, with special emphasis on assessing capacity gaps and achieving sustainability at the individual, entity and systems levels.

Coordination and Role of Resident Coordinator

UNDP can take a number of steps to improve the impact of UNDP-supported governance programmes and to ensure that the UN system and external partners better support national priorities in a coordinated manner. For example, it can become the lead agency in inter-agency collaboration and country-based aid coordination processes for one or more aspects of governance programmes; provide an impartial forum to discuss issues related to governance with national partners and to help forge local partnerships; provide data and electronic information services on national governance programmers to all development partners; help government to package and negotiate governance programmes for resource mobilization; and to facilitate coordinated UN-system responses and programmes in support of national goals or in answer to crisis situations — or both.

Conclusion

Since its inauguration under the Marshall Plan, development cooperation has continuously evolved to match economic thinking and the global political environment. There has been a gradual recognition and acknowledgement among donor agencies that development is more successful if it views people as both the owners of their problems and their solutions. Each successive phase in the evolution of development cooperation has moved more closely to defining a people-centred approach. Development cooperation has evolved from the top-down delivery of benefits by donors to beneficiaries to a more equitable and balanced approach where concerned stakeholders — state and local governments and authorities, civil society organizations, and the private-sector — can play a variety of contributory roles.

The effects of increasing globalization have also changed the ways in which states manage their affairs. Economic liberalization rests on the premises of competition, productivity, profitability, and efficiency. Market-based economics challenges governments to be more open, responsive, and, in many instances, more democratic. The inefficiencies of state organs in this climate have raised questions about the functions of government. Technological innovation and knowledge-based production demands a better educated and skilled work force, modern infrastructure, and adaptable and responsive private and public sector organizations.

The coming together of these influences has resulted in the emergence of a new development paradigm, which focuses on institutional efficiency, structural adjustment, concepts of sustainability, the mobilization and growth of human capital, and the globalization and liberalization of world trade. Economic development is seen as a process heavily influenced by a set of favourable legal and institutional environments, which form an integral part of the governance framework of a state. Structural adjustment seeks to liberalize markets, promote exports, deregulate trade, and relies on the private sector as the engine of growth. Environmental considerations have led to the concepts of sustainable development and of the harmonization of economic growth with other human aspirations. The quality of human capital is critical for this new approach. It is seen as a major factor in determining the rate of economic growth, particularly relevant in matters of innovation, entrepreneurship, and the ability of a country to integrate into world markets.

In the light of these global trends and forces, UNDP has been at the forefront and leading the broader understanding of development away from a sole economic growth and state-centred paradigm to one based on the principles embodied by sustainable human development (SHD). The major goals and thematic areas embraced by SHD — poverty, employment and sustainable livelihoods, gender, and environment — are indivisible from good governance. Indeed, good governance itself creates and facilitates the enabling environment whereby national socio-economic development objectives in general and SHD goals are achieved. The constructive engagement among the state, civil society organizations and the private-sector are critical for UNDP, and the implementation of technical cooperation for governance is characterized by participation, consensus-orientation, flexibility, and long-term development goals. The centrality of a governance approach to development for UNDP is well reflected by the level of UNDP resources allocated to governance programmes. Today, over a third of UNDP's total core resources are allocated to governance programmes worldwide.

The new development model does not deny a role for the state, but seeks a different role based on pluralistic structures, political legitimacy, and consensus. Progress in human development is dependent upon economic growth, political will to address the causes of poverty and underdevelopment, and strong policy frameworks, which facilitate growth with equity. Policymakers are recognizing that development must be people-centred, equitably distributed, and environmentally and socially sustainable.

Changes in the economic, political, and social systems around the world have brought both challenges and uncertainties for the advancement of human development. Against the backdrop of these changes and gradual acceptance of a new governance approach to development, the international development community has an unprecedented potential to build real partnerships with all of a nation's society to create and support an enabling environment for economic and social development.

References

ILO, *Employment, Growth and Basic Needs, A One World Approach*, Geneva, 1976.

Rostow, W.W., *The Stages of Economic Growth*, New Haven, 1960.

UNDP, *Governance for Sustainable Human Development*, New York, 1997.

UNDP, *Rethinking Technical Co-operation: Reforms for Capacity Bridling in Africa*, Regional Bureau for Africa, 1993.

UNESCO, *Capacity Building for Governance*, Paris, 1997.

World Bank, *Governance, the World Bank Experience*, Washington DC, 1994.

Index